John O'Farrell studied history at Desborough Comprehensive, where he got a B in his O level. He later continued his research by watching lots of programmes about the Nazis on the UK History Channel.

Apart from that he has published three novels, a memoir and three collections of his popular *Guardian* column. A former comedy scriptwriter for such shows as *Spitting Image* and *Smith and Jones*, he is the founder of the satirical website *NewsBiscuit* and can occasionally be spotted on such TV programmes as *Grumpy Old Men*, *Newsnight Review*, and *Have I Got News for You*.

He was encouraged to write this book after overhearing publishing executives agreeing, 'John O'Farrell? He *is* history.'

D1121305

AN UTTERLY IMPARTIAL HISTORY OF BRITAIN

or 2000 Years of Upper-class
Idiots in Charge

John O'Farrell

Doubleday

LONDON · TORONTO · SYDNEY · AUCKLAND · JOHANNESBURG

TRANSWORLD PUBLISHERS
61–63 Uxbridge Road, London W5 5SA
A Random House Group Company
www.rbooks.co.uk

First published in Great Britain
in 2007 by Doubleday
an imprint of Transworld Publishers

A CIP catalogue record for this book
is available from the British Library.

ISBNs 9780385611985 (cased)
9780385611992 (tpb)

Addresses for Random House Group Ltd companies outside the UK
can be found at: www.randomhouse.co.uk
The Random House Group Ltd Reg. No. 954009

The Random House Group Limited supports The Forest Stewardship Council (FSC), the
leading international forest certification organisation. All our titles that are printed on
Greenpeace approved FSC certified paper carry the FSC logo.
Our paper procurement policy can be found at
www.rbooks.co.uk/environment

Mixed Sources
Product group from well-managed
forests and other controlled sources
www.fsc.org Cert no. TF-COC-2139
© 1996 Forest Stewardship Council

FSC

Typeset in 11.5/14pt Ehrhardt by
Falcon Oast Graphic Art Ltd.

Printed and bound in Great Britain by
Clays Ltd, Bungay, Suffolk

2 4 6 8 10 9 7 5 3 1

For Freddie

Contents

Author's Note

During the writing of this book there were many occasions when I found myself flicking from one source to another, perplexed to discover that different historians gave conflicting dates for the same event. One respected scholar would assert that some ancient war lasted nine years, another might say eleven. It was at this point that I found phrases like 'around a decade later' incredibly useful. If the academics couldn't agree then I felt it was my duty to blur the facts further and make things as vague and murky as possible. When it comes to the audio book, I'll just mumble.

However, may I apologize now for any further errors that slipped through this process of checking and re-checking. My only defence is that these mistakes are fairly minor compared to the decision of the Scottish army to invade England during the Black Death.

Introduction

My history teacher went to the pub at lunchtime. You could smell the beer on his breath. History in the morning was irritable and short-tempered; it was no wonder there were so many wars and witch-burnings. But after lunch the history of Britain became suffused with a genial bonhomie and a slightly blurred sense of goodwill to all men (except the Germans). All the kings and statesmen down the centuries came across as bloody good blokes, although the nature of their predicaments seemed increasingly less clear as Double History entered its second hour. By the end of the afternoon 'The Causes of the Second World War' were mumbled in a sleepy, meandering monologue punctuated by extended silent pauses almost long enough for Britain to rearm. We'd glance up from our faithful note-taking, still awaiting the fate of Czechoslovakia, to see him staring out of the window. Had he just had a revelation about the annexation of the Sudetenland? Or was he thinking about a beautiful French girl he had left behind at Dunkirk in the summer of 1940? Either way, I still have this vague sense that the fateful meeting between Hitler and Neville Chamberlain didn't take place in Munich at all, but over a pub lunch at the Hand and Flowers in Queen Street.

The point is that the way we recount the past is deeply affected by how we feel now; whether our perspective is clouded by fierce religious fervour, a surge of patriotism or three pints of Brakspear's bitter. And so at a moment when we are feeling particularly sceptical and irreverent towards our leaders, I thought it was time for some edgy, hard-hitting satire aimed at King Eawa of the Angles. I don't care whom I knock, there are no sacred cows for me when it comes to sixth-century Mercia. It's just that it strikes me as odd that while we seem to have total contempt for today's politicians, a syphilitic wife-murderer like Henry VIII gets voted on to the BBC's list of all-time Great Britons. (He came in at number 40; 'greater' than Charles Dickens but apparently less great than Michael Crawford. Though to be fair Henry VIII's Frank Spencer impression was rubbish.)

When I said I wanted to write a humorous history of Britain, a common reaction was: 'What, like *1066 and All That*?' But unlike that comic classic, this is not a subversion of what we already know; this presumes that we never knew it in the first place. It assumes that when our history teacher slunk off to the staff room for another ciggie, mumbling the inspiring guidance 'Take notes from chapter seven' we did nothing of the sort, choosing instead to put to the test the bold claim printed on Timothy Johnson's 'shatterproof' ruler. I hope this book will provide the chance to put all that right, by going right back to basics and assuming the reader has only the sketchiest knowledge of the story of Britain. (*Britain*, you know; big island off the coast of Europe, rains a lot.)

My aim has been to write a funny, accessible history of Britain, for all those who weren't listening at school. And I have been amazed how many people said, 'That's exactly the book *I* need to read.' In fact I am still struggling to find a single person who *was* listening at school. This is a shame because unless you have the bad luck to be studying 'The Whig Oligarchy 1714–1763' the history of Britain really is a fascinating and compelling story, packed with one great character after another trapped in impossible dilemmas and gripping adventures which have you thinking: I wonder if he dies at the end? Obviously he *always does* die at the end; it happened hundreds of years ago, the 'ending-up-dead' bit is something of a foregone conclusion.

The '2000 years' in the subtitle take us from 55 BC to 1945. Clearly no history book can be comprehensive. Edward Gibbon's *Decline and Fall of the Roman Empire* took him fifteen years to write and was published in six fat volumes totalling one and a half million words. And then to wind him up, all his mates said, 'I can't believe you left out the Siege of Ravenna, Eddie.'

'What Siege of Ravenna?'

'God, that's crucial, that is, Ed, no Siege of Ravenna? That's central to the whole decline and fall thing, man.'

It's not possible to cover everything, and I apologize now to Scottish and Welsh readers for the way that English history tends to dominate these pages in much the same way that England has trodden all over her creative and enterprising neighbours. But all that stuff that you have vaguely heard about but never quite understood, all those niggling questions that seemed too obvious to ask: I will attempt to explain all of it here, trying to unpick the causes and the consequences before giving up and saying, 'Oh well, look, you had to be there, really.'

J. O'F.
Summer 2007

1

Ancient and Roman Britain

How the Romans established our template for 'civilization'
by killing anyone who didn't like it

There must have been a single day on which it happened. A definite moment seven thousand years ago when the strip of land connecting us to continental Europe disappeared under the waves to create a new island of Britain. Was there a last-minute rush to get across as people saw what was happening? An anxious wife trying to hurry her husband out of the prehistoric departure lounge as that last rising tide lapped at the disappearing causeway?

'This is the last call for anyone wishing to cross the land bridge to Britain! Last call for indigenous Britons: please proceed to gate one!'

'Come on, we're going to miss it!'

'Stop fussing, dear, we've got loads of time . . .'

Or did the isthmus just become increasingly treacherous over the decades, so that larger animals such as elks, bison and humans could wade through the increasingly boggy salt marshes, leaving all the hedgehogs and badgers sulking on the water's edge?* However it happened, 5,000 BC is apparently 'incredibly recent' in terms of the entire history of mankind. You have to ask what sort of timescale

---

* At low tide it is still possible to stand on the Goodwin Sands in the middle of the English Channel – though you might not want to pay the bloke with the boat until he's come back to pick you up again.

these historians and geologists are working to because I can't help feeling that 5,000 BC was ages ago. Last Tuesday was recent. Windows XP; that was quite recent.

This extreme period of climate change must surely have been a catastrophe for those who lived through it. Thousands of square miles of inhabitable land were suddenly claimed by the sea; a vast area now underneath the North Sea containing the villages and hunting grounds of long-forgotten societies disappeared under the waves. It was the same as when the tide finally washes over the little dam your kids have built on the beach, except that the next tide takes your entire village as well. The sea advanced at a rate of about two hundred yards a year (it would of course have been yards – the metric system came much much later) and no amount of recycling or car-sharing was going to stop it. The increased pressure on habitable land would have led to wars, famine and the breakdown of society, so thank goodness we are not going to have to go through any of that ever again.

Although we are all constantly evolving (with the exception of the readers of *Nuts* magazine), *Homo sapiens* are pretty much as they were 100,000 years ago, and the people who lived in Britain seven thousand years ago were not that different in appearance or intelligence to human beings today. They had language, tools, religion and culture, all influenced by and intermingled with the societies of other hunter-gatherers from all over the continent. And then suddenly they were cut off.* Immediately the debate began: Is Britain at the heart of Europe? Or should we keep our own currency until the conditions are right? Strictly speaking, those few thousand who found themselves isolated in these islands were the only original Britons. All the rest – Celts, Romans, Angles, Saxons, Jutes, Vikings, Normans – they were all immigrants. In fact there are one or two Conservative politicians who would still like to see a repatriation policy based upon this narrow criterion.

* The land that is now the British Isles had already been occupied and then become uninhabitable again according to the limit of ice sheets. The ice was a mile thick over much of the country. And still all the Geordie girls went out with bare legs.

The end of the Stone Age (a Thursday)

At the time that Britain became a separate geographical entity, the people of Northern Europe were in the last millennia of the Stone Age. They lived in caves, hacked at the earth with deer antlers and attached flints to arrows to hunt for food. Although contemporary culture has provided us with a very clear image of what everyday life was like for Stone Age man, many academics have begun to question the historical accuracy of our most popular source materials for this period. Apparently Stone Age man did not have pet dinosaurs, pterodactyls employed as gramophones or cars that ran on leg power. Nor did they have fur Wonderbras like the one worn by Raquel Welch in *One Million Years B.C.* The historical consultant on that film kept explaining that the dinosaurs died out 65 million years before *Homo sapiens* appeared on the earth, but the producer just nodded blankly and then said to the crew, 'OK, can we do that scene again, but this time the big dinosaur almost bites off Raquel's bra-strap!'

Our lazily absorbed view of ancient societies is that they must have been incredibly savage and brutal communities, totally without law and order, art, science or culture or any of the traits of what we would recognize as 'civilization'. People back then were savages; we, however, are highly sophisticated and civilized; ergo we are better than them. They'd never have used the word 'ergo', for a start. But this is of course arrogant and most certainly wrong. If the members of prehistoric British society were like that of any other society, then only *some* of them would have wanted to smash their neighbours' skulls in so they could steal all their possessions. But others would have cherished and developed the friendship, cooperation and mutual support without which they could not survive. And then once their neighbours' guard was down, *then* they would have smashed their skulls in. Then, as now, every member of society would have to battle with his inner caveman. Much of the journey of history is attempting to control the external factors that determine whether we win that battle or not. It's just that it was harder not to behave like a caveman when you were a man who lived in a cave.

Archaeological remains suggest that the greatest concentrations of human population were in the Fens, in the Thames Valley and along the South Downs, but we can presume that people hunted and ranged over much of the country. We know what people back then looked like from all those artists' impressions you see in the newspaper; the men were always walking around holding something they'd just killed and the women had very saggy breasts. Primitive attempts at agriculture gradually evolved where patches of land could be dug over with flint axes, and archaeologists tell us that animals such as the goat and ox were 'gradually domesticated'. How you gradually domesticate an ox, I don't know; you'd want to make pretty sure it was house-trained before you had it in the hut.

Britain's isolation would have made development slower, and for some reason British arrowheads got much, much smaller in relation to the European standard after the islands were cut off. But the continent was close enough for new ideas and technological advances to cross the widening channel. Without such cross-fertilization, it is quite probable that Britain would have remained in the Stone Age in the same way that the Australian Aboriginals did until the arrival of the rest of the world.

The Bronze Age: when the clever kids did metalwork

Historians have debated long and hard about which invaders came when, with the only consensus being that all of it occurred 'incredibly recently'. It is believed that the stone circle temple at Avebury was built by Neolithic man, but their supremacy was challenged by a stronger, larger race who originated in the Rhineland, reaching Britain in around 1,900 BC. These invaders have been dubbed the Beaker People, so called because of the pottery they brought with them. Since remains of the Beaker People have been found buried with their beakers, archaeologists believe that great significance was attached to the beakers. They were obsessed with bloody beakers; every birthday it was the same. 'You'll never guess what I've got you...' 'Ooh, thank you, darling, what a surprise! I'll put it with the others.'

4

It might be that the importance of the beaker was to do with what it was used for. Alcohol was a recent discovery, and the magical powers of this drink may have had religious meaning for the Beaker People. The drinking of fermented honey would probably have been a great religious ceremony with formal sipping being executed with great reverence as they paid homage to their gods. And then half an hour later it was all, 'Oi, you spilt my beaker!' 'Oh yeah, do you want some?' 'Right, outside, you beardy bastard!'

These were the people who built Stonehenge; after a long day dragging giant rocks into place you'd probably need a drink or two. Many of the stones were quarried in South Wales, 160 miles away from their destination on Salisbury Plain, and sunken stones have been found at the bottom of the Severn Estuary, which must have been the cause of a certain amount of prehistoric swearing. You spend months hacking a fourteen-foot rock out of the Welsh Hills, you drag it forty miles, and then halfway across the river Severn the bloke running the little ferry service explains that his raft wasn't quite as watertight as he'd thought.

'I'm terribly sorry, I seem to have lost your sacred stone.'

'Oh, not to worry, really. We can go back and get another one; it's no trouble.'

As a piece of engineering, Stonehenge is an incredible achievement and there is something rather symmetrical about Microsoft providing a photo of Stonehenge as a standard wallpaper for the twenty-first-century computer screen. No one knows quite why it was built, but it seems sensible to presume that some ancient ceremony took place there every year, hopefully slightly more meaningful than today's annual beating up of New Age travellers by the local riot police. The sheer scale of the monument and the logistics that must have been involved in constructing it tell us something of the society that built it. We know that they followed the movement of the stars and the planets, the presumption being that they worshipped the sun, which as religions go seems a bit 'first base', but then it was a long time ago. In fact the site was of religious significance for far longer than Christianity or Islam have existed. It is the temple of a civilization about which we know very little and so tend to presume was very simplistic. But they must have also had a fairly advanced social structure; in addition to a good number of labourers or slaves they would have needed managers, engineers, surveyors and designers. Basically they must have had a middle class. How Stonehenge managed to get planning permission with all those objections from 'The Friends of Salisbury Plain' is just another one of its ancient mysteries.

By this time Britain was following the rest of Europe into the Bronze Age. It is hard to imagine that one type of metal could have so transformed life for early man; today its only use is to make the medals for British athletes at the Commonwealth Games, but back then this new alloy brought about a revolution. Bronze Age man would have treasured the strength and versatility of this new resource and there would have been much debate about the evolving process of metalwork.

'So how do you make this "bronze" stuff exactly?'

'You smelt together the ore of two different minerals – copper and tin, see?'

'I thought that made brass. Are you sure we're not living in the *Brass Age*?'

'Nah, brass is copper and zinc, isn't it?'

'Or is it copper and lead?'

'What about this metal here, what's this?'

'Oh, that's iron. That's much better.'

'So isn't this the *Iron Age* then?'

'Well, it is *now* – but it wasn't when we started talking about brass. I mean bronze.'

The Iron Age actually arrived with invaders from Europe. Iron is much stronger, but consequently requires a far higher temperature to extract it from its mineral source. It took around a thousand years or so before they realized that that dial on the kiln went clockwise for 'hotter'. The Iron Age came to Britain around the seventh century BC. It is not just marked by the switch to stronger metal, but also by all sorts of development in society: advances in pottery, metalwork, woodwork and all the other subjects you choose because you think they sound easier than GCSE Physics.

In the centuries before the Romans made their first visit to these shores, complex and ornate objects were created by the Celtic metallurgists. Numerous metal artefacts have been recovered from British rivers: swords, axe heads, shields, helmets and a Sainsbury's shopping trolley, though this is thought to come from much, much later. There is a particularly fine Celtic shield in the British Museum which was taken from the Thames in Battersea. The Celtic warrior who forgot to take it home thought, Ah well, we conquered Britain centuries ago, I'm not going to need that now. Julius Caesar turned up with the Roman army the following weekend.

'Pah! Julius who?'

The Iron Age Britons described by Caesar were very similar to the tribes in northern Gaul. Jewellery was fashioned from shells and bronze, druids administered herbal remedies and hairy bearded craftsmen daubed bright colours all over their bodies and believed in the power of the sun and the stars. Basically the whole place was populated by hippies – the Romans definitely looked favourite to beat this lot. The British Celts faced their enemies stripped to the waist, which was a marginal improvement on the battledress of their cousins in Gaul, who went into battle completely naked. I'm no expert in classical military strategy, but if I was suddenly faced with thousands of heavily armed Romans with metal plate armour, iron shields and helmets, I'm not convinced that I would feel particularly invulnerable standing there with my genitals swinging about. Blushing and shuffling along with both hands covering your private parts can't be the most intimidating way to charge into battle.

Despite this typically slack French attitude to decency and personal hygiene, the Gallic tribes had been no pushover for Julius Caesar, whose attempts to conquer Gaul had been hindered by the military support they had been receiving from the Celts of southern Britain. Caesar decided that to secure northern Gaul he would need to crush their comrades on the other side of the Channel and so in 55 BC he sailed over the *Oceanus Britannicus* and landed near the white cliffs of Dover. This first visit may have been more of a reconnaissance mission than invasion because the following year he returned with eight hundred boats especially designed for the cross-Channel journey. Men in woolly hats waved each chariot driver to get his vehicle as close as possible to the one in front, and then it was a mad rush up to C Deck to claim their comfy seats for the crossing.

This campaign took Caesar much further inland. His army camped in the Thames Valley, which caused a certain amount of tutting from the local residents. In fact, judging by the number of places marked Caesar's Camp on the Ordnance Survey maps, he seems to have camped all over the place. Local farmers tended not to complain when he had over twenty-five thousand soldiers in the next field. But eventually he met fierce resistance and was nearly driven out of Britain by sheer weight of numbers. His absence from Gaul had also led to further uprisings there, and so with a handful of British Celtic chieftains now in the pay of Rome, he crossed back over the English Channel never to return. Contrary to popular belief, Caesar never did conquer Britain. He came, he saw, he went home again.

But the island was now in the sphere of Roman influence. Indeed it was argued in Rome that there was no point in conquering the territory while the British tribes were paying more in tributes to the Roman Empire than would have been raised in taxation if Britain had been conquered. So the decades following 54 BC were a relatively quiet time for Britain. While Caesar's best mates stabbed him in the back (and front), while Antony told Cleopatra that he didn't want to lose her as a friend, while the Roman Empire waited with bated breath to see what B C actually stood for,* various plans to complete the conquest of Britain were repeatedly postponed.

Of course, that's not to say that everyday life wasn't an enormous struggle. The ordinary Briton was at the mercy of forces way beyond his control and whatever life lacked in quality it made up for in

* For the Romans, year zero was the date that Rome was supposed to have been founded, so what we call 44 BC they would have called the year 711 or DCCXI. Like you care.

variety; generally alternating between cold, hunger and fear. Then, as for many centuries afterwards, the spectre of death constantly hung over every community. Most parents would have had to bury at least one child; at any moment you might succumb to disease, famine or murder. Basically, if you bought a five-year diary, you were considered an optimist. And to cap it all, in AD 43, you had to leave the farm to fight the greatest Empire the world had ever seen.

Kent Young Farmers' Association v Roman Empire: away win

Over the previous hundred years Britain had taken on a certain amount of glamour as the land that not even the iconic Caesar had been able to conquer. And so when the reviled Emperor Claudius came to the throne, facing military revolt and a desperate need to gain respect in Rome, the chance of glory offered by a conquest of Britain was too much to resist. Basically Britain was invaded because a weak dictator thought it would look good back home. As if having the Roman army turn up wasn't annoying enough.

Around forty thousand men arrived in Britain to face Celtic tribes who had become increasingly defiant of the Empire on the other side of the Channel. The British vastly outnumbered the invaders but, as is traditional in rural areas, hated their neighbours even more than they hated foreigners. If they could ally themselves with these Romans to gain an advantage over that tribe who lived up the road then they would do so. Caesar's old maxim of 'divide and rule' never worked so well as in the Roman conquest of Britannia. What's more, the Celtic warriors had farms to tend back home. Unlike the professional soldiers from Rome whose supply chains allowed them to fight year after year if need be, the Celtic smallholders could only spend a limited time on military service. So either they allowed the Romans to conquer the whole country, steal their land, murdering and looting at will; or they fought them in a protracted war that would see their fields unploughed and their people left to starve.

Well, that's what they claimed anyway, but then farmers are always moaning about something.

Boadicea rebels over incorrect spelling of her name

Within four years the Roman armies occupied Britain as far as the Severn and the Trent. The successful campaign was crowned by the public submission of eleven British kings to the Emperor and his triumphant entry into Colchester complete with a parade of elephants, which was more interesting than anything that has ever happened in Colchester before or since. However, the Romans' success on the battlefield was not matched by their skills of diplomacy. Had a regional commander in East Anglia treated the Queen of the Iceni tribe with a little more respect, the Romans might have avoided an uprising that saw tens of thousands of Roman settlers put to the sword. Within a few months 'Boadicea' was a name that struck fear across the whole province.

'Though you're not supposed to say *Boadicea* any more,' moaned one of the legionaries. 'It's Iceni-ist, apparently. We have to call her *Boudicca* now.'

'Honestly, it's just political correctness gone mad.'

Boudicca's dying husband had left half of his royal possessions to Rome, to ensure that his family and kingdom would be protected. As with all insurance schemes throughout history, however, the Iceni did not get what had already been paid for; instead the local commander immediately set about helping himself to the whole lot, including all of the bereaved Queen's personal possessions. When Boudicca protested, she was flogged, her teenage daughters were raped and the Iceni were driven off their land as the invaders began an orgy of destruction.* And then the Romans were surprised that she was really, really annoyed.

Allying herself with neighbouring tribes who had many grievances

* Or as the famous children's history book *Our Island Story* puts it: *The Romans were rude to her daughters.*

of their own, the striking red-headed Queen assembled a force of around 120,000 men; three times the number of the occupying army, most of whom were far away in North Wales. She swept through southern Britain burning Colchester, St Albans and London.* While the Roman army rushed back south and thousands of soldiers were sent over from Germany, her forces were estimated to have killed around seventy thousand Roman settlers and sympathizers. Finally, at an unknown location somewhere in the Midlands, the two armies came face to face in the Battle of Watling Street. Almost inevitably the military tactics of the disciplined Roman army proved superior to the chaotic charges of the assembled chiefs, and despite their massively superior numbers, the Celts were defeated and massacred. Rather than allow her daughters to fall into the hands of the Romans, Boudicca persuaded them to drink poison from a golden cup and then took the hemlock herself. When the Roman Governor finally beheld the dead Queen, he described her as lying peacefully, with an arm around each of her daughters. It's a beautiful and poignant image. The actual effects of hemlock are vomiting and diarrhoea, but you have to allow a certain amount of poetic licence.

Boudicca's rebellion was a major event in the story of Rome's conquest of Britannia; indeed it very nearly led to the Romans withdrawing from the island altogether. But her status as a British national icon is a fairly recent invention. When the Victorian propagandists were busy sifting through English history looking for some heroes they could stick on the plinths, they were attracted by the fact that this warrior apparently had the same name as their glorious Queen. Admittedly the Celtic spelling of 'Victoria' was a bit shaky, but back in AD 61 adult literacy still had a long way to go. 'Boudicca' is indeed the Celtic for 'Victoria', though after that it's hard to see many other similarities between the two. The Celtic Queen was much, much harder than her nineteenth-century namesake, but then Queen Victoria had the edge when it came to anger management. The fact that this English heroine came from a race of people who

---

* Thirteen feet beneath the pavements of the capital there is still a layer of the burnt remains left by Boudicca; part of it is exposed at the Barbican.

were later to be brutally displaced by the English seems to have been conveniently overlooked. Her status as one of our national heroes makes no more sense than if today's Americans were to get all patriotic about the bravery of Chief Sitting Bull. On the other hand . . . we really showed those bloody Romans a thing or two, didn't we? I think we can really pat ourselves on the back. Good old Boudicca, she was a true Brit and no mistake . . .

Within a couple of decades most of England and Wales was subjugated, although the island remained a very rebellious territory for the entire four centuries of Roman rule; requiring more occupying soldiers than any other province. At times, ten per cent of the entire Roman Empire's army was employed here as the rebellious Britons forced the Romans to put fortifications all around their cities, something that was not required in provinces such as Gaul where the indigenous population proved more willing to be Latinized. Several contemporary commentators mention the unusually defiant character of these Britons, their hatred of injustice and their determination to keep their liberty. Perhaps the geographical isolation of these particular Celts had made them value their freedom more than most, or maybe there really was something defiant in their national character that lives on today in the independently minded Celts of Ireland, Scotland and Wales. Hard to imagine Boudicca being satisfied with a regional assembly, but perhaps it was never suggested.

Hadrian's Wall: 'They promised it would be finished by Christmas'

The Scots can pride themselves that they proved to be completely unconquerable.* There was no pre-ordained plan to set the northern limit across the north of England and several wars of conquest of Scotland were undertaken, two of them led by the emperors

---

* Although at that time the tribe called the 'Scots' lived in Ireland, so they can actually pride themselves that they were not considered worth bothering with.

12

themselves. But the Romans who had crossed the Alps and the Pyrenees found the subjugation of the Scottish Highlands to be beyond them. In fact, having failed to extend the Roman Empire into Scotland, the mood in Rome changed and no further major expansions of the Empire were attempted. Scotland stopped the Roman Empire in its tracks. And all the Emperor had said was, 'So what exactly happens on Burns Night?'

So Hadrian's Wall is generally seen as the northern limit of the Roman Empire and remained the most heavily fortified boundary in the entire Empire. Anyone who remembers the Scottish football fans at Wembley in 1977 will understand why. The wall (some of which remains) starts at the Solway Firth and finishes up at Wallsend, which seemed like a sensible place to aim for. It was begun in AD 122 on the orders of the visiting Emperor Hadrian to keep out the Picts who kept crossing into England and deliberately calling him 'Adrian' to wind him up. It took ten years to build because the builders kept leaving at lunchtime to work on another job. To be posted to Hadrian's Wall was probably the bleakest posting a Roman soldier had to endure. 'Join the Army, they said. Travel to interesting and exciting places. Stand about on a freezing cold wall waiting to be skewered by a screaming bearded Pict.' Recent DNA samples have revealed that black African soldiers were stationed at Hadrian's Wall, who will no doubt have descendants living in Britain today being asked who they support when England play cricket against the Roman Province of Numidia. Some Roman garrisons were stationed beyond Hadrian's Wall at various times, and later on the Emperor Antonine built another wall between the Clyde Estuary and the Firth of Forth, but his ambition to extend the Empire a hundred miles northwards also proved to be unsustainable. Antonine became quite bitter that his follow-up wall was not such a big hit.

Romanized Britain: globalization starts here

Like many empires since, the Romans found that the most effective way to subjugate the locals was to get the native aristocracy to do it on their behalf. Britain's indigenous Celts were permitted to stick to their old-fashioned uncivilized ways, but began to notice their own tribal leaders walking around in togas and speaking Latin. Finally someone had to have a word.

'The thing is, boss, me and the lads were talking about it, and, well, we can't help wondering if you haven't, like, sold out.'

'Sold out! Don't be ridiculous. I'm a Celt through and through, from the sandals on my feet to the laurel wreath on my head.'

'You see, that's what I mean, all this dressing up like Caesar and lying on sofas eating grapes before throwing up in the vomitorium*
. . . It's almost as if you're on their side . . .'

'That's what we want them to think! But I'm doing this for you and the lads. If I can win their trust, and *appear* to be enjoying all the trappings of their civilization, then maybe I can change the Roman Empire *from the inside*.'

'Oh. Right. OK then.'

'Now pass the amphora, would you? I've run out of wine again.'

The British gentry thrived under Roman rule, building themselves huge villas in the countryside and growing rich on the slave labour they employed on their farms. There was the opportunity for a certain degree of social advancement in Roman Britain, particularly in the professional and educated classes. But even the ordinary work-men constructing the new Roman cities were expected to be able to talk and write in the language of the invaders. So while passing women may have had to endure the usual catcalls and obscenities from builders, at least all these lewd comments were in Latin: 'Wha-hey! Mamillae amabiles!'

At the very bottom of the pile in Roman society was the slave. Slaves in Roman Britain did not have the greatest of prospects. If they got themselves a life coach, there weren't many options to discuss. Slaves were owned in much the same way as cattle except you weren't considered a nutter if you ate one of your cows. They

---

* The idea of the vomitorium, a designated area where you went to empty your stomach when you had eaten and drunk too much, is actually something of a myth. This facility was not actually developed until much later when it became known as the 'pub car park'.

were poorly fed and clothed and had their owner's initials branded on to their forehead, which made it very difficult to maintain eye contact. It is reckoned that about one-third of the population of the Roman Empire was made up of slaves, although this became harder to sustain as Rome ceased to conquer new territories or capture prisoners of war. (It'll be the same when the EC stops expanding; eventually we'll run out of Polish or Croatian au pairs to do the ironing.) The masters obviously lived in fear of the latent power of this huge underclass, for the punishment for rebellion was swift and draconian. When one slave attacked his owner all the slaves in the household were put to death. So, as always, it was just a small minority spoiling it for all the others. There were gradual tiny improvements in the rights of slaves, and a few prosecutions of particularly cruel owners who obviously embarrassed the rest of this slave-owning society by going too far. Occasionally a Roman might even free one of his slaves, though this was probably done in the same spirit that someone might today dump a knackered old Ford Cortina. Much propaganda value was made of these *liberti*; holding out this tiny hope kept the majority of slaves from the total despair that would have had them slashing their masters' throats at the earliest opportunity and running off to join the circus.*

Artisans and craftsmen also arrived from all over the Empire and increasing numbers of retiring Roman legionaries were awarded land in Britain. Despite this, the vast majority of the population was still Celtic. They followed their religion and customs unchallenged; art-work from the period continued to be decorated with the distinctive swirly motifs favoured today by vaguely New Age students getting their first tattoo. The population of Britain grew to levels that would not be reached again until the Middle Ages, and although the Roman occupation depended on the creation of provincial cities, most of the people remained in the countryside. Britain exported minerals to the rest of the Empire: copper, tin, iron, lead, silver, gold and marble,

---

* Although this would have been a pretty stupid thing to do since all the gladiators were slaves as well. But then that's the slave class for you. Completely brainless. They've only themselves to blame.

as well as animal hides, pearls and slaves. The extensive growing of wheat provided the staple diet of bread. There were vineyards in southern Britain, but if it was anything like the British wine you can buy today, it's no wonder the Roman Empire eventually collapsed.

For administrative purposes Britain was divided into a number of regions. In the third century AD this was simplified into just two provinces governed from the regional capitals of London and York. The Governor of Britain clearly had a sense of humour because southern Britain became known as *Britannia Superior* and the North was named *Britannia Inferior*.

'Hang on a bluddy minute . . .' said all the grumpy Britons from York. 'What do you mean "inferior"? Typical bluddy Southerners, that is. Think they're so bluddy superior, just because they live in, er, *Britannia Superior*.'

Christianity was gradually making inroads into Roman society. The first English Christian martyr was St Alban, who was beheaded for his faith around 304 AD, on the site where St Albans cathedral now stands. The story goes that on the way to his execution, the bridge over the river was so crowded that they could not cross. Instead Alban ordered the waters to part so that they could walk across the river bed. This is clearly nonsense, but people would believe anything back then. Apparently Alban's executioner's eyes fell out when he had done the deed. Again, you can't help but think that this doesn't sound very likely.

A couple of years later the Emperor Constantine the Great succeeded to the throne (while in Britain, as it happened) and Christianity finally became tolerated throughout the Roman Empire. Back in Rome the old guard were blaming this fancy new religion and the abandonment of the traditional Roman gods for the increasing crisis in the Roman Empire. Although Roman Britain continued to flourish throughout the fourth century, the Empire itself was splitting and under pressure on all fronts. In December 406 the Rhine froze over, allowing thousands of barbarians to cross the ice, while their mums stood anxiously on the bank saying, 'Are you sure it's safe?' Armies were withdrawn from Britain to defend the imperial capital, making the province increasingly vulnerable to attack.

Last-ever Roman Emperor declares: 'It's the end of an era'

If you had to place a date on the point at which Britain ceased to be a colony of Rome, then the year 410 would be as good a date as any. With rebellious Britons becoming increasingly bold in their uprisings, Picts invading from the North and Saxons making tentative raids on the east coast, an appeal was sent to Rome for military assistance. A reply came back telling the Romano-Britons 'to look to their own defences', which is a polite way of telling someone that you are leaving them to be massacred.

But Rome was in greater need of soldiers than its remotest territory. In August of that year, the city itself was ransacked by the Visigoths; for three days the greatest city the world had ever seen was overrun by German hordes. In other parts of the once-invincible Roman Empire, frontiers were breached and new ruling tribes settled the land. From Eastern Germany came the infamous Vandals.

'Why are these invaders called *Vandals*?' asked the Romans.

'Because we think they originated from the Swedish province of Vendel,' said the Emperor, who always missed a comedy open goal when it was presented to him. Only in the East did the old order endure, based on the new capital Constantinople, where a shrinking Roman Empire actually survived right up until the thirteenth century.

The effect of all this in Britain was gradual. The Romans didn't suddenly all climb aboard the galleys and sail back across the English Channel. 'Right, we're off now, it's been a lovely four centuries, we would stay for the clearing up, but unfortunately we have to dash . . .' Britain was actually one of the least disrupted provinces during this turbulent period; there is even some evidence that anxious Romans from Gaul transferred their wealth to Britain. Other Romans buried their gold and silver deep in the fields hoping (in vain) to come back and reclaim it at some later date when metal detectors had been invented. These secret stashes still turn up from time to time, ploughed up by farmers who get interviewed on regional news programmes, looking a little worried that they might have to give it all to the local museum without being paid loads of cash for it first.

Archaeologists have dated new mosaics in British Roman villas to around 430 AD, so some of the landed gentry must have felt secure enough to think it worth getting the kitchen floor relaid. But Roman coinage had not been minted for some decades and with no centralized administration and no army to enforce the rule of law it was only a matter of time before Britain too fell into chaos and that the concept of 'civilization' was apparently packed into boxes and put in the loft until the Renaissance.

Civilization™ has encountered a problem and been forced to close

You can understand why at the end of the Middle Ages people started to hark back to Roman society as a high point. A thousand years is a long time to go without underfloor heating. But somehow the Roman way of life has endured as the prototype civilization, even becoming the default template for highly cultured outer-space societies in *Star Trek*. They just had to put on a toga, refer to their 'Senate' or 'Consul' and you knew Captain Kirk was dealing with some pretty advanced life forms here.

Civilization existed in Ancient Greece and the Roman Empire and then was suspended for a thousand years until Michelangelo became interested in interior decor. This is the condescending impression that we have been bequeathed by generations of scholars who hark back to the classical era as a benchmark of culture and sophistication. Perhaps the Romans are generally perceived in an overly positive light because our history has been written almost exclusively by former public-school boys who spent far too much time studying Classics at boarding school. Any sense of objectivity was distorted by a series of dodgy Greek masters who were slightly too interested in reminding the boys that Greco-Roman wrestlers were always naked.

But judging the Roman Empire to have been 'a good thing' because it brought order and engineering and literature and universal law is like excusing Mussolini for all the other stuff because at least he got the trains to run on time (which in fact he didn't). The reality is that the Roman Empire was ruled by a series of incredibly brutal and murderous regimes and if they hadn't lived quite so long ago, the Emperors might be regarded in much the same light as modern dictators such as Stalin and Pol Pot. Julius Caesar, for example, had four hundred thousand men, women and children massacred during his campaign in Germany. A decade earlier, a revolt in Judaea had seen six hundred thousand Jews murdered. The received wisdom is that this was the normal practice of warfare and that you cannot impose modern morality on to historical events, and indeed back then the victims were always saying, 'Yeah actually, things are different in sixty BC, we don't mind being massacred at all.'

In fact the struggle for civilization was not a battle between the cultured Romans and uncouth Germanic hordes. All these societies had many civilized aspects. But as Leo Tolstoy argued, man's on-going struggle for civilization occurs *within societies*, not between them (a battle I lost when I failed to finish that book by Leo Tolstoy). It is wildly over-simplistic to imagine that European history has been a straightforward quest for progress from the savagery of prehistory to the Romans, from the Dark Ages to the Renaissance, until we finally arrive at the Tate Modern, sipping a cappuccino looking out over St Paul's and the shiny new bridge feeling infinitely superior to everyone who came before. When we look back at Ancient Rome and say, 'That was civilization,' what we are really saying is, '*Aren't we civilized too?*' It is a way of flattering ourselves, of reassuring each other that having literature and great architecture, debating chambers and a legal system and advances in technology are the only things that matter; forget the levels of exploitation or inequalities of wealth upon which our 'civilization' is built. Both societies have their dark side, except our version of *Gladiators* is tackier than theirs was. Like the Roman world our society has incredibly civilized features coexisting with extreme brutality. Our slaves aren't in the fields around the villa, they are thousands of miles away working in sweatshops in Indonesia, but the principle is the same. We no longer occupy foreign territories to demand taxes, we reap the interest from indebted third world countries (which is pretty much the relationship that Rome had with Britain between Caesar and Claudius). If the mineral resources required by our economy look threatened, then, just as in Roman times, war will be the final resort. You watch: the moment that North Wales refuses to export all its pearls and animal hides, Washington will be invading Colwyn Bay under the pretext of the war on terror.

The other great myth used to justify all powerful empires, be they Roman, British or American, is that they guarantee peace. In fact by their nature they create injustice and exploitation and all the other things that make war ultimately inevitable. One British chief had the measure of Roman imperialism: 'Where they make a desert, they call it peace.'*

In fact in Britain the *pax Romanus* had never been that peaceful, and what is remarkable about the four centuries of Roman occupation of Britain is what little permanent impact it had on the country. Subsequent invaders left the villas to crumble, built their towns adjacent to the sites of Roman settlements and stripped the Roman walls and sections of the roads for building materials. Very quickly Latin ceased to be the *lingua franca* (except for that bit, obviously). This was in contrast to much of mainland Europe where the cultural impact of Rome endured long after the collapse of the Empire. In Britain, Celtic tradition and custom reasserted itself very quickly, even if some regional warlords may still have aspired to Roman ways.

Britain was finally free of a foreign power, though the ordinary Briton probably felt little sense of liberation or patriotic deliverance. Apart from the acute poverty endured by the ordinary peasant, which tends to distract from such unimaginable concepts such as liberty and self-determination, there was also the pressing fear that other more numerous invaders might at any moment exploit the military weakness of the island.

Just how bloody and cataclysmic these new invasions were it is

---

* The Roman historian Tacitus records this line in a speech by Galgacus to his troops, but Ridley Scott has it being said by Connie Nielsen to Russell Crowe in the film *Gladiator*. You make up your own mind.

hard to know, for no records were written, or if they were, almost nothing has survived. By the middle of the fifth century Britain had fallen into what is commonly known as the Dark Ages, when people travelling the countryside alone always emerged from swirling mists as a lone raven cawed eerily in the distance. Although we know less about this period than any time in the last two millennia, it is arguably the most significant period in the history of the British Isles. For this was when the English arrived. Never had an invading force queued so politely before killing everyone.

2

The Dark Ages

How wave after wave of immigration made (and continues to make)
Britain the rich, fascinating and occasionally suspicious country
it is today

It must have been hard being a liberal in the fifth century. You'd try to talk in encouraging terms about all the positive aspects of multi-culturalism, about the wonderful rainbow mix of ethnic traditions and customs, and then all the immigrants let you down by splitting every-one's head open with an axe, forcing you and your family to flee for your lives. 'Yes, well, you see, in their religion, murder and pillage is very much a matter of honour so I think it would be rather culturally élitist of us to attempt some sort of universal moral judgement based on our own ethical— Oi! The bastard – he just nicked my ox!'

By AD 500 conservative social commentators might have been justified in saying that they felt that Britain's native culture was 'being somewhat swamped'. No matter what the well-meaning lefties said about never prejudging people by the blondness of their hair, immigration in the fifth century meant conquest, robbery, homeless-ness and murder. Where the Romans had arrived four hundred years earlier to displace the ruling class, the Anglo-Saxons now displaced an entire society from top to bottom. They hadn't come to colonize the Celts or subjugate them or tax them; they were here to com-pletely replace them as the only inhabitants of what we call, thanks to them, 'England'.

Recent DNA studies have revealed that there was far more inter-marriage between Saxons and Celts than previously thought, but Britain's racial cocktail was still changed more fundamentally at this time than at any other. Most of the people who had lived here before were pushed out, and whole new races of people occupied the land in their place. Unlike the Romans or the Christian Celts, these new invaders were not literate, and so the most cataclysmic century in British history went completely unrecorded; no contemporary records were made, or if they were, they were destroyed in the rush for the best hut. The Dark Ages are so called because we know so little about them – we have literally been kept in the dark by the almost complete absence of contemporary accounts. But they were also very dark times politically speaking, with constant invasions, wars and slaughter. Plus it still got dark at around half past four in the winter, because daylight saving time wasn't introduced until May 1916.

The foggy mysticism surrounding these lost centuries means that the history books are full of vague supposition and phrases like: 'The invading Jutes must have felt a great sense of foreboding as they stepped ashore to make a new home in the fertile lowlands of Kent.' Well, maybe. But no one knows. You could just as easily write: 'The invading Jutes were feeling particularly ironic as they stepped ashore and proceeded to walk around making sarcastic comments about how rubbish Kent was.' If ever you are stuck writing about prehistory, just talk about their 'gods' in the plural and it sounds like you know what you're talking about. Anyway, these new invaders would have given thanks to their *gods* for their safe passage and would have made animal sacrifices in order to appease their *gods*.

It must have required an incredible amount of effort and organ-ization to venture across the North Sea with everything you needed to fight battles and then start a new life in a new country. If today it takes us about three days to decide what to pack for a week in Majorca, imagine how much planning must have gone into the wholesale emigration to an unknown and hostile foreign land: 'Right. Helmet, sword, shield, spear, axe, plough, yoke, seeds, scythes . . . are you sure we've packed everything?'

'I've only got one light jacket for the evenings. Do you think that will be enough?'

Hengist and Horsa: first, *two* Saxons move in . . .

The new arrivals were from the nearest part of Europe that had not been colonized (some would say 'civilized') by the Romans: northern Germany and the Danish peninsula. There had always been contact, of course, and as order collapsed in England, German mercenaries were hired by regional warlords attempting to cling on to power. The hired hands liked what they saw. Two Saxons, whom legend names as Hengist and Horsa, decided to stay, rebelled against their British commander and seized the land for themselves. This was at some point in the 440s and over the next fifty years wave after wave of Germanic and Scandinavian tribes landed along the coasts of England. Of course most of Britain was still forest – and not managed, National Trust forest with woody glades, picnic tables and information boards showing you what a badger looks like. England was covered in a thick impenetrable mesh of thicket, fallen trees and bramble which barely exists in Britain today outside the gardens of student houses. The few patches of Celtic farmland would have been very highly sought after; it takes years of toil to clear forests and drain marshes, whereas turning up, killing the farmer and moving into his hut takes about twenty-five minutes. The geography of south-eastern England makes it particularly vulnerable to invasion. The land closest to continental Europe consists of large areas of fertile lowland with countless navigable rivers beside which most of the arable land would have been concentrated. If the British Isles had been the other way up, and adventurers crossing the Channel had been suddenly confronted by the impenetrable Scottish Highlands, the history of these islands would have been very different indeed. However, this rather pointless observation does not seem to have made it as one of the great 'what if?' questions of world history.

But by 495 the invading Anglo-Saxons had pushed as far north as

York and west to Southampton. The sheer weight of numbers of these pagan warriors overwhelmed the indigenous Britons.* Unsurprisingly the Britons being driven west by the invading Angles and Saxons despised their oppressors, and held them in such contempt that even centuries later they had no interest in trading or converting them to Christianity. Today it is almost impossible for us to imagine the Welsh feeling any enmity towards the English, but back in AD 500, any Saxons thinking of getting a holiday cottage on the Gower peninsula would have been well advised to get a smoke alarm. Other Celts fled north across Hadrian's Wall creating the Celtic kingdom of Strathclyde, or south-west where Devon and Cornwall became known as West Wales. Some fled the country altogether with many Britons emigrating to north-western France, which became known as 'Brittany' as a result. Here they managed to forget the horrors of mass English invasions right up until Brittany Ferries introduced the Plymouth–Roscoff route in the 1970s.

King Arthur: as true an English hero as St George himself

It is during this catastrophic first century of Anglo-Saxon conquest that the immortal British hero King Arthur is thought to have lived. The legend recalls that in the face of this Teutonic onslaught, one chivalrous king gathered his court at Camelot† and then rode out to fight the pagan invaders with such heroism and Christian forbearance that his name has lived on for evermore. Clearly there

* Historically the name 'Briton' referred to the Celts who were pushed out by the Anglo-Saxons – it was over a thousand years later that the word 'Britain' was self-consciously adopted to denote all the countries that made up the 'British Isles'. The description is especially useful for describing Olympic champions from Scotland or Wales.
† 'Camelot' was an invention of Malory, whose *Le Morte D'Arthur* gives us most of the legend that we know today. The myth was further embellished by Geoffrey of Monmouth, Tennyson and Monty Python, although historians have questioned the historical accuracy of all of these versions, especially that bit where Lancelot is savaged by a little white rabbit.

would have been Celtic chiefs leading their people in defence of their lands and there was a battle at somewhere called 'Badon Hill' that seems to have halted the advance of the Saxons for around fifty years. But the name Arthur does not appear in any records until hundreds of years after he was supposed to have lived and the first account of his heroics says that all the 960 people killed in the battle of Badon Hill were slain by Arthur alone – so clearly a very reliable source.

But the romantic notion of this great British warrior grew with time, acquiring scholarly credibility from imaginative Norman historians. Then in 1191, the monks of Glastonbury dug in their cemetery and affected to have stumbled upon the body of a large man buried in a tree trunk. This was King Arthur, they proclaimed, and a forged inscription was produced as proof. The fact that their abbey had recently been destroyed by fire and the monks badly needed funds to rebuild it was neither here nor there. The association of Arthur with the West Country began as a money-making tourist enterprise and that remains the purpose of his legend today, as anyone who has paid for one hour in the Tintagel Pay and Display Car Park will testify. If we needed further convincing that King Arthur is just a legend we only have to look at the people who are keenest to believe that the fairy tale is fact. In the alternative bookshops the Arthurian legends are shelved alongside books on ley lines, crystals and crop circles. Give it another thousand years and the history books will be debating whether Luke Skywalker really existed or not.

England divided into separate kingdoms: no one wants Redditch

Another massive wave of Germanic immigration began around AD 550 and three main tribes were now firmly established in what now became known as 'Angle-land'. The Angles also gave their name to East Anglia and moved inland to create the kingdom of Mercia in the Midlands. The Saxons established kingdoms that evolved into English counties: the South Saxons ruled Sussex, the East Saxons, Essex and those in the middle created Middlesex (the 'sax' suffix was changed to 'sex' to make it harder for female history teachers to keep order in all-boy schools 1,500 years later). The largest of the Saxon kingdoms was Wessex, too large in fact to be remembered as a modern-day county, although bizarrely it did reappear when Prince Edward and his new wife gave themselves the title the 'Earl and Countess of Wessex'. (This has probably less to do with remembering an ancient English kingdom than it does with Sophie Rhys-Jones having done *The Mayor of Casterbridge* for English O level.) The Jutes, meanwhile, colonized Kent. You have to feel a bit sorry for the Jutes. No one ever talks about our Anglo-Jute heritage. Compared to 'White Anglo-Saxon Protestants', the acronym 'WJSP' never stood a chance. The Jutes (from the tip of the Danish peninsula) were numerically the smallest of the invading tribes; not content with occupying Kent, they also successfully conquered the Isle of Wight, a triumph which has failed to impress military historians as much as Stalingrad or Iwo Jima.

Another Saxon kingdom was established north of the Humber, unimaginatively named 'Northumberland'. The relative fortunes of these kingdoms ebbed and flowed, but for the first couple of hundred years there were around six or seven Anglo-Saxon kingdoms; worshipping the same gods, speaking similar dialects, but soon competing for land, influence and trade. Each of them had a series of kings – the main qualification for the job seems to have been based on who had the most unpronounceable name. Eawa of Mercia ruled at the same time as Eorpwald of the East Angles, whose brother was Raegenhere and father was Raedwald.

It was Raedwald's ship that was buried, probably with him inside it, in a huge barrow at Sutton Hoo in Suffolk. This discovery in 1939 was an incredible breakthrough in the study of early Anglo-Saxons.* For buried in this time capsule were countless royal treasures, Saxon tools, curious artefacts and a copy of the AD 624 *Blue Peter* annual. Raedwald had been buried in the same manner as the Anglo-Saxon

---

* The archaeologists were disappointed that their discovery got less coverage than they expected. They made their find in the last week of August 1939, and the news editors all decided to lead with this other story that was knocking about. 'The outbreak of World War Two'.

literary hero *Beowulf*: entombed in a ship facing out to sea. The hoard revealed that the early Anglo-Saxons had an extensive trading network with coins from Constantinople, Egyptian bowls, a Byzantine plate, Frankish coins and a shield, sword and warrior mask all made in Sweden judging by the little IKEA logo. Like the ancient Egyptians they buried their kings along with treasures and everyday objects, for even in 624, despite paying lip service to Christianity, these were still very much a pagan people, worshipping (among others) Tiw, the god of combat, Woden, the god of war, and Thor, the god of thunder.* There was no god of 'trying to get on with people'. Although the Christian Celts must have thought these pagan invaders to be utterly without morals, the barbarians had their own strict code of honour which allowed them to behave with such apparent cruelty. In the same way that a gangster will blithely torture or murder a rival but would be appalled by the immoral idea of betraying fellow gang members to the police, the Anglo-Saxons put loyalty to their 'kin' above all else. If one of your kin was murdered you were duty bound to avenge this death – failure to do so would bring shame on you and your family. Eventually a system of payments evolved, the wir-gild (or war gold), where money would be accepted instead of the life of the murderer, with strictly defined prices according to the status of the victim. You paid more for having murdered a thane than you would for having murdered a peasant (unless you had a really good accountant).

'Hello, have you heard the Good News about Jesus?'

Britain had of course been Christian once before and efforts had been under way for some time to convert it all over again. The story goes that in 597 the powerful Pope Gregory was in the marketplace in Rome and among the slaves on display were a couple of striking children with blond hair and blue eyes. On asking their origin, he was

* It is from these gods of course that we get many of our days of the week. Tiw's Day, Woden's Day and Thor's Day.

told they were Angles. The Pontiff looked at these innocent creatures and quipped, 'Not Angles but angels.' Being Pope, this pun got a slightly bigger laugh than it probably deserved; the cardinals were falling about at this one: 'Not Angles, but angels,' they repeated, wiping the tears from their eyes.

Encouraged by their enthusiasm, maybe he thought of taking it further. 'Perhaps I should do a bit of stand-up at the Coliseum?'

'Your holiness?'

'You know, go out in front of thousands of ordinary Romans and do my *non Angli sed angeli* gag.'

'Er, the thing is, sir, that the commoners may not be ready for that level of sophisticated humour . . .'

Instead the Pope declared that if these Angles looked like angels, then it was time their people were converted to Christianity. He sent his reluctant emissary Augustine to begin the work of the Lord and so southern England was converted to Christianity on the basis of a weak pun.

Many areas of the British Isles that had not been occupied by the Anglo-Saxons had been Christian for hundreds of years. The Celtic refugees living in Wales and Cornwall had been converted in Roman times. Meanwhile Patrick had converted the whole of Ireland in the middle of the fifth century, for which he got the top award of the day, being made a saint. 'And let the feast of St Patrick be celebrated evermore . . .' declared the Pope, 'by Irish theme pubs sticking up giant inflatable shamrocks as office workers are served too many pints of Guinness by puzzled Croatian barmaids wearing leprechaun hats.'

In 563, from a monastery he had established at Iona in the Western Hebrides, the Irish monk St Columba set about completing the conversion of the Scots and the Picts and soon Northumberland too was Christian. Although word of the gospel spread rapidly, the Anglo-Saxons took a few decades to get it. They believed in the one and only God as set out in the first commandment, while still worshipping all the other Norse gods just to be on the safe side. One pagan king said that if he had been at the crucifixion of Christ he would have avenged it and slain all those responsible. At which there was an embarrassed pause and the Christian missionary sighed and said, 'Right, let's start again . . .'

St Augustine (as he inevitably became) established the first arch-bishopric in Canterbury in 602 and Pope Gregory, glancing casually at an old Roman map of Britain, instructed him to found the other at York. Being thousands of miles away and about two hundred years out of date, the Pope didn't quite appreciate that York was now in a completely different country and that this was quite a demanding task. Especially as Augustine was so high-handed and arrogant towards the old British church that had clung on in the face of adversity for hundreds of years. However, by the middle of the seventh century, most of the country had rejoined Christendom. The only problem now was that there were two versions of Christianity: Roman and Celtic (that's 'Celtic' with a hard 'C'; people beating up Rangers fans in the name of religion came much, much later). Even the dates for Easter were different, which played havoc with the price of chocolate eggs. And so the first ever all-British conference was called in 664; the Synod of Whitby. The invitations caused quite a stir when they dropped through the letterbox.

'Darling, fantastic news – we've been invited to a synod!'

'A what?'

'You know, er – a synod.'

'What's a synod?'

'A synod is a, er – well, it's . . . well, it's hard to explain, you'll sort of pick it up when we get there . . .'

'OK, where's it happening? Venice? Paris? Ibiza?'

'Whitby.'

'Oh, spiffing. You promised to take me shopping in Paris and now you are saying we have to go to a synod in bloody Whitby.'

The conference was called by King Oswiu of Northumbria in AD 664. He followed Celtic Christian practice, which involved feasting at Easter; his wife who followed Roman practice was still fasting for Lent; the entire history of the British Church was rewritten because Mrs Oswiu was on a diet and she was annoyed that her husband wasn't. From all over Britain clerics, bishops and other Christians converged on Whitby; they say the drinking and feasting went on till half past nine at night. Finally the Synod came down on the side of the Roman traditions; King Oswiu (who sounds West African but this seems unlikely in Northumbria in 664) declared that he would prefer to go along with the traditions of St Peter, declaring that, *I dare no longer contradict the decrees of him who keeps the doors of the Kingdom of Heaven, lest he should refuse me admission.* Basically, always try to avoid offending the bouncer.

Of course these early Saxon Christian converts understood that the word of the gospel was not to be taken literally. Where it says, 'Thou shalt not kill', they were sophisticated enough to appreciate that this was a metaphorical commandment, and one interpretation might be: 'Kill everyone who stands between you and seizing power.' One brutal king who spared no one on his rise to the throne was King Offa (reigned 757–96). From his central kingdom of Mercia he acquired Sussex, Kent and East Anglia, while Wessex and Northumberland became passive neighbours. His contemporary the great frankish king Charlemagne recognized him as the ruler of all England, and agreed to a marriage between their two royal houses. Offa built churches, encouraged literacy and introduced the first widely accepted English currency since the Romans; his 'pennies' were accepted all over the country. Yet all we remember about King Offa is the enormous earthwork that still bears his name today. Having abandoned plans to conquer Wales he declared that the only thing that could stop the Welsh coming into England was a great big dyke. 'OK, what about Olaf's sister?' Once they had got that joke out of the way, work could begin on the largest fortified barrier since Hadrian's Wall. It was a huge undertaking: a deep ditch, then a raised earthwork rising twenty-five feet above that with wooden fortifi-cations on top and command posts along its 150-mile length from the Severn Estuary to west of the Wirral. In order to build it, Offa clearly needed to be in control of both sides and so he constructed the dyke some distance behind the front line, abandoning some Anglo-Saxon villages to their fate on what was to become the Welsh side of the border. This must have caused a certain amount of alarm to the English villagers who saw this enormous barrier going up between them and their only escape route from the marauding

Welsh: 'Erm ... excuse me, the solicitor said nothing about this when we bought the house. I mean this really ought to have come up in the search . . .'

With the threat of Welsh incursions now contained, with peace existing between the various Saxon kingdoms, with Christianity bringing a return to literacy and increased communication with the scholars of Europe, England seemed to be finally emerging from the Dark Ages. But then in 789, the year that Offa's daughter was married to the King of Wessex, some strange visitors turned up off the coast of Dorset. *And in his days came first three ships of Norwegians from Horthaland; and the reeve rode thither and tried to compel them to go to the royal manor, for he did not know what they were. And then they slew him.*

Viking Onslaught (and other heavy metal bands)

This reeve appears to be the first Englishman killed by the Vikings. His village was left with no one to do all the, well, all the reeving. This account of his death was recorded in the Anglo–Saxon Chronicle – the official record of events in late Anglo–Saxon England. Soon, readers of the Chronicle got fed up with reading the same depressing news year after year: *Vikings Raid Lindisfarne! (793) Jarrow Monastery Burned By Viking Thugs! (794) Iona Monks Murdered by Vikings! (795) Inside – Stop this Viking Misery says the Chronicle.**

When the planners had been trying to decide where to place the first monasteries they had decided that remote coastal locations would be best. 'Yes, where better to store all those golden religious artefacts and bejewelled Bibles than on an unfortified island?' The Vikings couldn't believe their luck as they plundered one monastery after another, murdering the monks while they knelt and prayed, destroying their beautiful handwritten manuscripts and ornate

---

* Most of these events were in fact recorded retrospectively by the Anglo–Saxon Chronicle, which did not begin in earnest until the reign of King Alfred.

gospels; entire libraries were burnt along with everything else. What was so terrifying about the Vikings was not just the suddenness with which they appeared, but also the savagery of their attacks. None of the usual European rules of engagement seemed to apply. King Edmund of East Anglia was tied to a tree and used for target practice by Viking archers, a Northumbrian king had his lungs ripped out of his chest, while another king was apparently hung from a tree by his testicles. Of course, our view of the Vikings is coloured by the fact that for centuries our only source material was the Anglo-Saxon accounts of their raids and so we have tended to stereotype the Vikings by presuming that they were all brutal and thuggish. And, of course, 'you don't get a second chance to make a first impression'. The earliest Viking raiders to leave Scandinavia tended to be the sons of farmers who had no land of their own. They were young, they were male, they had had a few beers. Imagine hundreds of football hooligans going on a booze cruise armed with swords and axes, and the wanton violence no longer seems so alien. Scandinavian society was, of course, as complex as any other, with great artists, craftsmen and storytellers. In fact the Vikings were only doing what the Anglo-Saxons had done to the Celts three hundred years earlier, who themselves had displaced earlier inhabitants and so on. In the case of the enforced lungectomy for example, it turns out that these Vikings were avenging the death of their father who had been thrown into a pit of poisonous adders by the Angles, so today a playground super-visor would say, 'Well, you're both as bad as each other.' But after centuries of gradual progress, of increased learning and prosperity, the Vikings were an utter catastrophe for Christian Europe.

For it wasn't just England that was suffering at the hands of these raiders; the Vikings sailed up the River Seine and ransacked Paris (to avenge a particularly rude waiter); they terrorized Spain and Portugal; their raids took them as far as Italy and Islamic North Africa. They were incredible seafarers, colonizing Iceland, Greenland* and of course discovering North America five hundred years before Columbus. Other

* A remote Viking community continued to live on Greenland until it mysteriously disappeared in the Middle Ages.

Vikings went East, founding Russia and besieging Constantinople. But the British Isles were in their direct firing line and felt the brunt of their attacks. For over two hundred years English society was on the verge of collapse; those that had escaped murder or slavery faced starvation as grain stores were burnt and livestock was slaughtered. So in fact, even if they did tell a few sagas and make nice jewellery, they were still a bunch of vicious bastards.

King Alfred: 'You think you're sooo great, don't you?'

Into this chaos a young English prince was born in Wantage in 849, who was to become the greatest king in Anglo–Saxon history. His father was the King of Wessex, by now the dominant English kingdom, who in three disastrous years had witnessed the Vikings completely overrun Northumberland and East Anglia. Two great English kingdoms ceased to exist, for the Vikings were no longer mere pirates returning back home for the winter, but were now set upon colonizing the whole of England. In 870 they camped at Reading ready to strike at Wessex, but Alfred and his older brother achieved the first military victory over the Vikings, even though Alfred's brother had been late to the battle because he would not leave mass until the priest had finished. Alfred became King of Wessex the following year and after suffering a military reverse, managed to buy off the Danes* for the time being while they turned their attentions to Mercia. The once great kingdom was easily conquered, leaving Alfred's Wessex standing alone against the ninth-century blitzkrieg of the Vikings. A demoralized and frightened people did not have much hope that this twenty-two-year-old king would fare better than the leaders of the other Saxon kingdoms, but at every turn Alfred proved to be creative and determined as he led

* The names 'Vikings' and 'Danes' have become interchangeable but generally speaking the Scandinavians who sailed down the west coast of the British Isles, founding Dublin and Cork and raiding Wales and Cornwall, were Norwegian Vikings, while those that attacked the east coast, Northumberland, Yorkshire, Lincolnshire and London etc. were Danish.

a fightback that brought hope to the whole of Europe. A grateful
Pope even sent him a piece of the original cross on which Christ had
been crucified.* King Alfred sought continental expertise on ship-
building and built a fleet of boats longer and faster than those of the
Danes, with the result that he managed to destroy a Viking fleet of
120 ships in the English Channel. The Viking leader Guthrum
signed a treaty saying they would leave Wessex alone, and he and his
men were allowed to join their countrymen in Mercia. Wessex it
seemed, was safe.

But Alfred's weakness was that he trusted the Vikings not to break
their word. At Christmas 877 he sent his nobles back to their estates
while he retired to Chippenham. On twelfth night the Vikings struck
with a massive army combining Guthrum's forces with the Vikings
who had taken control of South Wales. Alfred was taken completely
by surprise and was forced to flee and hide out in the Somerset
marshes.† Here, in disguise, he took refuge in a peasant's hut where
a housewife told him to watch the cakes while she went to fetch
water. So deep in thought was Alfred that he didn't notice the smoke
coming from the stove and when she returned she scolded him for
burning the cakes. He then revealed his identity and the woman
begged for forgiveness, but Alfred was humble and merciful saying
that she had every right to be angry.

There are those who doubt the authenticity of this story (i.e. *all*
reputable historians), but the account appears in the *Ladybird Book
of Kings and Queens of England* so it must be true. Either way, it is the
incident for which Alfred is most famous. You defeat the Vikings,
you found the navy, you establish a new legal system, creating the
shires and boroughs, you invent the candle clock, you learn Latin at
the age of forty so you can translate classical works into the language
of the common people, you set up the Anglo-Saxon Chronicle, you
restore the churches and the monasteries and then people say, 'Oh

* There were quite a lot of pieces of wood from the original cross in circulation at
the time – enough to make a few hundred crosses anyway.
† Nearly a thousand years later, a piece of jewellery was found here bearing the
Saxon legend 'Alfred had me made'.

yeah, Alfred – you're that bloke what burnt all those cakes.' But Alfred is also of course the only English king to have earned the title 'the Great'. He could have done a lot worse – his contemporaries in France were Charles the Bald and Charles the Simple (and his brother 'Charles the Hard to Pin Down to One Particular Attribute').

Now Alfred was to set the pattern for the preferred British template for historical greatness. When all seemed lost, at the nadir of his people's fortunes, he was to pull off the most spectacular of his military victories. Hiding in the marshes while the Vikings ransacked his kingdom, he sent out messengers that a new army was assembling. Amazed that their King had not fled or been killed, Saxons were inspired by him to fight one last time. Now, under Alfred's leadership, they utterly defeated the Vikings at Edington in the key battle of the war. Alfred was able to dictate terms and not only insisted that Guthrum be baptized, but made himself the Danish leader's godfather, so that Guthrum would not betray his new family loyalty. Every year after that Alfred had to try and remember to get his godson a present. 'Oh look, here's a fiver, buy yourself something.'

England was now divided in two. Alfred ruled Wessex and took much of Mercia, while everything north of the old Roman road between London and Chester, Watling Street, became what was known as Danelaw. Anglo-Saxons living under Danish law would not be persecuted and Alfred allowed some Vikings to continue to live in London. Today the Vikings constitute another key strand in our racial make-up. In fact there are those who put the independent nature of Yorkshire folk down to the fact that they are indeed a different race of people. Back in 870, they were all walking round Jorvik in horned helmets* slagging off southern beer and saying, 'Ee,

* In fact the idea of the horned Viking helmet is a relatively modern invention and no archaeological evidence has ever been found to support this popular image of the Viking. Early Celtic and Germanic tribes did have helmets with horns, wings or antlers for religious or ceremonial purposes, but such headgear would have been a hindrance in battle. Despite this, modern-day Scandinavians now wear horned helmets when supporting their national football teams, though these helmets are plastic and inflatable and frankly offer very little protection.

I think bluddy Danelaw is bluddy marvellous!' Viking place names abound in Lincolnshire and Yorkshire – anything ending in 'by' or 'ness' or 'thorpe' denotes a Viking lineage.

The history of randomly drawn political borders – Palestine, Northern Ireland and the partition of India for example – has always provided a very helpful pointer to indicate where the next war is going to be. Clearly Wessex and the Vikings would fight again, indeed Alfred fought many more battles, driving out another wave of Vikings who sailed up the Thames to Fulham. But thanks to Alfred, a solitary Anglo-Saxon kingdom had survived and he could turn his attention to securing what he had: fortifying the towns (including London), reviving the monasteries and churches that had been destroyed in the Viking raids; and trying to shake off the stubborn 'bloke who burnt the cakes' image. Alfred's ambition of unifying the Anglo-Saxon lands would not be achieved in his lifetime. But Alfred had a favourite grandson, and gave the little blond boy a great Saxon sword and belt and royal cloak before he died. It was this boy who would grow to become the most powerful Saxon monarch ever, finally uniting all the English into one kingdom.

Athelstan: great king, rubbish PR agent

Athelstan ought to be a famous king. But not having had as good an agent as Offa or Alfred, he never developed a gimmick or nickname.

'I could build a dyke? What about "Athelstan's dyke".'

'It's been done.'

'I could burn cakes.'

'Yawn. That is *so* 870s.'

'Oh well, at least I've got a really easy name to remember.'

'Of course you have, Al . . . satian?'

'Athelstan. Athelstan the Memorable.'

Athelstan was the king who conquered Danelaw for Wessex. It should be pointed out that for the Mercians or the East Anglians this was not necessarily seen as liberation so much as conquest by an alien power. There was no concept of being 'English', whether you lived in Durham or Southampton. Indeed, when Athelstan occupied the symbolic Viking capital York, there was shock that a southern king should have so exceeded his natural boundaries. Athelstan's father Edward had already pushed the borders of Wessex as far as the East Midlands, but now with the Vikings having become farmers rather than warriors, they were no longer the invincible army that had seized the land two generations earlier. Athelstan's army conquered Northumberland (which stretched well into modern-day Scotland) and the Kings of the Scots and of the Celtic kingdom Strathclyde acknowledged him as their overlord. He marched through Cumbria and defeated the Welsh, and the five kings who ruled within Wales met him at Hereford and agreed to pay him a massive yearly tribute of 20 pounds of gold, 300 pounds of silver and 25,000 oxen. His family were delighted with the 25,000 oxen to start with, but the trouble is they grow so big and need so much exercise. Athelstan also attacked West Wales (Devon and Cornwall), pushing these Britons back as far as the river Tamar, which is where the boundary of Cornwall remains today.

In 937 at Brunanburgh he defeated an unlikely alliance of Scots, Northumbrians, Icelandic, Norwegian and Irish Vikings; not even this impressive coalition of former enemies could defeat King Alfred's grandson and now Athelstan was recognized on the continent as King of all Britain; indeed, on his coins he described himself as *Rex totius Britanniae*. His sisters were married off to European monarchs; one got Hugh the Great, the other got Charles the Simple. 'Er, sisters; I can't think of a way of doing this fairly . . .' Two years later Athelstan died, and a succession of kings of the house of Wessex managed to hold on to what he had won. During the Middle Ages it was Athelstan, not King Alfred, who was viewed as the greatest of the Saxon kings.

The final Scandinavian onslaught (not including Abba)

But this new Anglo-Saxon state was a fragile collection of regional differences. Thousands of Danes resented the rule of a Saxon and looked to their homelands for possible leadership. It came from Norway, in the shape of the terrifying royal exile Eric Bloodaxe. Bloodaxe was just one of many Vikings whose names struck fear into the hearts of Christians. He had contemporaries such as Thorfinn Skullsplitter and Harold Wartooth. Obviously these weren't these leaders' real surnames; they were *noms de guerre* they adopted in order to intimidate their enemies. It wouldn't have been much good leading your men into battle with a name like 'Eric Flowerpress'. 'We cannot fail in our brutal slaughter of the Christians, for we are led by Olaf Tidyhouse.'

Eric Bloodaxe arrived as a Scandinavian saviour to the Danes of Northumberland, forging an alliance with the Vikings who ruled in Ireland with the intention of creating a Norse superstate which straddled the Irish Sea. For a while it worked; he declared himself King Eric, until finally the Wessex forces caught up with him and he was killed at the Battle of Stainmore in 954. But a massive new wave of Viking invasions was about to descend on the country. Now more than ever the country needed a king who would be ready. Unfortunate then, that the crown now came to Ethelred the Unready. In his *History of the English Speaking Peoples*, Sir Winston Churchill describes Ethelred as *a weakling, a vacillator, a faithless, feckless creature*, so he was lucky to get away with just being called 'unready'. 'Typical! Just when everyone else is ready to leave, Ethelred starts packing.' In fact the only thing we remember about Ethelred isn't even what was meant. His nickname was an elaborate pun on his own Christian name – 'rede' meant counsel, 'ethel-red' meant 'well counselled', so the joke is: 'Good-counsel the no-counsel'. Well, you sort of had to be there.

Of all the terrible leaders that this country has had to endure, Ethelred was up there with the worst of them, somewhere between King John and Margaret Thatcher. He had not got off to the best of starts: at his christening he had managed to crap in the font.* Ethelred had the ultimate in pushy mothers; when his half-brother King Edward

* This is according to a twelfth-century historian, William of Malmesbury, so may of course be a fabrication. But it is not the kind of detail you put in about someone you are trying to build up as a national superhero.

came round to her house, she had him stabbed to death, so that her boy Ethelred could be king in his place. But Ethelred was not up to the task. When Vikings landed demanding money, Ethelred gave it to them. Unsurprisingly they came back and asked for more and a frightened Ethelred paid them again. What his mother had clearly not told him is that you have to stand up to these bullies eventually.

'Tell me, Ethelred, this bully – Olaf, you said his name was. I bet he's not got many friends, has he?'

'Yes, he's got loads of friends, 'cos he's got all that money I gave him.'

'Maybe just try and avoid him, dear.'

'You don't understand. He's got thousands of mad, axe-wielding warriors who are going to cut each of my ribs away from my spine and then stretch my lungs out in the Viking sacrifice known as the blood eagle.'

'Well, dear, often the fear of pain is worse than the pain itself . . .'

The money Ethelred paid out was called the Danegeld; a word that entered the English language as a symbol of the coward's way out, best summed up in Rudyard Kipling's rather plonky poem:

> But we've proved it again and again,
> That if once you have paid him the Danegeld
> You never get rid of the Dane!

The Danegeld became such a burden for the country that thousands of free peasants had to give up farming their own little patches of land and were forced into serfdom by the crippling taxes Ethelred levied.

Finally Ethelred did stand up to the bullies, but in the most cowardly way possible. Instead of meeting the soldiers in battle, he hatched a plan that every Scandinavian in the country be murdered on the same day. There was a great difference between the young Viking soldiers who had just sailed from Norway, and the settled, Anglicized Danes who had been in the country for several generations, but Ethelred was panic-stricken and convinced that he was about to be assassinated. The St Brice's Day Massacre in 1002 was an orgy of co-ordinated, cold-blooded racial murder – England's own Rwandan genocide. Across southern and eastern England there were stories of babies being crushed under cartwheels, women being buried up to their waists in order that their breasts could be ripped off by dogs; when Danes in Oxford took refuge in a church, the locals burnt it down with all the Danes inside. Far from making Ethelred more secure the massacres provoked fury in Scandinavia. The King of Denmark's sister was one of the victims and now King Sweyn* sailed to England and for four years exacted a bloody and protracted revenge. Blinded or limbless victims of the Vikings' fury stumbled around southern England, a gruesome reminder of Ethelred's disastrous tactics. Ethelred paid Sweyn more bribes, this time 36,000 pounds of silver (about three years' national income). But Sweyn returned again, occupying much of southern England and seizing the Archbishop of Canterbury. When no more money was forthcoming, the drunken Vikings tied up the Archbishop of Canterbury and pelted him to death with cow skulls and animal bones. Frankly, it had all got very unpleasant.

Canute 'misquoted' over stopping tide claim

Sweyn's son was King Canute, who would soon become King of England, Norway and Denmark.† But there was to be one last flicker from the great royal house of Wessex. Before Ethelred's miserable reign had even come to an end, his courageous son Edmund Ironside was already making up for lost time. Disobeying his father (who considered Edmund a dangerous rebel) the young prince struck a series

---

* Sweyn's father had been Harald Bluetooth. It is this ruler of Norway and Denmark who inspired the creators of the wireless specification to name their product 'Bluetooth' – which unites mobiles, PDAs, computers, printers etc. in much the same way he united Scandinavia. Apparently. (The Bluetooth logo comes from Harald Bluetooth's initials in Nordic runes.)

† Many modern historians spell Canute's name Cnut, but I prefer the old-fashioned spelling as it doesn't make me think of French Connection's 'fcuk' campaign overstepping the mark.

of blows against the Vikings. When Ethelred made his best move yet by dying, the twenty-year-old Edmund became king – at least in the parts of the country that were not under the control of his contemporary and great rival Canute. After the Battle of Ashingdon (near Southend) Edmund struck a deal with King Canute, that whichever of them outlived the other would rule the whole country. Edmund mysteriously died soon after. The story goes that his assassins hid under his toilet and ran their swords into him from beneath as he was sitting there, even though from that angle he looked nothing like his picture. This means of murder did not remain fashionable for very long as they discovered that it involved hiding down there for ages with no guarantee that half a dozen people wouldn't use the toilet before the intended target.

With no proof that the chief beneficiary of his death was the instigator of it, Canute was now unopposed and English nobles recognized him as their king in 1017. It was over two centuries since those three strange ships had turned up in Dorset. Now the Scandinavians ruled all of England.

To provide some legitimacy to his claim to the throne Canute married Ethelred's widow Emma, the sister of the Duke of Normandy. Being a 'can-do' kind of monarch, Canute didn't let irritating obstacles like the fact that he was already married get in the way, and he sent his other wife to live in Scandinavia, saying to her, 'Honestly, what are you in a mood about now?' The churches seemed to forgive Canute for his bigamy, as his reign brought a period of much-needed peace to a war-ravaged and bankrupt England. The last Danegeld payment was made in 1018 and with England's King controlling the Viking homelands, a disastrous era of English history had finally come to an end. His empire eventually stretched across the North Sea uniting Denmark, Norway, England, parts of Wales, Scotland, Sweden and the Isle of Man, which he actually had the good manners to visit. The next English monarch to visit the Isle of Man after Canute was Queen Elizabeth II (though after her trip the royals thought they'd leave it a bit longer next time).

Today Canute's only claim to fame seems to be the legend of the power-mad King believing that he could order the tide to stop coming in, only to find it lapping around his ankles. In fact he was attempting to prove the opposite to his fawning courtiers, who had told him that he was powerful enough to command the seas.

'Did you hear about King Canute? Thought he could stop the tide coming in . . .' said everyone.

'No, I was demonstrating my humility . . . I said I *couldn't* stop the tide coming in . . .'

'Fancy thinking he could command the sea? Talk about an egomaniac . . .'

'Hello? Is anyone listening? I ORDER THIS RUMOUR TO STOP NOW!'

Sadly he wasn't all-powerful enough to turn back the tide of the gossip either. Canute died, probably out of exasperation, in 1035. His disparate empire did not survive his death, and although his two sons briefly ruled England neither of them produced heirs and so in 1042 the throne passed to their half-brother Edward the Confessor, the offspring of their mother Emma of Normandy and her former husband Ethelred the Unready. Even after his death Ethelred's policies would prove disastrous for England; it was this Norman connection that formed the basis for William the Conqueror's claim to the English throne.

Edward the Confessor: 'All right, it was me'

The penultimate Saxon king was actually a puppet of the dominant nobleman of the day, Earl Godwin, who had him marry his daughter while taking huge swaths of land for himself and his sons. Edward the Confessor's weakness led to two rival factions emerging at court, the Saxons under Godwin and the King's fellow Normans. 'Ah, it's nothing . . .' said the onlookers. 'I'm sure this whole Norman/Saxon rivalry thing will blow over . . .' Edward was a deeply religious man, attending confession every day, hence the rather unimaginative nickname. He commissioned the building of Westminster Abbey so that large groups of French children with identical rucksacks would have somewhere to visit on school trips to

London. During the period of the Danegeld, England's tax-collecting system had had to become very efficient and now large amounts of money were accrued that did not immediately disappear across the North Sea. But Edward spent much of it on pointless religious relics; Saxon wide-boys were queuing up to flog the gullible King bits of old rubbish that they claimed had immense religious value.

'Eddie, mate, have I got something here for you? This is yer actual skull of St Kenneth of Stevenage.'

'Really? It's very small; looks more like the skull of a badger or something?'

'Oh yeah, well, he was famously badger-like, St Kenneth. In fact legend tells how he transformed into a badger to escape the Romans.'

''Tis a miracle. I must have it. I shall keep it with the original self-assembly instructions from the one true cross.'

This was cash that might have been spent on strengthening England's defences, but the King left the country dangerously under-prepared for attack. On his deathbed he warned that a great calamity was about to strike his kingdom, as if this was an incredibly prescient prediction. Everyone just nodded and said, 'Yes, well, whose fault might that be?' After Edward's death an urgent ship-building programme was undertaken, but his successor simply would not have enough time. It was 1066 and everyone was saying, 'I'm sure that date is significant for something but I just can't remember what.' Then seven thousand Normans came sailing over the Channel and they said, 'Oh yes, that was it.'

Harold II – son of Earl Godwin – had not been an automatic choice as King of England when Edward had died in January 1066. But he had impressed on military campaigns in Wales and was popular and charismatic despite the absence of royal blood which would have meant handing the crown to Edmund Ironside's young grandson at a time of obvious national crisis. The Saxon throne had become something of an elective monarchy and Harold was seen as England's best chance against the Norman army preparing on the other side of the Channel. But England's last Anglo-Saxon king would be dead before the year was out.

Anglo-Saxon England had emerged from the chaos of the Dark

Ages and two centuries of Viking wars to become one of the most advanced and well-organized societies in Europe. It had a well-developed legal system, effective regional government, good trade networks, strong coinage and thriving churches and monasteries. But this society was about to be shattered. Everything Anglo-Saxon would become persecuted or suppressed for evermore – well, at least up until the 1970s when Saxon imagery became briefly fashionable with the designers of heavy metal album covers. In northern France the descendants of Viking settlers or 'Norsemen' had created the highly militarized dukedom of Normandy and it was from here that William eyed the rich kingdom which he claimed had been promised to him by his second cousin Edward the Confessor. William had been greatly angered by Harold's accession to the throne. In his youth Harold had been shipwrecked on the shores of Normandy, and William had made him swear on sacred relics to support the Duke of Normandy in his claim to the English throne. Now they would meet again, on a battlefield in southern England in what is generally considered to be the last successful foreign invasion of Britain.

The 'Anglo-Saxon' English (and other racial myths)

The period from the Roman departure to the Norman Conquest had seen the most dramatic and fundamental change in the racial make-up of England's population, and it would never be so sudden or violent again. Perhaps it was during that unhappy period between 410 and 1066 that our fear of new arrivals became hardwired into our collective psyche. Perhaps now when we see a family of asylum-seekers moving into a hostel in the town centre, there is a little bit of us still worried that they might tie us to a tree and pelt us to death with animal skulls (which apparently they do quite regularly according to the *Daily Mail*). This theory might hold true but for one significant historical fact. Though the racial DNA of the British was more or less created during those tumultuous five hundred years, *it has changed far more since then*. When we casually refer to ourselves as Anglo-Saxon, we are lazily ignoring the constant intermingling of the races that has continued ever since. 'One hundred per cent Anglo–Saxon with perhaps just a dash of Viking,' was how Tony Hancock described his blood group, but this line was of course satirizing this popular misconception of who we are.

So in the unlikely event that you are reading this book having just arrived in the United Kingdom from Somalia with nothing but the scars of war and an enormous sense of trepidation about what your new home will be like, there is something you should know about all the confident, busy people you see around you. *They are all immigrants too*. Everyone in Britain is of foreign stock. Some, like the Saxons or Vikings, arrived many generations ago, jumping out of longboats waving swords above their heads (which certainly saves all that red tape you had to go through at the Sangatte detention centre). But a far greater number arrived in the past few generations: refugees from other wars or revolutions or simply economic migrants looking for better wages and somewhere where you could get a pickled egg and a warm pint to wash it down with. There isn't a single person left in Britain who is a result of marrying and remarrying within the same tiny gene pool of those original Neolithic Britons (though there's a village in Norfolk where I have my suspicions).

Since 1066 our society has been continually enriched by thousands upon thousands of Dutch weavers, German bakers, Russian Jews, West Indians, Ugandan Asians, Bengali waiters and Premiership goalkeepers; all of them regarded with a certain amount of suspicion and disdain by the people who had got here a generation or two before them.

'I see some Huguenots have moved in at number 36.'

'Well, there goes the neighbourhood. Once you get one lot move in, another family takes over the house next door and before you know it the whole street is full of them, smelling of garlic and moaning about the Revocation of the Edict of Nantes.'

In fact the French Huguenots who arrived after 1685 soon accounted for one per cent of the English population. They continued to speak their own language for over a hundred years and still spoke French on Sundays in Victorian times. By then there had been another massive influx of European immigrants: thousands of

Germans came to Britain in the nineteenth century; in the 1800s there was barely a baker's shop in London that wasn't run by Germans. Since the nineteenth century census went online, thousands of English amateur genealogists have been discovering that they are not so English after all. Prince Charles was shocked. 'You mean there's German blood in the family!?'

But the greatest-ever wave of immigrants to these shores was not the Saxons in the fifth century, nor the Vikings in the ninth century, nor the Normans in the eleventh. It was Eastern Europeans in the twenty-first century. In terms of pure numbers, more Polish and other Eastern Europeans arrived in Britain in the years after EU expansion than any other racial group in the islands' history. The British economy boomed as a result, even if it did mean we had to surrender certain charming British traditions such as waiting three hours for the plumbers to turn up so that they could mix up the sewage outlet pipe with the taps on the bidet. In another age such a huge foreign influx would have caused riots and house-burning, but we have come a long way since the days of Eric Bloodaxe.

The depth of Britain's cultural heritage is reflected in its native tongue – English has a larger vocabulary than any other major language. This is just one legacy of all the diverse nationalities that have enriched our culture before *and after* the watershed of 1066. That same wealth of ingredients applies to everything else in Britain's make-up; the more skills, ideas, trades and cultures that you have in any one community, the richer that society will be. Especially as the people who upped and left their own homes to carve out a new life elsewhere were by definition among the most enterprising and dynamic individuals around. For every fifth-century Jute forging an exciting new life in the Isle of Wight there were probably a couple of unmotivated siblings lying around back in Jutland, saying, 'Yeah, well, I would have invaded Britain, but, like, I just never got my act together.' Imagine what the Isle of Wight would be like now if Britain had never had that constant renewal of immigration; imagine how dull and narrow-minded and economically stagnant Shanklin would be today. OK, bad example. But Britain has thrived *because* of its immigrants, not despite them. The evolution of the British people did not end with the Dark Ages or the Norman Conquest – that was just the starting point. The reason that 1066 is such a significant date in English history is that it is the last time a load of foreigners came over and really did take all our jobs and move into our houses. After that each influx of immigrants has started at the bottom of the pile rather than at the top.

The trouble with the Normans is that they had no intention of coming over here to scrape a living running late-night take-aways while their girlfriends worked as au pairs for the Saxon middle classes. And they didn't need any other immigrants to work as their servants either. They already had a very specific group of people in mind for that. The English.

3

The Normans 1066–1216

How the British class system became established and entrenched by some snobby French nobles whose descendants still have second homes in the Dordogne today

It happens all the time. You arrive at some genteel drinks party on a warm summer's day; you're hot and your mouth is dry but now you can almost taste that big cold glass of delicious beer. And then the host utters those dreaded four words: 'Red or white wine?'

'Er, I'd rather have a beer if you have one, please.'

'No, it's just wine, but there's mineral water if you don't want to drink.'

And you think, *Yes, I do want to drink*. I want to drink beer, thank you very much. Not red wine, not white wine: I want to drink the English national tipple and not stand around wincing as I sip some acrid plonk just because you think *vin rouge* is somehow more refined or civilized.

And it's all bloody William the Conqueror's fault. Coming over here with his fancy French ways and an entire new ruling class. He turned the free English into serfs, he seized the land, he laid waste whole areas of country massacring the local population, burning homesteads and food stocks so that the survivors would die of starvation or disease. But did he ever stop to think about the likes of me being forced to stand at some snooty bloody garden party sipping Piat d'Or and wondering just how cross my wife would be with me if

I popped down to the off-licence and came back with four cans of Hofmeister?

Because that's when Britain's bizarre class system got so distorted. We've still not recovered from having an alien upper class foisted upon us nearly a thousand years ago. And so affecting French sophistication is still *de rigueur*, while all our most offensive words are Anglo-Saxon. 'Shit' and 'excrement' mean the same thing, but one is Saxon, the other is French. That is why you will never hear a BBC newsreader saying, 'Several British beaches have lost their blue flags after EC inspectors detected unacceptably high levels of shite. The Prime Minister described the decision as "bollocks".' French vocabulary defines the language of refinement, law, government and finance. The very word 'parliament' comes from the French '*parler*', meaning 'to fall asleep on the back benches and have disturbing dreams about Ann Widdecombe'. Animals as looked after by the peasants in the fields are still known by their Anglo-Saxon names: pig, cow, calf. But once they are served up at the banquet they are referred to by their French names: pork, beef, veal. (And then they become McDonald's one hundred per cent Beef McDippers and go full circle to the bottom of the social scale again.)

Of course, every society has its social divisions, but the British class system is more peculiar and divided than most, and much of this dates back to 1066. In other countries, the class distinctions have evaporated more easily but here, where social classes became exacerbated by race, language, custom and appearance, there are still a thousand subtle nuances that distinguish the descendants of the Norman barons from the descendants of the Saxon peasants, all of them with some sort of insidious value judgement attached. Whether you look down on everyone else from a Norman horse or a Japanese 4×4, the principle is the same.

The Battle of Hastings: England finish as runners-up

Back in 1066, nobody would ever have guessed that they were living in the most famous year in English history. There had been countless invaders in the preceding centuries and there would surely be many more to come. But there was definitely a sense of crisis approaching. Saxon spies reported an invasion fleet being prepared over the Channel. Overhead, Halley's Comet blazed a portentous trail across the sky, while the threat of armed revolt from Tostig of Northumbria added to the Saxons' worries. The non-royal Harold II had only received the English crown a few months earlier in rather contro-versial circumstances and England was a divided and poorly prepared kingdom. Harold was doing his best to hold it all together but we all know what it is like trying to organize large groups of people to do anything.

'No, listen, everyone, listen. Can you *not* keep wandering off because we have got to stay here on the south coast in case we need to fight a big battle – excuse me, where are you going?'

'I'm just popping home to my estate, I won't be long.'

'No, no, that's what I'm saying – it's really important that we all stay right here. Hang on, I've got a message – Oh. Change of plan, listen, everyone, we all have to go up north to fight the Scandinavians . . .'

'But you said we had to stay here to fight the Normans . . .'

'I thought the Normans were Scandinavians?'

'Listen, Harold, is it all right if I meet you up there?'

'NO, IT IS NOT. Everyone, please try and stick together and listen for instructions.'

Harold II's army had waited on the south coast all summer for William. But isn't it always the way? You wait ages to fight one army and then three come along at once. Harold's disloyal half-brother Tostig had lost power in Northumberland and was sulking by pillaging the Isle of Wight, Kent, Norfolk and Lincolnshire. He then teamed up with the King of Norway who also believed the English crown to be his. Leaving the south coast undefended, Harold was forced to march north to take on this invading army. Tostig and Hardrada United had already won their first local fixture in the qualifying stages, which put them through to face King Harold in the second round. But the Saxon army was too much for the plucky part-timers from Norway. They were so comprehensively beaten that of the three hundred longboats in which they had arrived only twenty-five were required to take survivors back home. The Battle of Stamford Bridge finally ended the Scandinavian threat to England and would provide an easy headline for sports writers every time a Chelsea home game involved a minor scuffle.

But fixture congestion being what it was at this time of the season, Harold now had to rush south because William the Conqueror had just landed in Sussex.

'Er, why's he called William the Conqueror?'

'Oh, don't worry about that, it's just a nickname.'

In fact, during his lifetime, William's nickname wasn't 'Conqueror'; he was actually known as 'William the Bastard', owing to the scandal of his illegitimacy. Oh, and the fact that he was a complete bastard. It's hard to know how openly this nickname was bandied about. Since he was a ruler who thought nothing of having a man's tongue pulled out and nailed to his front door, you'd probably exercise a certain amount of caution before calling him 'William the Bastard' to his face. 'Oi, look, everyone, Bill the Bastard's here! Oi, Bastard, do you want a drink? Hey, I'm talking to you, BILL THE BIG BASTARD!' And yet you try repeatedly pointing out this nickname when you are at school and for some reason they decide you are a disruptive pupil.

William was the result of an affair between his father, the previous Duke of Normandy, and a lowly tanner's daughter. Many years before Hastings, when the Duke was besieging a castle at Alençon in France, the garrison inside mocked him with the origins of his mother's family, hanging animal hides over the ramparts and beating them. This little bit of topical satire did not go down too well with the Duke and when he captured the fort, he ordered that thirty-two of them had their hands and feet severed in front of the townsfolk. But apart from that, William liked a good joke as much as anyone.

Having convinced himself of his entitlement to the English throne, William considered Harold's acceptance of the crown to be an act of gross heresy. For Harold had sworn on sacred relics to help William become king. William had witnesses; hadn't those burly soldiers with the big swords been standing right behind Harold at the time? The Norman invasion force had been assembled using a sort of eleventh-century share issue. 'For just a small investment of a few hundred soldiers and horses, you could be the proud owner of this lovely estate in the famously sunny resort of Mercia. See brochure for details. (Please note: not all participants can be guaranteed an English country home. You may be horribly killed by axe-wielding Saxons.)'

Finally, after months of waiting, the wind was in the right direction. The ferry organizers apologized once again for the delay and asked customers to make their way to the embarkation points. Seven thousand Norman, Breton and Flemish soldiers boarded for England with weapons, armour, siege equipment and horses. Any weight limit on personal baggage allowance was overlooked.

When they finally did land there was another bad omen to add to the uncooperative weather. A Norman biographer tells us that William stepped ashore, tripped and fell, but turning misfortune to his advantage he declared, 'You see – I already have the soil of England in my grasp.' Since Julius Caesar is reputed to have made the same quip in response to the same misfortune, William either preplanned the stumble and the line, or the witness who reported this was very, very old and was getting his invaders mixed up.

It was just three days after Harold's victory near York. Now he had to march his battle-weary soldiers south again. He could have paused at London to wait for reinforcements, but William was already laying waste parts of Wessex – the historic seat of Harold's family. Perhaps this is why the tired Saxon army was rushed down to confront these Norman upstarts. Whatever the reason, it was a fatal mistake.

The famous battle didn't actually happen at Hastings but at a nearby place called 'Battle'. The Normans were walking around wondering where they were supposed to be fighting the Saxons when they saw the helpful signs pointing up the road saying 'Battle 3 miles'. 'Ah, look, it's this way, lads!' But they decided to call it the Battle of Hastings because they thought 'The Battle of Battle' sounded stupid. Oh, and also because the place was called Senlac until William ordered Battle Abbey to be built on the spot where Harold fell.*

It was the morning of 14 October and Harold continued to do his best to get his motley soldiers organized: 'Now, listen, we all have to stay on the top of this hill – Sorry, could everyone stop talking, I was just saying we all have to stay at the top of the hill and not chase any retreating Normans, OK?'

'Chase the retreating Normans – got it.'

'No, no, *don't* chase the retreating Normans, because we're all foot soldiers and they have cavalry, so if we come off the hill we lose our advantage. Did you all hear that at the back?'

'Something about foot soldiers have to come off the hill or something . . .'

William arranged his forces along the bottom of the hill, with his back towards the coast where his boats were waiting should he suddenly decide he needed them. With the two sides not sure how to begin, a Norman minstrel ventured into no man's land, juggled his sword and sang 'The Song of Roland'. Heckling was less witty in 1066 and the Saxons just killed him. Battle had begun. The Norman bowmen began to fire on the English position but made little impression on the well-defended English ranks, and so throughout the morning the Normans were forced to charge up Senlac Hill towards the English shield wall, where they suffered heavy casualties. Time and time again they charged and were forced back. With discipline and patience, it looked like the Anglo-Saxons might be victorious. Even on the left flank where the slope was gentlest and the Breton soldiers finally did reach the Saxon shield wall, they were forced to turn and flee.

'Come on, let's chase the retreating Normans!'

'Didn't King Harold say something about that?'

* This was a classic piece of annoying whimsy from a king. The top of a hill was a really stupid place to build an abbey because there was obviously no water supply. The monks wanted to build the abbey at the bottom of the hill but William insisted it should be on the spot where Harold died. 'Well, can't we just say he fell next to this handy stream, so we don't have to lug every last drop up the hill and we don't have a howling wind coming through the windows all winter?'

'Erm . . . maybe? Look, they're getting away!'

In a wild and undisciplined charge down the hill, the Saxons broke ranks, thinking the enemy was on the run. But the Saxons were the victim of a feigned retreat. Once the English were off the hill and out of formation, the highly trained Norman cavalry suddenly appeared and massacred the foot soldiers. This tactic was repeated on other parts of the hill until the English defensive line was completely exposed. Two of Harold's brothers died and finally King Harold himself was slain, though the accounts of how this happened vary. He is popularly believed to have got an arrow in the eye, but this might just be a case of mistaken identity on the Bayeux Tapestry. One eleventh-century account has Harold pulling this arrow from his eye and fighting on until a Norman knight skewered him through the heart, chopped off his head while his guts were strewn across the ground and his left leg was cut off at the thigh. Oh, and then his corpse was castrated just for good measure. Luckily these details didn't make it into the Bayeux Tapestry; they were worried about getting a 15 certificate and there was already a lot of controversy about all the gratuitous violence in these so-called 'tapestry nasties'.

It doesn't take much to work out that the Bayeux Tapestry isn't a hundred per cent reliable and honest. For a start it's not a tapestry and it isn't from Bayeux. The 'Canterbury Embroidery' (as it should be called) covers many of the events leading up to the invasion, presenting the Norman version of Harold's time in Normandy and the death of Edward the Confessor. The tapestry is 230 feet long and wasn't completed until the mid-1070s. Finally, this enormous work of art was laid out before King William.

'Your majesty, we present the Bayeux Tapestry – the largest embroidery in all of Christendom, hand-stitched by hundreds of artists from your new kingdom.'

An anxious pause while the King strode up and down, examining this epic work. 'Hmmm. These people here are the Norman soldiers, are they?'

'That's right, sire; hundreds of them, individually embroidered in lavish colour.'

'Hmmm. These figures, they're a bit . . . well, how can I put this? Well, they're a bit *rubbish*, aren't they?'

'Rubbish, sire?'

'You know – very badly drawn. Childish. Little stick men fighting each other. Just not very good.'

'But, sire, this embroidery has taken years of painstaking labour by dozens of devoted artists.'

'Artists?! Do me a favour; look at these horses, they look like a six-year-old did them.'

'But horses are really hard, I can never get the legs to bend the right way . . .'

'What's wrong with a few close-ups, or a bit of scenery here and there? It's a crap tapestry, let's be honest. No wonder you have to have all this writing across the top explaining who everyone's supposed to be.'

'But, sire, it was created to be displayed in your royal palace.'

'Look, I don't know much about art, but I know what I like. Why don't you guys keep it at Bayeux, maybe I'll come in and see it when I'm next over in Normandy. Not.'

Perhaps the reason that the Bayeux Tapestry isn't the world's finest work of art is that the brutish Normans were less concerned with what it looked like and more interested in what it actually said. The Bayeux Tapestry is an exercise in spin, a hand-stitched piece of propaganda, the *Pravda* of the eleventh century. Never was it more true that history is knitted by the winners.

Saxon England at the precipice: 'Time for a bold leap forward'

And lo, at the hour of England's greatest need, a child prince did step forth to lead them . . . Could it be that this young Saxon prince might sweep the English to a legendary victory? Could a mere child turn out to be one of the greatest war leaders this land had ever known, famously expelling the invaders and becoming a national folk hero who would inspire poets and storytellers down through the ages? Well, no, frankly. He was a complete waste of space. But the thirteen-year-old Edgar the Atheling was the only royal they had left; and they'd tried employing a king on merit, which just led to lots of arguments and military disaster.

But although the Battle of Hastings had been an unequivocal victory for the Normans, neither side could know for certain that the war was over. William waited in Sussex for the Saxon nobles to come and pay him homage but no one came. Instead the surviving earls declared Edgar their new king in an attempt to give heart to the English resistance. Given that Edgar was only thirteen years old, it probably had the opposite effect.

'This is not the end . . .' he might have implored them.

'Er, I think it may be . . .'

'This is not even the beginning of the end . . .'

'No, it's the end of the end.'

'We may have lost one battle. But have we lost the war?'

'Er, yes, we have.'

So Edgar surrendered, only to rebel unsuccessfully again several more times. (This begs the question: 'Why didn't William just have the Saxon prince put to death?' The most likely answer is that Edgar was so useless a leader that it was better for William to have his enemies rallying behind a no-hoper than any subsequent replacement who might actually pose a genuine threat.) Eventually William advanced towards London where he threatened to besiege the city and eventually the disunited and demoralized Saxons submitted to the conqueror. William I was crowned on Christmas Day 1066. This was year zero for the new British monarchy. Although there had been previous Edwards, for example, all kings are numbered from one upwards after 1066.

Westminster Abbey was surrounded by heavily armed Norman soldiers, so any parishioners who'd turned up to sing 'Little Donkey' decided not to complain about the double booking. There was some confusion inside the church when the oaths were read out in different languages, and the commotion prompted the Norman soldiers outside to slay bystanders and burn the surrounding buildings. It's very easy to criticize our security services but they only have a split second to make these decisions. Obviously they were mortified by their mistake and forever after the French riot police promised to be a model of restraint and fair play.

William had persuaded himself that he was the rightful king and heir to Edward the Confessor. But where his cousin had built Westminster Abbey, William felt the need to build another more foreboding London landmark. A few miles down the river, work began on the Tower of London, which, like so many Norman castles around the country, would come to symbolize the military power of the new regime. The first forts were motte and bailey castles, hastily thrown up earthworks with wooden fencing behind a moat. These defences could be very rapidly erected – the first one built at Pevensey was completed in eight days, which is even more impressive when you think how the French always stop for a two-hour lunch break. The large number of motte and bailey castles reveal just how nervous the Normans were about the local population and there was indeed enduring resistance in many parts of the country. Chester didn't fall to the Normans until 1070, while in the east the final stand was taken by the legendary Hereward the Wake who made his base on the impenetrable Isle of Ely. From a stronghold in the middle of the impassable Lincolnshire fenlands, Hereward held out until 1071, when he was betrayed by some local monks who were bribed into revealing a secret route through the bogs and marshes. English resistance to the Normans was over. But I'm sure it would have been a great consolation to the last Saxon hero if he'd known that nine hundred years later Peterborough's local radio station would be named 'Hereward FM'.

The motte and bailey castles were followed by more permanent structures of which over a thousand were built around the country under the Normans. The castle was the symbol of occupation, of Norman military power. As instruments of war no castle could be built without a licence from the King. Sometimes getting planning permission was a nightmare; the secret was to make friends with one employee in the planning office and always try and speak to them.

It should be stressed that England as such was still a fragmented place with divided loyalties which made a unified national resistance impossible. There were loyalties to local earls, Viking sympathies in the north and east, and within ten years of Hastings, Normans were rebelling against their Norman King. Basically, if you're ever stuck for something to say about any period of history, just say, 'Of course, it was far more complex than people generally imagine,' and you can't go far wrong.

William was not only vulnerable to rebellion from inside his new kingdom. Other foreign powers still fancied themselves as conquerors of England. During William's first trip back to Normandy, his former ally Count Eustace of Boulogne organized an invasion of England. 'Under my crafty leadership, my invincible French knights will conquer all of Britain, English dissidents shall flock to my banner, overthrowing William and making 1067 the legendary year of King Eustace the Conqueror.' He got as far as Dover, failed to take the new castle and went home again. Harold's sons landed from Ireland in 1068 and were easily defeated, and 1069 saw a number of landings, the most significant of which had a Scandinavian army joining up with northern earls who seized York and declared independence. William then arrived with an army determined to reduce the likelihood of any more rebellions in the North by killing everyone who lived there. During the infamous 'Harrying of the North' he laid waste entire regions, destroying every village and farm for miles around. Those that escaped the initial massacre were doomed to starvation as crops were systematically burnt, ploughs broken and livestock slaughtered. The death toll was thought to be around 150,000 and during the following winter survivors were reduced to cannibalism, reputedly cracking open the skulls to eat the brains of their former neighbours. Mind you, that's Northerners for you: black pudding, faggots; they'll eat anything like that. Fifteen years later in the Domesday Book, once thriving villages were recorded with a single word entry: *vasta* – meaning wasteland, or nothing.

These uprisings convinced William that only his fellow Normans could be trusted with any power. During the first decade of his reign around four thousand English nobles had been allowed to keep their land on payment of a tax to the King. But from the early 1070s onwards these ancient lands were seized and consolidated into much larger units that became the private fiefdoms of around two hundred Norman barons. Like so many corner shops being swallowed up by the supermarkets, this run of hostile takeovers marked a massive shift in England's social structure – within a decade one ruling class was entirely replaced with another, more powerful and more demanding of wealth and labour. Many English noblewomen became nuns to avoid being forced into marriage with Norman barons. There were minor battles as Anglo-Saxon nobles resisted their evictions – but eventually thousands were forced into exile.

'Don't worry darling, we shall smuggle our riches abroad with us – what is the source of all our wealth?'

'The land.'

'Damn.'

Everybody's gone serfin'

But at least the rich were free to leave. For the Anglo-Saxon peasants who had worked the fields as comparatively free tenant farmers, a new social order was gradually imposed which would see them legally tied to the land they farmed. The rapid spread of serfdom in England dates from William's social revolution and, for the next four hundred years, most of the population would become effectively owned by the local lord of the manor. Before 1066 many of these men had played a part in their local affairs; their grievances had been aired before and judged by groups of small landowners and farmers. Within a century they would have no rights in law and their grievances would be settled by their lord (who was of course the person they'd be most likely to complain about).

'Excuse me your lordship, I would like to object to this so-called droit de seigneur, whereby the lord of the manor apparently gets to deflower my fiancée the night before our wedding . . .'*

---

* The 'droit de seigneur' or 'right of the first night' appears in stories as diverse as *The Marriage of Figaro* and *Braveheart* but there is actually little evidence to suggest that it was widespread practice.

'Honestly, you serfs, you just moan about every little thing, don't you? So I get to sleep with every maiden in the village for evermore? What's the big deal?'

Although serfs could not be individually bought and sold at market like Roman slaves, neither were they free to leave the manor and work elsewhere.* If a parcel of land was sold, then the embittered, disease-ridden serfs went with it (or 'loyal, hearty farmworkers' as they were described in the estate agent's details). Serfs were allotted small parcels of land on which they could produce subsistence levels of food for themselves, but once they'd finished on their allotment they toiled the rest of the time for the lord of the manor.

Just to really rub their noses in it, the vast forests were now closed off to the common people, even if they had National Trust life membership. For centuries the woodlands had been a free source of food and fuel, but now they risked mutilation or having their eyes gouged out if they so much as caught a rabbit.†

The self-justifying philosophy of the feudal system was that 'the serf worked for all, the churchman prayed for all and the knight fought for all'. For it should be stressed that, unlike now, it was the upper classes who did the fighting in times of war. While England had a population of around three million, both William and Harold only had around six or seven thousand troops each at Hastings. If this system was still in place today, Andy McNab would be kept at home to watch the sheep while England would be protected by fearsome knights like Sir Norman St John-Stevas. It would be an enormous breakthrough some centuries later at the barons' 'Blue-sky Thinking Away-day' when some bright spark said, 'I know, let's get all the poor people to do our fighting for us as well!'

* If a serf did manage to escape from the manor to a 'chartered town' and evade capture for a year and a day, he was then released from his bondage to his lord. Just as with the *liberti* – the handful of freed slaves in Roman society – every exploitative system constructs the remote possibility of escape that prevents the oppressed from falling into total despair. Ours is called the National Lottery.
† Catching a rabbit wouldn't have been very likely, however, as they were not yet established in the wild. During the twelfth century the Normans brought them over and kept them in enclosed warrens. Then a few escaped and before long they were breeding like, well – whatever the simile was back then.

In the meantime, the King granted this land to the nobles with one major legal obligation: the barons had to provide a number of soldiers for so many days a year according to how much land they held. But isn't it always the way, you lend things to people and you never get them back in the same condition, there's always a leg or an eye missing or something.

By Christmas 1085, with his kingdom finally secure, the now rather corpulent King William held court at Gloucester, revelling and drinking and debating what the regime should do next. It was clearly a very fun Christmas because they emerged from the festivities with one really exciting, madcap idea; they were going to carry out a really thorough tax assessment.

The Domesday Book: 'No, you can't be ex-directory'

The Domesday Book was not the great survey's official title; the nickname stuck when some eleventh-century wag suggested that it was no less thorough than St Peter himself would be on the Day of Judgement. It was an enormous undertaking, quite unlike anything that had been attempted before. Surveyors came with their clipboards to every village, showing their plastic ID cards and reciting the same tired script: 'Hello, I'm calling on behalf of William the Conqueror. As you may have seen on the news, William is now King and has ordered that a thorough survey of the land be completed throughout his kingdom . . .'

'A new king? I never heard nothing about that . . .'

'Yes, well, it was only twenty years ago, and news travels slowly in these parts. So – how many oxen do you have?'

'Are they going to do something about those yobs who hang around the village green?'

'If you don't mind, we do have quite a lot of houses to get round, so if we could stick to the questions on the form . . .'

'And that bridge over the mill still hasn't been mended. You're all the same. First the Vikings get in, then back to the Saxons, the Normans; nothing ever gets changed . . .'

The assessments were agreed by juries in each village, who assembled in the open air; scribes would note down their estimates of land values and the number of pigs the woodland could support and which pubs did real ale and bar snacks. Today you can read the original entry for your own town or village on the internet, which gives you an idea of just how advanced they were.

The whole thing was written up by hand by one individual in Winchester, who rather brilliantly then managed to omit Winchester. The completed book is actually two books: Greater Domesday and Little Domesday. Little Domesday is actually the larger book, but is so called because it only covers the small area of East Anglia. The guys in data processing realized they were doing it all in far too much detail, and so rushed to the end before the deadline: 'Er Lake District, lots of lakes, some sheep probably and er, lakes.'*

If their aim was to complete the survey before King William died, then they failed. In 1087, during a military campaign to the south of Normandy, William's horse recoiled, having stepped on the hot embers of a town that William had just burnt down. He was thrown and suffered fatal internal injuries. His funeral was even more chaotic than his coronation. William's bloated body had already been robbed of jewellery and tipped on to the floor by his servants, and now the funeral mass was interrupted by an indignant man coming forward and complaining that William had stolen the land for Caen Abbey from his father without compensation. There was emphatic agreement from the locals, and given that a full-scale riot can some-times take the edge off a family funeral, William's son Henry paid the man off. Then came the dignified moment to lower the late king slowly into the specially made sarcophagus. The coffin wasn't big enough. They tried to force the swollen body in, splitting the corpse open and spilling out the internal organs that had been rotting in the heat of the late summer. The congregation fled in disgust covering their noses or screaming. And then later they all said, 'Aah, but it's what he would have wanted.'

* In fact Cumbria was not surveyed because in 1086 it was part of the kingdom of Strathclyde.

The Conqueror's sons: sibling rivalry gone mad

All brothers experience a certain amount of jealous rivalry. 'I sat in the middle seat on the way there', 'He got a bigger scoop of vanilla than me' or, 'I'm eldest, I should get England, Anjou AND Normandy.' But it doesn't mean you raise armies against one another or have your big brother assassinated so you can be King. Maybe William the Conqueror should have been firmer with his children, telling them that if they didn't stop arguing they would all get nothing. Instead the healthy competition that had his boys pouring urine on to one another from the castle ramparts evolved into full-scale military conflicts, with the eldest Robert instigating a rebellion in England to try and seize the kingdom from his younger brother William, while the youngest Henry bided his time before gaining the lands of both of them, most likely killing one of them and making the other his prisoner for thirty years. I blame the parents.

England's second Norman king was nicknamed William Rufus, owing to his red-faced complexion. He wore his blond hair long and parted in the middle and sported a moustache. William never married nor had illegitimate children and according to one Norman historian, was *a dandy dressed in the height of fashion however outrageous*. So definitely gay then. Another chronicler of the age bemoans the 'fornicators and sodomites' who were favoured at court during William's reign, so another little clue there for the eagle-eyed historian. However, this did not prevent him being every bit as ruthless as his father or brothers. He blinded and castrated those who opposed him, he funded his extravagant lifestyle with onerous taxes but unfortunately lacked the political skill that had helped his father turn Normandy from a minor duchy into one of the powerhouses of Western Europe.

William was a particularly irreligious man, whose lack of piety or any interest in the Church exasperated the clergy. He took years to get round to appointing a new Archbishop of Canterbury, during which time he took all the rents for himself. The monks who continued to record events in the Anglo-Saxon Chronicle were not particularly impressed that Church income should have been spent on fancy curly-toed shoes and Judy Garland records and said of William that he was hated by almost everyone in the land. His big brother Robert meanwhile was becoming the hero of Christendom as he liberated Jerusalem from the Turks in the first crusade. William got rather less credit for his campaigns against the Welsh; and those against the Scots, during which King Malcolm died and Carlisle was captured, which has been part of England pretty well ever since, to the extreme inconvenience of any English footy fan who has carelessly pledged to go to every away game in one season.

Like his father, William travelled the country imposing himself as a guest on various noblemen around his kingdom at little or no notice. These barons were expected to welcome their lord as their guest with all his retinue for as long as he cared to stay, laying on great feasts and entertainments, stabling all the horses, keeping the mini-bar well stocked and generally paying for everything until the King and all his hangers-on got bored and decided to move on. The expense of all this was crippling and sometimes noblemen would hide out in some lowly hunting lodge rather than appear to be at home when the King and his court turned up.

After a dozen years on the throne, William was unpopular with the Church establishment, despised at home and abroad and had behaved badly towards his younger brother Henry, the most likely heir to the throne. He became increasingly paranoid, particularly after his favourite nephew was killed by a single arrow in May 1100. All of which makes his own death three months later in the same place all the more suspicious.

Some saw it as God's judgement on a cruel and irreligious king. Others suspected a conspiracy that implicated the entire establishment. 'Why was that route taken for the hunt?' 'Was there a second bowman lurking behind the grassy knoll?' It is hard not to conclude that his mysterious death was indeed assassination, with his brother and claimant to the throne Henry the most likely instigator. Although Henry was with the royal hunting party, the King's body was left behind in the New Forest where it was discovered by a humble charcoal burner, a man called Purkess, who loaded it on to his cart and dragged it all the way to Winchester.* There was no public mourning and the body was buried without ceremony at the cathedral. The likely assassin, Walter Tyrrell, who had been with William during his last moments, slipped out of the country while Henry dashed to get himself crowned King just three days later.

Henry I: a very fertile king

As a mere prince, Henry had made great efforts to build bridges with the marginalized English nobility. He slept with no end of English women; his self-sacrifice in the cause of Anglo–Norman unity knew no limits. When one dispossessed English lady came to him in poverty after her husband died in prison, Henry went out of his way to help her. Their first child was born nine months later. Contemporary commentators, who were generally monks sworn to celibacy, jealously describe Henry's antics as 'chasing after whores' or 'brainlessly rutting like a mule'. Except that mules are generally sterile whereas Henry most definitely was not. He is known to have fathered around two dozen illegitimate children, nine of which were used as diplomatic pawns as they were married off to neighbouring royal houses from Scotland to France.

'But, sire, might it not be prudent to save your daughter's hand for a more powerful king?'

'Don't worry, there's plenty more where they came from . . . Just pull another one off the roll.'

Henry's anglophilia had even led to him taking an Anglo–Saxon Queen, a direct descendant of Ethelred, which united the Norman house with the ancient house of Wessex. While this union was celebrated by the English, the snobby Normans were appalled that their King had married below stairs. They couldn't possibly have a Queen called 'Edith', so she was forced to change her name to

---

* The Rufus Stone still stands on the spot in the New Forest where William was killed. As a great family day out, a visit to go and look at the Rufus Stone is hard to beat.

'Matilda' and do her best to chat in French at court. Any of her relations hoping to get a beer at the wedding reception could forget it.

Henry I was an effective and assiduous ruler. Unlike his predecessor he had little interest in lavish feasting and during his reign, a huge number of administrative and bureaucratic advances were made. The Exchequer became a distinct institution, so-called because they used a chequered piece of cloth as a basic abacus on which to do their sums. (Unlike the Arabs, the Europeans still had no symbol for the number zero, and so by the time they had finished trying to multiply MMMDCCXCIV by CMXLIX, it was the Renaissance.)

Advances were made in the legal system as judges began to tour the country in the circuit system that still exists today. The Normans had previously developed a custom of settling legal disputes by physical combat, in the belief that God would intervene on behalf of the righteous. 'Amazing! Yet again, God has chosen to agree with the champion all-in wrestler in his dispute with the little old lady who lives next door.' In the twenty-first century, it seems laughable to us that physical strength could be a factor in the matter of law; how much fairer today when law suits are settled on the basis of whoever has the most money.

Only physical force, however, could resolve the outstanding dispute of the day: who was the rightful ruler of England and Normandy. And so exactly forty years after the Duke of Normandy had invaded England, the King of England invaded Normandy and at the Battle of Tinchebray Henry united the two territories once again as his father William I had done. The battle itself was over in under an hour, with very few casualties. Henry's cavalry began by dashing in and capturing his brother Robert and after that there was not much point in carrying on. The crowd nearly asked for their money back.

Henry was now head of perhaps the most powerful empire in Western Europe; his kingdoms were prosperous and efficiently run; and his position was secured. So it was a cruel irony that the English monarch with the highest-ever number of offspring managed to die without a male heir. In 1120 his only surviving legitimate son

William died in a shipwreck in the English Channel, precipitating a succession crisis that would bring a decade of civil war.

Henry died in 1135 apparently from eating too many lampreys, which is a warning to all of us to eat lampreys in moderation. Never one for unnecessary glamour, he chose to be buried in Reading where the likely burial site is now a car park.

His daughter, also called Matilda, had been his favoured successor but to the less progressive Norman barons of the day this was not a very good plan. The reasons that it was simply not viable to have a female monarch in the twelfth century were manifold. For a start, marching to battle would involve stopping and chatting for ages with everyone you bumped into along the way. At the great feasts, roasted ox and wild boar would be replaced with a light salad. When asked for the specifications for a new warship she'd say, 'I'd like a blue one.' And so when news of Henry's sudden death spread it created the opportunity for another claimant, Stephen of Blois, to rush to England to try his luck.

'Sire, King Henry has joined his son and heir in heaven! Now is the moment to seize the throne for yourself.'

'Forsooth, how did he die? In battle?'

'No, sire, 'twas from eating too many lampreys. Your ship awaits . . .'

'Lampreys? What the hell are lampreys?'

' 'Tis a type of eel, sire. Your horse is outside . . .'

'If I may interject, m'lord, it's not actually an eel, it just looks like one. In fact a lamprey is a type of parasitic jawless fish that attaches its sucker-like mouth to trout and salmon and suchlike . . .'

'Sire, we must catch the tide or . . .'

'Eurgh! And people eat these lamprey things, do they?'

' 'Tis a great delicacy, sire. The food of kings.'

'What, they catch a salmon but think, "Yummy, it's got a big parasitic eel stuck on the side?" I'm not sure I want to be King now . . .'

By the time Stephen's disastrous reign was over, people were eating dogs, horses and anything else they could find as famine followed civil war and anarchy.

King Stephen v Queen Matilda: match abandoned after everyone killed

You could tell from his name that Stephen was never supposed to be King of England. 'King Steve' just sounds wrong – it would be like having 'King Kevin' or 'Queen Chloe'. But since many Normans weren't prepared to have a Queen Anybody, Stephen managed to persuade the key players that the country would be safer under his rule. They couldn't have been more mistaken.

Stephen's claim was not particularly strong; while Matilda had Norman, English and Scottish royal blood, Stephen hailed from the small county of Blois to the south of Normandy. But he was the grandson of William the Conqueror on his mother's side and qualification for the English throne was like the Republic of Ireland soccer team – one grandparent was generally enough. A more important factor had been how close to England Stephen had been when news broke of Henry's death. Stephen could slip over the Channel from Boulogne, while closer relatives were expected to remain in Normandy with the body of the late King.

Crucially, the Pope backed Stephen's claim. (The Church was still fairly conservative on the matter of equal opportunities. In fact the Catholic Church didn't finally allow female clergy until – oh, they still haven't.) But to talk of 'the reign of King Stephen' as if he always had complete control of the Empire in the way that his predecessor had would be misleading.

Taking advantage of Stephen's problems in England, French rivals took back chunks of Normandy, the King of Scotland invaded from the north while Matilda herself controlled large parts of the West Country and even held King Stephen as her prisoner after the battle of Lincoln in 1141. At this point Matilda briefly became the effective monarch, and was recognized as Queen by the Church, although bizarrely she preferred the title 'Lady of the English'.

But although this was a civil war between an English queen and a French usurper, there was little sense of national English resurgence. The Anglo-Saxon population didn't hate their oppressors because they were foreign, they hated the Normans because they oppressed them. The serfs who lived under Saxon kings (and beginnings of serfdom predate 1066) did not think, I don't really mind him taking all that wheat I grew because at least we can have a good chat about the cricket . . .

We've become used to the idea of war being tied to the idea of nationalism because for centuries that has been the easiest way for rulers to garner support. With a century of different propaganda it would probably be perfectly possible to get armies to march on the basis of, say, which sign of the zodiac they had been born under. 'The crisis in the Lebanon deteriorated further today, when a leading Sagittarian moderate was assassinated by a member of the Gemini militia. Hopes that the astrological ceasefire might hold faded when the Aries delegate walked out of talks, showing his characteristic impatience and incompatibility with other fire signs.'

Had Queen Matilda been able to call on the support of all the English in England there would have been no contest. But at any one point during the dozen-year conflict the advantage was generally held by whichever side had the most money to pay foreign mercenaries.

Matilda lost the upper hand when she was forced to release King Stephen in an exchange of prisoners that secured the return of her half-brother and the leader of her forces. Then she herself became trapped during the siege of Oxford. But by dressing all in white, she managed to slip unnoticed through the snow-covered landscape. A year later she was trapped again at Devizes and this time escaped by disguising herself as a corpse.

'Excuse me, guards, can you let through this cart carrying a body for burial?'

'Er, all right, but hurry up, we're looking out for a Queen dressed all in white. She'll be much easier to spot now it's not snowing.'

Despite her resourcefulness, Matilda (or 'Maud' as she was known to the Saxons) was a famously haughty and rude woman who managed to turn various possible allies against her with her charmlessness and obstinacy. She is sometimes considered the first Queen of England, if you discount the Celtic Boudicca and William Rufus.

But without one strong and universally recognized monarch

ruling England, private feuds between neighbouring barons also spiralled into violence with the poor often suffering the most during the chaos – as the Anglo-Saxon Chronicle recorded: *In the days of this King there was nothing but strife, evil, and robbery . . . and men said openly that Christ and his angels slept*. Strong words, but the Chronicle always told it like it was.

Exhausted by over a decade of war, and depressed by the loss of his wife and son and heir, Stephen eventually reached a compromise with Matilda. He would be allowed to rule unchallenged but upon his death the throne would pass to her son Henry rather than either of Stephen's children. Everyone thought this was a splendid plan, apart from Stephen's surviving son William.

Henry II: King bashes Bishop

Henry II was one of the greatest kings to sit on the English throne. He was an energetic, determined and intelligent operator who ruled for thirty-five years over a huge kingdom, stretching from Scotland to the Pyrenees. He brought peace and order to war-torn England, defeated rebels on all fronts, set down the principles of English law, established a Norman powerbase in Ireland, outmanoeuvred the King of France and secured his lands for his sons. But you kill just one archbishop . . .

So it is that all we remember about Henry II is a careless one-liner about a turbulent priest. Henry's primitive grasp of public relations meant he failed to foresee that killing Thomas Becket might not increase his poll rating for 'listens to others and accepts criticism well'. But apart from this PR disaster, Henry was a shrewd politician who excelled at war and diplomacy from an early age. When his great rival the King of France divorced Eleanor of Aquitaine for failing to provide him with a son, the nineteen-year-old immediately jumped in and married Eleanor himself. He fancied her because she had these *enormous* territories in the south-west of France. The English have been drinking Bordeaux and writing irritating memoirs about their holiday homes in France ever since.

Henry's Empire was so huge that it needed a king of great energy to govern it, but Henry was equal to the task, constantly on the move, always working, sitting down only to eat. Even his chaplain was chosen on the basis of who could say mass the quickest, so impatient was Henry to get on with the day's work. Already the ruler of about half of modern-day France, Henry inherited the English throne in 1154 at the age of twenty-one. One of the first tasks facing Henry was to face down the barons who had increased their power during the previous decades. Over a thousand castles had been illegally erected by independent-minded noblemen, but now Henry instructed them to pull them all down again.

'No, no, that's not a castle, it's a Wendy house. For the kids.'

'Why's it got battlements, turrets and a moat?'

'Well, it's a very big Wendy house, I'll admit.'

Having restored some sort of order in England, he dashed around Britain winning back the territories that had been lost to the Scots and Welsh.* It was also during Henry's reign that England began its disastrous eight-hundred-year campaign to colonize Ireland. After the King of Leinster was overthrown by rival chieftains he appealed to Norman soldiers to help him regain his kingdom. One Norman, who went by the name of Strongbow (after his favourite brand of cider), organized an invasion in 1169 and secured the former Viking settlements of Dublin, Wexford and Waterford for himself. Concerned at the possibility of a rival Norman powerbase over the Irish Sea, Henry invaded Ireland himself and eventually built a palace in Dublin. The area of Norman or English occupation around Dublin became known as the Pale, so that people could say to one another, 'You know, going beyond the clearly defined boundary of Norman occupation – that's really beyond the pale, that is.'

---

* Though of course neither Scotland or Wales were unified countries at this point. Wales was made up of a number of rival kingdoms, whose names reappeared during the 1974 local government reorganization; such as Dyfed, Gwynedd and Gwent. Similarly the Scottish region of Strathclyde is named after the ancient kingdom that occupied the west of Scotland, the Islands and the Isle of Man.

But Henry wasn't just a soldier. In the mini-renaissance of the twelfth century, Henry was a man of learning and culture. His subjects were to benefit from giant leaps in the concept of justice. Henry built a prison in every shire, and every sheriff had a sergeant with the power of arrest. The post of coroner was established to examine dead bodies when necessary.

'I am handing this body over to the coroner as I believe this death to be suspicious.'

'What makes you say that, Sheriff?'

'Look carefully, above his right ear, do you see?'

'Oh yes! A large axe sticking out of his head.'

Before Henry had laid down the basics of our legal system, one man could accuse another of theft or murder and if the lord of the manor felt so inclined the suspect would have his foot cut off. But exactly a century after the Norman Conquest, Henry established the principles of trial: by jury, of setting bail and a date for trial; all the basic pillars of basic justice were set in place as Henry added, . . . *and if he fail let him lose one foot*. So you still got your foot chopped off, but at least it was a fair cop.

However, improvements in the legal system heightened the problem of Church law versus secular law. If a priest nicked all the communion wine and went on a drunken rampage through the village, breaking his vows of celibacy with various farm animals, then was it enough for him to get a severe telling-off from the bishop? Henry thought not. This was just part of an ongoing power struggle between the monarch and the Church. The Pope was increasingly insistent that bishops be answerable only to him, while in the ultra-religious High Middle Ages, the King was determined that an institution as powerful and venerated as the Church should remain under his control.

Henry had the perfect solution to his battle with the Church. He would make his chancellor and best friend Thomas Becket,* the Archbishop of Canterbury. The established Church was appalled at

* Thomas Becket used to be known as Thomas à Becket, but that was apparently because of a mistake by a medieval historian getting him mixed up with someone else. Or maybe Thomas just thought it made him sound posher.

this prospect: Becket was not even a priest, he was not qualified to say mass, he had never gazed longingly at a choirboy in his life and yet here he was about to become the head of the Christian Church in England. The clergy was convinced that this was a catastrophe; that Becket was not sufficiently pious and would become a pawn of the King. Unfortunately for Henry, Becket was determined to prove them wrong. Almost immediately Becket transformed himself into the most devout and godly servant of the Church, zealously defending the interests of the Pope in defiance of the King who had put him in the job. Henry II was furious, reminding Becket that he was just a humble clerk when the King first took him on. Becket replied, 'It is true that I am not of noble blood but neither was St Peter.' So he was a smart-arse as well. No wonder everyone at court wanted to kill him.

After years of having his every move thwarted by dint of having given his best player to the opposition, Henry finally snapped. In a fit of pique he is alleged to have blurted out, 'Will no one rid me of this turbulent priest?' or something roughly equivalent in medieval French which (unfortunately for Henry) everyone understood back then. Four knights at his Norman court took his words at face value, and travelled across to England to assassinate Thomas Becket without waiting to see if the King still felt the same way the next morning when he had sobered up.

Finally they arrived in Canterbury. Rather bizarrely they stopped outside the cathedral to put on their armour – perhaps concerned about the nasty bruises you can get from elderly archbishops once they start waving that crook about. Then they marched inside to confront Thomas Becket. One of them realized that it might not play too well in the papers if they murdered him on consecrated ground and attempted to drag him outside. Becket clung to a pillar.

'Let go of the pillar.'

'No.'

Yet again, Becket had a clever reply, so they attacked him on the spot. Monks who had been saying vespers watched in horror as their Archbishop was struck in the head with a sword. Becket remained dignified, apparently pleading that no harm come to any innocent bystanders. The third blow knocked him to the ground where, according to the witness, the Archbishop said, 'For the name of Jesus and the protection of the Church I am ready to face death.' Though you have to wonder if it wasn't more likely that he just said, 'Ow!' When his skull was split open and his brains spilt out on the floor of the church the knights headed for the door, stopping on the way out to pick up a leaflet about the Alpha Course.

It was the scandal of all Christendom. The most powerful monarch of Western Europe ordering the murder of the head of the English Church, a defenceless man of the cloth cut down before the altar. Thomas Becket became the Princess Diana of his day. Everyone immediately forgot what a complete pain in the neck he had been and wept and prayed as they flocked to the place of his death. In the ongoing power struggle between the Church and the monarchy, the church milked this PR opportunity for all they could. The Pope excommunicated Henry and made Thomas a saint. The martyrdom of St Thomas secured the clergy's immunity from prosecution for another three hundred years.

Henry claimed the murder was all a terrible mistake (even though it is possible he knew exactly what his knights had set out to do). But eventually the King himself felt obliged to make the pilgrimage to Canterbury, approaching the shrine in the most humble manner possible. Barefoot and wearing only a sackcloth, he crawled on his hands and knees to Becket's tomb. Monks had been instructed to strike him with birch rods as he inched forwards. 'All right, all right . . .' he whispered, 'you don't have to do it *that* hard . . .' As part of his rehabilitation Henry planned to launch a crusade to recapture Jerusalem from the Muslim leader Saladin. To this end he instituted perhaps the first national income tax – the so-called 'Saladin Tithe' – which demanded ten per cent of all revenues and movable objects. Unsurprisingly the tax was extremely unpopular, increasing the bitterness towards King Henry, despite his rather transparent attempt to make people think this crippling new tax was all Saladin's fault.

'No, look, it's not the "Henry Tax", stop calling it that; it's the

"Saladin Tithe". Now make the cheque out to "Henry Plantagenet", would you?'*

Henry died before leading the crusade, eventually worn down by the campaigns of his four sons against him. Impatient to inherit his lands, his sons allied themselves with the King of France. Gravely ill and close to death, the previously invincible King Henry was finally defeated by his son Richard at Le Mans in July 1189. He died a few days later, muttering 'Shame, shame on a conquered king.'

Unlike his two sons who ruled after him, Henry II has failed to make much of an impression on the English popular consciousness, despite the enormous legacy of his reign, particularly in the field of English law. However, it should be stressed that for a couple of centuries after the Battle of Hastings, the Kings of England did not consider themselves English. The pride-inducing map of Europe that shows the King of England ruling lands from Scotland to the Pyrenees does not in fact depict English-held lands; it is the empire of a Duke from Northern France who counts England among his many territories. However, many French people do not realize this, so it is always worth scoring any points you can for the sake of a little historical accuracy. But all the news headlines during the 1100s and 1200s: the assassination of William Rufus, the murder of Thomas Becket, the Magna Carta; these are all matters of importance to a foreign nobility who ruled England from the safety of the stone castles that they built all over the country. The history of England during these centuries is the story of a territory ruled from abroad. This was never more true than with the next Plantagenet king, Richard the Lionheart, who somehow managed to become something of an English hero, which is quite impressive for a Frenchman who visited England twice.

---

* Henry II was the first of the royal dynasty known as the 'Plantagenets' after Henry's father had adopted the broom (*planta genesta*) as his emblem. The first coat of arms was sent back with the message, 'No, I mean the *flower* broom, you idiot.'

Richard I: Jihad, Christian-style

The dominant political theme of the late twelfth century and thirteenth century was the clash between Christianity and Islam. Today it is almost impossible for us to imagine there being endless pointless and unnecessary arguments between different religious faiths. It seems bizarre that Christian and Islamic leaders should use religion for political ends and – all right, you get the idea. In 1187, the holy city of Jerusalem was captured by Saladin the Great. Saladin came originally from Tikrit in modern-day Iraq, and for a moment the West was united in their efforts to remove this invader. Hmm . . . from Iraq, you say? thought all the political cartoonists from the *Daily Telegraph* eight hundred years later. And *Saladin* sounds a bit like *Saddam*, doesn't it? There must be an angle in here somewhere?

The crusades represented a massive popular movement that caught the imagination of medieval Europe. Ten-year-old sons would say, 'Can't we put a St George's flag on our cart?' and the parents would flinch slightly and say, 'No, dear, we don't want people to think Daddy is a builder.'

Many human lives would have been saved had the fairly minor city of Jerusalem not happened to be the central holy site for three of the world's major religions. It was where Abraham was supposed to have offered his son Isaac to God, where Christ was crucified and where Muhammad ascended to heaven. How much more peaceful might the world have been if these three events could have taken place hundreds of miles apart, say in Skegness, Reykjavik and Baden-Baden. Even though the two cultures were at war, Western Europe learnt a great deal from the Arabs during this period. The Islamic world gave Europe the decimal point, the triangular sail, the ogee arch plus much that the Arabs themselves had learnt from the Chinese. But in 1189, for Christians such as Richard the Lionheart, there was no more burning world issue than the fact that the 'infidels' were denying Christian tourists access to the popular Jesus of Galilee Theme Park and John the Baptist Gift Shop. Any of Richard's advisers attempting to talk to him about mundane domestic issues such as the appalling lack of pre-school nursery places in medieval England would have found the conversation returning fairly quickly to Richard's one big policy idea of getting a huge army together and travelling three thousand miles to kill all the Arabs.

However, in order to maintain a certain amount of balance, Richard's reign actually began with the murder of hundreds of Jews. During his father's reign the Jewish moneylenders* had become the easiest source of loans for knights travelling to join the pan-European effort against Saladin. They mortgaged their land without necessarily reading the small print about fluctuating rates and compound interest charges. And with prejudice against all non-Christians being whipped up by the Pope in response to the fall of Jerusalem, the Jews became the subject of an increasing amount of resentment. At the coronation banquet of Richard I, the arrival of some Jewish leaders bearing generous gifts to the King offended many Christians in the room, especially the ones who had only brought a bottle of wine and a card. They attacked the non-Christians (to whom most of them owed money) and soon a mob was attacking London's Jewish quarter, lynching its inhabitants and setting fire to their homes. So little was done to seek out and punish the perpetrators of this pogrom that copycat riots spread across the country with massacres in Norwich, Lincoln and Bury St Edmunds. It was in York, however, that the worst of the outrages took place; around one hundred and fifty Jews were murdered with the encouragement and in some cases the active participation of the local nobility. Huge debts were instantly cleared as a bonfire was made of all the bonds that had been stored in York Minster. After that early setback the Financial Services Industry incorporated certain safeguards and now it is no longer permissible to wipe out your debts by killing your bank manager, however tempting it might sometimes seem.

---

* The Bible forbade Christians to lend money and so it became the trade of the Jewish diaspora. Modern right-wing Christians citing the Bible's opposition to homosexuality do not seem to have the same enthusiasm for outlawing the money-lending on which the entire world economy is based.

But the English aristocracy wouldn't hold on to their money for much longer. Richard's plan to take an entire army all the way to the Middle East was clearly going to be an enormously expensive operation, and passing round the collection plate after evensong and selling jars of honey at the church fête simply wasn't raising enough. As well as levying onerous taxes, Richard was soon mortgaging much of his kingdom to pay for his big adventure. While his father had developed the role of the sheriff to tackle the problem of corruption, Richard now sold the office of sheriff. Where Henry had regained territory from the Scots, Richard sold bits back to them again. King William of Scotland paid Richard ten thousand silver marks for Berwick and Roxborough, although there was the usual argument about whether carpets and curtains were included. Richard joked that he would have sold the city of London if he could have found a buyer, which makes it all the more bizarre that his statue occupies pride of place outside the Houses of Parliament.

Perhaps the reason that Richard was so drawn to the prospect of military adventure was that fighting was what he did best. While other European monarchs had been ineffective and quarrelsome, Richard's arrival soon prompted enormous progress against the armies of Saladin.

Characteristically leading from the front, and making good use of the European secret weapon, the crossbow, he captured the strategic city of Acre, which became the capital of the precarious Christian kingdom in Palestine. But Richard's success only prompted more jealousies and rivalries within the allies and the King of France returned home to plot against him. Meanwhile negotiations with Saladin broke down, and Richard reacted angrily and ordered that nearly three thousand Arab hostages be massacred, which leaves you wondering just how much of the Bible these crusaders had actually read.* Having got within twelve miles of Jerusalem, Richard was finally forced to give up and go home, not least because of news that

* Medieval leaders could be absolved of their sins by getting monks to pray on their behalf. Many monasteries grew rich by taking on the atonement of those who could afford to outsource their penance.

his brother Prince John was joining forces with the King of France and other claimants to King Richard's various lands.

However, having fallen out with most of the other European monarchs, which is often the way when you go on holiday with people, King Richard was forced to change his route home to avoid travelling through the hostile lands. After being shipwrecked in the northern Adriatic, Richard was captured and held for ransom, despite his best attempts to travel in disguise as a lowly pilgrim, which apparently did not extend to taking off an elaborate gold ring that instantly gave him away. The Holy Roman Emperor demanded 150,000 silver marks for his safe return to England; around twice the annual revenue of the English crown. No one seems to have pointed out that he was never in the country anyway, and so enormous effort was put into raising this amount.

'If Richard is not released, the whole Angevin Empire might fragment . . .'

'Right. I see what you're saying. The thing is I already give to a set number of charities so I'm not sure I want to add any more at the moment . . .'

The silver crosses from cathedrals were taken and melted down and a crippling tax of twenty-five per cent was levied on every free man. His brother Prince John was as loyal as ever and offered the Holy Roman Emperor eighty thousand marks to keep Richard locked up, but the Emperor was holding out for the rollover jackpot. In public, of course, John made a point of setting an example by enthusiastically collecting these taxes himself. But did he a) pass this money over promptly to the 'Crusaders in Need' Fund? or b) keep all the cash for himself?

Finally Richard returned as a hero to his bankrupted country in 1194. He magnanimously forgave his brother and confirmed John as his heir. So grateful was Richard to his subjects for financing his return to England that he promptly disappeared again, never to return. Inevitably he died a soldier's death; besieging a castle in France he was struck by a bolt from a crossbow and contracted gangrene. As he lay dying, he summoned the archer from within the castle walls to his deathbed and publicly forgave him. Then once

Richard had croaked the archer was flayed alive and hanged. But it must have been a comfort to know that Richard hadn't borne him any ill feelings.

It is Richard's military prowess that has somehow afforded him heroic status, never mind the fact that he bankrupted the country fighting an insane crusade that he could never have won anyway. His body was buried beside his father in Fontevraud Abbey, after his heart had been taken to Rouen and his bowels had been removed and buried at the site of his last battle.

'Is that the custom of these times then?' whispered one of the soldiers at the colon-burying ceremony. 'To, like, remove the King's bowels and bury them?'

'Er, I'm not sure. It may just be that we have a nutter in the regiment.'

Bad King John the Bad

As rulers of England, both the sons of Henry II were a complete disaster. But in order to emphasize the spinelessness and cruelty of King John, historical commentators have contrasted these faults with the valour and courage of King Richard. This is just one of the many historical inaccuracies in Walt Disney's 1973 film *Robin Hood*. Neither were the royal family and their advisers talking animals, nor did they sing in American accents like that.

In fact, rather disappointingly, there is not even any historical evidence that a figure called Robin Hood took refuge in Sherwood Forest at all during these dark times when hoodies were no longer allowed in the shopping centre. A 'robbing hood' was a generic name for a career criminal, which evolved into stories of one individual folk hero and, as with the myth of King Arthur, generations of writers have endlessly reinvented the legends to reflect the values of their own times. So where earlier more idealistic versions of Robin Hood portrayed him heroically stealing from the rich to give to the poor, today the emphasis is much more on Robin working *with* the rich in a business/outlaw partnership for enterprise.

What we do know is that during this period King John pulled off the far more conventional scam of robbing from the rich *and* poor to keep for himself.

King John was clearly a very bad king. You can tell this from the appalling table manners displayed by every actor who has ever played him. Eating with his fingers, talking with his mouth full, throwing bones in all directions and probably manhandling the waitresses as well; this was clearly a monarch completely lacking in any nobility or chivalry.

Perhaps this is why when Richard died, many parts of his Empire opted for other leaders. England and Normandy got John, but Anjou, Touraine and Maine chose Arthur of Brittany, John's twelve-year-old nephew. John was duty bound to try and win back what he considered his rightful inheritance and at first he was successful, even capturing young Arthur himself. But being the cruel and tyrannical type he was, John had Arthur put to death (possibly murdering him with his own hands) and the courts of Europe were scandalized. John's lack of diplomacy or charm had already been alienating many of the barons whom he badly needed to help him hold on to his French territories and sometimes one minor incident like strangling your nephew can tip waverers over the edge. With the local nobility now allying themselves with the King of France, John was pushed out of huge swathes of French territory, eventually losing even Normandy itself. His father's Empire had included over half of France, about five times the land actually ruled by the French King himself. Now, from his ancestral Norman possessions, John only had the Channel Islands left. He tried to put a brave face on it: 'The Channel Islands, though? Lovely place for a holiday. Do you know there are no cars on Sark?' Unfortunately in 1205 this didn't make Sark particularly unusual. John's nickname had been 'Lackland' but now it was changed to 'Softsword'. It was a cruel judgement, but great satire is supposed to be hard-hitting as well as funny.

Clearly in terms of military and diplomatic prowess, John did not compare with his brother. But the main reason that history has judged King John to be perhaps the worst-ever English monarch is that he fell out with the Church, and it was the monks of course who wrote the history books. For much of British history, the media and the Church were effectively the same thing. Today, we get our information from television, radio, the internet, national newspapers and the local freesheet. Back in the Middle Ages, there was no local advertiser to report *Undaunted old person is doing things normally done by young people*. While monks did the journalism, writing their interpretation of what had just happened, the parish priest would do the editorial, telling the congregation what they should be thinking now.

So the monarchs that most pleased the Pope and the Church have tended to get the best write-ups (such as the crusading Richard), but kings like John (who were excommunicated) all got lousy reviews and stood no chance of getting their kids into the local C. of E. primary school. That's not to say that John wasn't a terrible king. Clearly he was spectacularly unsuccessful during a short reign, not only losing all his French territories, but also his absolute powers in England, and just to cap it all he even managed to lose the crown jewels in some quicksand in East Anglia.* He has also been remembered as cruel, vindictive, petty, tactless, lazy, lecherous and he was probably a goal-hanger as well. He imprisoned nobles and their wives and children in such conditions that they starved to death, he seized property at will and tortured and maimed. Other kings have shown similar excesses, but managed to keep the Church happy and so were forgiven for their massacres or mistresses.

When John fell out with the Pope the Vatican placed England under an interdict which meant that the whole country was effectively excommunicated. For five years all the churches were closed, there could be no Christian services at weddings or funerals and no church baptisms. The liberals tried to pretend that having a secular naming ceremony was an adequate substitute, but the grand-parents couldn't hide their disappointment. John responded by stealing more land from the Church (which helped ease his severe

---

* His baggage train sank into the tidal sands on the edge of the Wash, giving rise to the history teacher's joke that 'King John lost the crown jewels of England in the wash'.

financial difficulties) until the Pope finally excommunicated King John himself.

Now John's enemies held the moral high ground – any military adventure against the King of England and his territories could be spun as a religious crusade to bring the land back into the fold of Christendom. John's disastrous campaigns to cling on to lands in France had taken a financial toll and the King was particularly random and crude in his expropriation of other people's property. The problem of coin-clipping* meant that the value of the currency could not be relied upon and finally the nobility had had enough. The whole thing was a terrifying preview of the country under Labour in the late 1970s – England knocked out of Europe, real barons instead of union barons, rampant inflation, and with all the churches closed 'you couldn't even bury the dead'.

Magna Carta: King confronted by 'moaning minnies'

Normally any uprising against a king would centre on another claimant to the throne, but with Arthur dead, there was no clear figurehead under whose banner the rebels could march. Instead a number of barons drew up a charter listing their various grievances over the previous decades. Obviously there were many different agendas and it took a while to agree what to put down on the parchment.

'The King should not sleep with Horace's wife Marjorie, nor leave her with child, nor give her the pox.'

'I think that's a bit too specific, Horace.'

'Can't we put in something about how annoying it is when you decide to dig a moat around your castle and then you find there are loads of rocks and tree roots and everything?'

---

* Coin-clipping was exactly what it sounds like – chipping little bits of gold off the coins, so that their weight was less than the value stated on the face of the coin. Today it is no longer possible to devalue the currency using a hacksaw. You have to use the international money markets instead.

'Oh yeah, I hate that . . .'

'But that's not really the King's fault, is it, can we try and focus on the bigger issues here?'

Eventually there were over sixty articles agreed: some administrative niggles; others fundamental principles. For example Article Thirty-five states *that the measure for wine and corn and widths of cloth and other things be improved. And so with weights.* Whereas Article Thirty-nine demanded that *No free man shall be arrested or imprisoned or robbed of his land or outlawed or exiled or victimized in any other way, neither will we attack him or send anyone to attack him except by the lawful judgement of his peers or by the law of the land.* I would have put that one above the demand about widths of cloth.

The King tried to confuse his enemies by declaring his kingdom to be a fiefdom of the Pope, hoping this might split the clergy from the nobility, but it was too late. When the barons took control of London, the King knew he would be forced to go along with their demands. They met at Runnymede, a small island near Windsor, and in 1215 the King put his seal to the 'Article of the Barons', that would become known as the Magna Carta – the Great Charter. John had no intention of adhering to any of these demands (especially the one about new widths of cloth, he'd die before he conceded that one), but he thought it might buy him time until his military situation improved.

Class struggle 1066–1381 (Dress: formal)

The Norman Conquest had seen a significant widening in England's class divide, with a smaller nobility increasing its assets and the ordinary peasants finding themselves downgraded to serf class. Hopes of knocking the saloon bar and public bar into one looked more remote than ever. There is evidence of the peasant class showing occasional defiance; records of tenants refusing to plough the lord's land or turn his hay. But these courageous militants were prosecuted for going on strike, and legally speaking they didn't have a leg to stand on. Especially after they'd had their foot chopped off as punishment.

The power struggle between the King and the nobility would flare up regularly over the next century or so, until the Plantagenet kings were finally forced to share their power with the aristocrats in Parliament. It would be hundreds of years before the middle classes followed suit and politely asked if anyone would mind awfully if they had a say in things too. After that it was not until the nineteenth century that the working classes, now relocated in the cities, finally asserted themselves and demanded political representation. Perhaps one day the House of Commons will even include members from Britain's underclass? Annie's Bar will sell cans of Special Brew in brown paper bags and Prime Minister's Questions will feature MPs asking, 'Spare some change, please?'

Except that even eight hundred years after Magna Carta, the majority of British people still do not have very much control over the government of their own country. The figureheads may occasionally get voted out by popular demand but the way in which power and wealth is actually distributed remains stubbornly unjust. Current estimates of wealth inequality from the 2001 census suggest that the richest half of our society own around 95 per cent of the wealth. Estimates for the thirteenth century are not that different. Today's class system may be more fluid and complex, but new ways of trapping the poor in situations where they work harder for less money are continually devised. So in effect, the poorest in today's society are in much the same situation as the serfs under the Normans. Apart from having Sky TV, and a bathroom, and central heating, and a life expectancy of around seventy-five, their situation is almost identical. Oh, and they are technically free to leave their jobs whenever they want, of course, and have extensive rights in law and access to free healthcare and their children have the right to free education up to the age of eighteen and, if things go right for them, they can radically improve their situation and become rich and powerful and maybe Deputy Prime Minister. But apart from all the above, nothing has changed since 1215.

In 1066 England had fallen under the yoke of a brutal military tyrant who ruled as an absolute dictator, spending more time on the continent than in his new acquisition. A hundred and fifty years later, the King of England was finally forced to concentrate on England itself; the English Channel became a frontier instead of a narrow crossing between two parts of an empire. Just as significantly England's ruler had now been forced to concede that the person of the King was not above the law. The ideas of fundamental liberties and principles that England exported to America and the British Empire are often traced back to the one document that was sealed beside the Thames in 1215. In reality Magna Carta was about an aggrieved ruling class reasserting its privileges, but it might have seemed churlish to point this out to the bereaved Jackie Kennedy in 1965 when she came to Runnymede to unveil a memorial to her assassinated husband beside the apparent birthplace of political liberty.

After Magna Carta the King's power was no longer absolute and in the reign of John's son, a knight called Simon de Montfort would summon a Parliament to ensure that the nobles' voices continued to be heard. Whether any of the ordinary subjugated English were even aware of any historic development is another matter. If a Saxon had gate-crashed the party being held by the French-speaking barons to celebrate their new-found freedoms, would he have raised a glass of beer to toast the birth of English liberty? Probably not. Especially as the Normans would have said, 'Sorry, we don't have any beer, it's red or white wine or mineral water if you're not drinking . . .'

4

The Late Middle Ages 1216–1485

*How an independent, united kingdom eventually emerged from
centuries of civil war, bubonic plague and appalling spelling*

The thirteenth century was a time of class struggle. Not exactly the
sort of heroic conflict that Karl Marx advocated in which down-
trodden workers rebelled against exploitative factory-owners. The
social group that rose up and asserted itself in the 1200s was the
upper class. It was an inspirational moral fight between the 'Haves'
and the 'Have-even-Mores'. 'Landowners of the world unite . . .'
implored their leaders, 'you have nothing to lose but your sedan
chairs! And your castles. And your enormous estates. And your gold.
And your fine clothes and food and wine, your horses, your servants,
your serfs and your private armies . . .' In fact they had quite a lot to
lose but they rose up anyway.

At the time of King John's death, the battle between the nobles and
the monarch had been reaching a climax. Prince Louis, the heir to the
French throne, had invaded at the invitation of the barons who had
spotted his card in the newsagent window: 'Young royal looking for new
challenge. Good at waving. Will travel.' John's nine-year-old son had
been hastily 'crowned' at Gloucester; they had to use a gold necklace
since his dad had carelessly lost the crown itself. John had virtually lost
the Crown in the wider sense too: much of the country was now in the
control of Louis and his allies.

Louis I: a French exchange king

If John had lived it is likely that he would have been deposed and England would have become part of the rapidly growing French kingdom. Indeed there are those who argue that 'King Louis I of England' should be included in the list of English monarchs for in 1216 amid much pomp and ceremony he was proclaimed King in London. But King Louis was still fluffing up the cushions on the throne when the death of the beleaguered King John suddenly changed the picture. Louis did his best not to allow this unexpected turn of events to deflect the English barons he was leading to victory.

'Pah! I see King John's supporters are trying to make out that his nine-year-old son is now King . . .'

'Hmmm . . .'

'I mean, what sort of leader would he be for you all? He'd be weak . . . he'd be pushed around by everyone . . . Everyone would end up just doing whatever they wanted . . .'

'Er, actually, Louis, could we have a word?'

'*King* Louis, if you don't mind!'

'Yeah, it's sort of about that actually . . .'

When young Henry's court declared that they would abide by the terms of the Magna Carta the disloyal barons began to switch sides until Louis was finally forced to abandon his claim. He was furious: this new job had been a great opportunity for him; he'd relocated; his kids had moved schools; his wife had found a lovely palace and suddenly they were telling him that there wasn't a vacancy any more.

Louis was paid off with a nominal sum which he took home to France with his wife saying 'I can't believe you didn't read the small print' over and over again.

For a decade the English barons could get on with the vital business of exploiting peasants and trying to nick bits of land off one another, without being hampered by the petty red tape that required royal assent for even the littlest pet projects like invading Wales. In 1227 the young king began to rule in his own right, and the barons waited to see if this king was going to make his mark.

Henry III builds Westminster Hall: MPs say, 'That's perfect'

Henry III was a particularly unmemorable king. He ruled for fifty-six years from 1216 to 1272 but not even he could remember which Henry he was.

'Am I the one who killed Thomas Becket?'

'No, that was Henry II.'

'Ooh, I know, I'm the heroic one, who overcomes insurmountable odds to beat the French at Agincourt?'

'No, sire, that's Henry V. That doesn't happen for another hundred and ninety years.'

'Oh.'

While Genghis Khan was riding around conquering most of Asia, while Christians were fighting Muslims for control of Spain and possibly all of Europe, Henry III was chatting with the interior designers about the furnishings for Westminster Abbey. Henry's interest in the abbey was fuelled by his obsession with its founder Edward the Confessor. Henry was consumed by the cult of 'St Edward', he had a picture of Edward painted on his bedroom wall, an Edward the Confessor duvet cover and when he became a father he named his first-born Edward. He really should have grown out of it by now.

It is because of this obsession that England's seat of government ended up at Westminster rather than in the City of London or Winchester or Budleigh Salterton (which was frankly always a long shot). Henry had the Great Hall built beside the abbey unaware of the threat to royal power that would later emanate from that room. At this point England did not have a capital in the way that we understand today. The King was constantly on the move, putting down rebellions or inviting himself round to stay with various noblemen up and down the country. So while the treasury was at Winchester, and the largest city was London, the centre of government was wherever the individual person of the monarch happened to be; the seat of government was the King's saddle.

But now at least the King of England might be seen at home from time to time. Since 1066, England had been seen as just one of many territories in a Norman or Angevin Empire. For a century or so after Hastings, the Norman aristocracy had lands in England and estates in Northern France. Now the expats could not have both, and the psychological effect of this was a developing sense of independence and almost nationalism among the confused French-speaking English aristocracy. This was home now; the weather might be awful, the food disgusting and the public transport non-existent, but they were just going to have to make the best of it.

So it could not have been a worse moment for the King of England to pack his court with continental advisers and hangers-on. Henry III married Eleanor of Provence and soon her relations were snapping up all the plum jobs in the English establishment. One Frenchman, for example, Peter de Rivaux, simultaneously held the positions of Treasurer of the Royal Household, Keeper of the King's Wardrobe, Keeper of the Privy Seal and the sheriffdoms of twenty-one English counties. 'Well, if you want something done, ask a busy person,' he explained, adding together all his various wages.

Henry's French and Italian advisers led him to hanker after the lost lands on the continent, but the only continental military expedition that the King undertook led to a disastrous defeat. Henry's religious devotion had him agreeing to underwrite papal military campaigns in faraway Sicily, which did not strike the English aristocracy as the most pressing matter on the agenda and clearly must have involved some dodgy papal/Mafia conspiracy. Such a distant war cost a great deal of money, but crucially, under the terms of the Magna Carta, the King could no longer raise extra taxes without calling a council of barons.

Inevitably, the discussions widened to more fundamental issues of government and in 1258 the council refused to grant further taxes to the King unless he restored to them some of the offices of state. The barons drew up the 'Provisions of Oxford', which may not sound as important as the Great Charter, but are arguably just as significant.*

* These were replaced the following year by the 'Provisions of Westminster' but eventually overturned by the even snappier-sounding 'Dictum of Kenilworth'. Thousands rushed to arms at the thought of fighting for something called the Dictum of Kenilworth.

They stipulated that their 'Parliament' was to be called three times a year, that their council of fifteen ministers should take responsibility for royal castles and ministerial appointments; effectively that the King should share the government of the country with them. Significantly it was issued in English as well as French and Latin; for the first time the language of the people was acknowledged in the corridors of power.

When the King refused the council's demands, civil war looked inevitable. Half a century earlier, the struggle between the barons and King John had been known as the 'First Barons' War'. With a name like that, everyone had a hunch there might be another one along soon, and now finally the nobles rose again in the excellently titled 'Second Barons' War'. At the Battle of Lewes in 1264 the King was comprehensively defeated and now Simon de Montfort was effectively the ruler of all England.

Simon de Montfort asks: 'What's *coup d'état* in English?'

With all the hated foreigners dominating the court, it was ironic that opposition to the King should have been led by a French nobleman. Simon de Montfort had fallen out with Henry after marrying the King's sister without his permission, but the niceties of wedding etiquette had faded into insignificance by the time Henry and his son were being held captive. With forces loyal to the King gathering on all fronts, de Montfort felt a pressing need to garner wider support across the country and his next move is the act for which he has earned his hallowed status in English history. De Montfort summoned representatives from every county and borough; to this nascent House of Commons he called for two knights from every shire and two burgesses from every free town.

'What's a burgess?'

'I don't know, just make Malcolm a burgess; any excuse to be shot of him for a while.'

Along with the barons and the bishops (today's House of Lords) these representatives discussed the course of the struggle with the

King and the principle of defying tyrants, and then they all asked boring questions about their constituency so they could dash off a press release for their local paper. Although there had been other representative gatherings before and after the Norman Conquest, this assembly in 1265 generally marks the birth of the so-called Mother of Parliaments.

The ageing Henry may not have been much of an opponent to de Montfort, but his towering son, Edward, certainly was. Having managed to escape from captivity, he finally defeated de Montfort and his allies at the Battle of Evesham in August 1265. It was the last time anyone knew where Evesham is. De Montfort died on the battlefield but the idea of Parliament did not die with him. Even though de Montfort's body was publicly disembowelled and his head stuck on a spike outside the Tower of London, Edward still found it necessary to summon Parliament to Westminster when he became King. Although it was of course in no sense democratic, it was at least fairly representative in purely geographical terms, and by providing a check on the power of the monarch, this Parliament put England centuries ahead of most of Europe.

Edward I: enemy of the Scots, Welsh and Jews. Golf club membership accepted

Henry III died at the ripe old age of sixty-five and his body was placed in Edward the Confessor's tomb, which is more than a little creepy. His son Edward, who ruled from 1272 to 1307, was nick-named 'Longshanks' for his great height. He was on his gap year fighting the Fourth Crusade when he learnt that he was now King. He must have felt that his succession was pretty secure because he took a further two years to get round to returning home, which is a long time for the royal dignitaries to have to wait at the harbour.

His travels had taught Edward the value of trade and the new King encouraged England's booming wool industry. Vast areas of forest were cleared for grazing with the King making sure that he benefited personally, placing a tax on every bag of wool that was exported. Obviously this created new opportunities for organized crime, and in England's ports the customs officials were constantly on the lookout for the latest ingenious methods of smuggling wool.

'Hang on a minute, what's that jumper made of?'

'It's sackcloth, honestly . . .'

'It's wool, isn't it? Honestly, what will they think of next! You scum! Your sort make me sick, you're the lowest of the low . . . Now, let's have a look at this bobble hat.'

With the treasury looking more secure than it had done for years, Edward calculated that he no longer needed the Jews to lend the crown money. Pressure had increased on the Jews soon after he ascended to the throne and in 1275 it had been ordered that *each Jew after he is seven years old shall wear a distinguishing mark . . . of two tables joined, of yellow felt*. I.e. a yellow Star of David; the same badge the Jews were forced to wear in Nazi Germany. In 1290 Edward decided that they should all be expelled. They had been taxed so heavily over the previous century that they had been wrung almost dry; with anti-Semitism rife across Europe, it was an easy and pop- ulist move to suggest they went and lived in one of the many other European countries that had just banned the Jews from their shores. The deported Jews had to pay for their own passage, of course, and one charming entrepreneur put them on to the Goodwin Sands in the middle of the Channel, claiming that his ship had run aground, and then sailed off leaving them there to drown as the tide came in. 'Get your Moses to part the seas for you!' he called to them. Which was nice.

As if there was any sort of divine justice, Edward lost his beloved Queen Eleanor in the same year. The distraught widower travelled with the funeral cortège all the way to London, ordering an ornate stone cross be erected at every point at which they stayed; Lincoln, Waltham Cross and finally Charing Cross (*Chère Reine* meaning 'Dear Queen').

It was during Edward's reign that the independence of the various Welsh kingdoms effectively came to an end. Prompted by an attempt by the Welsh Prince Llewellyn to expand his territory into the border country, Edward invaded North Wales and imposed English law and custom. When this prompted further rebellions, Edward became less merciful; by now he was fed up that every time he went into a pub they would all turn their backs and start pointedly speaking Welsh. A ring of enormous Norman castles was built, such as Caernarvon, Harlech and Conway, and the country was divided into six counties. Edward's son and heir, the future Edward II, was born in Caernarvon Castle and the King is supposed to have shouted to the assembled crowd, 'I give to you a son who speaks no English!' Every eldest son of the monarch has been honoured with the title Prince of Wales ever since; it is because of this thirteenth-century piece of whimsy that poor Prince Charles was forced to learn Welsh.

Braveheart executed for 'major historical inaccuracies'

But though Wales would never be as independent again (save for a decade of rebellion at the beginning of the fifteenth century), it is for his wars against the Scots that Edward is remembered. Awareness of this period of history was raised in the mid-1990s with the release of Mel Gibson's *Braveheart*, a film based on the battles of the Scottish knight Sir William Wallace, and a movie that couldn't have been any more historically inaccurate if they had added in a plasticine dog and called it *William Wallace and Gromit*.

But even if they weren't all wearing kilts and covered in blue paint and waving claymores to end a 'century of tyranny' (the previous hundred years had been among the most peaceful in history), the Battles of Stirling Bridge and Falkirk really did take place in a war that marks the beginning of Scotland's 'auld alliance' with France. Edward I had been asked to arbitrate in a Scottish succession crisis which had been threatening to drag Scotland into civil war; he chose John Balliol as King and ordered him to support him in a war against the French. A council of twelve Scottish ministers met to discuss the complex diplomatic and geopolitical issues before them.

'I hate the English.'

'Aye, I really hate the English.'

'Och, the English – can't stand the bastards.'

They refused to go to war for Edward, and for good measure deposed the weak and pliant monarch Edward had chosen. Edward now declared himself King of Scotland and marched north because he suspected that just saying it might not be enough.

It was this crisis that caused Edward to copy the tactic of Simon de Montfort and summon an English Parliament that approved taxes for the war. *What touches all should be approved of by all*, he declared. Parliament was now an established feature of the English political landscape. Edward conquered the Scottish lowlands and, as in Wales, he reorganized the country along the lines of the English shires. To mark this transition, the famous stone of Scone, on which Scottish kings had been crowned since ancient times, was brought to London where it was kept until 1996.*

Edward left to defend his territory in France, but rebellion broke out north of the border under William Wallace. With his distinctive Gaelic/Australian accent, 'Braveheart' inspired the very Scottish-looking forces to put on their tam-o'-shanters and defeat the English by eating haggis and then tossing the caber at them as the film so accurately depicts. Edward returned and eventually captured Stirling Castle, the key to central Scotland's defences, and eventually Wallace himself was captured, hanged, drawn and quartered and his head stuck on a spike alongside the head of Prince Llewellyn outside the Tower of London. The idea of Welsh and Scottish representation in the capital still needed some development. But Scotland proved far harder to police than Wales, and every time Edward left, rebellion broke out again. Edward finally died within sight of the border during yet another attempt to crush the Scots. On his tomb were inscribed the words *Malleus Scotorum* which, although it

---

* It was returned to Scotland by John Major's government in the hope of raising the Conservatives' dismal ratings north of the border. In the general election the following year, every single Scottish Conservative lost his seat. This was not the first time that the stone had been back, however. In 1950 four Scottish students took the stone from Westminster Abbey (breaking it in the process) and avoiding road blocks and a frantic police search they smuggled it back to Scotland in the boot of their car. They symbolically placed it on the altar of Arbroath Abbey but the London police simply came along and took it back again.

sounds like some sort of venereal disease, translates as 'Hammer of the Scots'. Though it was usual for a king to be buried in a gold casket, Edward ordered that he be buried in a lead casket, and only upgraded once Scotland was conquered. The casket was never changed.

Climate change: government fails to act on global cooling

Despite the political struggles between the monarch and the barons, England had enjoyed a certain amount of prosperity during the 1200s. Dynastic wars would not necessarily impact on everyday life, and people were more concerned about the weather forecast than the news headlines. In a rural economy with little capacity to store food beyond the next harvest, the climate was of crucial importance to all, and so that polite mid-morning chat about the weather took on greater significance.

'Looks like rain again.'

'Yup, the crops are rotting in the field so we'll all be dead by autumn.'

'Still, mustn't grumble . . .'

But during the 1300s there were a series of disastrous summers that left millions without enough grain. The vineyards of southern England that had flourished in the 1200s were abandoned as a mini-ice age froze the river Thames. By 1315 the population had reached a peak of around five million, which is quite an achievement when the business of procreation faced so many obstacles. It was forbidden to have intercourse on the Sabbath day or on significant saints' days and the communal nature of the one-room family home meant that many couples must have struggled to find privacy (especially if they had teenage daughters, who tend not to be very tolerant of their parents doing it where everyone can hear them). There are various accounts of couples being spied 'doing what a man doth with a woman' in the open air, even in the rain and snow. There was of course no effective contraception, and coitus interruptus was only practised in defiance of the Church. Little was understood about the business of conception, particularly with regard to the female anatomy. The female *hath smalle ballokkys* as one gynaecological expert wrote, and it was also believed that conception was only possible when women themselves released their own semen. Millions of pregnant women who were sure they had faked their orgasms must have lived in a state of permanent confusion.*

With births outstripping deaths and little in the way of emigration England's population continued to grow right up until the disastrous harvests of 1315 and 1316. But then the trend changed. Every era has its own fashion, its own craze. In the 1300s the in thing was dying. Death would soon be all the rage: famine, endless war and most of all the Black Death would ensure that anyone who was anyone was dead. By the middle of the fourteenth century the population would have dropped by around forty per cent.

Edward II: winner of the 'grisliest death award'

Where his father had been interested in war and statecraft, Edward II's first love was show businesses.

'When I'm dead, son, I want you to take forty thousand men up north—'

'—to stage *Starlight Express*?'

'No, lad, to conquer the Scots.'

'Oh. And then do a musical about it?'

Just because Edward II loved minstrels and music and watching naked dancers more than fighting wars doesn't mean he was a homosexual. Just because he had an unusually close friendship with a man called Piers Gaveston, whom (contemporaries claimed) *he loved more than his wife*, doesn't make Edward II a big gay. We shouldn't necessarily infer anything from the fact that when his enemies got round to murdering the King, they did it by shoving a red-hot poker

---

* Because it was held that pregnancy only resulted after sexual climax in both partners, it followed that it was not possible to become pregnant if you had been raped, so thousands of pregnant rape victims must have suffered in guilty silence.

up his bottom. In fact, the unsavoury manner of his death is the only thing most people know about Edward II, but one hopes that wasn't the case before it actually happened.

'Will I be remembered for my statecraft and diplomacy?'

'That's not the actual headline on the obituary we were drafting, no . . .'

'Is it that during my reign came "the commonality of the realm" under which knights and representatives of the boroughs had to be consulted in important decisions that were to become law?'

'Nope, I'm afraid this red-hot poker up the bum is going to grab the front page every time.'

The story of how Edward II (1302–27)* came from inheriting the mighty throne bequeathed by his father to being deposed and horribly murdered is the subject of a tragic play by Christopher Marlowe which has been adapted into a ballet and a film by Derek Jarman set during the Stonewall riots. Oh, all right then, Edward was a homosexual. But had he been a strong and effective king such private matters would not have counted against him.

Things started to go wrong very quickly. His ostentatious favourite Piers Gaveston had been banished by Edward I, but was recalled upon the great King's death. Being lower-class, foreign and gay, the young King's boyfriend was always going to have to work on his popularity at court, although this was not something that came naturally to the Frenchman. As one commentator noted at Edward's coronation: *Piers, seeking not the King's glory but his own, as if contemptuous of the English, where the others were in cloth of gold, appeared in purple, decked with pearls, rode between the guests as if worth more than the King.* Well, clearly that was just asking for it, so Gaveston was confronted by a number of barons who ran him through with a sword and then beheaded him. A cross still stands on the site near Kenilworth today, perhaps the first permanent memorial to a homophobic murder.

* Dates that appear after the names of monarchs denote the years that they reigned rather than the years that they lived. Clearly William I was not born in 1066 or his battle strategy would have been rubbish.

But it was his disastrous failure against the Scots that seriously undermined Edward II's authority. Under the dynamic leadership of the famous Robert the Bruce, the Scots had now put their divisions behind them and united against their common foe. Bruce had originally been one of the Scottish barons who had cooperated with the English King, but he had been outraged by the behaviour of the English forces, particularly when they put a Scottish noblewoman in a big cage and dangled it over the castle ramparts.

Legend tells how Robert the Bruce was hiding out in a cave after an earlier defeat where he watched a spider weaving its web. Every time the spider's web fell apart, it simply started again and Robert returned to his troops and told them they should be more like that spider.

'Aye, so what you's saying, Robbie, is that we should build a great big sticky web to trap the English?'

'No, I mean I was inspired by the wee spider in a wider sense . . .'

'And then wrap them in a silky cocoon to eat them later?'

'No, no, I mean we should just keep trying. Like that spider did.'

'What? That's it? That's the spider metaphor? *Try again like a spider does?*'

Robert the Bruce did keep trying and eventually won Scottish independence after the famous Battle of Bannockburn in 1314. He lured the English cavalry into a trap, where they fell into hidden pits full of sharpened spikes. The English were already in a state of panic when over the ridge appeared massive reinforcements of Scottish soldiers. These were, in fact, women and various hangers-on in disguise but from down in the valley the English couldn't hear them all saying, 'I tried to get this armour in a size fourteen but they only had it in a size ten, I mean it's ridiculous, I'm going to take it back and get a credit note . . .' It was enough to make King Edward himself turn and flee, and seeing his example his army followed him in what turned into a complete and utter rout. Not only did the battle see massive casualties to the English nobility, it was also a milestone in the evolution of European warfare. It had been proved that a well-organized infantry could defeat cavalry, especially if the cavalry were led by a useless chicken like Edward II.

Private battles between rival barons broke out around the country, the North of England was plundered by the Scots and wet summers and bad harvests brought famine and disease so severe that even the royal household was short of bread. In the midst of this anarchy, Edward's estranged wife Isabella returned to England with their thirteen-year-old son, who proved a convenient rallying point for those seeking to restore order. The gates of London were opened to the Queen and her son, while King Edward was captured and taken in chains to Berkeley Castle in Gloucestershire. Here he was brutally put to death; it is said that his screams could be heard for miles around. To prove that he had not been murdered, his naked body was put on display and, indeed, there appeared to be no mark on his body, even if his facial expression did look more than a little alarmed.*

Edward III: 'I think "Black Death" is such a negative phrase'

Edward III (1327–77) ruled England for fifty years and was celebrated as one of England's greatest-ever kings. He brought authority back to the monarchy, strengthened the rule of law and the traditions of Parliament, won stunning military victories against the French and the Scots, established the Order of the Garter and asserted a new sense of Englishness as great architecture and literature flourished. It was a shame that nearly half of his subjects were wiped out by the Black Death but perhaps that's just being picky.

Although Edward III's pushy mother and her lover Mortimer had needed Edward to provide legitimacy to their military coup, they didn't seem too keen to relinquish power once Edward III had grown

* In 1878 a copy of the so-called Fieshci letter from the 1330s was discovered in France. This five-hundred-year-old account claimed that Edward had been aware of the plot to kill him and so had escaped and eventually lived as a monk in Milan. Local legend in that part of Italy had always maintained that a medieval English king was buried there. This conspiracy theory has now found its way on to the internet so it must be true.

up. Eventually the teenage King asserted himself. While his mother and her lover slept at Nottingham Castle, seventeen-year-old Edward stalked through the underground passages with a band of soldiers and dragged Mortimer from his bed. It was the classic teenage son in hostility-to-stepfather situation and the outcome is always the same. Mortimer was hanged at Tyburn and Edward's mother kept under guard for thirty years.

Almost immediately Edward set about rectifying his father's humiliating setbacks in Scotland. In 1333 he won a victory at the Battle of Halidon Hill, forcing Robert the Bruce's son into exile, to be replaced by a more subservient Scottish claimant. Territory was also returned to England, including the key strategic town of Berwick-upon-Tweed. Berwick had continually passed back and forth from English to Scottish control. Now they settled upon the compromise that Berwick would be part of England, but if somebody invented a game called football then the Berwick team could play in the lower Scottish divisions to save on travel expenses.

With Scotland no longer a threat, Edward turned his attentions to regaining the territory and trade that had been lost by his father and then his mother. With Edward's military flair and the skills of the English bowmen, there was no reason to believe that victory against the King of France would be any less swift.

'So tell me, what is the name of this new war against the French?'

'Er, the Hundred Years War.'

'OK. I've got a bad feeling about this one.'

King declares: 'Give war a chance!'

Edward was the grandson of the French King, and three of his uncles had been King of France. However, when the last of these died, the French got out the royal family tree and found a distant cousin to do the job rather than have some Englishman turn up and start passing laws about being nice to animals and women shaving their armpits. In 1340, an outraged Edward declared himself to be the rightful King of France and this claim subsequently dominated relations between the two countries for centuries.

But the war wasn't just about dynastic claims and territory. England's wealth was very dependent upon the growing wool trade, with Flanders the single most important market. French moves on Flanders threatened England's overseas exports and so military action was deemed necessary to protect this major source of income. Anti-war protesters would obviously have pointed this out: 'You know this war is actually all about wool? They'd never invade Iraq, would they, no, they've not got any wool. Everybody: NO BLOOD FOR WOOL! NO BLOOD FOR WOOL!'

In fact, with a shortage of coinage, military leaders were even paid in sacks of wool. 'Oh, a sack of wool, great. Me and the lads had been hoping for actual money on pay day so we could go into town, get drunk and find a brothel. But no, wool is fine; now we can stay in all night and do some knitting.'

The French began by blocking England's access to Flanders with a massive fleet of two hundred ships at Sluys. England's navy was a rather more haphazard affair of various converted ships that the King had managed to requisition. However, the rain of arrows from the English bowmen took the French by surprise. Hundreds were killed on deck or chose to jump into the sea where they were drowned. Mastery of the Channel was secured, and the French commanders were so embarrassed they got the court jester to break the news to the French King.

The English longbow was to prove the decisive weapon in the early phases of the Hundred Years War. It unleashed such a rapid volley of arrows that it more than made up for England's inferiority in numbers. But the key to its success was that the idea could not simply be stolen by the other side. Crafting a perfectly weighted six-foot-high longbow from English elm was a highly skilled trade. Learning to fire one accurately and effectively required training from childhood. England had the good fortune to have developed a battle-winning weapon of war that could not be quickly duplicated by the enemy. So concerned was Edward III that this advantage should not be lost that he banned all other sports on the village green. So come the church fête, you couldn't even throw a wet sponge at the vicar, though firing your longbow at him was probably fine.

It was at the Battle of Crécy in 1346 that the longbow's legendary status became assured. With King Philip VI of France attacking England's last possessions in south-west France, Edward decided to take the initiative. In 1346 he sailed across the Channel with a force of fifteen thousand men including his famous son. The young soldier was known as the 'Black Prince' after the dark armour he wore into battle. Legend says that the distinctive armour was intended to intimidate his enemies, although a more likely explanation is that he was just a sixteen-year-old goth-type and really into wearing black.* Philip was surprised by the English invasion and was forced to race back across France to meet him. Finding themselves outnumbered two to one, the English forces retreated towards Flanders. Eventually there was no choice but to stand and fight and Edward chose a hill near the village of Crécy. Fifteen times the French cavalry charged uphill and each time they were forced back by the intensity of the hail of arrows coming from the English longbows. The King of France's brother died, as did a dozen royal princes, 1,200 knights and around 15,000 French soldiers. The old King of Bohemia, King John the Blind, had insisted on taking part in the battle. It was pointed out to him that being blind might put him at a slight disadvantage, but he insisted that he be led to the front so that he might swing his sword in the direction of the English. Everyone was in awe of the King's courage (or 'stupidity' might be another word for it) and he of course was killed. Sometimes equal rights for the disabled can go too far. When the battle was won, the Black Prince stumbled across his body on the battlefield, and took the brave (stupid) King of Bohemia's crest for his own. The three ostrich feathers with the motto 'Ich Dien' ('I Serve') remains the emblem of the Prince of Wales to this day.

The shock victory of the English at Crécy opened up the path to Calais, which was captured after a year-long siege and remained an

---

* In fact, Edward was not known as the Black Prince during his lifetime and the black armour may well be a myth.

English possession for another two hundred years. During the siege six leading burghers of the city offered their lives to King Edward if the rest of the town's citizens were spared, which was quite a sacrifice on the part of the local authority considering most of us can't even get our local councillors to put in a pelican crossing. Edward said he would only accept the six burghers' offer if they walked from the city gates naked but for their shirts and clutching the rope with which they would be hanged. They agreed but at the last minute were saved by the intervention of Edward's wife. There is a statue of the famous six burghers in Calais which every year is pointed out to thousands of English schoolchildren on day trips before they disappear off to go shoplifting.

Age of chivalry replaced by 'respect agenda'

It was the chivalric code that had allowed Edward to bow to the will of his wife Philippa of Hainault (that's Hainault in the Low Countries, she didn't commute into London every day from the end of the Central Line). But Crécy is also seen by some to mark the beginning of the end for the age of chivalry. Peasants had been involved in the killing of knights, which the knights found most upsetting. The battle had shattered the myth of the invincibility of the mounted knight (the word 'chivalry' comes from the French word for horse). But Edward understood the propaganda value of being an honourable knight. He was much taken with the legend of King Arthur, and devised his own round table. On his return from France he created the Order of the Garter, made up of twenty-four knights, himself and his son, which remains the pinnacle of the British honours system to this day. It takes its name from the lady's garter that was dropped by the Countess of Salisbury at a ball in Windsor Castle. Perhaps neglecting to consider how the Countess was going to keep her stockings up, Edward picked up the garter himself and put it around his own leg. When there was sniggering at the King's flirtatious behaviour, he said, 'Honi soit qui mal y pense.' ('Shame to him who evil thinks.')*

This famous motto was only one slogan among many embroidered on the clothes of the King and his courtiers. There was also the less than profound pub-bore's motto: 'It is as it is' (which actually sounds better slurred), and the bizarre: 'Hey, hey, the white swan; by God's soul I am thy man', from which we can only conclude that though corn yields were down, it was a bumper year for magic mushrooms. Indeed large birds seem to feature prominently in the life of Edward III. In the worst year of the Black Death, Edward showed due respect and reverence for the catastrophe by turning up to a tournament dressed in a giant bird costume. A few years earlier, when the serious moment had come to declare war on France, a contemporary poem tells how Edward did so by swearing an oath on a roast heron. Fortunately this does not seem to have been a diplomatic convention that stuck.

'Mr President, it's war! The Japanese have bombed Pearl Harbor!'

'Yeah, but is it technically war? I mean have they actually *sworn on a heron*?'

After the victory at Crécy in 1346 and the capture of Calais the following year King Edward was riding high. England had secured her territory and gained new ground in France, Parliament was willing to grant the King further taxes for the pursuit of the war, his son and heir had won his spurs at Crécy, and Edward had cleared out corrupt and inefficient officials from his government. What could possibly go wrong? And then somebody complained that they didn't feel too well, that they had these big lumps under their armpits . . .

---

* No succinct translation of this motto quite does it justice for there is more than a hint of existentialism to it. Is it better to base your moral code on the behaviour of those around you, or should each of us act according to our own consciences? Either way, stealing items of ladies' underwear is surely bang out of order.

The Black Death: 'I don't see why Timmy shouldn't have a rat'

The Black Death was surely the single greatest calamity ever to befall the British Isles. The invasions of the Vikings, the brutal tyranny of the Normans, the bloody battles of the English Civil War and the bombs of the Luftwaffe all killed many thousands, but none of these even approached the scale of devastation wreaked by a tiny flea in the fur of the black rat. After repeated epidemics throughout the late 1300s the population was eventually halved. Massive social and cultural changes were inevitable. The subsequent labour shortage sounded the death knell for serfdom, the scale of the disaster challenged people's religious faith and a mood of great despondency and depression settled over Europe. And the popular image of the rat took a bit of a knock as well – it was over six hundred years before Roland Rat got a slot on Breakfast TV.

The disease is generally believed to have been the bubonic plague caused by the bacterium *Yersinia pestis*, carried by the black rat (*rattus rattus* – it was late on a Friday afternoon at the office of Latin animal names), although there are those who dispute this: Iceland did not escape the ravages of the Black Death even though the island remained free from rats, and there are well-researched arguments proposing that the pandemic was closer to anthrax or the ebola virus. However, the disease was clearly highly infectious. It crossed Asia during the 1330s and finally arrived in Europe at the trading ports of Sicily. The first outbreak in England was reported in Dorset and the disease soon spread through Devon and Somerset, finally infecting Bristol. Gloucester refused to let anyone from Bristol into the city, but no part of the British Isles escaped infection. Soon it had reached Oxford and then London.

The symptoms came on rapidly. Swellings under the armpits and in the groin oozed blood and pus as the body became covered in blotches. Intense headaches, high temperatures, aching joints and nausea were followed by vomiting and the victim died within days. Not everyone who displayed the weeping pustules died, though they did find it hard to get invited to parties. In its first year 1348–9, about one fifth of the population were killed.

Hearing of the calamity that had befallen the English, the Scots decided this would be a good time to invade England. No one seems to have spotted the one flaw in this cunning plan. 'Yes, with England being ravaged by a highly infectious disease, this is our chance to rush into England and grab everything for ourselves! Their clothes, their hairbrushes – why, even the flea-bitten rats in the bales of hay will be ours!' The Scots had believed that they would not be affected by the plague because it was God's punishment upon the English. Sometimes in history you wish you could just go back in time and put them straight on a few basics. Soon the Scots too were dying in their thousands. Wales had already succumbed; only the remote mountainous areas of Ireland held out, until they were suddenly infected a decade later.

Across the British Isles whole villages were abandoned and the dead buried in great public pits. The mortality rate was particularly high among priests who selflessly tended the sick and dying, but this only made the wider populace more suspicious of the Church. Religious sects sprang up, most notably the flagellants, who went around flogging their own bare flesh to atone for their sins, a bizarre practice which can still be observed on certain specialist websites. People's religious faith was severely tested and the search for more secular answers to philosophical questions nudged Europe towards the Renaissance.

With the sudden shortage of labourers, landowners found themselves in competition for farm-workers. Edward III tried to defy the laws of supply and demand, passing a statute fixing wages at pre-plague levels, but the economic landscape was too radically altered. Serfs could no longer be tied to abandoned farms and across Europe labour became a commodity to buy and sell, which some analysts define as the beginning of modern capitalism. So if you a see a poster for a Socialist Workers' Party meeting on 'The Black Death: First Crisis in Capitalism?' you don't need to go any more; you can just go to a Julia Roberts movie and then go for a curry instead.

France was even more drastically depopulated and it was not until the 1350s that England and France gathered themselves up again and said, 'Right, thank goodness all that dying seems to have abated. Now, where were we? Oh, that's right, killing each other in Europe's longest-ever war.' It was not the best era to be in life insurance.

Hundred Years War: 'What do you mean there's still over a century to go?'

The country was sixteen years into the Hundred Years War and there were about a hundred years left. (Arithmetic was still very much in its infancy in the Middle Ages.) In 1356 the Black Prince won another stunning victory at Poitiers, capturing King John II of France, who was held in the Tower of London. He joined King David II of Scotland who had been in there for ten years. So the most secure prison in England was shared by an outraged French King and an embittered Scottish monarch; and still no one has written a sitcom about it.

The French conceded various un-English sounding territories and ransom for the French King was set at an unpayable three million gold crowns (eight times the annual revenue of the English Crown in time of peace). Most of this money has still not been paid, which might be worth mentioning next time they are discussing EC rebates.

But this was to be the high point of Edward's reign. The French had learnt their lesson and avoided meeting the English in pitched battles with the result that the English army exhausted itself on endless local campaigns. The Black Prince became diverted by a wasteful military adventure in Spain, growing increasingly cruel (and indeed unchivalrous), demanding the execution before his eyes of hostages including women and children. He contracted an illness in Spain and eventually died the year before his father. Queen Philippa had been killed by another wave of the plague in 1369 and Edward's final years were marred by his descent into senility.

'Do you know who I am?'

'Ask Matron, dear, I'm sure she'll tell you?'*

---

* This was a new joke in 1377.

As the once-great King lay dying in Sheen, he was abandoned by courtiers and relations who rushed to stake their claim in the court of his successor. Even his mistress deserted him, having gathered up whatever valuables she could carry, not forgetting to pull the precious rings off the dying King's fingers.

But Edward III's reign had been a remarkable half-century. Many English institutions date back to this period and Parliament itself came of age, gaining its first Speaker and separating itself formally into the two chambers of the Lords and Commons. The war with France had helped foster a renewed sense of Englishness at home. St George had replaced Edward the Confessor as the patron saint of England, and in 1362 English officially replaced Latin as the language of the English law courts. The Romans had only left England a thousand years earlier, but the legal profession has never been the quickest to react to change. The English language was evolving rapidly at this point and Geoffrey Chaucer became the most famous scribe of the time to write in the new Anglo-French dialect, even if his public readings met with a mixed reaction.

> *A frankeleyn was in his companye.*
> *Whyt was his berd as is the dayesye . . .*

'I'm sorry, Geoff, I can't understand a bloody word you're saying, mate.'

'You should see his books. He can't spell neither . . .'

Richard II: the peasants are revolting*

Richard II (1377–99) ascended to the throne at the age of ten. His father the Black Prince had died a year earlier, and during the final years of King Edward III's reign, Richard's uncle, the immensely wealthy and influential John of Gaunt, had become the effective centre of power. John of Gaunt was so-called because he was born in

---

* See footnote on previous page.

Ghent. So why wasn't he called John of Ghent, you may ask? Er, well, obviously I do know the answer, I just choose not to pass it on. John of Gaunt was the key figure in the fifteenth-century royal family tree. If one of the Tudors were doing the celebrity genealogy show *Who Do You Think You Are?* Great-uncle John would be the ancestor the BBC focused on, as Henry VII wiped away a tear when he learnt how many of his relatives were killed in the Wars of the Roses.* John lived in the magnificent Savoy Palace on the banks of the Thames (where the Savoy Hotel† and Theatre stand today), until it got burnt down during the Peasants' Revolt while he was fortunate enough to be away on business.

The Peasants' Revolt of 1381 may be the one event that we remember from the reign of King Richard II, but modern interest in this chaotic uprising has less to do with its actual historical significance than our romantic notions of democracy and 'the voice of the common people'. There was indeed a successful revolt during the reign of King Richard, but it was yet another *coup d'état* by one branch of the aristocracy against another. In 1381 there was no sense that power was wielded on behalf of or indeed with the consent of the masses. Kings did get overthrown in the Middle Ages, but by the rich not the poor.

The roots of the Peasants' Revolt lay in the social changes that had occurred since the Black Death had virtually halved the population of Europe (there were similar uprisings across the continent). In England wages had been legally pegged back to pre-plague levels and workers demanding any more were put in the stocks – an idea that Mrs Thatcher was later dissuaded from using on members of the Transport and General Workers' Union. However, what the government of the 1380s and 1980s did have in common was the idea of the

* In William Shakespeare's excellent and underrated play *Richard II*, it is John of Gaunt who gets the famous patriotic speech about 'This blessèd plot, this earth, this realm, this England'.
† An interesting fact about the approach to the Savoy Hotel is that it is the only road in Britain where you should drive on the right. This is a fairly useless piece of trivia, unless of course you happen to be driving at speed up to the doors of the Savoy Hotel and another car is coming towards you.

poll tax. This had proved to be the final straw for the rebels heading up the Old Kent Road; they believed it to be fundamentally unjust that a standard charge of one shilling be levied on every citizen of the realm irrespective of income.

'It's not a "poll tax", it's the "Community Charge",' insisted the Lord Treasurer as he was hacked to death by the rebels storming the Tower of London.* The Archbishop of Canterbury (who was also closely associated with the tax) had also taken refuge in the Tower and he too was killed. Marshalsea, Fleet, Westminster and Newgate Gaols were all broken into and the inmates released to swell the numbers, which did little to improve the image of the mob. For the thirty thousand rioters who had spent their entire lives in poverty and servitude, the sudden intoxicating sense of power as they rampaged through the capital must have been like nothing they had ever experienced. Contemporary chroniclers were appalled by the rabble, saying they behaved like *the maddest of mad dogs* and their leader Wat Tyler came in for some particularly harsh criticism for his uncouth manners and the way he glugged his drink when he finally came face to face with the boy King.

Wat Tyler was, as his name suggests, a roofer and – according to the rather biased accounts of the time – a notorious criminal who was *both lustful and vengeful*. His apparent misdeeds had led to a flogging by one former master, who was now hunted down and beheaded. We've all had bosses we didn't like, but it doesn't mean you kill them and carry their heads on spikes through the streets of London. Other leaders were Jack Straw, whose name made the rebels suspicious that he might not be as radical as he claimed, and John Ball, a dissenting priest who had been touring the country preaching sedition utilizing his unusual gift for rhyme. (So he was basically a rapper.) However, the rebellion was uncoordinated and disorganized, and the mob ram-

---

* Perhaps if the revolt had been successful we would mark the Storming of the Tower just as France's National Day celebrates the storming of the Bastille that occurred four hundred years later. In both uprisings the mob also looted buildings that were thought to contain large amounts of alcohol – but for propaganda purposes the Storming of the Off-Licence does not carry such a symbolic resonance.

paged through the capital killing foreigners, bankers and any city merchant who wouldn't give them the keys to the wine cellar.

The climax of the crisis came on 14 June 1381. After much anxious deliberation, the young King was volunteered as the best person to go and talk to the rebel leaders, since no one else fancied having their head impaled on a nine-foot spike. So rather bravely the fourteen-year-old boy rode out to meet them with the Mayor of London and various other nervous dignitaries who were all secretly wearing chain mail underneath their clothes. And so the King asked the ringleaders what it was that they wanted.

In *Monty Python's Life of Brian*, the People's Front of Judea demanded the complete dismantling of the entire apparatus of the Roman Imperialist State. In the Peasants' Revolt, the claims were not much less ambitious. They called for the end of feudalism and the abolition of all laws save 'those of Winchester' (most probably the laws of England under Alfred the Great); demanded that all church lands be confiscated for the benefit of the people and that they themselves be pardoned for all the killing and looting to take place during the revolt. Richard appeared to think about this for half a second, and then said, 'All right. Granted.' This rather threw the rebel leaders, who couldn't help suspecting that Richard was just saying this, but, not having anticipated all their demands would be immediately agreed to, didn't quite know what to do next.

'Er, right. OK, and we want the abolition of the poll tax. And fair rents for all. And freedom and equality for everyone.'

'OK, no problem, I'll add that to the list.'

'You're not just saying that, are you?'

'Look, I've agreed to all your demands, haven't I? What else can I say?'

Accounts vary as to how the meeting turned nasty but it appears that a member of the King's party suddenly claimed to recognize Tyler as one of the most notorious thieves in all Kent. Taking umbrage at such a slur on his reputation Wat Tyler attempted to prove what a fine and upstanding citizen he was by stabbing his accuser with a dagger. The Mayor of London was rather alarmed at having these Class War demonstrators stabbing nobles in such proximity to the King, and so he attempted to arrest Wat Tyler on the spot, only to have Tyler stab him as well. Tyler was wrestled to the ground and the rebels raised their bows ready to shoot; this was the moment at which the ordinary people of England came closest to overthrowing their monarch. If one rebel had shouted 'Fire!' the King and his retinue would surely have been killed, but instead the crisis was diffused by somebody claiming that Wat Tyler was actually on the ground being knighted by the King. By the time confused word was spreading that he had actually been killed, the King was riding up and down telling the mob that he was their King, 'their captain and their leader', and that they should all go to open country in Clerkenwell Fields. Not knowing what else they could do, most of them obeyed, and it was there that they were confronted with the vision of Wat Tyler's head on a spike to convince them to give up their rebellion. The boy King had agreed to all their demands, and so there was nothing else to do but go home and tell their wives the good news.

'How was your rebellion, darling?'

'Excellent. The King agreed to everything we asked for. An end to serfdom, church lands to be confiscated for the good of the people, fair rents for all . . .'

'Jolly good. And you got all this in writing, did you?'

'Er, well, it wasn't really like that, I'm not sure if anyone had any paper . . .'

'Oh, so your leaders got the King to put his seal to all your terms on a formal charter before you disbanded?'

'Er, well . . . actually our leader got killed.'

'Wat Tyler was killed?'

'Yes, and his head displayed upon a spike, but I don't think we should infer too much from that. The King said there would be no more injustice or something something, it was quite hard to hear . . . Honestly, why can't you just say *well done*?'

Once the mob of peasants were all back at home waiting for the equality and liberty promised, their former leader John Ball was being hanged, drawn and quartered in front of the young King. Jack Straw was tortured into naming the other surviving leaders, and serfdom eventually withered through economic necessity over the following century. The poll tax, however, was abandoned. 'And no British leader will ever be so stupid as to try that again . . .' said the Minstrel with a knowing look to the audience as his assistant held up a sign saying 'Irony'.*

Nobles show peasants how it should be done

The courage Richard had shown in facing the mob was remarked upon by many chroniclers, but very few had a good word to say for him after that. As he grew into adulthood and took responsibility for his kingdom, he developed into a bad-tempered, dishonest and vengeful monarch who failed to manage the nobility with the dexterity required. There were about sixty significant families across the country, most of them possessing their own private army. The King had to keep a majority of these barons on his side or see a rival candidate for the throne emerge from his own family. But you promise the Liberal Democrats one thing, and that just annoys the Green Party; Richard II lacked the skill required to play the elaborate chess game of patronage, diplomacy and occasional suppression.

When the Lords demanded that he sack his corrupt chancellor, Richard II said that he would not dismiss the lowliest kitchen servant to appease Parliament; the stand-off escalated and finally Richard declared war on the Parliamentary party. But in the ensuing battle at Radcot on the banks of the river Thames, Richard's small army was overcome and he took refuge in the Tower. The country was now ruled by a Parliamentary council, with Uncle John of Gaunt returning to the country to smooth things out.

'Why's he called John of Gaunt?'
'Because he was born in Ghent.'
'So why isn't he called John of Ghent?'

* In fact, Mrs Thatcher was not the only subsequent leader to impose a poll tax. It was also levied by Henry VIII, so clearly the idea has consistently been the product of a fair and balanced mind.

'Er, well . . . oh look, there's a greenfinch!'

When Richard passed the age of twenty-one he gradually reasserted his position as supreme ruler although an abiding sense of his incompetence remained. He has been criticized for his vanity – he was the first king to demand that he be addressed as 'your majesty' and was also the first to have a lifelike portrait commissioned.

Richard had been married to Anne of Bohemia, a well-connected European royal whose brother was actually King Wenceslaus. (She had come to England to get away from that bloody song, she was completely fed up with it.) Richard was apparently devastated when she died in 1394 during another wave of the bubonic plague and became increasingly irrational and prone to bad temper.* Two years later Richard married the French King's daughter, but the couple failed to bond in quite the same way, possibly because she was six.

And so Richard was without an heir, unpopular and increasingly tyrannical. One by one he was taking his bloody revenge on the Lords who had defied him early on in his reign. On a flimsy pretext he banished his cousin Henry Bolingbroke for ten years, later confiscating all the family lands. Richard had made one powerful enemy too many.

When Richard had been ten years old he had been admitted to the Order of the Garter at the same ceremony as his eleven-year-old cousin Henry. Side by side the two young royals would have sworn to defend other Knights of the Garter, to remain loyal to fellow members of this exclusive order and never to take up arms against his companion. But if Rolf Harris had written 'Two Little Boys' about Henry and Richard, the final verse might have been a little different, with one grown-up warrior coming across his former childhood friend in battle, imprisoning him, seizing his crown and then having him put to death.

Henry Bolingbroke landed near Hull in July 1399, and marched across the north of England where, as the Duke of Lancaster, his

---

* When the Earl of Arundel turned up late to his wife's funeral, King Richard went across and struck him in the face. If his mobile had gone off during the service he'd have really been for it.

family's support was historically strongest. Henry had originally launched the rebellion with the intention of reclaiming his inheritance, but the unpopularity of the King was such that the uprising snowballed into a full-blown military coup. Richard returned from campaigning in Ireland to face Henry in battle, only to find that nearly all of his supporters had deserted him and now he had little choice but to surrender to his cousin.

Parliament, now as strong as it had ever been, forced the tyrannical King Richard to abdicate, and Henry IV was declared King. It was a momentous act: the rightful monarch had been deposed by the Lords and Commons; Henry was acceptable because he would rule in co-operation with Parliament rather than in defiance of the laws of England. Henry addressed his Parliament in English, the first King ever to do so.*

Henry IV: 'Uneasy lies the head that nicks a crown'

The new King had his predecessor imprisoned at Pontefract Castle; but when a plot was exposed to kill Henry IV and return the former King to the throne, Richard must have known he would not remain alive for much longer. The official version was that Richard went on hunger strike, though it is more likely that he was forcibly starved or poisoned. In order to end any thoughts of further uprisings in his name, Richard's emaciated body was put on public display in the old St Paul's Cathedral, which took some of the romance away from all the weddings taking place that Saturday. He was interred in a shoddy tomb in King's Langley, where legend has it that a schoolboy was able to squeeze his hand through the gaps in the coffin and take the King's jawbone home as a souvenir.

England had rid itself of an unpopular King, but by placing a

---

* Note for pedants: all right, it wasn't technically a 'Parliament' because that would have required the monarch to be present and Henry didn't yet have the crown; this Parliament was the step to achieving that. Just stop being so picky; no one is impressed.

monarch with a weak claim on the throne, the seeds were sown for decades of civil strife that would resurface as the Wars of the Roses. As the Bishop of Carlisle warns in Shakespeare's Richard II:

> *And if you crown him, let me prophesy,*
> *The blood of English shall manure the ground,*
> *And future ages groan for this foul act.*

But the nobles did not heed this warning as they, of course, never read Shakespeare's play. They only read the Brodie's Notes. And so on the feast of Edward the Confessor, 1399, the stolen crown was placed upon Henry's head. It was not the best of omens that the new King's head was crawling with head lice.

The terrible reputation of Richard II owes much to the fact that the chroniclers were writing under the watchful eye of the vulnerable King Henry, who needed all the anti-Richard propaganda his spin doctors could produce to bolster his weak claim to the Crown of England. Under instruction from Henry's court, monks set to work busily writing about how terrible Richard II had been and by the end of the first week had finished embellishing the first letter. All our history is of course subject to this sort of distortion – eighty years later the next King Richard would be redrawn as a child-murdering hunchback, in order that everyone felt inordinately grateful to have his successor on the throne. Plus it would have been a bit boring to see Laurence Olivier play Richard III as a pleasant but dull chartered accountant.

Henry IV had been talked into seizing the throne and once he was in the job there was not much evidence of him particularly enjoying it. He was the John Major of his age, the surprise ruler, failing to fill a power vacuum, constantly troubled by plots and rebellions. He was so nervous of assassination that on military campaigns he sometimes slept in his armour.

Plaid Cymru (Paramilitary Wing)

By far the most enduring rebellion of his reign was the last great Welsh uprising against England, which began around 1400 under the leadership of Owen Glendower, which should be spelt 'Owain Glyndwr' if you don't want to annoy Welsh speakers.* So anyway, Owen Glendower began his rebellion as another indignant landowner, much as King Henry himself had been, fighting because he believed he was being denied land (and therefore wealth) that was rightfully his. But his rebellion lit the fire of Welsh nationalism. Without ever facing the English in open battle, Glendower succeeded in uniting much of Welsh nobility (including the Tudor family, whom the English royals might have been well advised to keep their eye on). His forces harried the English supply lines, raided over the border and for nearly a decade he ruled most of Wales. He declared himself 'Owen IV', called a Welsh Parliament and instituted a Welsh church, two Welsh universities and put up bilingual road signs on the M4.

For a moment it seemed as if his rebellion might threaten to displace King Henry himself when the King's English former allies changed sides and joined with the Welsh rebels. Henry could not have taken the throne without the support of the Percy family of Northumberland but here too things turned sour fairly quickly, even though Henry did his best to keep the Percys sweet by giving them little presents like the Isle of Man. Northumberland's son was the famous 'Hotspur' and by the time of Henry's coronation he was noticeable by his absence.†

As Owen Glendower was achieving fame with his guerrilla war in North Wales, Hotspur marched to join forces with the rebels,

* The militant Welsh nationalists who set fire to English holiday homes in the 1970s and '80s called themselves the 'Sons of Glendower'. But their campaign petered out in the early 1990s, so if you're looking for a cheap second home, Wales has got some real bargains; none of the locals can afford them.
† Tottenham Hotspur take their name from this medieval knight, who had lived on an estate in this part of London. He may well have still been playing for them the last time they won the title.

indignant that his family had not received land and money they had been promised for their former support. Henry IV's forces moved quickly enough to prevent the two groups of rebels coming together and the young Prince Hal, the future Henry V, defeated Hotspur at the Battle of Shrewsbury in 1403. Hotspur died when he opened the visor on his helmet to get a breath of fresh air and an arrow flew into the gap. The Welsh rebellion continued erratically throughout Henry's reign although Glendower became increasingly elusive, finally disappearing altogether in 1412, never to be seen again. Welsh legend states that when Wales is threatened once more then Owen Glendower will rise from his unknown resting place in order to lead its defence. But clearly this is not going to happen.

Against Scotland Henry had an uncharacteristic piece of good luck. While James I was sailing to France he was captured by pirates, who sold this valuable hostage to the English. The indignant King of Scotland spent much of his reign as a prisoner in the Tower of London, where he joined Owen Glendower's wife who also happened to be staying there at the time. After many years of being locked up together, they finally discovered they shared a mutual interest: 'That's amazing, because I really hate the English too!'

Relations with France were more troublesome. By 1400 Richard II's widow had reached the grand old age of eleven, and the tricky matter of her return to France produced a diplomatic stalemate. The French royal family wanted her returned and her dowry repaid; Henry IV thought she had value as a potential hostage in the event of war, and so certainly didn't want to pay out large amounts of money to send her back, especially when he was a bit short of cash himself at the time.*

Unlike the monarchs of medieval Europe who enjoyed absolute power, Henry IV's policies were subject to the approval of Parliament. With the House of Commons including small

---

* Henry had come up with the creative solution of marrying her to his son, but Isabella wanted nothing to do with the usurpers who had murdered her first husband. When the tragic figure of Isabella did finally return to France she was married off to her cousin, dying in childbirth a few years later.

landowners, lawyers, merchants and the like, England became pretty well the only country in Europe where the middle classes as well as the aristocracy influenced policy and legislation. This broad power-sharing was a source of some pride to the free-born Englishman of the early fifteenth century.

'So how shall we best use this progressive form of government that guarantees us freedom from tyranny?'

'I know, let's introduce the burning of heretics.'

Are the Popes Catholic?

In 1401, Henry IV agreed that members of the religious movement known as the Lollards could be classed as heretics and publicly burned.

The Lollards had emerged several decades earlier as followers of the Oxford theologian John Wyclif. Long before the Reformation, Wyclif had translated the Bible into English and proposed the revolutionary ideas that piety could exist in lay people as well as priests, and that Christians should take their guidance from the scriptures rather than the clergy. The popularity of these anti-establishment ideas were a contributory factor in the rebellious national mood that led to the Peasants' Revolt, and now the Church establishment was determined to stamp out this attack on their monopoly of holiness by burning people. Ordinary churchgoers had previously been taught not to question the nature of their religion but simply accept the word of the Pope. This became harder after 1378 when suddenly there were two Popes. Clearly this situation was not sustainable, they'd have to put another named driver on the Popemobile insurance, so in 1408 they had a go at ending this ridiculous situation and emerged with three Popes. One was at Rome (the papacy recognized by England and Ireland), the other in Avignon (recognized by France and Scotland) and the extra, reserve, just-in-case, back-up Pope was in Pisa. The resolution of the Papal Schism finally came in 1417, with Henry IV's heroic son Henry V playing a significant part.

The young Prince was already showing himself to be something of a military prodigy and as his father became ill, Henry was eager to take more responsibility upon himself. The King was struck with a recurrent illness, thought to be leprosy or perhaps syphilis, and the royal accounts are full of payments to physicians for blood-letting and balms to treat the hideous pustules that now covered his face. It is thought that Henry had a nervous breakdown in his later years; Shakespeare portrays him as an insomniac racked by guilt for the savage steps he took in order to seize and secure the throne. *Uneasy lies the head that wears a crown*, he says. Especially if it's crawling with bloody head lice. Despite the nits and the erupting pustules, the crown still looked an attractive-enough item of headgear for the impatient young Prince to take it from the sleeping King's pillow to try it on. This scene, famously dramatized by Shakespeare, really did take place, with the sickly King waking to see his estranged son already sporting the symbol of his royal office. The King is only forty-five at the end of *Henry IV Part 2*.

'So, er, is there going to be a *Henry IV Part 3*?'

'Um, well, your majesty, I'm afraid the ratings haven't been that good. But we are going to do a spin-off show featuring some of the characters from your life story.'

'Great! What's it called?'

'Er . . . *Henry V*.'

Henry V: the secret of heroism – one big success, then die young

For centuries Henry V (1413–22) has been perceived as England's ultimate heroic warrior king. Courageous, inspiring, egalitarian and, most importantly of course, victorious; in 'English Heroes Top Trumps' he would definitely be right up there with Boudicca, Bobby Moore and the Prime Minister from *Love Actually*.

As Edward III had done before him, Henry V defeated the French against all the odds. Unlike Edward III he died while the memory of his heroics was still fresh; he didn't grow old and senile, which rather tends to tarnish the image of the dynamic matinée idol. No one would have posters of James Dean on their wall if he'd grown into a fat old baldy doing adverts for stairlifts.

Over the centuries a certain quota of heroes and villains has been required by the historians as the simplistic rules of storytelling have been imposed on to the uncooperative complexity of British history. Henry V has been lucky enough to be cast as one of the great iconic heroes, a process that owes much to the talents of far greater Englishmen such as William Shakespeare and Laurence Olivier. But another director, applying more modern values, could just as easily have portrayed Henry V as a villain. He persecuted religious dissenters, invaded a neighbouring country as an aggressor, starved the people of Harfleur to death and had all the French prisoners of war put to death at the battle of Agincourt.* By making his son King of England and France he guaranteed decades of war, death and suffering, plus he had a stupid pudding haircut and a hideous scar on his face. It would have been easy to make Henry V into one of the bad guys. Except that the script, once it has been written, is very hard to change. By modern standards poor Richard II should be venerated for his renaissance values and his avoidance of war, and yet for some reason success in killing foreigners is still the criterion by which modern historians rate figures from history. Academic historians seem such gentle scholarly types in their normal lives, all half-moon glasses and leather patches on their elbows, but as soon as you get them writing history books they turn into *Sun*-reading white van drivers: 'Up yours, Frenchies! Our 'Enery bops the wops, and make In-ger-land champs of Euro 1415!'

The Battle of Agincourt: Henry atones for haircut

The event for which Henry V is so revered is the Battle of Agincourt. Henry's revival of the Hundred Years War in pursuit of his tenuous

---

* The English nobles were aghast at this order, not out of any high moral principle about the honourable rules of war, but because there were huge profits to be made from demanding enormous ransoms for captured aristocrats.

claim to the French throne and the resolution of English trade disputes was enthusiastically welcomed by Parliament, who seemed to have forgotten what an expensive business war always turned out to be. France was racked by internal disputes and was ruled by a King who was given to periods of madness, so this seemed as good a time as any to take an army over to pick up a load of stubby lagers and a big cheese for the missus.

Much of what is dramatized by Shakespeare has a basis in contemporary chronicles: Henry really did go out amongst his soldiers on the eve of battle; he really did encourage an almost democratic sense of common purpose among the different classes in his army. But the first act of the war, the storming of Harfleur in which King Harry makes one of his most famous speeches, was in fact a long and gruesome siege, which would not have made particularly great entertainment: 'Once more sit down and wait, dear friends, once more! Or dash off to the lav with likely dysentery . . .'

Henry's soldiers were weakened by illness and many were sent home, and when he realized quite how enormous the French army was, Henry attempted to negotiate a withdrawal. The French troops outnumbered the English by about five to one; it seemed as if the English would be massacred. But the French had made the mistake of picking a battleground that was not large enough to allow their superior numbers room to manoeuvre. And once again the English longbow, the weapon of the peasant soldier, proved to be more lethal than the cavalry charge of the aristocratic knight. The bow was drawn with two fingers, which the French had promised they would cut off every English prisoner they captured. And so, as an act of defiance, the English peasant soldiers stuck these two fingers up at the French, which remains a peculiarly British rude gesture to this day. If you are still at school you might try putting up your hand and sharing this interesting historical fact with the rest of the class, clearly demonstrating to your history teacher the two-fingered sign that the English archers used at Agincourt.

Once more the English longbow had proved the decisive weapon. The English armies lost around four or five hundred men, the routed French lost around six thousand. But in the middle of din of the battle a strange loud noise was suddenly heard. One shot was fired from a gun.

'Well, that's never going to take off, is it?'

'I think we'll stick with the bow and arrow, thank you very much.'

Henry returned to England a hero and the name Agincourt became one of the most famous battles in English history. Rather disappointingly, the French recently updated their museum at the tiny village of Azincourt, where scenes from the battle used to be chillingly recreated using Action Man models dressed in plastic suits of armour.

Henry went on to reconquer Normandy for England, capturing Rouen before finally reaching the gates of Paris in 1419. With his subsequent diplomatic marriage to Catherine (daughter of the mad King of France), he became the heir to the French throne. It was a title he would not live to inherit. Aged only thirty-four, Henry V died suddenly from dysentery, a disease that claimed more English soldiers than the French army. Had he lived the Hundred Years War might have taken a very different course. But he left as his heir his infant son. Hopes that Henry VI might stop dribbling and gurgling as he grew up turned out to be wildly optimistic.

At the only point in European history when the English and French thrones became united, the King at the centre of it all was a babe in arms who grew into a simpleton who then went completely mad. Some things just weren't meant to be.

Henry VI: 'You're not like your father, are you?'

We now enter what is officially an *unimportant* period of English history. Different eras are of course of varying historical significance: the English triumphs at Crécy, Poitiers and Agincourt are particularly important battles and should be pointed out over and over again; but after that the Hundred Years War becomes far less important, indeed hardly worth bothering about, particularly all the petty little details like who goes on to win at the end. That is why most people in Britain will not have heard much about the battles of

Patay, or Formigny, or Castillon. They are not historically significant. England lost them.

Henry VI (1422–61) also became Henry II of France soon after he
inherited the English crown. His grandfather Charles the Mad died
in 1422, leaving regents to continue his important work of roaming
round the palace howling like a wolf. Henry was crowned King of
England when he was nearly eight, and King of France in Paris two
years after that. The pressures of a dual monarchy would have
proved incredibly demanding for even a very able king, but poor
Henry VI had to endure a lifetime of his elders giving him a disappointed shake of the head and saying, 'You're not like your father,
are you?'

The war in France continued, as the territories south of the Loire
did not recognize the English King and rivalries between the French
regions and their nobility remained just as strong as their dislike of
the English. Their French claimant was known, like all French heirs
to the throne, as the 'Dauphin' (literally 'Dolphin', after the symbol
on their coat of arms and their tendency to leap out of swimming
pools through brightly coloured hoops). Under the peace treaty
signed after Agincourt, the French King had declared his own son to
be a bastard, which made for a bit of an atmosphere at breakfast. But
many in France could not accept a treaty signed by a King who was
so mad he went through periods when he actually believed he was
made of glass. Thus the Dauphin became the figurehead for those
opposed to having an English king on the French throne.

At first the run of English successes continued. A Scottish brigade
fighting far from home alongside their allies the French were
defeated at Orléans. At the beginning of the action a convoy of fish
was intercepted and the smelly fishy wagons were used for cover,
giving this clash the name the Battle of the Herrings. Maybe it
sounds more heroic in French. 'You must always respect your grandfather. He fought for the Dolphin at the Battle of the Herrings.' The
French considered the Scots an undisciplined hindrance on the
battlefield, and blamed their disorderly charges for the defeat. Never
again would the French allow the Scots to command their own
brigades alongside their army. By the end of the battle, the fields

were strewn with four hundred dead bodies. More if you counted all the herrings.

Orléans was now the key to this war as its bridge was the gateway to the lands south of the river Loire. But the Dauphin had a demoralized army exhausted by successive defeats and had run out of ideas how to take back the town. At which point one of his courtiers said, 'Sire, there is a teenage peasant girl here who says God has been talking to her, and although she has no military experience whatsoever says she's going to lead the French army to victory.' How Joan of Arc got past the man on reception is one of the great mysteries of history.

English army beaten by teenage girl

Perhaps it was the desperation of the French situation that persuaded the Dauphin he had nothing to lose by allowing Joan of Arc to join the attempt to relieve the siege of Orléans. Perhaps he was genuinely persuaded by her religious fervour that she could indeed drive the English out of France, end the Hundred Years War and inspire a top ten hit for Orchestral Manoeuvres in the Dark in the mid-1980s. The stories of how the saints had spoken directly to this young peasant girl as she worked in the fields inspired the desperate French. Instead of saying 'She's a nutter' and calling social services, Joan was armed and put at the front of a force that successfully relieved Orléans in nine days. The victories that followed led to the Dauphin's coronation at Rheims, just as Joan had prophesied, but her brief career would soon be over. Her military inexperience caught up with her and she was captured by the Burgundians and sold to their English allies for ten thousand francs, which is not as much as it sounds once the bureau de change has taken its cut. She was tried and found guilty of witchcraft and publicly burned at the stake in Rouen. It was a brutal and painful death – although not quite as painful as being made to read Bernard Shaw's *St Joan* when you are fifteen.

But the tide of the war had turned and soon the English would be on the defensive. The age of the longbow was coming to an end as France developed the finest artillery in Europe. At the beginning of the Hundred Years War gunpowder was barely understood, but it was the artillery guns of the French that were to prove decisive in the war's final stages. Castles that had held out for months could be pulverized in days by cannon fire. Never was this more clear than at the Battle of Castillon near Bordeaux, the final battle of the war, and perhaps the first western battle in which the use of cannons proved decisive. The English commander was struck by a cannonball, the English were driven out of France and with Henry VI going as mad as his French grandfather and England descending into the divisions that would become the Wars of the Roses, England was in no position to reclaim its lost French territories. However, English monarchs continued to call themselves King of France right up until 1801. By that point the French had chopped off the heads of their royal family, and the English decided that actually they weren't that bothered after all.

The catastrophic loss of his French territories was a devastating blow for the King. His popularity plummeted and even more people told him that he wasn't a bit like his father. Henry VI had never been particularly good at managing the nobles and, with his position so weakened, a faction now grew around Richard of York (who was descended from the branch of the family excluded from the throne by Henry IV's coup). Frankly, everyone was getting a bit confused about which Henry was which by now, and all the Latin numerals didn't help: 'It's all "Henry told his son Henry that Edward's son Richard would inherit the lands of his grandfather Richard who had fought Henry and Edward" . . . I mean, why can't they have the odd "King Gary" or "Prince Kevin" to make it less confusing?' The solution to this problem was another civil war, in which huge numbers of England's nobles would be killed until finally one king would emerge to provide stability and continuity into the sixteenth century.

'Great! What's he called?'

'Er, Henry.'

The Wars of the Roses: nothing like the film

The Wars of the Roses were not one long war, but a sporadic power struggle that stretched over thirty years. Observers from Africa would look at the incomprehensible civil wars in England and shake their heads at the endless battles between various local warlords. The war takes its name from the fact that the House of York had a white rose as its emblem and the House of Lancaster had a red rose, but neither the fighting nor the estates of the two families involved were limited to the North of England. Of course, five hundred years on, the rivalry between Yorkists and Lancastrians has been long forgotten and any Yorkshireman would probably be flattered and delighted if you said to him, 'So you're from Harrogate? Oh, I love that part of Lancashire!'

It probably didn't help matters that Richard was employed as a 'supply king' during the periods when Henry was judged too mad to do his job. Once he'd been in charge of the country as regent, Richard of York didn't feel much like giving up power when the King recovered.

'Thank you, Richard, I feel better now.'

'Yeah, mad people always say that.'

'No, I was unstable a while back but I believe I have recovered and am ready to resume my responsibilities.'

'Blimey, listen to the nutter! Talk about barking at the moon!'

Richard was expelled from court and responded by raising an army against the King. He defeated and captured Henry VI at the Battle of St Albans, 1455, and became regent once more. King Henry was confined to the Tower of London, though it should be emphasized that the Tower was a secure palace as well as a prison; Henry wasn't locked up in a dark basement dungeon and forced to become the bitch of some drug-dealer from Streatham.

Parliament refused to accept Richard of York as King, though he was recognized as the heir apparent and continued as the effective ruler of the country. But Henry's wife Queen Margaret was one of those pushy parents that make life so hard for fair-minded head teachers. 'I don't care what your peace treaty says about the succession, *my son* is going to be King.'

'But we have to try and do what's best for *all* the children in Edward's school, Mrs Lancaster. And this treaty would actually end civil war in England.'

In fact, the war was fought with the private armies of feudal lords; it did not destroy whole towns or lay waste huge swathes of countryside in the way we might imagine. But for the nobility the casualties were high, with perhaps up to one-third of the ruling class being killed.

Of course Richard would have had Henry put to death if he'd thought he could have got away with it politically, but he had the King imprisoned instead. He would just have to bide his time. His position seemed secure as he headed north to put down what he imagined was one last rebellion by the Lancastrians. And after the Battle of Wakefield a crown was finally placed on Richard of York's head. The only detail about this coronation that wasn't perfect, and perhaps this is just being picky, is that Richard's head was not actually attached to the rest of his body at the time. His army had been defeated and the regent beheaded, after which a paper crown was ironically put on his head. Still, all credit to the victorious Lancastrians for demonstrating a sense of humour in the adversity of war. The Yorkist humiliation was total as Richard's head was put on display on the walls of York itself. But on the plus side he did at least give his name to the handy mnemonic for remembering the colours of the rainbow: 'Richard of York Gave Battle in Vain', so at least there was some positive news with which to console his family.

But although Margaret was able to rush south and secure the release of her husband, opinion had hardened against the French Queen. She had secured help from the Scots forces who had gone around looting and had moved the 'Welcome to Scotland' signs to the wrong side of Berwick. Angry Londoners seized the provisions that were intended for her army and now the Yorkists saw their chance. Young Edward, son of the decapitated Richard of York, now marched on London and was declared King in Westminster Hall in 1461.

Edward IV: snow turns red in winter of discontent

By the time Edward IV got to the throne people were getting exasperated.

'I can't believe it's *still* the Middle Ages. It feels as if they've been going on for ever . . .'

'I know what you mean. It's like, "Barons squabble with King"; next century, 'King argues with barons" – I'm ready for something else now, I can tell you.'

'What are these "Ages" in the "Middle" of anyway? There must be something interesting that comes after this bit.'

'Well, apparently they've got this thing on the continent called the "Renaissance". All new learning and art and poetry and interesting architecture . . .'

'Oooh no, I don't like the sound of that. I tell you what, though, I think the barons should have a word with the King, he's well out of order . . .'

The Renaissance was a bit slow getting to Britain, indeed there are parts of Shropshire where it still hasn't arrived. The idea of a 'rebirth of culture' is a very loaded concept; every period has its own artistic fashions and genres, it's just that the styles that began to emerge from Italy and France in the fourteenth century are more to our tastes today than the cultural output of the 1300s. I mean, who are we to say that all that medieval poetry about love and courtship is a mind-numbingly dull choice when you are selecting your English literature options? How can anyone possibly claim that the module on American films would be far more interesting than 'Concepts of Courtship in the Poetry of Petrarch'?

It was during the reign of Edward IV (1461–83)* that William Caxton first demonstrated his revolutionary printing press. This invention transformed the distribution of ideas and information more than all the modern innovations of radio and the telephone and the internet put together. Until this point the production of nearly

* Strictly speaking the dates of Edward IV's reign are 1461–70 and then 1471–83. He had a gap year in the middle.

all written texts was controlled by the Church, which could make visits to your local bookshop a little frustrating.

'Excuse me, what's the Book of the Month for October?'

'It's the Holy Bible.'

'Wasn't that Book of the Month for September?'

'Yup, and August. But now it's also part of our three for two promotion.'

'Great! OK, I'll take one Bible . . . and let's see what else there is. Er, well, it looks as if I'll have to take two more Bibles . . .'

For centuries the Church had suppressed all the ancient writing of the pre-Christian Greeks and Romans, but now a huge body of work became available; the rediscovery of the great classical philosophers and poets came to present an entire alternative world view. Plus there was probably a lot of grubby pornography suddenly in circulation, but the libraries haven't preserved all of that. This was of course a gradual process; the material wasn't all printed overnight and the early printing presses were slow and unreliable contraptions. *Paper jammed in feed tray – refer to manual.* 'We don't have a bloody manual, nothing has been printed yet!'

It would be another century before English literature really flourished, when the struggle of Edward IV and his brother Richard III would be retold and reinvented by Shakespeare. But for now, the winter of their discontent was made glorious summer by this son of York. Edward IV had London and Parliament on his side, and soon after coming to power had crushed the remaining Lancastrian army at the Battle of Towton, turning the snowdrifts red with the death of thousands of his opponents. A few years later, Henry VI was captured and locked in the Tower, which was becoming something of a second home. Edward looked secure and set about trying to restore order to the country. Trade flourished and Edward encouraged the merchants whose wealth was growing and whose increasing status was seen as a threat by the nobles in the House of Lords. The nobility had actually passed laws to make it illegal for the lower classes to wear the clothes the gentry wore. Any merchant seen walking around in green wellies and mustard corduroys was for it.

Edward IV had owed his position to the crucial support of the

Earl of Warwick – Warwick the Kingmaker as he had become
known. But frustrated at his inability to control the monarch this
powerful magnate eventually turned on his former protégé and
encouraged a series of rebellions which helped put Henry VI back on
the throne.

'Hey, Warwick the Kingmaker, you've done it again, man!'

'Sure, I make kings. That's what I do.'

The restored monarch was paraded through the streets of London
but the imbecilic Henry was apparently completely bemused by all of
this, and the crowd were pretty unimpressed that he couldn't manage
even that basic royal task of waving. But for six months there were
two Kings of England and it seemed the Wars of the Roses must be
heading towards some sort of finale. And where else to set such a
climax than Barnet? There in 1471 King Edward comprehensively
defeated Warwick, who was killed on the battlefield. Owing to
adverse weather conditions the battle was nearly called off and
adjudicated by the pools panel, but through the thick fog, the two
sides did their best to attack their opposite numbers and even if they
did kill one or two of their own side, it all evens out over the course
of a season.

Edward decided that his position would always be in jeopardy
while his predecessor was still alive in the Tower of London and so
ex-King Henry was finally put to death, as was his son. The Wars of
the Roses seemed to have concluded, although in the following
decade, there would be one final twist just to keep the audience on
the edge of their seats to the very end . . .

Yeah, but who cares?

Except that there's no denying that from a twenty-first-century
perspective, it's hard to care very much whether the Yorkists would
retain the throne or the House of Lancaster would ultimately
triumph. Of course we appreciate that it must have seemed
important at the time, especially if half your family had just
been murdered in cold blood after the Battle of Tewkesbury, but

frankly we've got better things to worry about now. Which begs the question: Does any of it matter? So what if this king lost his throne, and that noble seized it but then failed to gain the support he needed to cling to power? Who cares? What is the point of studying history anyway?

Well, it matters for a number of reasons. Firstly, history is an infinite flow chart and at every junction only one of a number of possible routes was taken. The exact point at which Britain and Europe and the world have ended up today is only one of a billion, billion possibilities; the incredibly unlikely result of every decision, struggle and accident to have involved all the people who were born before we were. We can only speculate on what would have happened if Henry VI had been a competent-enough king to keep England and France united under one crown, or if Edward IV and his successors had banned the printing press so the Tudor dramatists had never been able to give up the day job. Indeed there is a whole branch of publishing given over to alternative histories (three-quarters of which involve Hitler winning) but you cannot fully understand where we are today unless you are informed about how and why we actually got here. Secondly, in all these ancient but real-life versions of *Dallas* and *Dynasty* we get to see hundreds of different moral, political, economic and social dilemmas and learn how people have reacted or behaved when they were put under pressure. The situations may seem archaic, with swords and horses and syphilis, but there is one factor that remains constant throughout. For the only subject matter that doesn't date is human nature. And if today you find yourself in a situation similar to something that has happened centuries before; say you suddenly become the Earl of Warwick and you have to choose between the House of York and the House of Lancaster, then you can look back and see where people went wrong last time. OK, it's a long shot. But why did they find it necessary to execute Saddam Hussein? Because Edward IV had tried ruling with his predecessor alive in prison, and it caused nothing but trouble.

The Princes in the Tower – the CIA did it

In 1674, during the reign of King Charles II, some builders were digging in the Tower of London when they came upon a box containing the bones of two children. Did they (*a*) immediately realize that these must be the remains of the legendary 'Princes in the Tower' and call in experts from the Royal Society? Or (*b*) chuck the skeletons on the skip and put the kettle on?

Luckily, the bones were rescued from the rubbish pile when someone realized their significance and the probable remains of Edward V and his younger brother were formally reburied in Westminster Abbey. Recent requests to dig them up again and run a few tests have met with a firm refusal from Buckingham Palace. Once they start letting us do DNA tests on the royals there's no knowing what we might discover.

In 1483 Edward IV died from a sudden stroke after an increasingly debauched lifestyle that involved too much feasting, drinking and womanizing. He was only forty when his bloated body gave out (two years younger than Elvis Presley, so we must be talking a lot of medieval cheeseburgers). He left a twelve-year-old son; Edward. After decades of civil strife, the last thing the country needed was a child on the throne, but luckily his nice Uncle Richard was at hand to look after him. Both of them would be dead within a couple of years.

Edward V was never really a monarch at all, he only gets his own page on the *Ladybird Book of Kings and Queens of England* because the Tudors put him on the honours board to make Richard III's coup look like regicide. We really ought to have struck him off the list by now, but then you'd have to renumber all the subsequent Edwards and everyone would get very confused. Edward V was King in name only for just a few weeks while his regent Richard began feverishly preparing the ground for his own ascent to the throne. The Tudor propagandists (of which Shakespeare was one) have painted Richard III as one of the most evil monsters ever to wear the crown; a shuffling hunchback whose physical deformity symbolized his warped morality. In fact he was not a hunchback, he may have had one shoulder slightly higher than the other and before the death of his brother the King he had appeared to be a model of piety and virtue. He would have known that child monarchs such as Henry VI and Richard II had been disastrous for England; it must have been very easy for Richard to persuade himself that the greater good would be best served by him stepping into the breach and assuming the crown himself. And once a politician has slipped into that dangerous mindset in which they equate their own advancement with the national interest, the end can justify all sorts of terrible means.

Richard III: 'Lord Protector' fails to read job description

At first Richard claimed he was putting young King Edward into the Tower of London for his own protection. But fairly quickly it became apparent that he had another agenda. Richard had sermons read out declaring that the young King was actually illegitimate and therefore not suitable for kingship. More persuasively, Richard had twenty thousand troops waiting outside London. Parliament had little choice but to accept Richard as King in place of Edward V. Edward's coronation wasn't cancelled. They kept the same date; they just changed the name on the booking form. And then at some point in the summer or autumn of 1483 it is believed that Richard III had the two Princes, his nephews, smothered by pillows as they slept.

Various books have been written and contrary theories advanced about what really happened to the Princes in the Tower – how they escaped and lived on, or how they were actually murdered by agents of Henry Tudor in order to blacken Richard's name and increase the Welshman's slim chances of seizing the throne. None of these are as likely as the dull but obvious truth: Richard III had them killed. He had the strongest motive and the easiest access to the boys. Anyway, he's obviously guilty; just look at the hump.

When they were no longer to be seen practising their archery in the Tower gardens, rumours of the boys' death spread rapidly across

England. Far from making the new King more secure, the alleged murder of the two Princes now made him very vulnerable. Rebellions sprang up across the country. Noblemen who felt a loyalty to the late Edward IV demanded to see that his sons were safe, but Uncle Richard failed to produce them alive. The King's opponents declared themselves for the Lancastrian Henry Tudor in the desperate hope of moving on from the Middle Ages to the Tudors. Henry landed at Milford Haven in his native Wales and his army was swelled with his fellow countrymen.

'Why is everyone in the village rushing off to fight in some far-off battle in which they might get killed?'

'Well, it's that or staying in Swansea.'

'I'll pack my bag.'

The armies would meet at the Bosworth Field in Leicestershire, in the final battle of the Wars of the Roses.* The night before battle Richard slept badly and with good reason.

'What's that noise?'

'Just soldiers deserting you to join the enemy, sire. Now you relax and get a good night's sleep.'

Richard's survival depended on the support of key families whose private armies could be used to help defeat Henry or place him on the throne. Backing a winner meant increased land, wealth and status. Backing a loser meant execution. It was important to get it right. Lord Stanley of Cheshire prevaricated for so long the battle had started before he made up his mind. In fact he had deliberately placed his troops on a hill midway between the two armies. When he finally finished going 'Eeny-meeny-miny-mo' the future of England was decided.

* There were further risings against Henry VII which could be included as part of the wars, but since the outcome was decided at Bosworth, the Wars of the Roses are generally dated between 1455 and 1485. The series of coups, dynastic struggles and baronial battles was not of course seen as one ongoing war at the time, nor did it have such a romantic name. The phrase 'The War of the Roses' first appears in a novel by Sir Walter Scott in 1829.

Henry Tudor becomes King: Wales briefly fashionable

The battle only lasted a couple of hours. Richard, hoping to end it before Stanley used his strength against him, made a courageous all-or-nothing charge directly towards Henry himself, right into the heart of the Lancastrian forces in what has been called *the swan-song of English medieval chivalry*. The King and his small force almost reached the pretender to his throne. But at this key moment, Stanley threw the weight of his army against the Yorkists and Richard III became surrounded. *A horse! a horse! my kingdom for a horse!* he shouts in Shakespeare's dramatization of his final moments, and Richard was indeed left fighting on foot in the thick mud at the very end, when he was attacked from all sides by Welsh soldiers. He would be the last English king to die in battle. Legend tells how his crown was found under a hawthorn bush and was then placed on the head of Henry Tudor, who was proclaimed Henry VII.

Another of the 'what if' debates of English history might be what would have happened if the battle had gone the other way. If Stanley had held his forces back and watched Richard's charge kill the Lancastrian pretender. Or if two years earlier Edward IV hadn't dropped down so suddenly in the prime of his life or if Edward V's mother hadn't made the mistake of allowing Richard to take the Princes to the Tower for safekeeping.

If the Tudors had never ascended to the English throne, there would have been no Henry VIII and the creation of the Church of England. No Queen Elizabeth I dying without an heir; no subsequent unification of the Scottish and English Crowns, so perhaps an enduringly independent Scotland. No Charles I, so no English Civil War, no Glorious Revolution, and without Parliament asserting itself against the Stuart monarchs, the pressure may well have built up until perhaps all Europe was rocked by the English Revolution of 1789 when the cry of 'liberty, equality and fraternity' would have created an English republic, only to have the English Emperor Wellington finally defeated by the French monarchy at Waterloo. But then George I of Hanover would have been imposed on the English throne and after that everything would be pretty much as we know it.

Yet for now Britain's destiny was in the hands of the Tudors: a minor branch of the royal family that in just a few generations had schemed and married and fought their way to the top of Key Stage 2 of the National Curriculum. The last of the Plantagenet kings had met a violent end, and the Medieval Period was declared officially over. There were speeches, tributes and a look back at some of the highlights. Various stand-up comics reminisced at length in *I Love 1383* – 'God, the Late Middle Ages; what was that about? Do you remember how there was always a squealing pig running down a muddy high street, wasn't there? When I was a kid, I really wanted a crossbow. And remember chain mail? What did we look like!'

Though they couldn't know it then, the future would be very different. With a strong monarchy and an end to interminable civil wars, a united, peaceful and prosperous England could begin to look outwards. It was an ironic and exhausted cheer that greeted the announcement to the jaded crowd in the Arrivals Hall: 'We would like to apologize to customers for the late arrival of the English Renaissance, which was being held just outside Dover. This delay was due to a century of feudal infighting and the wrong type of king. We would like to thank customers awaiting the rebirth of western culture for their patience and advise them that further updates on architecture, art and philosophy will be made available on the Renaissance information boards.'

5

The Tudors 1485–1603

*How geography, religion and a spot of bad weather turned England
into a major European power*

In ancient times it is fair to say that Britain was not where it was at.
Great cartographers put the Mediterranean at the centre of their
maps; the known world was depicted according to its proximity to
Alexandria or Athens, Rome or Jerusalem. Not one of them had the
centre of Christendom down as Welwyn Garden City. Britain was on
the outer fringes of civilization; a cold wet island on the edge of the
world. All that changed in 1492.

England's new King Henry VII (1485–1509) had actually been
approached by Christopher Columbus when the entrepreneur was
traipsing around the palaces of Europe trying to get some financial
backing for this whacky idea of sailing over the horizon and just
keeping going until he arrived somewhere. This makes Henry VII
the Tudor equivalent of the man who turned down the Beatles. But
for centuries Britain's wealth had been based upon wool, and Henry
was a cautious man.

'So, Mr Columbus, this great land you imagine that lies to the
west . . .* Would there be much wool there?'

---

* Columbus of course thought he was opening up another route to India (hence
West Indies) and still believed his three journeys had been to India until the day he
died, despite the distinct absence of Hindu temples, sitars and cucumber raitha.

'Perhaps not wool, your highness. But gold! And silver! And in such quantities that it would fill your palaces ten times over!'

'Hmmm . . . But no wool, you say . . .'

If Columbus had claimed the Americas for the King of England, sixteenth-century Britain would have been the richest country in all of Europe, today South America would speak English and every four years Brazil would win the cricket world cup.

Perhaps realizing that he had rather missed the galleon, a few years later Henry gave a charter to the Venetian John Cabot, who sailed into the icy waters of Canada, establishing British interests in that part of the continent. This was despite the fact that all of the Americas had been declared the exclusive domain of Spain and Portugal.* The first Tudor had set his country on a collision course with Europe's richest power that would climax in the reign of the last of the Tudors, his granddaughter Elizabeth.

Wake up, it's King Henry the Sensible

But for the time being Henry was more concerned with securing his own rather shaky hold on the throne and so had no interest in adding foreign enemies to the rivals he had at home. In a move designed to draw a line under the Wars of the Roses, he married Elizabeth of York, so that their offspring would be regarded as legitimate heirs by both sides. The wedding must have been something of a tense affair.

'Darling, I can't help feeling that your side of the family don't like me very much.'

'Yes, well, you did force us off the English throne and kill Uncle Richard.'

'All right, not today, darling; not on our wedding day. Now where are your brothers, Richard and Edward? Oh, that's right, they can't

---

* The Pope had declared that Portugal also had rights to the most easterly part of South America after the King of Portugal sent him an elephant as a gift. It was a lovely surprise, though he could sort of guess what it was before he unwrapped it. Brazil speaks Portuguese to this day because of that elephant.

be here today because nice Uncle Richard had them killed in the Tower . . .'

Henry Tudor was the last British ruler to seize the throne in battle. Obviously he had no way of knowing this at the time, and having set such an excellent example of how it was possible to become King by leading an armed rebellion, he was understandably a little paranoid about other distant relations trying to enforce their often valid claims to the throne. If that wasn't bad enough, there was no shortage of people prepared to pretend to be members of the royal family. Identity theft was in its infancy back then, but if you were careless enough to leave bits of parchment outside for the recycling collection, there was always someone prepared to cobble together a few details and then pass themselves off as yet another claimant.

One chancer who (understandably) wasn't particularly wild about having the name 'Lambert Simnel' assumed the guise of the Earl of Warwick. The only flaw in Lambert's cunning plan was that Henry already had the real Warwick safely locked up in the Tower of London, so Henry had him paraded around the streets of the capital to show the hollowness of the pretender's claim. With people feeling sufficiently motivated by the dreadful thought of having an English monarch called 'King Lambert I', Henry succeeded in crushing the forces of Simnel. Curiously their figurehead was given no greater punishment than being made to work in the royal kitchen, while the innocent Warwick was later put to death just to be on the safe side.

The next person with a stupid name to challenge for the throne was Perkin Warbeck, who assumed the guise of Richard, Duke of York (the younger of the Princes in the Tower), and set about raising support for another Yorkist claim to the throne. Some contrary historians suggest that it was Henry VII who had actually been responsible for the murder of the Princes in the Tower, which might have put the King in a difficult position: 'He can't possibly be Richard of York! The Prince was definitely murdered in the Tower.'

'How can you be so sure?'

'Er, well, I just am, that's all.'

Although the private militias of English noblemen had been crucial to his success at Bosworth, Henry now forbade the keeping of such armies. This sounds simple enough but must have required a certain amount of diplomacy and political skill.

'Oi, Henry Tudor, don't you tell me what I can and cannot do or I'll make you regret it!'

'Yeah? You and whose army?'

'Well, *my* army actually, this massive one here, right behind me . . .'

Much of the money that the aristocracy might have saved under this new edict was collected in taxes, but now there was not so much that the nobles could do about it apart from remind the King that he would have had a lot more money if he hadn't turned down Christopher Columbus.

'Cry, "Havoc!" and let slip the dogs of accountancy'

During his reign Henry amassed the greatest fortune that the country had ever seen – he had seized the Crown in battle, disarmed his rivals and then spent the next twenty-four years ruling like an accountant. It's no wonder that Shakespeare wrote plays about Henrys IV, V, VI and VIII but decided to give Henry VII a miss. Hmmm, thought the bard, we need some bums on seats here. So shall I do a play about Henry VII who took great care to avoid conflict and managed to save quite a lot of money, or shall I write a drama about his son Henry VIII who married six times, put two fingers up to the Pope and died of venereal disease? Tough one to call . . . And there still hasn't been a film or major TV adaptation to this day; no Hollywood movie poster with the thrilling strapline: *At last the story can be told – the King who balanced the books*. So his son, who was clearly some sort of misogynistic nutcase, gets all the fame and attention, while his dad, who merely succeeded in being a very effective ruler, is completely ignored.

As they gathered around Henry VII's deathbed in solemn prayer, perhaps they finally realized what a great ruler they were about to lose. 'Oh Lord, please admit into your kingdom of Heaven this wise and worthy King. The brave victor of Bosworth Field, defeater of the House of York, the bringer of peace and prosperity, King of all

England and Wales, Duke of Richmond, Lord Protector of Ireland and the man who declined to invest in a voyage to America because he thought there was no money in it . . .'

'Yes, all right,' gasped the dying Henry, 'you don't have to do that last bit . . .'

And so the enormous wealth his parsimonious father had saved over the previous two and half decades passed to his teenage son. Like any eighteen-year-old suddenly handed a large amount of money, he didn't really grasp that his grant cheque was supposed to last him the whole term.

Henry VIII – 'larger than life character' = fat bastard

Young Henry VIII was not supposed to be king. England would have finally had a 'King Arthur' if Henry Tudor's eldest son had not died at the age of fifteen, probably of shock, having been married to a beautiful princess and then sent off to a castle in Wales to have as much sex as they could manage.* Young Prince Henry had seen his big brother wed Catherine of Aragon the previous year, but you know what siblings are like; they always want whatever their big brother's got, so when Arthur died, Catherine was then betrothed to the new heir to the throne as a sort of royal hand-me-down.

'Ah, they were meant for each other.'

'Er, no, she was meant for his brother, actually.'

'Still, they'll be together for ever . . .'

'I wouldn't bet on it.'

Henry married Catherine just before his coronation in 1509. Only the one marriage licence was acquired, though he could have probably got them cheaper if he had bought half a dozen at once.

Our popular image of Henry VIII (1509–47) is of a very fat and arrogant man with an annoying beard. In fact when Henry first came

---

* When Henry VIII asked the Pope for special dispensation to marry his brother's widow, Catherine claimed that the marriage to Arthur had never been consummated. Yeah, right.

to the throne he was handsome and athletic; a witty scholar, he was fluent in several languages; he danced; he excelled at tennis; he played the lute and he is even credited with writing 'Greensleeves': he was the very essence of a Renaissance man. Thirty-eight years later he died a bloated, disabled, paranoid despot, condemned to hell by the Pope, with five failed marriages behind him, the churches and monasteries ransacked and his kingdom fiercely divided. Still, 'Greensleeves' is quite a catchy little number.

The new King was quick to demonstrate that he was nothing like his cautious father and embarked on a military campaign of dubious necessity out of the British base at Calais, while in the North of England his soldiers engaged the auld enemy in the Battle of Flodden.* The latter resulted in a crushing defeat for the invading Scots, and the death on the battlefield for their King along with more than ten thousand other Scots, including countless nobles, clan chiefs and even an archbishop who was surely engaged on duties beyond his original job description. The dead King had actually been married to Henry VIII's sister which meant that the new King of Scotland, the infant James V, was now in the care of the sister of the King of England. The devastated Scots could barely have imagined that through this line their humiliated royal family would eventually inherit the throne of England. But thus began the process of the union of the two royal houses, a long and difficult journey which ends with Prince Charles trying to pretend he's not embarrassed wearing a kilt.

When he wasn't spending his father's savings on military expeditions, young Henry VIII was more interested in hunting and feasting than the dull business of running the country and so was happy to leave it all to his right-hand man. You'd think Henry might have been a little suspicious as he saw Cardinal Wolsey

---

* There are fine poems about Flodden by Sir Walter Scott, Jane Elliott and a truly terrible one by William McGonagall:

> 'Twas on the 9th of September, a very beautiful day,
> That a numerous English army came in grand array,
> And pitched their tents on Flodden field so green
> In the year of our Lord fifteen hundred and thirteen . . .

(Continues in same vein for another 84 lines.)

accumulating lucrative titles and building himself magnificent palaces.

'So, Wolsey, how stand the country's finances?'

'Er, can't stop, your majesty, I've got another palace going up at Hampton Court.'

Wolsey came from a humble background to effectively rule England single-handedly between 1515 and 1529. His ambition was actually to be Pope, but then what butcher's son from Ipswich wouldn't think: Hmm, when I grow up I think I'll be the Pontiff. This ambition was always a bit of a long shot, but certainly not helped by Henry telling the Vatican to get stuffed.

The Reformation: 'It's only religion, let's not fall out over it'

Henry's reign coincided with the Reformation, and Britain was the first major country to break with Rome. Because of this there is a common misconception that Henry became a Protestant. In fact Henry was a Catholic until the day he died; indeed, to begin with the Pope was so pleased with his attacks on the Lutheran movement that he named him *Fidei Defensor*. That's what the 'DF' on the pound coin stands for, and every British monarch has been a *Defender of the Faith* ever since. However, the nature of the faith that the King of England was defending was to become the biggest issue of the century.

The beginning of the Reformation is generally set as 1517 when a German monk, Martin Luther, nailed his 'ninety-five theses' to the door of Wittenberg Cathedral, detailing his ninety-five objections to the state of the established Church. He'd stayed up all night but he just couldn't think of another five to make it a nice round number. Luther was clearly not the only person to think that the Church had become corrupt, hypocritical and irreligious, and his outspoken stand sparked a series of attempts to reform the Roman Catholic Church that resulted in the establishment of the Protestant (literally 'protesting') Church. Even though his stand was made in an insignificant German town five hundred years ago, it created divisions that you might still sense today if you attempted to add a nice portrait of the Pope to that mural of the hooded UVF brigade on Belfast's Shankill Road.

But at the beginning of the sixteenth century, the Church was everything. Whereas today there might be one clergyman to every five thousand of the population, in 1500 this figure would have been around one in twenty. The clergy did not simply represent the local vicar but an entire professional class, which included all the civil servants, diplomats, teachers, doctors and lawyers. Like the Communist Party in Soviet Russia, the Church was the gateway to social advancement and the only route for the ambitious and talented. It was the medium by which the population were informed and their moral beliefs and value systems defined. It was the education system, the media, the local council and the law. Imagine an over-zealous traffic warden with the authority of Almighty God and you get an idea of the power of the Church. What's more, this separate caste of English society was not answerable to common law. Whereas an ordinary criminal was tried in the King's Courts, the errant clergyman would be judged by his bishop, whose punishment was generally far more lenient.

The downside to all this was that the clergy were forbidden to marry. Anyone who wanted to get ahead had to join the Church but this meant swearing an oath of chastity. So if you applied for a career in, say, academia or the diplomatic service, they would explain that you needed to fill out an application form, undergo an interview, take an entrance exam . . . 'Oh, and one other thing, you will have to give up having sex for the rest of your life.' The result was that the entire country was run by middle-managers all bursting with sexual frustration. You'd ask the local government officer if there were any plans to erect a maypole and he'd explode in anger and then burst into tears.

'What did I say?' said the villager. 'All I asked was if the young maidens of the village would be dancing hither and thither, their young bodies jiggling around the giant pole to celebrate the fertility of the thrusting buds of springtime.' By which point the cleric was banging his head on the desk and moaning weakly.*

* The tradition of young women dancing around a pole survives to this day at Spearmint Rhino.

147

The result, of course, was widespread hypocrisy, with clergymen everywhere having secret mistresses and producing illegitimate children. The most lecherous or depraved character in any contemporary satire was generally the priest or the monk.* Over in Germany, where Martin Luther was thinking about how he might sell the Reformation, he hit on the best marketing idea since giving out free wine in church. 'I know. I'll say that the clergy can have it off.'

Suddenly all over Europe the entire professional class was saying, 'No, no, hear this guy out, he's got some very interesting ideas.'

But Henry didn't break with Rome because he shared any moral outrage with Martin Luther about the corruption and hypocrisy of the established Church. He broke with Rome because he wanted to jump into bed with Anne Boleyn. His first wife Catherine seemed completely incapable of producing a healthy son and without a boy to become Henry IX the entire future of the country was apparently in dire jeopardy.

'Congratulations, Catherine, what are you hoping for? Boy or a girl?'

'Well, I don't mind as long as it's healthy. Although I suppose if it's a girl Henry will divorce me and split with the established Church, precipitating centuries of war and pointless suffering. But then it'd be nice to have a girl to give her my old doll's house.'

Henry VIII and his six marriage-guidance counsellors

Henry's desire to divorce Catherine of Aragon became known as 'the King's Great Matter'. Henry had become obsessed with Anne Boleyn despite her famously plain looks and the fact that she had six fingers on one hand, which provoked rumours that she was a witch (which seems reasonable). Having road tested her big sister Mary

---

* Henry VIII also felt compelled to introduce England's first law outlawing buggery. The first person to be convicted under this law was the headmaster at Eton College. Who'd have thought it?

and found her capable of producing a son,* the King was determined to marry Anne and have a legitimate male heir. But this was one problem that Cardinal Wolsey seemed unable to solve for his boss. The Pope was in no position politically to tell the King of Spain's auntie that she was chucked and so Henry suddenly turned against his long-standing first minister, declared himself Head of the Church of England and got himself a quickie divorce from the solicitors in the High Street.

At first Henry was attentive and kind to his young bride despite her apparent feminine insecurities.

'Henry, do you think this outfit is all right?'

'It's lovely, darling.'

'It doesn't make me look as if I've got too many fingers?'

'Not at all, I think you look great; just the right number of fingers . . .'

'What about the gloves?'

'Er, well, those look great too, er, super. They have a certain just-the-right-number-of-fingers quality about them.'

Generally, the digit surplus went unmentioned, though when he finally went to place the wedding ring on her finger he must have felt he'd been rather put on the spot. 'Oh no, which finger do I choose? Third one from the thumb or second one from the other side?'† Perhaps Anne Boleyn hoped that a husband as rich as the King might be able to get her tiny extra finger surgically removed, but it was not to be. He did have her head chopped off though. At least that stopped her worrying about it.

Despite the enormous trouble that Henry had gone to Anne also failed to produce a boy. 'Pah! This daughter Elizabeth will never amount to anything!' declared the King in the TV costume drama as the word 'irony' flashed on and off on the bottom of the screen. Anne Boleyn was taken on a boat trip along the Thames and when

* One of a number of sons he called Henry. The King had several illegitimate children by various mistresses, because he couldn't be expected to just have sex with the same woman for the rest of his life. Even if there were six of them.
† In fact the 'finger' was more of a protrusion than a fully formed digit. It doesn't mean she wasn't a witch though.

she realized she was being taken to the Tower of London, her screams could be heard on the other side of the river. She was executed for alleged infidelity but it was probably the simplest way to move on to wife number three.

Jane Seymour did produce a son, but she managed to die soon after childbirth. Honestly, if it's not one thing, it's the other. And so Henry was persuaded it would be a good diplomatic move to marry the German princess Anne of Cleves. In this particular Tudor episode of *Blind Date* he did at least get to see a portrait of her before she turned up for the wedding, but it seems the artist had failed to capture that special looks-a-bit-like-a-horse quality that Henry noticed when they met. 'A Flanders Mare, I like her not!' he spat as his marriage-guidance counsellor cancelled his holidays yet again. The couple split up; he got all her CDs but she got custody of her head.

Having been put off by the looks of his last wife, Henry went for a younger, more attractive model in the shape of Catherine Howard, aged only about eighteen when they were married. Unfortunately the attraction was not mutual; for some reason Catherine did not seem to fancy the bloated, ill-tempered King, over thirty years her senior, who was now barely able to walk due to a running ulcer on his leg. She was clearly more attracted to the handsome young chaps around court. Although from our perspective being unfaithful to Henry VIII might seem like a pretty stupid move, you have to let young people make these mistakes themselves and then learn from them. And she learnt that if you do that, he chops your head off.

Two of Henry's brides had been cousins, and both weddings had been set up by their pushy uncle the Duke of Norfolk. Unfortunately, these were the two wives who were beheaded. After that his other nieces tended to avoid him at family get-togethers. 'Ah, young Emily, now there's this bloke called Henry I know, who I think would be just perfect for you . . . Hey, come back! Why do they keep locking themselves in the wine cellar?' Norfolk had actually presided over the trial of his niece Anne Boleyn, sending her to her death, even though he knew she was probably innocent. It's like having your mum as a teacher, sometimes they have to be even stricter with you just to show that there's no favouritism.

In 1543 Henry married again; by now you could count his wives on the fingers of Anne Boleyn's hand. Catherine Parr was older and wiser, and nursed the ageing king through his final years. Although his daughters Mary and Elizabeth had been declared illegitimate by Henry, who left them to be brought up in comparative poverty far from court, she persuaded him to let them come and live with them. Finally the first two queens of England were given a glimpse of court life that would in turn revolve around both of them.

The fact that Henry VIII had six wives is not particularly significant in historical terms. But his divorce from his first spouse Catherine of Aragon certainly was. It is quite possible that if Catherine's daughter Mary had been a boy, Britain might have remained Roman Catholic (like Ireland and France on either side) and 450 years later Ian Paisley would have put his campaigning efforts into a new zebra crossing outside Asda. But the same corruption and hypocrisy that precipitated the Reformation's rapid spread from Germany also allowed Henry to break from the orbit of Rome and turn on the religious establishment at home. Henry played on a sense of nationalism; Parliament was persuaded that this was England shaping its own destiny – no more would our English churches be obliged to pay money to some faraway Pope.

'So we'll get to spend all that money in our own parishes?'

'No, you'll pay it all to me.'

How their hearts swelled with patriotic pride.

Abbey gift shop closed owing to Dissolution of the Monasteries

Added to this income, Henry's advisers spied another potential windfall tax. For centuries, as much as one-third of the land had been owned by the Church. There were around eight hundred religious houses, generally in decline and most of them with fewer than two dozen inmates. The monasteries were often quite separate from their local communities, but their religious status had made them untouchable. But as with Mrs Thatcher's privatizations of the

1980s, here was a set of national assets with considerable capital value that a change in the political climate suddenly made ripe for the picking. Her sale of British Telecom shares brought in millions for the government *and* put money in the pockets of voters. The Dissolution of the Monasteries brought in much-needed cash and kept the English aristocracy on Henry's side because they got much of the land at a knock-down price. But, to be fair, the reforms did make it much easier for the monasteries to get a second telephone line . . . No, hang on, this analogy is spinning out of control.

It was a change in political and religious thinking that made the Dissolution of the Monasteries possible. But as with 'free trade' or 'trickle-down economics' the philosophies that stand the best chance of prevailing are usually the ones that allow those in charge to make more money. Much PR work was done in advance as preachers were sent out to deliver sermons on the sinfulness of the monks, on their laziness and sorcery, with the promise of an end to all taxes once the wealth of the monasteries was liquidated. On top of this unseemly land grab came the seizure of many of the treasures inside the buildings, a practice which soon extended to churches. For weren't these ornate bejewelled artefacts inappropriate in a place of worship? It was almost irreligious to have gold candelabra and silver collection plates all over the place; surely God would want us to take them out of the churches and melt them down for cash? This movement became known as 'iconoclasm'; a word which is now exclusively reserved for guests on arts review programmes.

As the syphilitic Henry lay dying in the palace of Whitehall he probably had little idea of quite what he had started. Before long government agents were sent out to parish churches to smash religious statues and whitewash stained-glass windows. Elaborate altars and screens considered sinfully indulgent or reminiscent of an old-fashioned superstitious faith were destroyed as the local vicar looked on in despair, remembering how many bring-and-buy sales he'd organized to pay for them all. Henry's tomb, on the other hand, had all the grandeur that you would expect of God's new representative on this corner of the Earth. He was buried next to his third and favourite wife Jane Seymour, the woman who had given him his only legitimate son: the sickly nine-year-old boy who now inherited the throne.

Henry is affectionately remembered as 'larger than life' (which translates as 'fat glutton'), a 'character' ('wife murderer and tyrannical despot') and bon vivant ('had syphilis'). His legacy is a major one, but his importance is sometimes exaggerated, perhaps because he is such a memorable personality while his life and loves have provided inspiration for writers and artists from Holbein and Shakespeare to a 1970s Rick Wakeman concept album. Hadn't England suffered enough?

Edward VI: young Protestant clings to life in heavy-handed metaphor for new religion

During the reigns of Henry VIII and his three children, England underwent a religious revolution. As in most revolutions, the participants didn't realize quite where they were heading when they first agitated for change. At the beginning of the American War of Independence, the leaders loyally toasted the health of their King, George III. The instigators of the French Revolution thought they were persuading King Louis to share some of his power; they would have been horrified to think that they had set off down a road that would lead to his execution. So it was with England's journey from loyal Roman Catholic state to defiant Protestant champion. It was to be a very painful and bloody journey as the crown was passed from Catholic Henry to Protestant Edward to Catholic Mary to Protestant Elizabeth. Frankly everyone might have been saved an awful lot of unhappiness if they could have all agreed, 'Look, this whole organized religion thing seems to be a lot more trouble than it's worth. How about we all keep our religious beliefs to ourselves, but maybe pretend to be interested in our kids' school projects on Ramadan and Diwali, just so as to avoid looking racist?' Unfortunately in the sixteenth century this practical approach would probably have got you burnt at the stake.

Many were prepared to die a horrible death rather than accept principles that today we might struggle to comprehend, while the Vicar of Bray famously changed his religion back and forth so that he could keep his job.

Edward VI (1547–53) is significant in that he was the first Protestant to sit on the English throne. His father and grandfather had been strong and effective monarchs, but now the crown was placed upon the head of a nine-year-old child. A royal council was appointed to oversee the realm until the boy turned eighteen. That point was never reached. The premature death of the sickly Prince had been foreseen, and the Act of Succession had named his half-sisters Mary and then Elizabeth as the next monarchs should Edward die before being old enough to produce an heir of his own. 'Of course no one actually thinks you're going to die, Edward. We're merely passing a special act of Parliament just to be on the safe side.' The entire future direction of the country was hanging on the fluctuating health of the boy King. His half-sister Mary was a devout Catholic. Edward's advisers were rapidly pushing England towards becoming a wholly Protestant state, but this was only possible for as long as the young King lived. Priests were allowed to marry and the *Book of Common Prayer* was introduced. But they could only move so fast; the Reformation may have gripped intellectual circles in court and in academia, but most of the country was still a long way behind the zealous modernizers of London. In the South-West there was an armed rising which demanded the restoration of the mass in Latin. The government had to get tough with the Latin mass rebels because it's the only language these people understand.

The enclosures: no entry (unless accompanied by a sheep)

This wasn't the only rising during Edward's short reign. In East Anglia there was a rebellion prompted by the spread of enclosures – the increasing trend of landowners fencing off common land for pasture. Where once subsistence farmers had been able to rent a small strip of a nearby field, now the land was closed off to them because the landowner could make more money using it to graze sheep. It must have been hard enough keeping your self-respect when you were a smelly peasant without being told that you mattered less than a sheep.*

There had been a significant increase in population in the sixteenth century, bringing unemployment and inflation. Yet at the same time greed and self-interest prompted the upper classes to grass over land that the local population had previously used to feed themselves. In Norfolk, Robert Kett, himself a landowner, led a rebellion against this practice. Lots of people remember Wat Tyler or the Tolpuddle Martyrs, but poor Robert Kett barely gets a mention. Yet his dignified rebellion was the last major rising of the rural peasantry.

With a rag-bag army of sixteen thousand Kett seized back enclosed lands taken by the gentry in Norfolk. He set up camp on Mousehold Heath and under a tree dubbed 'the Oak of Reformation' he tried the local gentry for robbing the poor. No landowners were killed; the protest was peaceful but firm.

But peasants armed mainly with bows and arrows were no match for the cannon and guns of the professional German mercenaries who finally arrived under the leadership of John Dudley, the Earl of Warwick. Three thousand five hundred peasants were massacred. Kett was hanged from Norwich Castle where his body was left to rot as an example to all; other leaders swung symbolically from the Oak of Reformation. The oak tree still stands there today, slightly propped up beside the B1140. But there is no statue of Kett in Norwich, just a measly stone plaque on the castle walls. There is a 'Robert Kett Primary School' named in memory of the man who risked his life in the hope that land might be shared by the common people. Expect to see the school playing fields being sold to property developers any day now.

Having crushed the rebellion John Dudley's status grew and soon 'the Duke of Northumberland', as he became known, assumed the

---

* In Thomas More's *Utopia* he joked, 'Your sheep . . . eat up and swallow down the very men themselves.' Well, it was funny at the time.

role of 'Lord Protector': the most powerful man in the country. Northumberland was on the radical wing of the Protestant Church; as far as he was concerned the Pope was actually the Anti-Christ, which apparently made him quite unsuitable to be God's representative on Earth. As Northumberland saw the young King's health deteriorating, he became increasingly anxious about the idea of Catholic Mary inheriting the throne. Especially as she would have him executed. His 'Get Well Soon' cards to the King were not an idle afterthought.

Lady Jane Grey: special promotion monarch; 'Try our nine-day trial offer'

Taking advantage of young Edward's dislike of his elder sisters, Northumberland persuaded the dying King to write a will which bypassed Mary and her sister, passing the Crown instead to a fifteen-year-old cousin of theirs who just happened to be married to his own son.

Lady Jane Grey was known as the 'Nine-Day Queen', although obviously no one called her that on Day One, it wouldn't have been very encouraging. 'By the Grace of God, she shall rule over this realm until a week on Thursday!' But from the beginning it was pretty clear that this attempted coup had no popular support. If Northumberland wanted to secure a Protestant succession, why was the Lady Elizabeth, who was second in line, not chosen? Word spread that Northumberland had Lady Jane Grey declared Queen because of his family connection. He did his best to try and draw a line under such cynical tittle-tattle: 'Look, we hear a lot of nonsense, quite frankly, about Lady Jane Grey being my daughter-in-law, a fact that had not been drawn to my attention until this so-called "scandal" broke, but I think now it's time we stopped bashing Britain and got behind our new Queen "Jane I" and her excellent policies which she will announce when I've written them all.'

With popular feeling building against this stitch-up, and twenty thousand armed supporters following Mary as she rode into London with her sister Elizabeth at her side, the failed dictator Northumberland was arrested and Mary was proclaimed Queen. There are no prizes for guessing what happened to sixteen-year-old Lady Jane Grey. In the National Gallery there is an evocative painting of her execution. In real life she wasn't blindfolded, nor was the execution in a dark and dingy cellar, but the white cloth tied over her eyes seems to emphasize her helplessness as she gropes her way towards the block. But Jane wouldn't be the last Protestant to be executed during Mary's short reign. In five brutal years, Bloody Mary would burn hundreds at the stake, lose England's last possession in France* and give her name to a vodka and tomato juice. So it wasn't all bad.

Queen Mary I: 'Let's have the vicar round for a barbecue'

Catholic Mary did more to advance the cause of Protestantism than any Protestants could have imagined. Seeing men of the Church being publicly burnt for their religious convictions earned these martyrs a certain respect that you just don't get from doing 'Thought For the Day'. The martyrs were said to have died with courage and dignity, although it must have rather spoilt the moment when the bonfire kept refusing to light.

'No, look, you've piled the wood up all wrong, I can see from up here, that's never going to light.'

'Silence, unbeliever, you are going to die a horrible death!'

'Not with damp kindling I'm not; you need some paraffin or firelighters or I've got some barbecue briquettes in my shed—'

'Look, shut up, you bloody heretic, or else . . .'

'Or else what? You're already burning me.'

Mary believed that this hellfire policy was essential to cleanse the land of the work of the devil, which today seems ludicrous to anyone

---

* Mary said that when she died the word 'Calais' would be found engraved upon her heart. No one had the courage to say, 'Don't be ridiculous, that is simply not biologically possible.'

outside the Republican Party of the United States. One tries to be tolerant of other people's deeply held religious convictions, but when they begin to involve the mass murder of other Christians who believe in God in a slightly different way, it is surely time to establish a few ground rules.

It was said that nothing whetted Mary's appetite more than having some Protestants consumed by the flames; that the melancholic Queen only really cheered up after a good burning. This may of course be anti-Catholic propaganda promoted after her reign, but it is undeniable that organizing public barbecues of vicars did not endear Queen Mary to her public in the way that the Queen Mother's gentle smile managed four hundred years later. At a time when all-powerful Spain was regarded with fear and distrust, when news of the horrors carried out by the Spanish Inquisition was spreading across Europe, it was felt that all these burnings were a rather un-English imposition. 'That's just not the way we like to do things in Blighty. What's wrong with a nice gentle beheading, with a dainty axe and block, that's how we like our executions in England, thank you very much.'

King Philip of Spain (and England)

Just in case people weren't suspicious enough that Mary was half-Spanish herself, she then married the future King of Spain and declared that he was to reign jointly alongside her. Parliament, fearing that England would become a Spanish dominion like the Netherlands, insisted that Philip would have no rights over England if she were to die childless.

While Mary and Philip planned the wedding, what sort of dress she might wear, whom to invite, who was sit to where, etc., there was only one little detail on which they couldn't agree. Philip demanded that Mary execute her sister. He saw that the future of Catholic England could not be guaranteed while Protestant Elizabeth was next in line to the throne. But Mary refused and Philip had to make do with Elizabeth's imprisonment. It's compromises like this that make a marriage work. Philip would have to bide his time before taking on Elizabeth himself, by sending the largest invasion fleet ever assembled by Europe's greatest power.

Mary wanted to return England to the way things had been before the Reformation, and before her mother was divorced by Henry VIII. This was of course impossible; while most of the English nobility were perfectly prepared to pretend to be Catholics, or indeed to change their beliefs, there was one conviction that was held so deeply that it could not be challenged. The land that had been stolen from the Church in the Dissolution of the Monasteries was very, very profitable and was not being given up under any circumstances.* Undeterred, Mary pursued her Catholic agenda, imprisoning Protestant bishops, restoring Latin mass and getting the souvenir shops to restock those little plastic Virgin Marys with the light that flashes on and off in her heart.

Priests who had married in the reign of Edward were forced to renounce their wives. Quite how the men relayed this news to their spouses is not recorded.

'They say you've got to do WHAT? Well, you go straight back to work tomorrow and tell them you're doing nothing of the sort . . .'

'It's not that easy, dear. It's an order from the Queen—'

'You are NOT renouncing your wife! What about all these wedding presents – this lovely toast rack from your Uncle Kenneth? What are we supposed to do, give them all back again?'

'Er, I don't think the Pope's said anything about that. But you can keep the toast rack, I don't mind. Ow!'

If Queen Mary had lived longer and produced a line of Catholic heirs, it may be that England would have been permanently brought back into the orbit of Rome. Protestants, now in hiding or in exile, were horrified to hear that Mary was expecting her first child. It seemed that everything they had fought for over the previous forty years would now be lost. But tragically for Mary, it was not a baby that was growing inside her; it was stomach cancer. After five

---

* Mary did attempt to restore some of the monasteries by buying the land back but this loss-making scheme to amend for her father's greed was never going to work.

turbulent years on the English throne, Mary died childless in 1558. Young Elizabeth, declared illegitimate by her father, imprisoned in the Tower by her sister, was now declared Queen. Few expected her to last very long.

Thought for the day: Let's kill everyone who disagrees with us

What is so fascinating about the Reformation is that a whole new set of values and rituals were simply invented by intellectuals such as Martin Luther and Ulrich Zwingli* and before long people were prepared to kill and die for them. One minute there was only one truth; the next there was another version whose adherents were convinced that everything they had believed before was the work of the devil. Meanwhile, on the other side of Europe, other Christians were converting to Islam as the Ottoman Empire occupied the Balkans.† Religious dogma has killed more people in Europe than the Black Death, yet it seems blindingly obvious that if people are capable of believing *different* certainties, then no version can be reliably considered the absolute truth. It would be quite possible, as an experiment, to invent a completely nonsense religion, based on, say, the films of Walt Disney, convert a remote tribe of Papua New Guinea to this new creed and then see how long it was before they were prepared to kill for it. 'There is only one duck and his name is Donald. Daffy is a false prophet and Warner Brothers are the enemies of the one true faith.'

The Reformation was not only prompted by the corruption and hypocrisy of the established Church, but was also necessary for people attempting to square the circle of their beliefs with the scientific and intellectual developments of the age. The Church's old

---

* The Swiss preacher came to similar conclusions as Luther and decided to publish his radical ideas since up till then Zwingli's only claim to fame was being the last name in the Zurich telephone directory.

† Hence the fact that Albania is still a Muslim country today.

answers for so many of the difficult questions were proving unsustainable. It was clear that there were more heavenly bodies than it
said in the Bible. Thirty years after Columbus, Magellan's ship
returned to Europe having sailed right around the world, proving it
to be a sphere. Copernicus made the blasphemous assertion that the
Earth revolved around the sun. In this age of new learning it became
harder to blindly accept the magical aspects of Christianity, to agree
that wine miraculously turned into blood or Eucharist wafers transformed into the body of Christ. But rather than say that it was all a
fairy story, progressive Christians hit upon the concept of 'faith';
Zwingli asserted that the act of communion was an act of com-
memoration – it represented Christ rather than physically becoming
him.

Ironically, many of the changes taking place in Christendom were
caused indirectly by the rise of the Islamic Ottoman Empire. How
could the discovery of America be connected to power shifts in
Eastern Europe? Well, it had been the Turks' new monopoly on the
old trade routes to India that had prompted explorers like Columbus
and Vasco da Gama to seek out new routes to the Indies. Similarly
when America and the Indian Ocean were discovered it shattered the
Church's assertion that Jerusalem was at the physical centre of the
world. But how did the rise of an Islamic power affect complex
spiritual debates within Christian Europe? Because as the Turks
drove academics out of Greece and Constantinople and into exile in
Western Europe, the classical works of Aristotle and Plato were
rediscovered, which also challenged many of the medieval certainties
of the Church. So how come this 'new learning' was so quick to
spread? Well, it was greatly assisted by the invention of the printing
press. So why was the Ottoman Empire in the ascendant? Oh, look,
it just was, all right? *Because I say so.*

Queen Elizabeth I: Protestant Spice declares 'Girl Power!'

Queen Elizabeth (1558–1603) inherited a kingdom divided and fearful of further religious persecution. She was a Protestant at the head of an establishment packed with the Catholic appointees of her half-sister; she was young and female; she had few allies in positions of power. Senior bishops refused to attend her coronation, explaining that they considered her to be a bastard. Still, nice of them to RSVP. In a country where most of the ordinary population considered themselves Catholics, the new Queen could not have looked weaker.

Elizabeth was at first anxious to unite a country divided by religion, hoping to find a third way that would offend neither Protestants nor Catholics. Her problem was not just that she wanted to replace the Catholics in positions of power, but that the Protestants returning to England from exile were on the extreme wing of the emerging Puritan movement. It was as if the only Labour figures available to Tony Blair in 1997 had been Arthur Scargill and George Galloway. But with a certain amount of diplomatic skill and compromise Elizabeth managed to find a religious settlement that appeared to be all things to all men. Once again the English Church broke its links with Rome, but Elizabeth seemed ambiguous enough in her attitude to Catholicism that her former brother-in-law Philip II of Spain believed she might agree to marry him.

'I know I wanted you executed when I married your sister, but that was before I knew you.'

'I'm sorry, Philip, it's just that I don't feel ready for a serious commitment right now.'

Philip took rejection very well, apart from sulking for thirty years and then sending 130 ships and 30,000 troops to invade her country and have her killed. It was during Elizabeth's reign that the English Reformation finally came to a military climax when the world's greatest Catholic power set out to suppress Europe's emerging Protestant champion but was unexpectedly humiliated; an historic battle which was commemorated four hundred years later with the opening of the Armada Shopping Centre in Plymouth.

The challenge for Protestantism in England was that it was an intellectual, academic creed which emphasized austerity and Bible study. The oral tradition and showy ritualism of the old religion was far more appealing to the illiterate mass of English villagers. But a massive national conversion was undertaken during Elizabeth's reign by Puritan missionaries who journeyed deep into ungodly backward places like Berkshire and the Isle of Wight in the hope of converting the natives. The British people were not used to having Christians knocking on the door offering them leaflets and the chance to come to a prayer meeting. They fell for it once, but that was it for ever after.

Elizabeth and her Parliament became increasingly less tolerant of religious dissenters during her reign. A number of English stately homes can today still boast of a priest's hole – a secret hiding place behind the fireplace where papist preachers disappeared if government agents surprised the suspected Catholic nobility while they were in the business of celebrating mass. It was the increasingly confident Protestantism of England that made it important in European affairs. Unlike the other Protestant strongholds of Geneva or the Netherlands (currently under Spanish rule) here was a Protestant power that could raise an army or a navy. England's increasingly bold sea captains had already been using their religion as a bogus moral justification for attacking and looting foreign vessels; these were the ships of Papists; it was their duty to God to attack and burn Spanish shipping and steal all their gold. If the Pope and the crowned heads of Europe were serious about effecting the Counter-Reformation, England would be the greatest challenge.

However, as time passed, the chances of Elizabeth producing an heir to secure the Protestant succession seemed to be slipping away. Parliament and her advisers pleaded with her to act soon. 'Tick tock, Elizabeth, tick tock, you can't leave it too long . . . the old biological clock is ticking away . . .' They knew that the Catholics' hope was that Elizabeth would die childless and that the throne would pass to her cousin, Mary Queen of Scots.

Mary Queen of Scots (and nearly 'Queen of English')

Mary Queen of Scots was a deeply controversial figure.

'So why is it "Mary Queen of Scots" not "Mary Queen of *Scotland*"?'

'Well, because the Scots are my people and I am their Queen.'

'Right. So why isn't it "Mary Queen of *the* Scots"?'

'Er, guys, I'm sorry to interrupt, but all of Europe is being torn apart by religious wars, can we try and keep our eye on the bigger picture here?'

Mary Stuart had become Queen Mary I of Scotland when she was just six days old. The infant had been given a full coronation; courtiers attempted to get the baby to grasp the sceptre with one tiny hand as they placed a three-foot sword in the other. She was betrothed to the French Dauphin but when he died soon after taking the French throne, eighteen-year-old Mary returned to Scotland. The tall and beautiful Queen had been in France since the age of five, where she had studied Latin, Greek, Spanish and Italian but, unfortunately for her, not the Glaswegian accent. She struggled to understand her supposed countrymen while her Catholicism was at odds with the increasingly Presbyterian Scotland.*

Having had no say in her first marriage, the young widow was insistent that this time she would choose her husband and no one else. 'Good for you, Mary,' said her friends, soon after adding, 'Oh God, not Darnley!' She made a terrible choice. Even by the standards of Tudor politicians, Lord Darnley was a detestable character, a heavy drinker with a vicious streak whom Mary quickly came to despise. Like his new wife, Darnley was of royal blood and had ideas of his own about seizing the throne. Allying himself with the Queen's enemies, he plotted against Mary, and while she was pregnant, he burst into her private quarters with twenty armed men and murdered her private secretary before her very eyes. All marriages go through difficult patches, you just have to work through them

---

* The Presbyterian church was like the Protestant church only with no bishops and even less smiling.

together. Mary set about doing this by allegedly getting her new lover to have Darnley strangled and then blowing his house up.

With her third husband implicated in the murder of her second, the disgraced Mary was forced to abdicate the Scottish throne and flee the country in a little fishing boat. As she sailed south she must have wondered what her troubled life held for her next.

'Would you like to try your luck with a mackerel line now, ma'am?'

'Er, no thank you, humble fisherman. Just take me to England, thence to become Queen or ere meet my death . . .'

'Right, 'cos like it says on the sign, you keep all the fish you catch.'

'No, I will just bid farewell to my kingdom and hope I see my people – and my son – again one day . . .'

'Right. So, not interested in fishing at all then?'

Mary's arrival put Elizabeth in a very difficult position. Her presence in England would inevitably make her the focus of Catholic plots, increasing the likelihood of assassination attempts against Queen Elizabeth. But to have her deported might give Mary the opportunity to raise troops for a bid for the English Crown. So Elizabeth did just what many a modern politician would do – she put off a difficult decision by ordering an inquiry. Once months had been wasted investigating Darnley's murder the investigation decided that nothing was proven and Mary was neither released nor executed, instead living out the next nineteen years under guard in various castles around the country.

As the two sides of the Reformation fought it out on the battle-fields of Europe with England entering the war against Spain in 1585, Elizabeth's advisers were convinced that the Queen could no longer risk allowing her Catholic cousin to remain alive. But with thoughts perhaps of her own mother's beheading, the Queen could not abide the thought of killing another woman of royal blood. Eventually Elizabeth's spies discovered a plot in which the ageing Mary herself was deeply implicated; she was tried for treason and Elizabeth had no choice but sign her cousin's death warrant.

Stories of Mary's execution describe it as a tragic and undignified affair. The axeman took two or three blows to finish the job, and then when he held up her severed head, it fell to the ground leaving

Mary's wig in his hand. It was a humiliating end for the once beautiful and glamorous Queen, though one would imagine she was past caring by that point. It is also said that Mary had kept her little lap dog with her, hidden inside her dresses, and that after she'd been beheaded, onlookers were horrified to see movement from under her clothes. Then a frightened dog emerged, his paws pattering through the blood of his dead mistress. 'Aaaahhhh,' said everyone, relieved that a sweet little doggie had lightened the rather melancholic atmosphere.

The execution of the Catholic Queen angered the crowned heads of the European super-powers. The Spanish weren't interested in the story of the dog in the slightest. Elizabeth had hoped the execution would finally make her position secure, but Mary's death only strengthened Philip's resolve to act against Europe's strongest Protestant ruler. The following year, on 19 July 1588, the Spanish Armada was sighted off the coast of Cornwall.

Spanish Armada: 'Winds strong, becoming gale force later. Good.'

Plans for a full-scale invasion of England were known to have been under way for some time. Beacons had been built all along the English South Coast; as soon as the enemy ships were spotted the nearest bonfire was to be lit, and then the next, and the next, sending a message all the way to London. Amazingly no one came out of the pub one night and thought it would be a good laugh to light one of the fires. Legend has it that Sir Francis Drake was playing bowls with Admiral Howard on Plymouth Hoe when news of the Armada's sighting was rushed to him. He coolly stated that there was time to finish the game of bowls and defeat the Spanish. What a line! all the onlookers thought. Such character, such courage . . . But then the longer the game went on the more they must have realized how stupid this was as they deliberately played really badly to get the game over with as quickly as possible. Around one hundred and thirty Spanish ships sailed over the horizon. On board were 30,000 troops, 2,500 guns and a Spanish edition of *Great Days Out in London and the South-East*. The ships were to sail to the Netherlands to pick up a further 16,000 crack, élite Republican-guard-type mercenaries who would then land somewhere in Kent where Elizabeth was waiting with her inexperienced soldiers wondering if this finally was the end.

It is very unlikely that England could have withstood the full might of Spain's professional army, so Howard and Drake had to stop the ships that were heading to pick them up. And yet the English ships did not attack. Onlookers from the South Coast despaired at England's apparent powerlessness to do anything but watch this seven-mile-wide fleet proceeding to collect the mercenaries that would kill them all. Apart from a couple of minor skirmishes, the English ships did little but follow the Spanish all the way from Cornwall to the Straits of Dover.

But the invaders' ships were too large to enter the shallow ports of the Spanish Netherlands (a fairly basic flaw in the plan, by any standards) and so they anchored off Calais to take on supplies. Finally Drake saw his chance. In the dead of night he sent in 'fireships'; smaller, less valuable craft packed with tar and explosives that were set alight and then directed towards the giant wooden galleons tightly anchored off the French coast.

'So hands up who wants to sail a fireship towards the Spanish?'

'Why are they called fireships?'

'Er, well, don't worry about that for the time being – just make sure you take a load of gunpowder, some matches and your swimming costume . . .'

No Spanish ships were actually burnt by this tactic, but it created confusion among their fleet; many cut their lines and set sail, suddenly finding themselves upwind of Dunkirk where they were supposed to be heading. Now the scattered ships could be engaged individually by the English, whose smaller, more manoeuvrable galleons could come close, sometimes below the level of the cumbersome Spanish cannons. A strong south-westerly wind prevented the Spanish ships from turning and engaging the English who bombarded them from the rear. The weather had made it impossible for the Armada to get to their intended destination, and the Spanish now had no choice but to continue into the North Sea, and then round Scotland and Ireland to head for home.

At this point Spain's massive navy was still intact to fight another day; in military terms the engagement in the English Channel had not been much more than a tactical draw. But the worsening storm proved disastrous for the Spanish. The fleet sailed into one of the fiercest hurricanes ever recorded at such a northern latitude, driving ships on to the rocky coast of Scotland and Ireland, where two thousand bodies were found in Sligo Bay alone.* Only half of the great fleet returned to Spain, where the outcome of the ill-thought plan caused enormous damage to King Philip's reputation. But England's seemingly miraculous deliverance from mighty Spain secured the reputation of Elizabeth I, an heroic status that has actually grown down the centuries. But only in England has the Spanish Armada of 1588 been held up as a great English military victory, the rest of the world has always understood that Spain was defeated by a terrible storm. However, the idea of Drake's little ships harrying the giant Spanish galleons fitted the mythic narrative of 'Britain the Underdog': England triumphing against the odds, the country that produced its greatest victories when its back was against the wall.

The Golden Age (of spin)

It is partly because of this that Elizabeth's reign has been remembered as the Golden Age. For surely not only did England defeat the mighty Spanish and thus set in motion the decline of Spain and the emergence of England as master of the seas and the dominant colonial power, but also the wise governance of Good Queen Bess left this happy land a united, wealthy and peaceful nation, whose sailors

* Others survived and made new lives in Ireland, giving rise to the myth of 'the Black Irish', the dark-haired Celts who are supposed to be descended from shipwrecked Spanish sailors.

and poets brought us potatoes, tobacco and the chance to stage a school production of *A Midsummer Night's Dream*.

Well, it was certainly a golden age for one branch of government; Elizabeth had the best spin doctors the country had ever seen. Elizabeth is remembered as one of our greatest monarchs because so much effort was put into creating and sustaining this myth. No wonder it is seen as a great time for English literature with the amount of imaginative storytelling that came out of Elizabeth's court. Where her failure to marry and secure the succession created deep anxiety and the fear of future war, she propagated the fiction of the Virgin Queen, married only to her people. The image of the wise and cautious ruler was used to mask the reality of a very indecisive monarch who drove her advisers to despair with her procrastination and equivocation. Hers was far from being a peaceful and prosperous reign; she burnt many more religious dissenters than her sister while her protracted wars left the country millions of pounds in debt with no military or strategic gains. Wages reached their lowest level in real terms for hundreds of years – around forty per cent of the population's income fell below basic subsistence levels – there was widespread malnutrition, increased crime and homelessness. In the middle of this 'Golden Age', people were suddenly starving to death in the heart of London. Spain retained mastery of the seas, beating England in successive battles on land and at sea, and even landing a force in Cornwall, which burnt and plundered Penzance and the surrounding villages, and celebrated a Catholic mass before setting sail again. The England of Elizabeth I was a long way from the 'happy land' of Shakespeare.

It was undeniably a golden age for literature, and often the spin and poetry overlapped, as in Spenser's interminable eulogy *The Faerie Queene*, which you might care to read all the way through if, say, you are being held prisoner by Al-Qaeda and you have already read the Basra telephone directory three times. But Elizabeth can hardly take credit for the talent of Shakespeare, Marlowe and the other poets and playwrights who flourished during her reign.

The adventures of England's seafarers were more directly attributable to her government, as not only did their voyages require the royal blessing, but the largest investor in the trips was usually the Crown. Francis Drake was effectively a pirate whose thieving and plundering was given retrospective legitimacy once Spain and England were at war. He was the first man to captain a ship all the way around the world and on his return the Devon racketeer was knighted.* They were not so embarrassed by 'cash for honours' back then; Drake became 'Sir Francis' because Elizabeth's share of his stolen gold surpassed the rest of the crown's income for the whole of that year.†

Sir Walter Ralegh attempted the first English colony at Roanoke in North America which was an unequivocal failure.‡ But a more successful enterprise was Jack Hawkins's establishment of the slave trade, hardly an endeavour to bring a patriotic lump to the throat of a modern Briton.

England emerged from the Tudor Age as an important European player because its defiant Protestantism made it a thorn in the side of Europe's Catholic super-powers. Meanwhile simple geography made it well placed to exploit the new sea routes to the Atlantic. The defeat of the Armada did not shift the balance of power in Europe, but it would have been a major setback for English independence and the Reformation had it succeeded. Elizabeth's legendary status was guaranteed after the seemingly miraculous defeat of Spain in 1588, though the Queen's governance was increasingly ineffective the longer she stayed alive.

Elizabeth died at the age of sixty-nine. One modern theory is that she may have inadvertently poisoned herself. The white powder that she put upon her face was a lethal lead compound. The more she put on and the worse her skin became, the more of this poisonous powder she applied. England's last Tudor had survived smallpox, the

---

* Magellan's ship had done the trip, but Magellan himself had been killed on the way.

† The Spanish still consider Drake a pirate and a thief. He had no right to steal all that gold, it belonged to them – they had stolen it off the Aztecs.

‡ This was later named Virginia after Elizabeth, even though her name wasn't Virginia, it was Elizabeth; it was so named because she was a virgin, even though she almost certainly wasn't.

might of Spain, assassination attempts, plots to replace her with Mary Queen of Scots, but in the end her undoing may have been her own vanity.

Her cousin Mary had failed in her ambition to claim the English throne. Her life had been as tragic and hopeless as Elizabeth's had appeared glorious and successful. But Mary Queen of Scots did at least produce an heir – and it was her offspring, not any close relation of Elizabeth's, who now inherited the English throne.

Nearly forty years earlier when Mary Stuart had witnessed the murder of her private secretary by her drunken, brutal husband, his supposed plan had been to force her to miscarry. But the baby lived, while its father had been strangled and then blown up by Mary's new lover. It was into this domestic bliss that the baby James was born. No wonder, then, that the Stuarts were even more screwed-up than the Tudors.

6

The Stuarts 1603–1714

*How Britain's Kings were so appalling that Parliament was
forced to step in and take things over itself. Twice*

Tudor England did not suddenly turn into Jacobean* society
overnight – people didn't wake up one morning thinking, Forsooth,
we have a new dynasty upon the throne, I shall forsake my dandy
tights and codpiece and dress in the dark sombre clothes of this new
Puritan fashion. People carried on tilling their fields, going to church
and dying of hideous diseases. Shakespeare continued to write plays,
although now he was free to write one about Elizabeth's mad father†
and with all things Scottish suddenly fashionable he wrote *Macbeth*
(tactfully changing history to make King James's ancestor Banquo
innocent of the murder of Duncan).

But despite the apparently repetitive routines of daily life, society
is always in a continuous state of evolution. Some changes are
temporary – for example, abolishing the monarchy or putting your
washing powder in a little plastic ball to get right to the heart of the

---

* The word 'Jacobean' comes from the Latin for 'James' – 'Jacobus'. What the
Latin is for 'Jacob' is anyone's guess. The words 'Jacobean' and 'Jacobite' are used
to refer to the whole Stuart dynasty, whether they were called James, Bonnie Prince
Charlie or Kevin (though none of them were).
† It was during a performance of *Henry VIII* that the Globe theatre burnt down in
1613. It was reopened in 1997. Apparently it took ages to get the insurance money
through.

wash: these were both experiments that our society attempted before deciding to go back to the earlier system. Other changes are irreversible, such as the fundamental shift in power from the King to Parliament that occurred in the seventeenth century. This would have happened eventually whoever had sat upon the throne. It's just that the Stuarts were such a useless bunch of untalented, incompetent, arrogant, upper-class thickos that it happened a lot earlier than might have been expected.

The English Parliament that the Stuarts had been bequeathed by Elizabeth was of course a very different institution to the wonderfully democratic assembly that we all love and respect today. The Tudors ruled as individual dictators, with counsellors and advisers who either agreed or disagreed with the monarch, depending on whether they wanted a new dukedom or their kidneys nailed to the gatepost. The monarchs still needed the English establishment on their side, of course, and Parliament ensured that every part of the country was represented in a debating chamber which the King or Queen had to summon when new taxes were levied. There was no army or police force; law could only be effected with the support of the noblemen who were effectively minor monarchs in their own part of the country. A Tudor gentleman might selflessly serve as a Member of Parliament among the many public duties that added to his status and his influence. Often civic leaders were reluctant to send anyone to Westminster because of the enormous burden of paying living expenses and travel and accommodation costs, so when it came to selecting their local representative, they would listen to worthy arguments from various honest and loyal citizens but as soon as the rich bloke stood up and said, 'I'll pay my own expenses,' they knew they'd found their man. A member of the House of Commons was supposed to come from the borough he represented, but though this principle was much debated it was often ignored. As the Commons became more influential, members of the Lords even got themselves a seat in the lower house as well. Parliaments did not sit regularly but were summoned by order of the King for one purpose only. Parliament and the monarch had roughly the same relationship as the parents of a grumpy son who's just gone off to university.

'You only call us when you want money . . .'

'Yeah, whatever. Can I have three thousand pounds?'

'Of course, dear. Er, have you thought any more about sanctioning a new translation of the Bible?'

'Stop bloody telling me what I should be doing!'

'Sorry, dear, sorry, we just want what's best . . . You'll call us again soon, won't you?'

Parliament would seize the opportunity of these intermittent gatherings to raise all sorts of issues; one outspoken MP declared in 1576, 'All matters that concern God's honour through free speech shall be propagated here . . .' However, the assertion got him locked up in the Tower, so still a little bit of work to do on the free-speech concept at that point. Elizabeth, like all monarchs, had found the idea of having to listen to Parliament an effrontery at the best of times. To attend to the everyday business of government she had her Privy Councillors, the equivalent of today's cabinet, which Elizabeth reduced from thirty-nine members to just thirteen. They were her ministers, her executive officers, appointed by her just as the monarch nominally appoints the Privy Council to this day.* But the crucial difference between then and now was that power and consent came from the top down. Everyone had their place in society as allocated to them by God; there was no notion of democracy, of owing your position to the people below you or having a duty to represent those without a voice. For every single member of Parliament, his electorate was God. Come election time He must have got pretty fed up with the number of canvassers asking for His vote. The Bible was the starting point for all the laws passed by Parliament; so any bill saying, for example, that it was a really good idea to covet your neighbour's ox was never going to stand a chance.

---

* Any politician referred to as 'Right Honourable' is a member of the Privy Council – just in case you thought they had that prefix because they were always right and honourable. This anachronistic committee is part honorary and part constitutional – for example it is still actually the supreme court for Commonwealth countries such as Belize and Jamaica.

James VI: the last King of Scotland

James I of England (1603–25) already had over thirty years' experience of being monarch of the country next door, so he came with certain fixed ideas about how the job should be done. He had been used to the rather more compliant Parliament of Scotland and had even written a book which asserted his belief in the Divine Right of Kings. This concept, that God placed the monarch on the throne, was to tear the country apart in a bloody civil war forty years later. At the time of James I's accession, many English Parliamentarians shared this belief, but their faith in this concept must have been challenged by the way that God had chosen to rule through such a disgusting and brainless specimen.

In his *Child's History of England* Charles Dickens describes James I as *cunning, covetous, wasteful, idle, drunken, greedy, dirty, cowardly, a great swearer, and the most conceited man on earth*. James's parents had been cousins and it showed. His tongue was too big for his mouth, with the charming result that he slobbered when he spoke, a habit not helped by him being half-pissed most of the time. Not having had his mum around to teach him the basics of good manners or personal cleanliness, James was also scruffy and smelly; he wore the same clothes until they fell apart and scratched himself continually, particularly in the groin area. Apart from all that he was a deeply attractive individual. If James had been the preferred choice of the English Privy Council, it makes you wonder if the other candidates were some sort of baby-eating trolls. The new King fancied himself as a bit of an intellectual, writing tracts on tobacco and the problems of demons (his rule in Scotland had seen a national panic about witchcraft with hundreds of women being burnt). The critics were not particularly impressed, however, and the French court dubbed James 'the wisest fool in Christendom'. James took a particularly severe line on homosexuality, reaffirming the Buggery Act and listing sodomy as one of those *horrible crimes which ye are bound in conscience never to forgive*. His firm public stance failed to fool anyone about his own homosexuality. He surrounded himself with handsome young men; the Duke of Buckingham being a particular favourite, whom he knew as his 'sweet heart' and his 'dog'; and although he was married to Anne of Denmark, they eventually agreed to live apart.

James was the first monarch to be King of both England and Scotland, although they remained very separate countries for another hundred years. On his accession to the English throne he became 'James I' while in Scotland he was still called 'James VI', which must have been a nightmare to explain to the bank. He was warmly welcomed as he travelled south, freely dishing out titles to whoever pleased him along his journey. One particularly fine loin steak was knighted on the spot, and that cut of beef has been known as 'sirloin' ever since.

English Catholics had waited a long time for the death of Elizabeth with great hope that the new monarch would bring an end to their persecution. Although James was a Protestant, they had believed him to be far more sympathetic to their plight, and in the first few months he did attempt to be all things to all men. He did away with fines for not attending the Anglican church but then found himself under pressure from the increasingly puritan Parliament to bring the fines back again. Within a couple of years bitter dis-illusionment had set in among certain Catholics. 'Hmmm . . .' they said, 'we don't like this new King, and his Parliament is even worse, but it's not as if there would be any way of getting rid of the whole lot of them in one go.'

A thoughtful sip of beer and then someone said, 'Unless . . .'

The Gunpowder Plot: government wins war on terror

The first meeting of the Gunpowder Plot conspirators was on 20 May 1604 in the Duck and Drake in the Strand. Normally when you wake up the next morning, you realize what a complete load of rub-bish you'd all been talking the night before. The mistake the Gunpowder Plotters made was to stick with the plan once they had sobered up. The idea was to tunnel under the House of Lords and hide barrels of gunpowder underneath the spot where both Houses and the new King would be gathered for the state opening of Parliament and then blow them all up. And then, er, have a rebellion, and well . . . we'll cross that bridge when we come to it.

However ill thought out the second part of the plan, the murder of the King, all his ministers and the Members of Parliament came pretty close to succeeding. Even half as much gunpowder would have wiped out the entire ruling class of the country in one moment: all the noblemen who effectively kept order in the shires, the Privy Council who managed the country's finance and foreign policies, all the bishops who ruled over the Church, even Black Rod would have perished, leaving the country without anyone to, um, do whatever Black Rod does.* England did not possess a standing army to step into the power vacuum and anarchy would surely have followed, with the innocent non-conspiring Catholics the most likely target for any backlash.

The leader of the conspirators was Robert Catesby; by rights he should be the figure burnt on bonfires around the land on 5 November, but 'Penny for the Robert!' doesn't have quite the same ring to it.† Guy Fawkes was a former soldier who had gained experience with gunpowder when fighting in the Spanish Netherlands. Guy now needed to go undercover, so after much thought he hit upon the imaginative alias 'John Johnson'. Security at the Palace of Westminster was slack to say the least and when the conspirators discovered that a coal cellar directly underneath the House of Lords was available for rent, it was quickly leased and then this trustworthy-looking John Johnson chap promptly started filling it up with barrels of gunpowder. Thirty-six barrels of explosives were all ready for 5 November, plus a packet of sparklers, mulled wine and some overcooked jacket potatoes.

In fact the original date for the opening of Parliament had been

* It depends on which one you are referring to. Black Rod is either the personal attendant of the Sovereign in the House of Lords or a male strippergram, available for hen parties operating in the West Midlands area.
† Because of the tradition of making effigies of Guy Fawkes out of old clothes, in America the word 'guy' came to mean any scruffy man; eventually becoming slang for 'man'.

early October, but following an outbreak of plague in the capital it was put back a month. It has recently been argued that having now sat around for so long the gunpowder would have 'decayed' and thus would have failed to detonate. There is no way of knowing this for certain, but the ritual of dramatically lighting a fuse and then wondering why nothing is happening is still re-enacted every Bonfire Night. The delay also created time for more anxious conspirators to have second thoughts. One of them sent an anonymous note to Lord Monteagle (a relation by marriage) warning him to keep away from Parliament on the day of the state opening. The letter prompted a search of the Palace of Westminster where at midnight on 4 November, a man was discovered beside a surprisingly large amount of wood. He said his name was John Johnson and that he was standing guard over his master's supply of winter fuel. They pulled away a few bushels of sticks to reveal thirty-six huge barrels of gunpowder.

'Oh that – yes, well, er, the shop had run out of firelighters . . .'

The discovery was a sensation. Every lord and bishop was staying in London that night, anxiously wondering whether if they ordered a wench up to their room it would be itemized separately on the hotel bill or just be added to the total. When news spread that 5 November was intended to be the last morning they would ever see, they shared a sense of moral outrage and divine deliverance. It is quite possible that the letter to Monteagle was a forgery by the security services, who had known about the plot for some time but were waiting until the last moment to expose it, thus creating the maximum impact and giving themselves the widest rein to act against the conspirators and any other Catholics they didn't like the look of. If this was the case then it was certainly very effective. But current conspiracy theories that the whole thing was cooked up by the Protestant establishment (probably with the help of the CIA and the Israeli security services) don't really stand the test of looking at any source material that is not on the internet. Guy Fawkes was initially brazen in his proud admission of his murderous intentions, although bearing in mind what they went on to do to him he might have been better off saying he was very, very sorry. There are famously two signatures by Guy Fawkes, the neat and legible 'before torture' example, and the pathetic, shaky, scrawled 'after torture' sample. They eventually learnt the names of the other conspirators – and that days and days of unendurable agony does nothing to improve a man's handwriting.

Robert Catesby and the other plotters had been in the Midlands declaring that the King and his heir were dead as they tried to gather support for a Catholic uprising. No one was very interested. Their plan to kidnap the King's nine-year-old daughter had failed miserably, and eventually they made a last stand at Warwick Castle. Here they discovered that their gunpowder was damp and with the genius that had marked every stage of the project, they hit upon a brilliant solution.

'I know, we could put all our gunpowder by the fire to dry out!'

'Yes, putting gunpowder really close to the fire – that seems like a totally flawless plan to me.'

It seems tragically appropriate that their Gunpowder Plot literally blew up in their faces. One of the conspirators was blinded, making him useless for the final shootout, although judging from their competence up to that point they probably appointed him Chief Lookout. James I, no doubt shocked as to how close he and his family had come to death, declared that the date should be celebrated evermore, by 'ye hoodies letting off airbombs at two in the morning from September onwards'.

Drunk gay King 'losing Puritan vote'

This shared experience might have been the opportunity for James to build an excellent relationship with his Parliament, but the King quickly managed to alienate and disillusion the people he needed to rule effectively. He made no secret of his contempt for this presumptuous institution; he didn't just ignore Parliamentary bills, he tore them up in members' faces. His son Charles, whom he had put in the House of Lords as part of his education, looked on and saw the art of kingship at first hand.

It didn't help James's cause that while asking Parliament for money he seemed to waste it so brazenly. Not only did he give away thousands to court favourites or nobles in Scotland, James was a king who liked to party. When a feast was held for James's visiting brother-in-law, the two monarchs led the guests in getting so drunk that most people could hardly stand. There were hopes that the tone might be raised a little with the performance of a charming little morality play, but the women playing 'Faith' and 'Hope' were found vomiting in the hallway, while 'Peace' starting whacking everyone with her olive branch. This sort of behaviour did nothing to endear James to the Puritans who now dominated Parliament. Their idea of having fun was extra praying; they considered the idea of Christmas to be a papist indulgence; they didn't approve of wedding rings or church organs or bright colours or decorations. Getting pissed and vomiting during morality plays was definitely out.

James called no Parliament between 1614 and 1621 and virtually gave up trying to rule towards the end of his reign, leaving it to his son and the Duke of Buckingham. He had arrived in England with grand ideas of political unification of his two kingdoms, but lacked the skill or personality to achieve his aims. The painting of James in the National Portrait Gallery by Daniel Mytens displays the shell-shocked expression of a bewildered old Maths teacher who has just had class 5C on a Friday afternoon. Despite his ineffectiveness, his time on the throne has left us with plenty that survives. Apart from the quaint custom of watching Catherine wheels failing to spin around on Guy Fawkes' night, James himself claimed to have come up with the name 'Great Britain' and the idea of combining the cross of St George and St Andrew to create a new national flag. He also authorized the King James Bible, the standard English text for three hundred years and still considered a great piece of literature by those who have managed to get past all the 'begats'. The new Bible was not enough to satisfy one group of Puritans, however, and in 1620, despairing at the sinfulness of England and their inability to preach as they wished, they sailed away on the *Mayflower* to establish a new life in North America. James made no secret of his dislike of Puritans and would have wished that more had joined them. 'Good riddance! If you don't like it in England, go off and create your own land then. Let's see what becomes of that!'

There is one other legacy that is still with us today. His predecessor Elizabeth had begun a policy of 'plantations' in Ireland, seizing land from the Irish and awarding it to Protestant nobles who would support the English monarch's hitherto empty claim to be Lord of all Ireland. During this process Catholic farmers had generally remained to farm the land of Protestant landowners, but in Ulster, then the most rebellious and Gaelic of the provinces, James thought it might be a good idea to make a conscious effort to displace the Irish and pack the land with Scottish Presbyterians.* 'Let's get the one group that hates the Catholics more than anyone else to kick them off their land and then see how they all get along together down the centuries . . .' A siege mentality was soon created and by 1640 there were fifty thousand Ulster Protestants, all marching and banging drums and singing 'The Sash my Father Wore' to celebrate the anniversary of the Battle of the Boyne even though it hadn't happened yet. James failed in his plan to create a united Britain; but he did manage to sow the seeds for a divided Ireland three hundred years later. Without James getting his fellow countrymen to pioneer ethnic cleansing in Ulster, there would have been no Northern Ireland, no Troubles and George Best could have played in the same football team as Johnny Giles and taken the Republic to the World Cup in 1970.†

James died in 1625, nursed by Buckingham to the end. His reign had been a failure, but not so much so that they decided to abolish the monarchy altogether. That unique achievement belongs to his son and heir. Charles I came to the throne at the age of twenty-four, a deeply unimpressive figure both intellectually and physically. He is listed in the Guinness Book of Records as Britain's

---

* Wealthy individuals and corporations were allotted land; Derry, for example, was sponsored by the Corporation of London, who stuck their name at the front of the town to annoy Nationalists for ever after.

† Actually, hang on, George Best's ancestors would have stayed in Scotland, so he would have played in the same team as Denis Law and Jimmy Johnstone; except that's three strikers: one of them would have had to drop back into midfield. Anyway, back to the Stuarts.

shortest-ever king. He was even shorter once they'd chopped his head off.

Charles I: Head of State 'to separate from Body Politic'

If you were attempting to devise the worst possible system of government for a country, you would be hard pressed to come up with anything more stupid than the idea of a hereditary monarchy. The concept is appealing only in its simplicity; one man is in charge of *everything*: the government, the economy and the Church. The best man to nurture the nation's religious well-being is apparently also the best man to lead the army into battle; he is the legislature, the executive and the judiciary all rolled into one. That man's qualification for the post is simply the fact that his dad did it; he then rules for his entire life irrespective of how well he performs until the job passes to his eldest son, whatever his suitability for the position. At best you would be concerned at the random quality of individuals that this system threw up. But of course it is worse than that, because the formula is almost guaranteed to create arrogant, blinkered and over-protected individuals who have never been criticized, corrected or had to consider the possibility that they might not know best. In this sense the heir to the throne was possibly the very worst person in the entire country to become ruler.

Charles I (1625–49) combined all the arrogance and certainty of the English upper classes with an acute lack of intelligence and a natural tendency to deceive. Basically, if he were alive today he'd be an estate agent. Historians attempting to appear even-handed have pointed out that he did buy some nice paintings, but that hardly makes up for chopping off the ears of his critics, torturing his enemies and then declaring war on his own people. He was only five feet four, he stammered and he argued furiously with his wife over such matters as whether or not it was raining.

The dismal relations that his father had had with Parliament continued uninterrupted and the three Parliaments at the beginning of his reign were fractious and bitter affairs. Charles's dependence upon his father's favourite, the wild and idiotic Duke of Buckingham, was a disaster which was obvious to everyone except the King. Parliament demanded that he rule with a council of advisers rather than acting upon the whim of his dad's old boyfriend. Charles dismissed Parliament for its presumptuous behaviour, resolving to rule without it, and attempted to raise money by means other than taxation. One method was 'forced loans', a sort of compulsory lending scheme whereby you lent the King large amounts of money or you were arrested and went to prison (as hundreds of indignant squires did). Another method was reviving the concept of 'ship money': a charge that had historically been levied on ports to pay for defences against raiding pirates or enemy invasions.* A gentleman in Buckinghamshire refused to pay this charge, perhaps feeling that the chances of pirates landing in Buckinghamshire were a little remote, unless perhaps they sailed up the Thames and then got into little rowing boats for the last bit of the journey to Marlow Bottom. Resentment grew across the country but without Parliament there was no focus for opposition to the King's illegal extortion, while criticism of the King was brutally punished. Many emigrated, up to thirty thousand Puritans sought freedom from Charles's religious persecution by sailing across the Atlantic to 'New England'.† But for those that remained there was a very real fear that Parliament might have been effectively abolished as it had been in France.

War with Scotland: pre-season warm-up tour

Charles had of course also inherited the throne of Scotland and it was north of the border that his authority was first seriously

* In 1627 Islamic pirates captured Lundy in the Bristol Channel and for five years used it as a base for raiding. Whole villages were kidnapped and shipped off to North Africa, most notably at East Looe in Cornwall and at Baltimore, County Cork, with British men, women and children becoming white slaves in Muslim North Africa. But the *Daily Mail* was quite laid back about it.
† A harsher but perhaps truer analysis of this exodus is that the Puritans left this country not because they were being persecuted, but because they were not being allowed to persecute everyone else.

challenged. Urged on by William Laud, his over-zealous Archbishop of Canterbury, the absentee monarch attempted to impose a new Anglican prayer book on to the Presbyterian Scots without consulting the nobles or the Scottish Parliament. As the new prayers were read at St Giles's Cathedral in Edinburgh, a footstool was hurled at the Dean and pandemonium broke out in the church followed by riots in the streets outside. Apart from that it was a lovely service. Civil disorder rapidly spread across Scotland and leading nobles effectively took the government into their own hands, resolving to protect Scottish Presbyterianism and ignoring Charles's orders to disband their assembly.

Charles was determined to march on Scotland and impose his will, because once you let people start choosing their own prayer books, anarchy is surely just around the corner. For the first time in over three hundred years the King went to war without summoning Parliament. Hoping to rely on anti-Scottish sentiment and the English aristocracy's deep love for their King, he called on peers to march north with their local militiamen. A large number of lords said they couldn't come because they were ill (and they didn't even have a note). There were mutinies and some officers were lynched by their own men. In their first major victory since Bannockburn, the Scottish army trounced the English at Newburn in 1640, and occupied Northumberland and Durham. Now, with no army and no money to raise one, the King was finally forced to call the English Parliament after eleven years of attempting to rule without it. To Charles's surprise it wasn't one big happy reunion with everyone giving him presents and showing him pictures of their new grandchildren. An angry Parliament was determined that they were not going to grant the King money without first ensuring he desist from imposing illegal and invented taxes. Charles was forced to agree a bill that Parliament would be called regularly; neither could he dissolve Parliament without its consent, and forced loans and ship money were abolished, leaving Charles dependent on Parliament for income.

However, at this point Charles still had many supporters in both Houses of Parliament, indeed many were offended by overt hostility towards the monarch.

'You shouldn't criticize the royal family because they can't answer back.'

'Yes they can. William Prynne was branded with red-hot irons and had his ears chopped off.'

'Oh yeah. But apart from that, they can't answer back.'

Indeed, within Parliament there was emerging a 'Royalist' Party that sought to defend the established social order and blamed previous mistakes by the King on his advisers (which is of course exactly the same defence made by royalists today). On the other side, the Parliamentary Party was led by John Pym, a West Country Puritan who fought a determined campaign on behalf of the rights of the House of Commons and then went and spoilt it all by being the ancestor of one of Margaret Thatcher's ministers.*

While the House of Commons was not particularly concerned about the Protestant Scottish forces occupying the North of England (Pym even secretly liaised with Scottish Parliamentarians), a rebellion in Ireland was another matter. The Catholics who had been driven off their land in Ulster finally turned on the Protestants and in scenes that are still depicted in Orange Order banners today thousands of the colonists were brutally massacred. Parliament was united in agreeing that an army had to be raised to put down this Catholic uprising but Pym and his supporters knew the King would probably use this force against his Parliament.

With the King's authority non-existent in Scotland and anarchy in Ireland, law and order began to break down in England. Enclosures were pulled down, deer in royal parks kept disappearing as the locals suddenly started having lots of barbecues, while in London a mob outside the House of Commons harangued anyone who was not with Pym and the Parliamentary Party. At one point Charles's Catholic wife rushed to confession thinking that the mob would storm the palace and kill them all. The French ambassador remarked that in any other country, buildings would already be on fire and blood

* Francis Pym, Minister for Foreign Affairs 1982–3. John Pym wasn't as pure as his puritan label suggested, however – he was involved in some pretty shady business deals before he died in 1643.

would be running in the streets. This being England, however, most people generally tutted and looked skywards.

Power-sharing talks break down over who gets the army

The King had already proved that he could not be trusted with the armed forces and so the Commons passed a bill that the army and navy be controlled by Parliament. It was the boldest assault yet on the ancient powers of the monarch, and came with Pym's 'Grand Remonstrance', an exhaustive list of the King's misdeeds since he had come to the throne. The debate was heated and passionate. The member for Cambridge, a man called Oliver Cromwell, told a colleague that if this vote was lost, he would leave England for the New World. It was passed by just eleven votes. But this was all going a bit too far for many of the Royalists in Parliament and the King believed he now had enough support at Westminster to seize the initiative. With his wife haranguing him, calling him a coward and urging him to deal with these upstarts, Charles took four hundred soldiers to the House of Commons to arrest John Pym and four other leading Parliamentarians. Any loyalty and sympathy felt towards the King evaporated with this insane act. Freedom from arrest in the chamber was an historic right of Members of Parliament, reaffirmed at the beginning of every session by monarchs down the centuries. 'Privilege of Parliament,' shouted the crowds outside the Palace of Westminster, who knew a snappy slogan when they heard one. The five MPs had been forewarned and had taken flight so Charles failed to make any arrests while totally alienating both chambers.* With four hundred armed militiamen behind him, it would have been hard to pretend he had only come round to visit the gift shop.

The King's action prompted open rebellion on the streets of London. Thousands of citizens armed themselves and many surrounded Parliament allowing the five MPs to take their seats once

* Because of Charles's actions the monarch is still not allowed into the House of Commons to this day.

more to cheers from their fellow MPs. Charles fled the capital, never to return until he was tried and executed seven years later. It is a commonly held belief that England has never had a revolution, but the events of 1642 to 1649 were no less revolutionary than what occurred in France in 1789.* We just call our revolution the English Civil War so as not to appear too radical. Oh, and to annoy the Scots and Irish who played a crucial part in its causes and its outcome.

The English Civil Wars: neither English nor civil

Charles marched to Hull to seize the largest arsenal outside the capital, but the gates of the city were shut against him. He attempted to commandeer the navy, but the fleet declared itself for Parliament. Finally he raised his standard at Nottingham Castle, and the flagpole blew over. Things weren't going very well. This declaration of war didn't mean that hostilities began immediately; the country drifted along for some months with both sides preparing forces while others sought to negotiate some sort of peace. Most of the country wished that this crisis would go away, and hovered on the edge of the fight saying, 'Leave it, Charlie, it's not worth it!' Some areas tried to declare themselves neutral despite the fact that armies don't have a habit of saying, 'Oh, hang on, lads, we can't march down here; it says "Welcome to Lambeth, A Civil War Free Zone."'

For the minority who were committed to one side or the other there were more than just constitutional issues at stake. Inevitably religion was a major factor. It had been something of a miracle that England had managed to avoid civil war between Protestants and Catholics in the previous century, but now thousands would lay down their lives in a struggle between the Anglican Church and the ultra-Protestant Puritan and Presbyterian movements. Parliament's army in particular was driven by religious zeal, hard though it is

* Though by the end of the French Revolution things had clearly got far more radical. Trying to do away with the twelve months of the year and replacing them with decimal months with stupid names like Thermidor and Fructidor – that's just Euro-bureaucracy gone mad.

today for us to imagine Puritan squaddies. 'Great, the pub's open! I'm gonna order ten pints and then pour them down the sink!' 'Oi, barmaid! Your neck is showing; 'tis an offence against God!' Class was also a factor: men who had made their money from trade were more likely to favour Parliament than the landed gentry; indeed, the richer the noblemen the more likely they were to be on the Royalist side. As for Charles's nephew, well, with a name like Prince Rupert he didn't have much choice in the matter. Pwince Wupert was an expert and experienced cavalry commander. The preference for fighting on horseback is what gave the long-haired Royalists the name 'Cavaliers' – not a cavalier attitude to ruling the country even though they had that as well. The Parliamentarians were dubbed 'Roundheads' after the pudding-basin haircuts of the City apprentices organized by Pym. Basically it was mods v rockers, but with much more at stake.

Our half-remembered view of the English Civil War, in which Cromwell and Parliament defeat Charles and the Cavaliers, is not particularly accurate. There were actually two English Civil Wars and during the first (1642–6) Cromwell was not the leader of the Parliamentary forces. By the time of the Second Civil War (1648) it was more a case of Cromwell and his New Model Army* versus everyone else. But the whole business was irritatingly complex and confusing, with people changing sides, and patches of support for one side or the other all over the place instead of everyone helpfully agreeing to have one front line, which would have made the maps in the history books look much neater. In Ireland and Scotland the war was an opportunity for rival clans and factions to revive old feuds, though Charles's Catholic sympathies generally pushed the Scots into assisting Parliament while Ireland's support for Charles failed to endear the country to Oliver Cromwell.

The first battle at Edgehill in October 1642 was a score draw, although both sides tried to claim victory in the post-match

---

* The New Model Army was a modern professional force led by trained generals rather than aristocrats. They should not be confused with the 80s radical rock band led by 'Slade the Leveller' (real name Justin).

interviews. Charles attempted to advance to London but was halted at Turnham Green, and he withdrew to establish his headquarters at Royalist Oxford, which welcomed the King until he started melting down all their silver. Both sides lost support in areas of the country that they controlled as the cost of the conflict led to taxes far more severe than the levies and charges that had been a factor in the build-up to war. One new tax was called 'the scot' and those that managed not to pay got off 'scot-free'. Money was a key factor in the outcome of the war – when Charles abandoned London at the beginning of hostilities, he left behind the city that was responsible for seventy per cent of the country's trade. It's all very well having the West Country on your side, but he was never going to raise much cash taxing cream teas and holiday lets.

Minor battles and sieges took place all over the country in order to give dull provincial towns something to put on the brown signs for people driving through them 350 years later. Today these skirmishes are regularly re-enacted by the Sealed Knot, the curiously English historical organization whose members dress up as Cavaliers and Roundheads to give us a clearer idea of what actually happened in the 1640s. So it would appear that the Battle of Newbury ended with a victory for the Parliamentary forces, but then in a surprise twist all the dead Royalists got up and went to the beer tent to drink real ale out of plastic glasses and shout, 'Darren! That musket is not a toy!'

By 1644 Parliament had realized that the two armies were simply too evenly matched, but Pym* had negotiated the support of twenty thousand Scottish troops by promising to make Presbyterianism the only tolerated faith in England. The result was probably the largest-ever battle to have taken place on British soil, a disaster for the Royalist forces who had over 4,000 soldiers killed with another 1,500 taken prisoner at the Battle of Marston Moor. The death toll of the English Civil Wars was catastrophic: when you add in related deaths

---

* Pym had died of natural causes in 1643 and was buried in Westminster Abbey. Charles II later had his remains dug up again, despoiled and dumped in a common pit. There's no point in bottling it up.

from disease and Cromwell's massacres, a larger percentage of the British population was killed in this conflict than in even the First World War.

Cromwell's own nephew was killed at Marston Moor and Cromwell wrote to his brother, *You have cause to bless the Lord*, which gives an idea of the sort of religious nutcase who was about to become the military dictator of the British Isles. Oliver Cromwell, a burly man with a nose like a potato, had been an ordinary Cambridgeshire Member of Parliament before the outbreak of hostilities, but during the course of the first war it became apparent that the Roundheads had in their number a soldier of enormous ability. Despite having no military experience he quickly learnt to read any situation through the chaos of the battlefield, deploying his forces skilfully and effectively as each engagement saw his reputation grow. He commanded forces from the Puritan heartland of his native East Anglia, and his devout soldiers sang hymns as they marched into battle. Trying to remember the words to the middle bit of 'Lord of all Hopefulness' is one way of taking your mind off the fact that people are firing cannonballs at you.

Cromwell's influence was crucial at the Battle of Naseby the following year which proved to be an even more comprehensive defeat for the King's forces. Not only were Charles's armaments captured but also secret letters proving that the King was promising to suspend anti-Catholic laws in return for help from Catholics in Ireland, and that his wife and son were also trying to secure an invasion of England by foreign troops. After Naseby, Royalist towns fell one after the other until in June 1646 Oxford was captured and the war was over.

But instead of surrendering to Parliament, Charles gave himself up to the Scots in the hope of creating divisions among his enemies. In this he was successful, and the gap between the politicians and the army grew throughout the following year. The problem for the victors was that the defeated King simply refused to agree to any settlement.

'Oh, now come on, that's not fair. *We won*, you have to do what we say.'

'Yeah, but I'm still King though, aren't I? And there's absolutely nothing you can do about it . . .'

Cromwell was one of the few people to see the shocking reality of where this was heading – that they might have to remove the King from the equation altogether. But in 1648 many Parliamentarians were sufficiently alarmed by the religious extremists in the army that they allied themselves with former Royalists and Scottish Presbyterians, and when separate Royalist uprisings erupted in Kent, Essex and Wales the country was at war once again. But now Cromwell's experience and total control of the army was decisive. He crushed the revolts, defeated the Scots at Preston and established himself as Britain's first and only military dictator.

Oliver Cromwell: England's Ayatollah Khomeini

Quite what Cromwell's statue is doing in pride of place outside Parliament is one of our democracy's great mysteries. A number of today's MPs still seem to have a misplaced notion that 'Old Noll' was some sort of benign saviour whose leadership made Parliament's authority supreme. But where the King had attempted to arrest five MPs, Cromwell now arrested forty, and forcibly ejected another sixty. Many more stayed away in protest. The House of Lords was abolished altogether and with his remaining yes-men in the so-called Rump Parliament, Cromwell set about having the King put on trial for his *treason, blood and mischief.* ('Treason and blood' sounds serious enough, but I would have let him off the 'mischief'.) A self-styled 'Court of Justice' was created; not one of its members was a judge and no defence witnesses were to be allowed. No one actually called it a kangaroo court, but that might be because Australia hadn't been discovered yet.* Beyond Westminster Hall, the rest of the country was appalled at the presumption of the army. Justice had always been sought in the name of the King in the King's Courts.

* Actually the Dutch explorer Abel Tasman had sailed along the northern coast of Australia earlier that decade, but the postcard hadn't reached England yet.

'What gives you the right to put the King himself on trial?'

'The fact that I have five hundred men standing behind pointing muskets at your head.'

'No, actually, looking at it that way, you may have a point . . .'

For once Charles overcame his stammer and spoke loudly and clearly. As is traditional in these situations, the deposed leader refused to recognize the authority of the court. He declined to plead despite being asked forty-three times. Many of those involved still hoped that he might make some conciliatory offer or be exiled or deposed, and so even those inside the hall were shocked when the King was sentenced to death *by the severing of his head from his body*. Fewer than half of those present were prepared to sign his death warrant, this from a commission created by a tiny minority of just one House of Parliament.

Despite this spurious legality, on the morning of 30 January 1649, the King was led to the scaffold that had been hastily constructed outside the Banqueting House in Whitehall. Charles wore two vests against the cold that morning, for if people saw him shivering they might have thought it was through fear. Hundreds of thousands of people had gathered, kept at bay by lines of armed soldiers on horse-back. Charles made a short speech, and then placed his head upon the executioner's block. (And then you remember the *one* person you forgot to thank.) A single blow from the hooded axeman was enough, but instead of cheers there was a terrible groan from the crowd. Many began to weep openly. Realizing the unpopularity of what they had done, the army moved quickly to disperse the thousands of appalled witnesses still struggling to come to terms with what had happened. Instead of sticking the King's head upon a spike, Cromwell allowed it to be sewn back on again. However, it failed to make the King better.

Despite the public relations disaster and the political uncertainty, Cromwell had what he had wanted. The King was dead. Britain had become a republic. Cromwell must have slept well that night. Especially as by now he was sleeping in the King's bed.

The Commonwealth – but no games

During the decade following the execution of Charles I, England was ruled by the Protestant version of the Taliban. England in the 1650s was a country ruled by Christian fundamentalists, whose religious mission was to search out anybody who might be having a good time and put a stop to it at once. Theatres were closed down, music was banned, even Christmas was abolished – which is one way of explaining away why you forgot to get Mrs Cromwell a present.

'Here you are, Oliver – is my present downstairs?'

'Present? Um, well, no, Christmas, you see, is actually a sin against God. Yes, that's it, a papist indulgence, so I haven't bought anything and neither should you, though I might as well keep this since you've spent the money.'*

Easter too was abolished; fines were imposed for sporting activities, for swearing, gambling and excessive drinking as countless pubs and inns were closed down. Even the private business of sex was adjudged to be sinful if it was enjoyed, which by the look of Cromwell can't have been much of a problem for his good lady wife.

Although historians generally date the end of the civil wars as 1648, this reflects a particularly Anglocentric viewpoint since the wars continued in Ireland and Scotland into the next decade. Cromwell soon turned his attention to Ireland where a Royalist army had remained to threaten the English republic. No one can accuse the dictator of being ambivalent in his attitude to Ireland. Between the lines one can definitely detect a certain lack of enthusiasm for their Catholic clergy: *Your covenant is with death and hell*, Cromwell told them. *You are part of the Anti-Christ, whose kingdom the Scripture so expressly speaks should be laid in blood, yea in the blood of the saints . . . ere it be long you must all have blood to drink, even the dregs of the cup of the fury and wrath of God, which will be poured out unto you.*

---

* In fact the tradition of giving Christmas presents didn't actually take off until the Victorian era. The gifts from the Three Wise Men to the infant Jesus were sort of joint Christmas and birthday presents.

'Oliver, I'm picking up a lot of hostility here,' said his anger-management coach.

Cromwell's name is still uttered with contempt in Ireland and with good reason. His conduct of the war there would embarrass a modern-day Serbian warlord. At Drogheda he had thousands of civilians put to death; women and children taking refuge in the church were burnt alive while the commander of the town's forces was beaten to death with his own wooden leg. The handful of survivors were deported to Barbados, which was not as nice as it sounds. Shortly afterwards, at Wexford, a similar massacre took place, priests bearing crucifixes before them were mown down by English soldiers. Even by the brutal rules of war of the time these were exceptionally barbaric episodes. Anyone who imagines that some fundamental decency in the English national character would somehow make it impossible for the brutality of the Nazis or the Khmer Rouge to happen here should remember that the English military have committed plenty of horrendous war crimes of their own that somehow didn't make it into *Our Island Story*. Any race or people are capable of obscenely inhumane acts once they have been persuaded that their victims are subhuman – and such was the propaganda directed at Irish Catholics in the seventeenth century.

A massive programme of land seizure was now undertaken as the Irish were driven 'to hell or Connaught'. The plan was to completely banish the native Catholics to the west of the River Shannon. It eventually proved over-ambitious as the new landowners found they needed local labourers, but in terms of property it was the greatest land grab since 1066; farms were confiscated from their rightful owners and this *Lebensraum* given over to the very soldiers who had gone round murdering everyone. Even without the benefit of hind-sight you'd think that they might have realized they were storing up a certain amount of resentment for later on. But the immediate mil-itary threat from Ireland had been removed, and now Cromwell turned his attention to the uncooperative Scots.

When news of Charles I's execution had reached Edinburgh, Charles II had immediately been declared King of Scotland. Charles I had been their King too, and the English failure to consult the Scots before killing their monarch had really annoyed them. Before long, Charles II was at large in Scotland and although he was in no position to actually rule (the divided country was still controlled by a collection of nobles), his presence alone was enough to provoke Cromwell to march north. Not even the Romans had successfully conquered Scotland, but Cromwell pulled off a spectacular victory at Dunbar which gave him control of the capital and all of the lowlands. Refusing to accept defeat, young Charles provocatively had himself crowned King at the ancient coronation seat of Scone and then slipped past the New Model Army and marched on England, hoping that the presence of the actual King might rally closet Royalists to his cause. It didn't. By now most people had worked out which side to back in any battle involving the New Model Army. Cromwell finally caught up with the twenty-one-year-old Charles Stuart at the battle of Worcester where another crushing victory finally ended any chance of a Royalist revival. Charles escaped, and in the grounds of Boscobel House hid up an oak tree while the Roundheads trudged around underneath all day looking for him. After the Restoration countless pubs were renamed 'The Royal Oak' in memory of this adventure and all the old people moaned about them changing pub names. 'What was wrong with the good old "Slug and Lettuce", that's what I'd like to know!' Eventually Charles slipped out of the country, sailing from Shoreham in Sussex in the dead of night disguised as a manservant. He would not set foot back in England until he returned nine years later as King.

Cromwell's brilliance as a military commander was not matched by comparable skills as a ruler. He was hesitant then petulant; he sought godliness over talent and intelligence in those he appointed. He initially deferred to his Rump Parliament, but dispensed with that when it irritated him. An attempt to pack Parliament with suitably pious individuals (whose qualifications for the job included the number of times they prayed every day) left him with a bunch of dolts who wanted to abolish lawyers, priests and just about every branch of government, and so he was forced to dismiss them. Several written constitutions were drafted but none was settled upon. Meanwhile the 'Commonwealth' was of course nothing of the sort.

Here was the greatest-ever chance to radically change the nature of government and society but instead of turning political revolution into social revolution, the conservative Cromwell concentrated on making sure that nobody was doing anything subversive like smiling. During the civil wars a progressive group called the Levellers had debated notions of democracy and equality, proposing the then radical ideas of the extension of voting rights in fair elections, the right to trial by jury and, rather wonderfully, a reduction in the price of beer. Declaring that *by natural birth all men are equally and alike born to like propriety, liberty and freedom*, they called for a secular republic with the abolition of censorship and complete religious toleration. Having had considerable support within the army (many had marched into battle believing they were fighting for a more just society), they now hoped that the execution of the King might be followed by the realization of their lofty ideals. But Cromwell was a landowner and acted in the interests of his own. When Leveller soldiers (who had been happy to fight the tyranny of the King) refused to be part of his invading army to murder and displace the Irish, Cromwell had leading Levellers arrested and imprisoned in the Tower. Other radicals were also suppressed, notably the even more radical Diggers who had advocated an early version of agrarian communism. (Obviously the Levellers and Diggers hated one another; the Left splitting into bitter factions is a tradition that goes back many centuries.) Though the Levellers failed in their own lifetime their pamphlets, petitions and speeches went on to inspire Rousseau, Thomas Jefferson, the Chartists and the beardy composers of countless pub folk-songs.

Cromwell had his political philosophy already – it was called the Old Testament. Perhaps it was this that made the man who despised Catholics surprisingly tolerant of Jews. Edward I's anti-Jewish legislation was repealed and Jewish communities began to spring up in England. He did not require the consent of those he ruled while memories of the wars were so fresh and his New Model Army was so feared. As 'Lord Protector' Cromwell had even more power than the King he had overthrown; ironically Parliamentarians actually offered him the throne as a way of limiting his powers. He wrestled with this idea for weeks at his new home in the royal palace at Hampton Court and finally declined it. He hadn't fought to remove the King only to establish another form of monarchy, and he hoped his chosen successor, his son Richard, would think likewise.

Cromwell famously told his portrait painter to 'paint me as I am, warts and all'* and yet in England at least, it would appear that all the warts have been removed from popular folk memory. There is a misplaced notion that Oliver Cromwell was the defender of a democratic Parliament against a tyrannical King, but his motivation was not liberty for the free-born Englishman, but a fanatical obsession to pursue *jihad* against all Catholics and possible sympathizers. In the end his religious bigotry was also his undoing. There was only one known treatment against the malaria that had plagued him since the Irish campaign, which had been discovered by Jesuits working in South America. Trying to prescribe something called 'Jesuit powder' to a Puritan like Oliver Cromwell was always going to be tricky; he adamantly refused it and died in September 1658. You'd think they'd have had the sense just to change the label.

The regime imploded without him. His son was unable to reconcile the rivalries between the army and Parliament and quickly packed the job in to retire to his country estate. Political chaos ensued and eventually the taciturn General Monck, who commanded the occupying army in Scotland, marched south, with no one quite sure of what his intentions might be. If you felt like being contrary you could argue that the British Civil Wars were in fact finally won by the Royalists. For in 1660 it was an army marching into London that finally put Charles II on the throne. With the country demoralized and miserable after the joyless piety of the interregnum, a return to the certainties of monarchy was a popular choice.

Charles was brought across on a ship called the *Naseby*, hastily renamed the *Royal Charles*, and he finally arrived in London on the day of his thirtieth birthday. So thick were the crowds in the street that it took his procession seven hours to pass through the city. The

---

* This is in fact a paraphrase of what he actually said: 'I desire you would use all your skill to paint my picture truly like me . . . warts and everything as you see me.'

roads were strewn with flowers, church bells rang out and music was heard once again along the length of his route. Charles was convinced that providence had brought him here. His own belief in the Divine Right of Kings had been vindicated by events; he was God's appointed ruler and the Almighty would demonstrate His approval by smiling upon his kingdom now that it had come to its senses. Before long half the country was dying of plague and most of London had burnt to the ground.

Charles II regains throne, prefers bed

Charles II (1660–85) always dated his own reign from the death of his father way back in 1649. Glances would then be exchanged around the room and the pedants subtly discouraged from putting him right. Of course he didn't deny Cromwell's existence. In fact he had the late Protector's body dug up again, hanged, drawn and quartered and his head stuck upon a spike. That must have been a pleasant morning's work for somebody, unearthing the half-decomposed body, lugging it up the scaffold and decapitating it. ' "Get a job with the government . . ." they said. "Do something really worthwhile." ' A dozen or so former members of the Commonwealth government were executed while many others, including Cromwell, Jr., suddenly developed a passion for foreign travel.

Power had completely shifted since the death of the Lord Protector and the new House of Commons became known as the 'Cavalier Parliament'. It really was most peculiar, Charles never seemed to meet anyone who hadn't been in favour of the Royalist cause all along. Determined that the Puritans would never again get such a grip on power, Parliament forced the nation's clergymen to swear an oath designed to weed out all the non-conformists, and suddenly around two thousand clerics were out of a job. They got what work they could elsewhere and for a brief period attractive young women would walk past building sites to find that all the labourers were averting their eyes and then kneeling down to pray.

Meanwhile Charles did his bit to support the backlash against Puritanism by having sex with as many actresses and duchesses as he possibly could. It is ironic that having been so determined to be the ruler of England, Scotland and Ireland, Charles did so little actual ruling once the crown was his. Instead he enjoyed himself yacht racing and betting on the horses, but most of all going to bed with beautiful women. His eleven-year quest to become monarch had seen him raise armies, risk his life in daring escapes, traipse around the royal courts of Europe and now his motivation was clear. He had wanted to be King because chicks dig it. His most famous mistress was Nell Gwynne, a one-time orange-seller who won the seventeenth-century equivalent of *Fame Academy* by being chosen for a starring role in Charles's bedroom. Meanwhile his poor Portuguese wife was unable to produce an heir – it was clear that the fertility problem lay with her (either that or all the ladies at court were walking around with pillows stuffed under their dresses). Though the number was probably higher, Charles officially fathered fourteen illegitimate children, most of whom were given dukedoms and whose descendants continued to sit and vote in the House of Lords until the end of the twentieth century.

But the overthrow of Puritan England in 1660 sparked a new sense of liberation in London and for decades later young people would have to put up with old bores saying, 'Wow, man, you should have been here in the sixties.' Music flourished; theatres reopened, with bawdy comedies a particular favourite. (Scientific advancements since Shakespeare's time meant that for the first time jokes were now actually funny.)* Architecture flourished; Christopher Wren was full of exciting ideas for magnificent new buildings: 'I'm sorry, Mr Wren, but nothing needs building in London at the moment. We'll keep you on file just in case anything comes up.' Isaac Newton developed his theory of gravity and Boyle developed Boyle's law, which was

---

* The Tudor crowd watching Shakespeare's comedies only ever got the jokes after an English professor explained each one by reading out footnotes from his Arden Shakespeare. And then they all went 'Oh I see', and attempted a retrospective laugh.

that, um . . . well it was a very important law anyway and Charles II gave his blessing to all these developments with his patronage of the Royal Society founded in 1660.

England's status in Europe had risen during the Commonwealth. Trade was continuing to flourish, particularly following brief wars with Holland and Spain that had gained England the colony of Jamaica and had seen England emerge as a formidable naval power. New colonies were founded in America with William Penn founding Pennsylvania and Charles's brother the Duke of York capturing New Amsterdam from the Dutch, which in his honour was renamed New York. He then declared that it was a wonderful town, and the Bronx was up, whereas the Battery, was, in fact, down.

Plague and Fire: religious zealots look smug

However, the new sense of optimism did not last for long. In 1665 the Great Plague killed around a hundred thousand people and many believed this was God's judgement upon a sinful land. In the face of such a catastrophe, suspicion and rumour replaced the new-found faith in science and learning and a brisk trade was done in bizarre masks and amulets that would supposedly protect the wearer. 'No, no, what you need to do is walk around sniffing flowers,' advised the doctors, while great pustules erupted on their necks and they dropped down dead. No one quite realized that the fleas on the black rat were to blame for this disaster. In fact the first thing they did was have all the dogs and cats of London put to death – the rats couldn't believe their good luck. The rich of course escaped from the capital; Charles and his court decamped to Salisbury and then, when the plague struck there, they all moved to Oxford. The poor meanwhile were forcibly kept in their homes where carts would come around to pick up the bodies and then dump them in plague pits.

'But should one tip the man with the corpse cart? It's one of those embarrassing social dilemmas, isn't it?'

'Well, I only did so he'd take away the recycling at the same time.'

With the coming of winter the flea population declined and the worst was over. The plague had thrived in London's narrow unhygienic streets and questions began to be asked about the terrible, cramped living conditions within the city. But nothing had prepared Londoners for the radical solution that presented itself on the night of 2 September 1666. In Pudding Lane, a baker's wife woke up her husband in the middle of the night: 'Darling, you did put the fire out in the kitchen, didn't you?'

'Nah, that's just one of those over-the-top health-and-safety fixations. I mean, really! What's the worst that could happen?'

Before long flames were spreading through the house and the couple escaped over the rooftops, leaving behind their maid who became the first casualty of the Great Fire of London. The inferno soon spread to surrounding buildings and to his irritation the Mayor of London was woken up. He took one look and famously uttered, 'A woman might piss it out!' Whether this was actually attempted is not recorded, but by morning the situation was becoming serious. The fire might have been contained to a few streets had it not been for the indecision and incompetence of his local government.

'Lord Mayor, the fire is spreading rapidly! If we act fast and destroy a few buildings in its path, we will create a gap and save many many more!'

'Absolutely. As soon as this proposal has been submitted to the Housing Safety Sub-Committee, which meets on a bi-monthly cycle, although it may be too late to get anything on the agenda for the meeting on the twenty-eighth.'

The Mayor refused to pull down any buildings without the owner's consent and so unsurprisingly householders refused to have their homes blown up, hoping the fire might miraculously change direction. But the densely packed wooden houses with their thatched roofs could not have been more inflammable, and the fire was well on the way to consuming pretty well every building between Fetter Lane and the Tower of London.

The diarist Samuel Pepys fled his home, having taken the trouble to dig a big hole in his garden to bury a Parmesan cheese and a few bottles of wine. He rushed to inform the King and the Duke of York, who became involved in directing efforts to save the capital. But for three days the fire burnt, eventually destroying 13,200 houses, over 80 churches, 44 company halls and the old St Paul's. There were surprisingly few recorded deaths, though many of the anonymous poor were probably cremated in their homes.* But five-sixths of the area within the city walls was destroyed. It was a calamity without equal; central London was reduced to a pile of smouldering ashes. And the baker from Pudding Lane said, 'All right, all right, you don't have to go on about it.'

In fact such a catastrophe demanded a more meaningful scapegoat than a common house fire, fanned by a strong wind in a dry summer. Rumours spread that the fire had been deliberately started by Jesuits, by the Dutch, by Spaniards; a Frenchman was virtually dismembered by a London mob, while the King's Guard took it upon themselves to start attacking people who spoke poor English. Eventually a French watchmaker Robert Hubert confessed to starting the fire, though it became clear during his trial that his story was nonsense. The King's Chief Minister commented, *Neither the judges, nor any present at the trial did believe him guilty; but that he was a poor distracted wretch, weary of his life, and chose to part with it*. He was publicly hanged at Tyburn. Though he was a Protestant, an official plaque was later put on the monument to the fire blaming 'the popish faction' for the inferno, where it remained until 1831 (soon to be replaced with a plaque blaming Muslim extremists).

Within weeks Christopher Wren produced exciting drawings for a whole new London; a majestic and confident city with classical squares and imposing boulevards with a grandeur and scale that could match anything in Europe. But his ambition was stymied by vested interests. Many basements had survived and too many landowners wanted to cling to the patches they had had before the fire, and so the City of London today remains a modern conurbation built on a medieval street plan. Many beautiful buildings were commissioned, however, including Wren's famous St Paul's

---

* The official death toll of the Great Fire was only eight. Sixty years earlier a tsunami in the Bristol Channel had resulted in the deaths of over two thousand people but this is completely forgotten. A great hurricane in 1703 is thought to have killed over eight thousand people.

Cathedral (which was not declared finished until 1711), but this time the city was rebuilt mainly in stone, not the combination of wood, thatch and firelighters approved by the safety officers last time.

Civil War averted as King 'can't be bothered'

But the Plague and the Great Fire were not the only reasons that the optimism of the Restoration evaporated so quickly. Charles's own behaviour as King had much to do with it. The following year the King failed to put out a fleet despite reports that Holland's navy were approaching. The Dutch then sailed up the River Medway, burnt the pride of the King's fleet and captured his flagship the *Royal Charles*. Samuel Pepys records that while Londoners were in a state of near panic, Charles was with his mistress chasing a moth.

Charles shared the Stuarts' disregard for Parliament, failing to summon it every three years as the law demanded. He preferred to rely on a small cabal of favoured nobles; indeed, the very word 'cabal' comes from the initials of the five advisers who made up Charles II's inner circle.* On one of the rare occasions when he was persuaded to give in to the House of Commons's wishes, Members of Parliament were so euphoric that they left the chamber and walked in an orderly procession to Whitehall Palace where the speaker gave their formal thanks. The King then invited MPs down to the royal wine cellars where they spent the rest of the day getting drunk. For Charles II had something very precious that his father had lacked and such an asset can make as much difference as a personal fortune or a power-ful army. Charles II had charm. Where his father had been arrogant, rude and remote, Charles II was witty, persuasive and likeable. If the first Charles had had the good sense to invite Parliament to his walk-in drinks cabinet to get sloshed together, a brutal civil war might have been avoided.

Once they had sobered up the Cavalier Parliament became

---

* Clifford, Arlington, Buckingham, Ashley and Lauderdale; together these advisers tended to form something of, well, a 'cabal', there's no other word for it.

203

increasingly anxious about the King's foreign policy. Just like his father, Charles went to war without calling Parliament and although Protestant Holland would have seemed like a more natural ally against the alarming ambitions of Catholic France, Charles secretly negotiated with his cousin Louis XIV asking for military support if he publicly converted to the Catholic faith. Had this scandal become public it would have been disastrous for the King, but Charles managed to keep his papist sympathies a secret until he finally converted on his deathbed.

'No Sex Please, You're Catholic'

However, with no apparent legitimate heir amongst his countless children, the next in line was his brother the Duke of York, whose Catholic tendencies were less cautiously concealed. When James Stuart married the Catholic Mary of Modena, Parliament passed a resolution to ask the King that the marriage should not be consummated. The motion that 'This House requests that the Duke of York restrains from having it off with his good lady wife' (or however it was worded) was unsurprisingly ignored by the royal family.* But by the end of the 1670s the prospect of James's accession to the throne had created a constitutional crisis. His Catholicism was no longer a secret and England faced the prospect of its first papist monarch since the disastrous Queen Mary. On one memorable night in 1679 two hundred thousand people gathered in the City, where an effigy of the Pope was burnt and floats featuring murderous Jesuits and randy nuns were paraded through the streets. Guy Fawkes' Night in Lewes is not much different today.

James's unpopularity was briefly alleviated when his daughter Mary was married to William of Orange, the Dutch Prince who led the Protestant forces against Catholic France. James could have had

---

* Though the episode demonstrates how taboos change down the centuries. In the 1670s Parliament was appalled that the heir to the throne might have sex with a Catholic. Today we would be appalled by the fact that she was only fifteen.

little idea of the political ramifications that this union would eventually have.

'So, young William, what are your intentions towards my daughter Mary?'

'Well, obviously I want only the very best for her, sir, so I thought I would wait until you were King, land an army in Devon and chase you out of the country, thus making her Queen of England, but more importantly making myself joint sovereign, thus taking over your kingdom and leaving you to die in exile, a bitter and humiliated man.'

'Jolly good – as long as you weren't intending her to take in washing.'

As long as James's Protestant daughter Mary was next in line after James, the prospect of the fifty-year-old Catholic briefly sitting on the English throne was not worth risking civil war over. Parliament of course was not completely united in its approach to the future of the monarchy, and during what became known as the 'Exclusion Crisis', two distinct parties emerged in the Commons, the more pro-Royal Court Party were dubbed 'Tories' and the Country Party in favour of excluding James were dubbed 'Whigs'. Both names were originally insults: a 'tory' was an Irish bandit, while a 'whiggamor' was a Scottish cattle driver, but these became the accepted names of the two groups that evolved into the Conservative and Liberal Parties. Perhaps our modern insults will evolve into accepted political labels: 'In the House of Commons today, the record of Gordon Brown's Lefty Scumbags Party was attacked by Mr David Cameron, leader of the Fascist Bastards.'

When the Whigs tried to introduce a bill excluding his brother from the English throne, Charles suspended Parliament and for the last few years of his reign ruled without it. Cromwell would have been turning in his grave – if Charles hadn't had him dug up and chopped into pieces. The remarkable thing about the restoration of the monarchy is that Parliament had fought and won a war and in 1660 had held all the cards. The powerless royal exile had had no bargaining power at all when he was invited back, and yet the upper-class idiots who made up the Cavalier Parliament made the fatal mistake of investing all their faith in his good character, in the naïve hope that he could be trusted to behave honourably. This imbalance of power never works; in any situation, if total authority is given to one individual and the only check upon the abuse of that authority is trusting the person to police him– or herself, sooner or later it always goes horribly wrong. It is why company chairmen are held to account by boards of directors; it is why head teachers are monitored by governing bodies; it is why Darth Vader has to explain himself to the Jedi Council.

One Parliament won a war against an absolutist monarch. The next Parliament blithely handed his son absolute power and then saw the same tensions re-emerge. It was the terror of slipping into another civil war that prevented many from objecting to the subsequent behaviour of Charles II, even though he tested the patience of Parliament to the very limit over the twenty-five years that he reigned. His brother, on the other hand, overstepped the line within the first five minutes.

James II: not as popular as the other Jimmy Stewart

Today it seems insane that so much energy and indeed life was wasted over whether someone chose to be Protestant or Catholic. To us it is as if our ancestors might as well have had major constitutional crises, massacres and wars over which football team they happened to support:

> The 'Superhoops' crisis of 1679 arose because the King insisted on his right to marry a supporter of QPR. Parliament was adamant that only Crystal Palace fans could sit upon the throne of England and now feared that the King's heir might grow up supporting the Rs. So on the anniversary of Palace's cup-final replay against Manchester United, Parliamentary forces assembled at Selhurst Park wearing their distinctive red and blue stripes, shouting 'Eagles!' at the arrival of their mascot, a man in a comedy bird costume.

Although there were those who could see how ridiculous these endless religious battles were, when James inherited the throne most of England sincerely believed that the Catholics were out to get them. The century had begun with a Catholic plot to blow up the Houses of Parliament, they had been told that the Papists had burnt down most of London, and now in 1685 on the other side of the English Channel a terrible persecution of Protestants was unleashed as Louis XIV revoked his grandfather's 'Edict of Nantes', which had previously granted them freedom of worship. French Protestants or 'Huguenots' fled in their thousands to England, bravely recounting the horror stories of their persecution and then finally breaking down in tears when they realized they were going to have to eat English food for the rest of their lives. Into this atmosphere arrived the first Catholic to take the throne since Bloody Mary and England became a very nervous place.

Britain might have been able to tolerate James II (1685–88) if his Catholicism had been a private, personal matter, but he had converted from Protestantism some years earlier, and there is no zealot like a recent convert. ('Excuse me, your cigarette smoke is drifting over the fence into my garden,' says the man who was on eighty a day before 1 January.) To the alarm of many life-long English Catholics, who feared James's actions would provoke a back-lash, James appeared determined to try and make England a Roman Catholic state. He filled official positions with Papists, rejecting the best candidates in favour of those who would promote what he believed to be the one true faith. In his mind, he was merely redress-ing an existing imbalance: 'James II is an equal-opportunities employer, and applications are particularly welcome from those with a preference for rosary beads and Eucharist wafers.' With all the political nous that his father had shown in the run-up to his execution, James issued the so-called 'Declaration of Indulgence'. By modern standards this would be a very progressive document, allowing freedom of religion, removing the bar on Catholics occupy-ing official posts and removing penalties for failing to attend Anglican services on a Sunday. But back in 1687, this was like a declaration that Al-Qaeda, the IRA and Gary Glitter should be allowed to run our Civil Service, schools and hospitals. It appalled mainstream opinion and a number of senior clergymen refused to read it out. Being a King who badly needed to win over public opinion, James thought it might be a good idea to lock these seven bishops up in the Tower of London. But amazingly that only made things worse; nothing he did seemed to increase his popularity. Now even the Tories who had supported him as heir to the throne were turning against the King. The sense of crisis was already reaching a crescendo when the final straw came in the shape of a little baby boy.

'With deepest sympathy on the birth of your son'

In June 1688 James's wife gave birth to a son, James Francis Edward Stuart.* Never had the birth of a son and heir to the monarch been greeted with such abject depression; the boy would clearly be brought up a Catholic and his gender put him first in line ahead of the Protestant daughters from James's first marriage. The prospect of a long line of Catholic Stuart monarchs stretched out into the indefinite future. A conspiracy theory quickly spread about the parentage of the child; it was soon widely believed that the baby boy was not royal at all, but had been smuggled into the royal bed-chamber in a warming pan.† The 'warming pan' detail was the inspired extra touch that any good propagandist knows is required to give a complete fiction the air of truth. By managing to convince themselves that James was deceiving them, James's opponents acquired some vague moral authority for the illegal, treasonous course that they were about to pursue.

Before the birth of the baby prince, James's Protestant daughter Mary had been next in line to the throne. She was married to the man who'd made it his life's mission to oppose the rise of Catholic France.

---

* He would one day be known as the 'Old Pretender' – father of 'Bonnie Prince Charlie'.
† 'Warming pans', for those modern people who prefer to use hot-water bottles or electric blankets, are those great big circular copper dishes with long handles that today hang on the walls of olde worlde pubs.

William of Orange had only married Mary in the hope of adding England to the military alliance he had forged against the French and now he received a letter from a group of leading English Protestants inviting him to invade England. Although these senior figures were from all parts of the country and included Members of Parliament and the Bishop of London, they had no legal authority, nor were they acting upon any mandate from the Commons, Lords or the Privy Council. But the invitation was all that William needed to fulfil his long-term ambition to secure the English Crown. On the day that the letter was dispatched, the seven bishops were formally acquitted in court; James could see his power already slipping away.

William landed at Torbay on the totemic Protestant anniversary of 5 November 1688. James marched west to meet him with an army that was large and well equipped. But although James was militarily well prepared, he had already lost the propaganda war.* As towns across the country declared themselves for William, officers quit James's army to join the other side. The navy came out itself for the Protestant cause. James got as far as Salisbury Plain where he paused and waited. He dithered and fussed over minor details. He kept getting nosebleeds and his high command found themselves pre-occupied with trying to find something to stem the bleeding.

That was the only bloodshed there would be. James suddenly abandoned his post, sent his wife and baby to France, and then pre-pared to follow them. On the night of 10 December he tiptoed down the back stairs of Whitehall Palace to the Thames. From a little rowing boat he threw the great seal of his royal office into the river, somehow imagining that this would make the government of the country impossible, and then he headed for the coast in disguise.

William didn't want James in the country to become a rallying point for Royalists, nor did he want to kill him and create a martyr.

* As well as 21,000 soldiers, William had also brought a printing press. He quickly distributed pamphlets in English declaiming James's shocking mistreatment of churchmen and repeating the scandalous story that the royal baby was an impostor. Plus recipes, horoscopes, sudoku puzzles and much much more . . .

James's decision to sneak abroad was the best result he could have hoped for and William was jubilant at the ease with which this had all happened. Except a couple of eagle-eyed yokels on the South Coast identified James and brought him back to London.

'We've caught 'im, sir! Tryin' to flee the country he was, but we was too sharp for 'im!'

'Spiffing. Really excellent, thank you. Now why don't we keep him prisoner in this room here. The one with the open window and the horses loosely tied up outside.'

James then escaped a second time and, with him finally having fled the country, his opponents somehow surmised that this amounted to an abdication of the throne.

The Glorious Revolution (or Protestant consortium wins hostile take-over bid)

It is commonly believed that no foreign army has successfully invaded Britain since 1066. However, this is not strictly true. Whatever we think about James II, he was the rightful King of England and Scotland; William of Orange himself had no legal claim to the Crown and his invading army consisted of his fellow country-men from Holland, with German, Danish and Huguenot reinforcements. There may have been no battle, but James did not flee his realm because he thought William might tease him about his nosebleeds. An invading foreign army was the key factor in this illegal *coup d'état*. The last foreign power to invade England was not the Normans but the Dutch in 1688.

So why weren't Britons forced to wear clogs, grow tulips and speak impeccable English? Well, although the English were shocked to see Dutch guards standing outside the royal palaces and William's army was kept close to London during the ensuing election, the whole revolution was achieved through negotiation between two groups of European Protestants who cooperated against a common enemy. They put their religion above nationalism or respect for the law. It is a cliché that history is written by the winners, but if James had beaten William in battle that year, today we would celebrate the event as another great patriotic victory, like the Armada or the Battle of Britain, when the British saw off a foreign invader and remained a proud and independent sovereign state. Instead it has been spun as the 'Glorious Revolution', or the 'Bloodless Revolution' in order to accommodate the uncomfortable truth that a foreign Prince took the British throne by turning up with a huge army.

In his propaganda William had claimed that he had merely come to assist the English resolve their grievances in their own way and now the politicians began to debate the legal niceties of how this might work: 'Legally James would have to remain King, but his daughter Mary will act as regent in his absence . . .' or, 'If we say James abdicated, we can crown Mary with William as her regent?' Only now did William make his intentions clear. The English establishment was shocked. 'Durrr! I thought he was turning up with a massive army just to be helpful. But now he's saying he wants to be King himself.' Well, who would have thought it.

William III says, 'Let's go Dutch'

When Mary had first been introduced to her future husband she had cried for a day and a half. He was a short, hunched, wheezy man, twelve years older than her who lacked charm and spoke poor English. But though the Princess was only fifteen and repelled by her suitor, William was determined to marry her. She had that special 'heir to the English throne' characteristic that is so hard to find in a girl; that elusive 'going to be queen of major European power' quality that none of the girls from the dating agency had so far seemed to possess.

William III (1688–1702) was a ruthless continental politician who acquired the English throne as part of his life's project of fighting a virtually permanent war with Louis XIV. Because Mary was actually the one who had the claim to the throne, it was eventually agreed that they would reign 'jointly' – the first (and still the only) 'dual monarchy' Britain has ever had.* But of course this was a complete sham; William alone was granted executive power and for us still to refer to the reign of 'William and Mary' as if she had a say in anything other than the colour of the bedroom curtains is going along with a bit of seventeenth-century spin dreamt up to mollify some long-dead Tories. James II was succeeded by William III, Mary was no more joint ruler of England than Cherie Blair was. Actually, bad example; Denis Thatcher then.

There were many who were deeply uncomfortable about the unconstitutional nature of what had just happened,† but they comforted themselves with the thought that the asthmatic usurper looked certain to die before his royal wife. Even these hopes were dashed when the thirty-two-year-old queen died of smallpox in 1694 leaving William to rule alone.

By passing an act to hand William the Crown while James and his heir were still alive, the monarchy and Parliament inadvertently crossed a major staging post in the evolution of British democracy. The Crown was in the gift of Parliament. At the time this was just an embarrassing compromise to keep out James and placate this Dutch bloke who still had his army camped outside London. Parliament did its best to pretend that James had abdicated, even though he made it clear he thought the Crown was still his. The principle was taken one stage further when the Bill of Rights stipulated that the Crown could only pass to a Protestant. This law is still in place today. Camilla Parker-Bowles's first husband was a Catholic; had she converted Britain would have later had a mini-constitutional crisis, but for some reason she never made the jump.

---

* Philip II of Spain was to be called 'King' when he was married to Mary Tudor, but Parliament had ensured that he lost any claim to the English throne once she had died. It is one of the curious anomalies of English royal tradition that the wife of King George V was 'Queen' Mary but the husband of Queen Elizabeth II is 'Prince' Philip. There is probably a reason for it, but any enquiry might involve having to listen to 'constitutional expert' Lord St John of Fawsley and frankly life is too short.
† The Archbishop of Canterbury actually refused to crown the new King and Queen. They had to get in an agency archbishop.

'Camilla darling, have you thought about converting to Catholicism?'

'I'd rather not, Andrew dear. I'm having a secret affair with the future King of England, and if I converted I'd be excluded from eventually marrying him by the 1689 Bill of Rights.'

'Oh, fair enough, I just thought I'd ask.'

The Bill of Rights: 'Let the People Be Free' (from Catholics)

Not only did Parliament do away with the principle of a hereditary monarchy, it also exercised this right by outlining the path of succession for the foreseeable future. If William and Mary produced no heirs, the crown would pass to Mary's younger sister Anne. In the event of Anne dying childless, they had managed to track down a German family in Hanover who would no doubt be delighted to learn that they were distant relations of the British royal family and had inherited a large island off the north-west of Europe. All this of course was to make it abundantly clear that any Catholic Stuarts who had previously sent in their CVs need not reapply for the position. Despite Tory opposition to the abolition of the hereditary principle, dozens of Catholic contenders to the English throne would be bypassed, including Louis XV of France, Louis XV of Spain, and Charles VI, the Holy Roman Emperor.

Apart from their now-embarrassing sectarian overtones, the Bill of Rights and the Act of Settlement were major steps forward in Britain's journey from absolutist monarchy to Parliamentary democracy and forms a major part of Britain's famously 'unwritten constitution'.* During the following years a number of progressive measures were established, including the freedom of the press, all of which served to inspire political thinkers in France and the American

* Like America's constitution a hundred years later, the Bill of Rights also contained a clause upholding the citizens' right to bear arms. It's just that Britain later realized that it might be sensible to change that bit.

colonies. Parliament had learnt the lesson of the Restoration in 1660 when they had foolishly recreated a dictatorship and trusted to the King's good nature. Now Parliament's supremacy was set down in law. It would be illegal for a monarch to collect taxes by Royal Prerogative or to maintain a standing army without the consent of Parliament. The King could not suspend or dispense laws; he could not intervene in debates in Parliament, nor interfere in justice by tampering with juries or setting up his own courts. One Christmas message on the telly and that was it. Foreign policy remained in the hands of the monarch, but the cost of William's wars against the French made him even more dependent on Parliament to fund them.

Before William could use this new kingdom that he'd acquired for his obsessive crusade against Louis XIV, there was the matter of his predecessor James to deal with. James had landed at Kinsale in Ireland and summoned a Catholic Parliament that recognized him as King. With French support, James planned to use Ireland as his base to reconquer England; the Irish meanwhile saw this as a chance to assert their independence from the English and claim back the lands that had been stolen from them. Attacks began on the Protestant landowners who fled to Derry and Enniskillen where they were besieged for many months and learnt of the many interesting ways that you can cook rat. Public opinion forced William to intervene personally and in June 1690 he landed with an army of continental mercenaries patched up with a few Ulster volunteers who flocked to his cause. On 12 July the two Kings met on the banks of the River Boyne. Both men had been crowned King of England, but anyone suggesting a compromise involving some sort of job-share would have had their work cut out. Before the battle even began a cannon-ball fired from across the river hit William on the shoulder. Had it struck his head and killed him Irish and British history might have taken a different course. The King was injured, but not so seriously that he could not continue to direct his troops, and James's in-effectiveness as a leader was exposed once again as his forces were routed. The Battle of the Boyne was decisive, but only because James decided so. Despite there being considerable support for the Stuart cause, once again the cowardly and defeatist James fled to France, earning himself the Irish nickname Séamus á Chaca ('James the shite').

Euro-Superstate blocked by Britain

Now William could turn his attention to his first love: fighting Europe's major Catholic power and the personification of that state in Louis XIV. The PR company charged with coming up with a name for this nine-year conflict rejected all sorts of suggestions before they hit upon the title that captured the essence of it. 'The "Great Religious War"?' 'No.' 'The "War of the Faiths"?' 'Nope.' 'I know, what about the "War of the League of Augsburg"?' 'Ooh yes, that's catchy; sort of memorable, isn't it, yes, the "War of the League of" – sorry, what was it again?' In fact events in Ireland and on the continent were all part of one giant European war, which would among other things determine whether William or the exile James sat on the British throne, and so another name for this conflict is the 'War of the English Succession'. It has also been called the 'War of the Grand Alliance' and 'King William's War'; in fact there were so many names for this war that it's a wonder they ever managed to agree what to put on the peace treaty without hostilities breaking out all over again.

William had allied his new kingdom with a coalition of German Princes who were set upon halting the expansion of France, and the country now found itself involved in a continental land war. But with William and his army over in the Netherlands, Britain itself suddenly became vulnerable to invasion. In April 1692 British agents suddenly realized with some alarm that twenty thousand French and Irish troops were waiting in Cherbourg and the entire French fleet was gathered in the Channel ports.

'Please, you must tell King William that his kingdom is in dire peril.'

'I'm sorry,' said the receptionist, 'King William is away in Holland at the moment. If you would like to leave a message he will deal with it on his return.'

The French fleet had already comprehensively defeated the English in the Battle of Beachy Head and if they could assert their control of the English Channel, there would be nothing to stop the French occupying England and putting Catholic James back on the throne. However, the French navy were routed at the Battle of Cape La Hougue; *the Trafalgar of the seventeenth century* as Churchill described it. For five days after the engagement, smaller English boats sailed into French ports destroying much of the French invasion fleet, as James watched the destruction of the ships he had hoped would carry him back to his former kingdom. James remained exiled in France for the rest of his life. He was set up in a little château in the French countryside where he lived out his years with all the bitterness of a former celebrity who'd had their long-running TV series cancelled by the BBC. Louis XIV offered to have James II elected King of Poland, but he declined. 'That's very kind, Louis, but I can hardly accept the throne of Poland if I'm going to be returning to my old job as King of England.' At which there was a bit of embarrassed coughing and various courtiers wondered whether they ought to explain that it wasn't going to happen.

The land war did not go so well for England, and Parliament reacted furiously at successive defeats of English armies led by Dutch generals. 'We need a British manager,' said the pundits, 'these continentals don't understand the English game.' Resentment against the Dutch King William increased after the death of his English Queen, and Parliament made it illegal for a monarch to declare war on a foreign power without Parliament's consent. The protracted European war was also incredibly expensive, prompting one creative Whig to hit upon the excellent idea of creating a 'national debt'. 'We'll invent this thing called the "Bank of England", get people to lend money to the government and pay it all back when things have sorted themselves out.' Which should be any day now. The Bank of England also issued banknotes, although each one had to be handwritten until 1725, which made for quite a queue at the cashier's window.

The enormous cost of keeping an army of ninety thousand could not be justified after the war ended in stalemate in 1697 and so eighty thousand men were demobbed overnight, without of course any government plan to integrate them back into paid employment. The result was that thousands of them spotted the same card in the job centre. *Remote road seeks Highwayman to shout 'Stand and deliver!' and then be annoyed when victims start singing the Adam and the Ants hit.* Peace brought a massive crime wave to Britain, and incentives were offered for members of the public to name active thieves and vagabonds in an eighteenth-century version of *Crimestoppers.* Hundreds of men who had borne arms for their country were hanged when in desperation they had turned to crime on their return.

Before long, however, the prospect of another war with France loomed on the horizon even though William would not live long enough to take part himself. In 1702 his horse tripped on a molehill, he fell and died soon after. The most powerful man in the world had not been able to defeat him, but in the end he was killed by a little mole.* William of Orange still has iconic status among the Orangemen of Northern Ireland; today if someone from East Belfast is called 'Billy' it is a pretty safe bet that he is a Protestant, especially if he's wearing a Rangers shirt and painting the kerbstones red, white and blue. Elsewhere in the UK his status has rather faded, even though at the time he was the single most important figure in European politics after Le Roi Soleil. William's popularity plummeted after the death of his wife, who had at least had some claim to the English throne. Her husband made little effort to hide his preference for Dutch advisers and friends and gradually the fiction of the 'Glorious Revolution' evaporated as the country realized it had a foreign King pursuing a foreign agenda. It didn't help that William gave English titles to his favourite Dutchmen who were widely believed to be lovers of the bisexual King. He had been forced to accept a Crown with greatly diminished powers, but it was worth such sacrifices to throw the weight of England against his

* Ever after the Jacobites would give thanks to the mole by toasting 'the little black man in velvet'. Either that or they'd had a spookily accurate premonition of the Artist Formerly Known as Prince.

arch-rival the King of France. He must have envied the increasing absolutism of Louis XIV. But this centralization of power would eventually lead to the demise of the French monarchy. It would take a bloody revolution to address the imbalance of power that had just been grappled with in England. However, before the monarchy finally became wholly subservient to Parliament, there would be one last appearance from the ugly face of Stuart intransigence. That face belonged to Anne.

Queen Anne: gives name to chair, then breaks it

The Stuarts had never been known for their striking good looks and the wheezy hunchback with the Dutch accent was followed by another shocker from the Ugly Agency. Fat Anne had a neck like a tree trunk and became so obese that eventually she had to be carried into meetings. Looking at her portraits you can almost hear the painters thinking, Well, there's no point in even trying . . . Luckily for her she was so short-sighted she could barely see their efforts. Her fondness for a tipple earned her the nickname 'Brandy Nan' and probably contributed to the gout which helped finish her off. At her death her body was so swollen that she had to be buried in a square coffin.

Of course you should never judge a person by their looks – the important question is: 'Was Anne an interesting and pleasant person on the inside?' And the answer is 'No'. Grumpy, boring and un-intelligent, she lacked wit or charm and her writings are riddled with basic grammatical errors and spelling mistakes. She attempted to present herself as the new Queen Elizabeth, but historical pedants spotted subtle differences between the two queens – namely that Elizabeth had been a striking redhead with a fierce intelligence and ready wit, whereas Anne was a big fat thicko who was as dull as ditchwater. To be fair to the last Stuart, few modelling agencies recommend that you are almost permanently pregnant and then suffer the endless misery of miscarriages, stillborn infants or seeing all your children die. Anne endured around eighteen pregnancies, giving birth thirteen times without a single child surviving her. If it was the first duty of the monarch to provide an heir, then Anne gets an 'A' for effort and an 'E' for achievement.

The best that can be said for Queen Anne (1702–14) was that she provided some sort of focus for national unity during a war with France that lasted for nearly her entire reign. With the army now free of King William's questionable skills as a general, Anne was able to employ the outstanding military commander of the day in John Churchill. On this appointment she was dispassionately advised by her best friend, confidante and possible lesbian lover Sarah Churchill. For most of the war, the general's wife was able to use her unique position at court to lobby on behalf of her talented husband until she and consequently the general fell out of favour at the end of Anne's reign. The Duke of Marlborough, as he became, was among the greatest military commanders Britain ever produced, and in 1704 he won a stunning victory against the French at the Battle of Blenheim. At three successive victories he recreated this triumph, and though each sequel was slightly less successful than the last, the war marked England's arrival as a major military power on land as well as at sea. The French were never again to threaten German territory (except in 1945 when they were allowed to pretend they were one of the powers overthrowing Nazi Germany just to shut Charles de Gaulle up for five minutes). When John Churchill fell from favour in 1711 he turned his attention to building the spectacular Blenheim Palace where his famous descendant would be born the following century.*

The so-called 'War of Spanish Succession' was also another war of English succession, since Louis XIV had recognized James Edward Stuart as the rightful monarch of England and defeat in this war would probably put Catholic James back on the throne as a French puppet. With an entire alternative royal family waiting in the wings, the survival of the sickly Protestant wing of the Stuarts was of major

---

* Sir Winston Churchill was very proud of his ancestor. When it was said to him that the Battle of Britain was his Waterloo, he replied, 'No, it was my Blenheim.' Yeah, whatever.

religious, political and strategic importance. But Anne's last surviving son, the Duke of Gloucester, died of smallpox long after she was capable of producing another heir. The death signified the end of the line for the Stuarts as a ruling royal dynasty stretching back to their accession to the Scottish throne in 1371. More significantly the death of this eleven-year-old English boy also precipitated the death of Scotland as an independent nation state.

The Act of Union: Scotland marries abusive partner

For the previous century or so Scotland had grumbled about the English forgetting to consult them over minor constitutional niceties such as chopping the heads off their monarchs. But the death of the Duke of Gloucester prompted a succession crisis and resolution in England that was a step too far for the Scots. The English Parliament passed the Act of Settlement which confirmed that the throne would pass to someone called Electress Sophia of Hanover, who, though a granddaughter of James I/VI, had so little interest in Scotland that she had not even been there to stage a madcap student revue during the Edinburgh Festival.

The Scottish Parliament reacted by asserting its right to choose its own monarch. This defiant show of independence put the last nail in the coffin of Scottish independence. For England the declaration held out the possibility of the revival of the 'Auld Alliance' and England being threatened by Catholic France to the south and her historic ally led by a Catholic Stuart to the north. The English government generously decided that the safest course was to subsume Scotland into one larger country, which would be known as Great Britain – the name coined by James I. It was a great deal for both sides; England would get all the Scottish scientists, philosophers, engineers, oil and footballers while Scotland would get to have little gift shops at the airport selling smoked salmon and malt whisky.

In fact the Scottish economy was in dire shape following years of bad harvests, in-fighting amongst the clans* and a disastrous attempt to found a Scottish colony in Panama, so the prospect of passing all their debts to the wealthy English was an attractive one. The total failure of the Scots' colonial adventure had confirmed just how much the Scottish economy was dependent on England. Now, with England threatening to cut off all trade and confiscate land in England owned by the Scots, a majority of the landowning Scottish MPs (though not the Scottish people) saw this Parliamentary merger to be in their best interests. The two most crucial groups of opinion-formers – the clergy and the lawyers – were mollified by promises that the Scottish legal system and Church would remain untouched. These institutions were proud of their high standards: only a few years earlier they had combined to ensure that an Edinburgh student was executed for the heinous crime of blasphemy.† And so the Act of Union was passed in 1707, and under its terms forty-five Scottish MPs came to Westminster and sixteen Scottish peers joined the House of Lords. In Scotland there were massive demonstrations against the legislation on the day it was passed and martial law was declared in Edinburgh. Before long it became apparent that the instincts of the Scottish population had been sound – as one English Parliamentarian put it: *Have we not bought Scotland in order that we may tax her?* When a school of whales was beached off the east coast of Scotland it was interpreted as a symbol of the death of Scotland. It would have worked better if it had been Wales, but the Welsh had been absorbed two hundred years earlier.

And so the process that had begun with the first Stuart to sit on

---

* The most infamous incident was the massacre at Glencoe in 1692, when dozens of the MacDonald clan were murdered in cold blood by their house guests, the Campbells. The Campbells had been staying with the MacDonalds for two weeks and families always start to get on each other's nerves after a few days. King William knew of and approved the pre-planned massacre – the MacDonalds had been slow to declare their allegiance to the new King – but the scandal it provoked meant that no union could be possible between England and Scotland during William's lifetime. The animosity between the two clans survives to this day; the Clachaig hotel in Glencoe still has a sign saying 'No Hawkers or Campbells'.
† Nineteen-year-old Thomas Aitkenhead had asserted that religion was nothing more than invented nonsense and he was tried and hanged in 1697.

the English throne was completed under the last. When all the power had been in the hands of the King, it had been the two monarchies that had been united. Now that the power belonged to the second and third estates, it was the union of Parliaments that counted. The country had a new name and a new flag; a common market and monetary union and somewhere in the small print of the act it must have stipulated that if any Scottish sportsmen won anything, the London media would always refer to them as 'British' just to annoy the Scots.

The Scottish MPs arriving in Westminster found a Parliament very unlike their own. Party political divisions were now at their fiercest ever. Whigs and Tories read different papers, drank in different taverns, went to different clubs and even frequented different race meetings. Violence occasionally erupted between supporters of the two sides; after closing time, they would square up in the pedestrianized high streets and chant: 'Two, four, six, eight, Your view of a divine and magical monarchy is synonymous with Catholic superstition and a medieval papal state!' But the Tories knew that their idea of a sacred monarchy anointed by God would die with the last Protestant Stuart. One of the unforeseen successes of the Glorious Revolution was the way it altered the concept of power: everyone from the King down no longer had their place as allocated to them by God. This would be important as the coming revolutions in industry and agriculture would make millionaires out of ordinary tradesmen, who would in turn demand political power to match their financial muscle. As they stumbled down this progressive path, the landed gentry who had ruled the country for centuries can have had little idea that it would end up with them having to open up their historic manor houses to the general public, offering cream teas, kiddies' korners and rather disappointing exhibitions of old farm machinery.

Had Charles II or William and Mary or Anne produced any surviving legitimate heirs, the old-fashioned monarchy with its strict hierarchy might have survived a little longer, but gradually the cult of reason was eclipsing centuries of blind faith and superstition. The last woman to be tried and executed for witchcraft was killed in

Scotland in the 1720s* and Queen Anne was the last monarch to practise the 'royal touch'. This was a bizarre custom dating back to Edward the Confessor which held that the monarch possessed the magical power to cure his subjects of the hideous disease of scrofula. It only took them seven hundred years to work out that being touched by the King actually made no difference whatsoever.

More importantly, as the House of Stuart era lumbered to its undignified end, the monarch's dead hand could still be felt on the body politic. In 1708 Anne refused to grant the royal assent to Parliamentary legislation, becoming the last British monarch to do so. The Queen was still the effective centre of government, the first minister or chief executive whose personal approval was required for all legislation. But this considerable personal power was not finally seized from the Crown by an indignant Parliament or revolutionary mob. Instead it withered owing to practical considerations. When Anne was replaced by a foreign King, the government discovered that it could function perfectly well without the monarch having the faintest idea what was going on. This is a tradition that has continued into the modern era; today the Prime Minister has a weekly audience with the Queen, and he explains the economic policy of the government in relation to the exchange-rate mechanism, fluctuating global interest rates, petro-dollars and Sino-Indian expansion in the digital service sector, and she just smiles and nods politely. Of course, ever since the end of the Stuarts, various royals have hankered after a time when they had real power. Tony Benn's diaries reveal how the Duke of Edinburgh used to go around suggesting to senior ministers that he sit in on cabinet meetings as members of the Saudi royal family do. But after a battle of wills that lasted a hundred years, the

* Though illegal mob executions of supposed witches continued. Nor was this the last prosecution for witchcraft; during World War II the Witchcraft Act of 1735 was used against the Scottish spiritualist Helen Duncan who, it was alleged, was using her powers to reveal military secrets. One of her séances was raided by the police, who charged her with conjuring up spirits. She was found guilty and sent to Holloway Prison. Witchcraft of any description was not decriminalized until 1951, though that did not stop the police from raiding Helen Duncan one last time in 1956. You'd think she would have seen it coming.

executive power of the monarchy died with Anne in 1714 and the role of Prime Minister emerged to fill the vacuum. The Stuarts had begun the century insisting that they were chosen for the monarchy by an act of God. But because they had exercised that right with such crass stupidity, they now owed their position to an act of Parliament.

It was Britain's system of government that gave her a vital head start as Europe unknowingly stumbled into the modern era. A less feudal hierarchy allowed talent to flourish, while limited freedom of the press challenged corruption and incompetence. Unlike the absolute monarchs in France and Spain, the English Parliament had rigorously ensured that Britain had a modern and effective tax-collecting system. This meant that England was able to mobilize surprisingly large amounts of money at times of war; punching above its weight on the battlefields of Europe and on the high seas. France's population was nearly four times that of England's but Louis XIV's finances were archaic, chaotic and corrupt and the growing debts of the French monarchy would be a major factor in its destruction at the end of the eighteenth century. This was to be the key to Britain's eventual triumph over France during the coming century as Great Britain became the most powerful country in the world. *C'est l'économie, stupide.* With success in war on land and at sea, with British trade booming, her colonies growing across the Atlantic alongside newly won possessions of Gibraltar and Minorca, at last a newly unified Great Britain could feel a strong sense of security and national pride as they patriotically celebrated the accession of the new King of England. It was a shame he didn't actually speak any English, but you can't have everything.

7

Revolutions 1714–1815

How agricultural, transport and industrial revolutions allowed Britain to fulfil its manifest destiny of duffing up the French

Wanted: 'Prime Minister' for emerging world power. YOU ARE: hardworking, innovative and extraordinarily adept at bribery and corruption. WE ARE: Protestant country with large army and navy having recently completed leverage buyout of northern neighbour and with plans for further expansion. The position of 'Prime Minister' is a new executive post created following recent appointment of a new King who doesn't speak a word of English. Great Britain PLC is an equal-opportunities employer, although we will only consider applications from white English upper-class males, who are Whigs not Tories, and if you are a Catholic, I can't believe you've even bothered reading this far.

The modern concept of a Prime Minister as head of a government evolved as a practical necessity after the accession of George I. Government ministers trying to discuss complex economic, diplomatic and trade issues found progress difficult when the head of government didn't speak any English and they didn't speak any German.

'Marvellous to have a king who shares the name of England's patron saint!'

'*Wie, bitte?*'

'St George. You have the same name. St George and the Dragon.'
'*Draggen?*'
'Oh, it doesn't matter.'

George I (1714–27) was fifty-four when he became King of Great Britain, and was not particularly interested in changing his ways. He never bothered to learn English, and annoyed his new subjects by considering Great Britain to be of far less importance than Hanover. Robert Walpole, who eventually emerged as the dominant politician of his age and Britain's first 'Prime Minister', communicated with the King in Latin. Unsurprisingly, the vision of a big fat German King talking to a big fat Norfolk aristocrat about matters of state in Latin has yet to be recreated as a high-budget costume drama. George had arrived in England with his two mistresses of contrasting physical appearance, who were soon nicknamed 'the Elephant and the Maypole'. His wife would not be joining him for the tour of his new kingdom since George had had her locked up in a German castle where she was imprisoned for thirty-two years for having an affair as he had done.* Her lover disappeared on the same day, rumoured to have been killed, chopped up and buried beneath the floorboards.

Although the head of state had ceased to be the central figure in the British Government, the monarch was still more than the symbolic figurehead of today. It was the King who appointed ministers (including henceforth the Prime Minister), so getting the right sort of chap at the top still mattered. George I had not been the first in line to the British throne, nor the second or third. In fact there were over fifty people with a better claim to the Crown than the obscure German Elector of Hanover, but they were all ruled out on

---

* Her son, the future George II, had been a small boy when his mother was condemned to stare endlessly out of the window of the tall tower, hoping that one day her prince would come. And then one day her son did finally journey to the castle. In a heroic rescue mission he dived into the moat and swam across to the battlements, ready to climb the walls of the castle and whisk her away. Except that he was simply apprehended by the guards and sent packing. The Prince hated his father George I, a pattern that seemed to continue through the generations of the Hanoverians.

the grounds that they were Catholics. And so the search had begun to find one person who would win the 1714 version of *The X Factor*.

'I definitely feel I have got what it takes to be King of Great Britain,' whined a pale Scottish man clutching rosary beads and bearing a strong family resemblance to James II.

'Next!' laughed the judges with patronizing contempt.

'I'm going to prove you wrong!' he angrily told them as he went off to launch the Jacobite Rebellion of 1715.

'Oh yes, I'm the Old Pretender'

It had been James Stuart's birth in 1688 that had precipitated the Bloodless Revolution and the Protestant settlement that still forbids a Catholic monarch to this very day. In 1688, opponents of James II had claimed that the 'warming-pan prince' had been smuggled into the bedchamber, and was not of royal blood at all. But James Stuart now proved that he was indeed his father's son by being every bit as useless, indecisive and weedy a hypochondriac as James II had been. The effete French-educated Prince was late to arrive in Scotland and failed to show much leadership when he finally got there, appalled by the lack of sophistication of his Scottish 'subjects'. The Jacobites had already suffered the ill fortune of having their most likely sponsor Louis XIV die in the week they raised their standard. After an inconclusive battle at Sheriffmuir the Jacobites suffered a rash of desertions, but marched on into England presuming that the general population shared their outrage that the rightful heir to the throne had been disinherited. But faced with the burning issue of the day: 'Whom do you wish to be your King and ruler – the rightful heir King James III or this unknown German impostor,' the majority of English did not seem particularly bothered.

'What is it you're doing exactly? Sponsored walk, is it?'

'No, we're invading. You must join us as we march to London in a fight to the death for the one true King.'

'Right, I see. Look, I'm happy to sign a petition or something but I'd rather not get involved with anything political, if you don't mind . . .'

Pretty soon it became clear that the rebellion would amount to nothing more than a damp squib. A few die-hards held out in the hope that it might turn into some other sort of squib, but it transpires that there is no other variety. James fled and lived out the next fifty years of his life in Rome where he was buried at St Peter's Church. No one has yet dug up his bones to do the DNA test which would settle the warming-pan mystery once and for all, but surely a *Time Team* special can't be far off.

Although 'the Fifteen' (as the rebellion became known), never posed any serious threat to the Protestant establishment, it was a useful crisis for those in power looking to secure their own positions. Elections would now be held every seven years instead of every three and the Whigs could now portray the Tories (traditional sympathizers of the Stuarts) as potentially violent traitors, and so for the next half-century the Tories were a broken force. The Whigs tried to explain what was happening to George I but by the time they had worked out the correct Latin verb endings for 'James, having rebelled, will be imprisoned if he is captured, in case he were to rise up again in the future', well, the whole thing was already over.

Era-naming committee decides on 'Georgian'

The national corporation of which George I had just become honorary chairman was an attractive financial proposition. Great Britain was enjoying considerable economic growth, the population was increasing and improvements in roads and agriculture were about to precipitate an industrial revolution that would totally transform Britain, and eventually the whole world. At the beginning of the eighteenth century, the British road system was still inferior to the network left by the Romans. It took three days to travel from London to Exeter, or more if there was a contra-flow on the Basingstoke bypass. In 1706 Parliament had passed a Turnpike Act, allowing local businessmen to extract tolls on a section of the main

London to Chester road (the old Watling Street). This precipitated a whole series of entrepreneurial road-improvement schemes, each of them requiring an individual act of Parliament to set up a board of trustees who were allowed to charge tolls where people had previously travelled for free. The 'turnpike' was the barrier at which the toll was collected and hundreds of extremely bored-looking men had to be found to sit in the gatehouses all day to slowly lift the barrier without returning a smile. There was great resentment from locals who were forced to pay to use old byways, even if these roads were now properly paved and had occasional milestones telling you how far it was to the next Little Chef. The toll house was often the first place to be burnt down during any local riot. But thousands of miles of road were built within a very short time.

'I know, shall we lay down gas pipes and cables and everything before we put the road on top?'

'Good idea. I haven't written that down, but I'll definitely remember to tell the contractors.'

Suddenly Britain had some sort of transport infrastructure, people and goods could be easily moved around the country and trade and communications were vastly improved. Stagecoach companies established regular routes and timetables: '8 a.m., leave London for Bath; 12 noon; change horses at Maidenhead; 2 p.m. get held up at pistol point by lone highwayman, who wears mask but looks a ruggedly handsome, rebellious type beneath mask and causes ladies to heave their bosoms and flutter their fans as they coyly hand over priceless pearls.'

The Agricultural Revolution: when the Country Show and Craft Fayre was cutting edge

The new roads were much in demand to transport foodstuffs to London which was rapidly growing to become the largest city in Europe. Thousands of people flocked to London thinking that the streets were paved with gold, when, as we know, they are in fact paved with discarded chewing gum. As Britain's population grew, more and more food was required and the pressure was on for farmers to increase yields. One of the first milestones of the Agricultural Revolution was the invention of the seed drill by Jethro Tull. It is one of the great sadnesses of modern history teaching that classrooms of school students no longer start singing 'Living in the Past' and miming the flute every time the history teacher says 'Jethro Tull'. Now they have to wait until they get to the origins of the First World War and start singing 'Take Me Out' whenever the teacher mentions Franz Ferdinand. But long before he was a hippy folk-rock band, Jethro Tull transformed agriculture with a contraption that planted seeds in orderly lines, making it easier to hoe out the weeds that had previously choked the wheat and barley.* It was *the* must-have Christmas present for farmers in the early 1700s.

'Happy Christmas, darling. Here, I got you an iPod.'

'I don't want an iPod, I wanted a seed drill.'

Up to this point farming methods had changed very little since medieval times when the ancient crop-rotation system had left one field in three fallow to recover after a year growing barley or oats. This was clearly a very inefficient use of available land, unless the farmers were particularly enterprising and managed to hire it out for paint-balling or quad bikes. But now the youngsters were getting into the groovy new methods of crop rotation being imported from Flanders.

'Oh, Dad! Leaving fields fallow is, like, *soooo seventeenth century* . . . We should use the extra field to grow clover or turnips, that's the latest thing; they actually add nutrients to the soil.'

'Ooh, I can't keep up with all this change. First horses replace oxen, then iron ploughs, what will Heathrow Farm be like in two hundred years, I wonder!'

The first commercially successful iron plough had just become widely available, which frankly you'd have thought they would have invented back in the Iron Age. These were now pulled by big power-ful horses, which everyone thought they ought to adorn with lots of

---

* In fact Jethro Tull 'reinvented' the seed drill; a similar device had also been developed in Ancient China.

brass symbols on leather straps, and luckily there happened to be a load of these hanging on the wall of the village pub.

Some historians argue that there was no 'Agricultural Revolution' as such, just a rapid evolution of methods that greatly increased food production. Others insist that the transformation of farming methods in the eighteenth century was every bit as radical as the changes that followed in industry. Then one of the historians gets over-emphatic and starts to prod the other one in the chest, and before long punches are thrown and the police have to be called out.

But one highly significant effect of the Agricultural Revolution was the change it provoked in the role of women in society. With fewer hands needed to work the land, women ceased to toil in the fields alongside the men. The traditional idea of a woman's place being in the home is only a few hundred years old; the social conservatives who hark back to some golden age when the men tilled the fields while the women brought them a ploughman's lunch are describing a world that never existed.* The low status of the ordinary worker would have been obvious from their bronzed skin; before the Industrial Revolution pale skin was a symbol of wealth and status for both sexes as it demonstrated that you were too rich to have to work outside. Today darker skin is more fashionable because it shows that instead of being stuck inside a factory all week, you have been lying on a beach in Lanzarote in a determined effort to get a sun tan and skin cancer.

The South Sea Bubble (*not* a ride at Chessington World of Adventures)

Unsurprisingly the idea of becoming extremely rich for very little effort has always been an attractive one. At regular intervals throughout

---

* The 'Ploughman's Lunch' of course is itself a marketing invention from the 1970s. Very few medieval ploughmen actually stopped work to extract a measly piece of processed cheddar from its polythene before sticking it on a piece of white sliced bread having paid £5.75 for the privilege.

history, completely new investment opportunities have come along seeming to promise easy riches for lazy, greedy people (i.e. all of us). In the late 1990s it was the so-called dot com boom, but in 1720 the hot investment was the South Sea Company, which had been granted a monopoly to trade with the Spanish territories in South America. The government saw a chance to offload some of the national debt, and encouraged people to invest in the company while accepting bribes and taking shares themselves. All over the country, nervous investors were quizzing their financial advisers about this new money-making scheme: 'Hmmm, I'm possibly interested, but tell me, are these investments entirely ethical?'

'Well, it's impossible to invest in stocks and shares and remain purer than pure. Most of the South Sea Company's trade is in abducted African slaves, so, morally speaking, that's one of those grey areas, isn't it? But let me just show you the chart with your projected profit on it . . .'

With the value of shares increasing ten-fold in the course of one year, a kind of investment madness gripped the nation. People mortgaged their houses to put the entire value into the South Sea Company; servants and ordinary tradesmen risked all to grab a slice of the spiralling profits. All sorts of other bizarre investment opportunities were launched; people invested in a scheme to develop square cannon balls and even in one case 'a company for carrying out an undertaking of great advantage, but nobody to know what it is'.

Rather unsurprisingly, an endless supply of free money could not be sustained and in September 1720 the 'bubble' burst; confidence in the shares plummeted; hundreds of thousands of people faced financial ruin; and the country was plunged into a desperate financial crisis. Sir Isaac Newton, who lost twenty thousand pounds in the scheme, commented, *I can calculate the movement of the stars, but not the madness of men*. The government was in disgrace, and the Chancellor of the Exchequer was dismissed from the Commons while another minister did the honourable thing and committed suicide.

There was a great deal of retrospective moralizing and people were reminded that there is no substitute for hard work and that with any venture, you only get out as much as you put in. Except, of course, that you don't always get out as much as you put in: on that basis everyone who entered the National Lottery would win a pound. The slaves who'd been transported by the South Sea Company put in a lot more effort than the investors, but must have been a bit puzzled when they heard people say, 'Remember, the harder you work, the more you'll get out of it.' The reason that we still continue to fall for scams like the South Sea Bubble is that sometimes they *do* come off, sometimes people do reap much more than they sow, while others reap much less. Sadly Jethro Tull never went on to invent a karma seed drill to make sure we all reap exactly the right amount.

Is it a bird? Is it a plane? No, it's Sir Robert Walpole, 1st Earl of Orford, KG, KB, PC

One former Chancellor of the Exchequer had been critical of the scheme from the very beginning, and now was everyone's pick to step in and take over the government. Robert Walpole was a short, twenty-stone Norfolk squire, who was the natural choice to lead the country, and over the next twenty years proved himself to be far more adept at bribery and corruption than all the upper-class idiots who had gone before him.

   Sir Robert Walpole was not the most exciting politician to ever lead the country. His motto was 'Let sleeping dogs lie' but to make it sound duller he said it in Latin. Under his cautious stewardship, there were no exciting wars, no major power struggles between monarch and Parliament, no further financial catastrophes or sordid sex scandals; just a steady rebuilding of prosperity and confidence. He is generally considered to be the first 'Prime Minister' although at the time this phrase was coined for Walpole as a mocking term of abuse. He remains the longest serving 'First Lord of the Treasury'; still the official title of the PM, it is engraved on the front door at 10 Downing Street, which Walpole was the first leader to occupy. On the stairs at Number 10, Walpole's is the first portrait that visitors encounter, before having to endure the likes of Neville Chamberlain,

'Skullface' Douglas-Home and Maggie Thatcher grinning back at them. No wonder the Blair family moved into Number 11.

Walpole wisely chose to remain in the House of Commons, while most of his government were in the Lords. The Commons supported him for over twenty years, because they recognized his outstanding managerial abilities, his firm grasp of economic and diplomatic issues and also because he fixed every general election for his entire time in office. Once at Westminster, MPs were bribed with titular posts and sinecures and sometimes with straightforward handouts of gold. Walpole was the master of the compromise; his solutions rarely excited anyone but worked just well enough so that everyone could live with them. With his government in such competent hands, the King was able to spend more and more time in his beloved Hanover and in 1727 he travelled there for the sixth time never to come back. He suffered a massive stroke and was buried in his homeland. Although the majority of English people thought they would probably get over his demise eventually, his surviving mistress, 'the Maypole' was completely traumatized. When a raven flew into her home shortly after his death, she convinced herself that it was a reincarnation of the dead King; she spent her last days curtseying to the royal bird and trying to understand what his croaks might be saying to her.

George II: der englischer König nicht deutscher

The Prince of Wales had hated his father and by association all his ministers, so it was with some trepidation that Walpole went to wake up the new King with the news that his father was dead and that he was now George II. Walpole struggled to lower his huge weight on to one knee and when he finally managed to convey the news to the stirring king, George was reputed to have shouted, 'Das ist von big lie!' Walpole expected to get sacked by George II (1727–60), but he had taken the trouble to develop good relations with his wife, Queen Caroline. If ever you are at some important function and all the sycophants are trying to grab their two minutes with the boss, spend half an hour chatting to the boss's partner instead, and you'll be the only one they'll talk about on the way home. 'God, he was a sycophantic git; thought he could get on the right side of the Chief Executive by flattering his wife all evening . . .'

Walpole kept his job thanks to the Queen ('I have the right sow by the ear,' he said, rather charmingly) and gradually the new King came to respect and admire him. Walpole's dominance was secured a few years later when his brother-in-law Viscount 'Turnip' Townshend retired from politics to concentrate on his exciting ideas about root vegetables. Townshend had been dismissed as Foreign Secretary because he was not sufficiently cautious in his dealings with foreign powers. Walpole was a good leader for Britain for the very reason he had failed to make much of an impression on the public consciousness. He was determined at all costs to keep Britain out of war. It is one of the injustices of history that diligence and effectiveness seem to register less than foolish military adventures or avoidable political conflict. Anyway, that's enough about Walpole, he was a boring old bastard.

Decades without war created a trading boom that in turn elevated a whole class to a level of wealth that rivalled the aristocracy. The Georgian nouveaux riches bought themselves large estates and coats of arms, and many were eventually admitted into the House of Lords themselves. The established nobility looked down on them, of course, but could not prevent them buying themselves the finest clothes, shoes and the extravagant horsehair wigs that were all the rage in the early 1700s. For some reason no one has informed today's judiciary that these wigs are no longer the height of fashion, and so judges, barristers and the Lord Chancellor continue to wear them.

While the government was happy to help those who already had wealth and influence, for the mass of the populace life was not becoming any easier. At the beginning of the eighteenth century, one in five babies died in their first year, with a third failing to reach the age of five. For their parents life expectancy was around thirty-five, increased mechanization combined with a growing population kept wages low and the gradual drift to the cities did nothing to improve the quality of life or prevent epidemics such as measles and smallpox.

Added to all of this was a particularly unpleasant new killer: gin. In the 1720s low taxes and unrestricted distilling meant that cheap gin had become widely available and the suppliers didn't even bother with the insincere 'Please drink responsibly' tag line at the bottom of their ads. The problem of public drunkenness was a growing worry in Georgian Britain. Today it is almost impossible for us to imagine men and women binge-drinking and fighting in the town centre of a Saturday night, etc. etc., you get the idea, but back in the early eighteenth century it was a serious social problem. What is interesting is that they managed to legislate the problem back to manageable levels by heavily taxing the drink responsible. 'The Abolition of Bacardi Breezers Bill' of 1736 coupled with the 'Blue WKD and Smirnoff Ice Act' of 1751 drastically reduced public drunkenness and alcohol-related illnesses as impoverished drinkers were forced back to beer, which was far less alcoholic and dangerous. It took the brewers another 250 years to come up with Special Brew and Diamond Lite.

But this sort of 'nanny-state' intervention was the exception rather than the rule. On the whole, Britain was a far less regulated and restricted society than most of Europe. Apart from the obvious difference in the power of the monarch in relation to Parliament (which was a source of great national and Protestant pride to the privileged minority who noticed it), Britain's economy benefited from lower taxation, greater social mobility, fewer restrictive practices and less red tape. A trader moving goods around France would have to pay tariffs as he crossed from one region to the next (the equivalent of having a customs barrier at Watford Gap service station). Trade in Britain was unimpeded; you were allowed to bring whisky down from Scotland, along with smoked salmon and shortbread; it was only Catholic armies where they drew the line.

Meanwhile, greater freedom of speech expressed itself with the first national and local newspapers and a boom in satirical theatre and pamphlets. When Daniel Defoe was placed in the stocks for overstepping the mark with a satirical attack on the government, the crowd threw flowers instead of stones and rotten vegetables. The first lending libraries opened around this time, although middle-class parents fretted that their children weren't interested in them: 'The kids are just staring at the Hogarth cartoons, why can't we get them to read any novels?'

'Because the novel hasn't been invented yet.'

'Oh. Hang on, here we are: *Robinson Crusoe* by Daniel Defoe.'*

In fact, the advent of the novel created concerns about young people lying around all day reading when they should have been outside being active or doing something useful. In a hundred years' time, parents will be worrying that their children are not spending long enough on the PlayStation.

The War of Jenkins's Ear: At last, something worth fighting for

The policy that had kept Walpole in power for so long eventually saw him lose office. The country simply got bored with peace, and Walpole was clearly no war leader. Parliament was spoiling for a fight with its Atlantic trading rival Spain, and the excuse finally came in the shape of a shrivelled ear that had formerly belonged to a Captain Jenkins. Its enforced removal had allegedly been carried out by an over-zealous Spanish boarding party who were searching Jenkins's ship for illegally traded goods. The shrivelled ear (by now a few years old) was passed around the House of Commons in a bottle; Members affected outrage at the treatment meted out to an English sea captain by the barbaric Spaniards and so the bizarrely named war began. We should just be grateful that they didn't castrate him or it would have been the 'War of Jenkins's Bollocks'.

Walpole did not leave office gracefully; he attempted to cling to power against all the evidence, even after he had lost a vote of no-confidence in the House of Commons. As Walpole finally took his

---

* The claim to be the first novel in English is of course a fiercely contested one; other contenders are John Bunyan with *The Pilgrim's Progress* (1678), Sir Philip Sidney with *Arcadia* (1581) and a rather weaker claim from Jeffrey Archer with *First Among Equals* (1984).

leave of the King, kneeling and kissing the royal hand, George II burst into tears and was unable to instruct his former minister to rise, and so the bloated politician remained in that position until the King finally recovered himself. Inevitably, the war became more complicated, gaining the far less interesting name of the 'War of Austrian Succession' as Britain found itself dragged into some pointless continental land war caused by Prussia's invasion of Silesia. Now George II's enthusiasm for the military finally came into its own. At the Battle of Dettingen in 1743, he became the last 'English' monarch to lead an army into battle; dressed in his armour sporting the pale-blue colours of Hanover, George led the allied forces to a decisive victory over the French. The Palace's PR department were delighted with the outcome and his popularity greatly increased as a result of the victory. George's decisive leadership, his heroism, his mastery of the battle-field: the King was more than happy to describe any of these features of the battle over and over again to anyone who would listen.

Before long the conflict with Spain became a side-show as the war evolved into a struggle between the traditional enemies of Britain and France. As Austrian armies marched against the Prussians and the British navy fought sea battles with the French and Spanish, Captain Jenkins might have been forgiven for feeling that his original grievance was being somewhat overlooked. 'Shut up about your ear, Jenkins, it's bigger than that now.' The war brought a surge of patriotism to England and Georgian pop-pickers first heard the lyrics of the smash new number-one hit: 'Rule Britannia! Britannia, rule the waves' (note the comma, 'ruling the waves' was an aspiration, not a statement of existing fact). But soon, England would be invaded by a more traditional enemy and another patriotic song would be penned which included a final verse urging Marshal Wade to crush the 'rebellious Scots'. These lines in the sixth verse of 'God Save the King' remain part of Britain's and therefore Scotland's official national anthem.*

---

* The same tune is also used as the Liechtenstein national anthem, and so when England played Liechtenstein in the qualifiers for Euro 2004, the same tune was played twice. Confused England fans didn't know which one to boo.

The Jacobite Rebellion of 1745: last chance to wear tartan till the Bay City Rollers

A British naval defeat (which we prefer not to talk about) had suddenly made a French invasion possible, and with Britain's forces tied up on the continent, a French army assembled in Dunkirk ready to set sail. As so often in Britain's history, the weather was the ally that made all the difference. Perhaps that's why the English are so obsessed by the weather forecast – long before it determined whether or not we planted out the geraniums, the reading on the barometer was often the difference between war and peace. 'And if we look at tomorrow's weather map, we can see a strong wind coming in from the north-east, so if you're planning to sail across the Channel with a massive invasion fleet you might want to leave it till after the weekend . . .'

Waiting with his French hosts was the legendary Bonnie Prince Charlie, leader of the Jacobite cause since his father had retired to spend more time with his malt whisky collection. When the French eventually gave up on the invasion plan, the 'Young Pretender' decided that he would invade without the help of a major European power because that worked so well last time. The Highlanders had high hopes of their new Scottish hero, but were a little perplexed when he landed with half a dozen supporters. And having been raised in France, it appeared that this new ruler of Scotland was every bit as Scottish as cognac itself.

'Bonjour, I am your nouveau King of L'Écosse. Pleeze, why are all ze soldiers wearing ze skirts?'

'Och, those are kilts, your majesty. Traditional dress of your Scottish subjects.'

'So, my army is all, 'ow you say – "ladyboys"?'

The effete Prince Charlie was shocked by what he saw as the unsophisticated savagery of the Highland chieftains, and confidence was not helped with both sides saying, 'Er, I thought you were bringing the army?' But many of the clans still rallied to the cause and the Jacobites marched to Edinburgh where they defeated a government force at Prestonpans.

Suddenly the situation was taken seriously in London. George II was told he ought to come back from Germany and at least pretend he was interested in being King of Great Britain. There was a run on the Bank of England, with the final amounts being paid out in sixpences. In September 1745 Bonnie Prince Charlie crossed the border, bypassed the English army and soon took Carlisle before pressing on for Manchester. Wearing his traditional Scottish regalia of a beret, a stripy shirt and a string of onions, le Bonnie Prince Charlie ordered his forces to march to London, even though many were losing confidence in the whole venture and turning back to the Highlands. The depleted army reached Derby, only 125 miles from an undefended London, and the English establishment was planning its evacuation.

But by this point Charles Stuart had lost the confidence of his men. So many promises about the impending French invasion had failed to materialize and with an English army chasing them, they acrimoniously resolved to head back to Scotland to regroup. The English forces finally caught up with them in the Highlands at Culloden; the last battle ever fought on British soil in April 1746. The exhausted Jacobites were routed and the survivors murdered in cold blood by 'Butcher' Cumberland (the younger son of George II), who ordered his soldiers to bayonet every injured Jacobite lying on the battlefield. The savagery of the English revenge was an indication of the alarm that had been felt within the English establishment, and the whole culture of the clans was thereafter systematically destroyed. Highlanders were forbidden to wear their traditional tartan, to carry daggers or ceremonial swords, and deep-frying Mars bars was definitely out.

But the Stuart claim to the British throne was finally extinguished; the autocratic absolutist monarchy that it represented could never return. In a sense the 'Forty-Five' rebellion was just another front in the War of Austrian Succession; France had subsidized Bonnie Prince Charlie and had been close to invading on his behalf. But although Britain fought with a certain amount of vigour when defending the throne against totalitarian Catholic invaders, by the time they were eight years into the war, the issue of the Austrian

Succession didn't seem quite as important as it had back in 1740.

'Do you know what, Smudger? I'm not sure I'm still that bothered whether the Empress of Austria inherits the Habsburg dominions or not.'

'I know what you mean. When this war was about Jenkins's Ear, you knew what you was fighting for . . .'

The ensuing peace treaty failed to settle the real issue of the mid-1700s: 'Who is top dog in Europe? Is it still France, or is it finally England's turn?' The period between 1688 and 1815 has been called the 'Second Hundred Years War', so protracted was the struggle for supremacy between the two nations. There is of course no roll-call or national memorial for the thousands upon thousands of lives that were lost so that businessmen from one country would have the advantage over traders from another; no appreciation of the enormous human sacrifice or acknowledgement of the suffering during the endless decades of war. Still, at least we beat the French in the end, and that's the main thing.

The Enlightenment: 'Surely Astrology can't survive this'

Despite England's ability to duff up the French on the battlefield or high seas, when it came to the Philosophers' World Cup, the English lads were always the underdogs against the overpaid rationalist superstars of the French or German teams. Immanuel Kant was the captain of a very efficient and highly disciplined German squad while the flair of the French masters Voltaire and Rousseau saw them dominate European abstract thought for decades (except for 1756 when they lost to the Austrians on penalties).

'The Enlightenment' was not an organized movement; people didn't turn up at Benjamin Franklin's house and say, 'Hello, I'd like to join the Enlightenment please.'

'Certainly, here's your application form, we meet on the second Tuesday of the month in the room above the library.'

But it became the height of fashion to apply the power of reason and logic to the laws of both nature and man and to challenge everything that had previously been accepted because of tradition or superstition.

'So these great big curly wigs – you don't think these might be a bit silly, do you?'

'*Au contraire*, 'tis the summit of all logic and reason to stick a great big horsehair wig on your head until you find there's a rat's nest in it.'

The seed for the Enlightenment had been the huge advances made in physics and maths by Sir Isaac Newton, one of the two great minds to come out of Grantham, Lincolnshire. No, actually, the *only* great mind to come out of Grantham, Lincolnshire. Isaac Newton explained the movement of the stars, formulated the laws of motion, developed calculus and invented the refracting telescope. And then people said, 'Oh yeah – you're the apple bloke. How's your head?'

'For the last time, the apple didn't hit me on the head. I observed it in my garden, which prompted me to develop my theory of gravity.'

'Right, so before you invented gravity . . . was everyone just float-ing around, like, trying to grab hold of things?'

Other major British influences came from philosopher John Locke, an early champion of the social contract between government and the governed, and later the political agitator and pamphleteer Thomas Paine, whose writings greatly influenced the American and French Revolutions. Edinburgh-born David Hume was one of the major advocates of 'naturalism' (meaning that he argued against belief in the supernatural, not that he was a creepy fat nudist who played table tennis in the buff). Another Scot, Adam Smith, turned economic theory on its head with his seminal work *The Wealth of Nations*, the proto-capitalist manifesto in which he proposed that the greater good was served by individuals pursuing self-interest (which certainly struck a chord with the millions of slaves being transported across the Atlantic).* The great Mary Wollstonecraft was a prolific

---

* Published in 1776, in the same year as the declaration which created the United States of America, which, by pursuing the philosophy espoused in Smith's book, would become the wealthiest nation ever.

philosopher, historian and author whose work established her as the founder of modern feminism.* If you are a young man about to head off to college it might be worth reading her *Vindication of the Rights of Women*. It may give you an insight into the ways in which women have been oppressed and exploited down the centuries, plus that gorgeous politics student you fancy will be really impressed when you casually drop it into the conversation.

Most of these scientists and philosophers were not atheists but 'deists', believing in one supreme being, but rejecting the organized religions that depended on faith and belief in divine revelation. Everything must be tested and proved; the universe had natural laws and these same principles must be applied to government and society. Organized religion was not without its champions however. Away from the intellectual élites in London and Edinburgh, John Wesley headed a great evangelical revival, doggedly travelling thousands of miles on horseback preaching Methodism to the masses, living a devout and pure life dedicated to God. Rather disappointingly he was never once accused of using money from his collection plate to pay hush money to prostitutes and drug-dealers. Despite the new mood of reason and tolerance, public hostility to Catholicism was never far below the surface. When the government attempted to repeal some of the more extreme anti-Catholic laws on the statutes, the so-called Gordon Riots resulted in around three hundred deaths.

Today it may seem difficult to comprehend the intense hatred felt towards Catholics; we imagine that if we'd been alive then we would never have succumbed to such prejudice and bigotry. But the anti-Catholics weren't simply the equivalent of today's racists, they saw themselves as the defenders of cherished English freedoms and the opponents of the totalitarian monarchies of France and Spain. It would have been quite consistent to consider yourself a liberal and to be against the Catholics; just as many on the left are hostile to all things American. The great poet and artist William Blake was

---

* Mary Wollstonecraft died after giving birth to her second child, who would grow up to become Mary Shelley, author of *Frankenstein*.

actually caught up in the so-called Gordon riots, although his own religious beliefs were slightly more bizarre and complex than the mob shouting 'No Popery'. Often claiming to have had visions of angels or the face of God, Blake himself was involved with an obscure and bizarre religious sect that maintained that Christ has come to England. The words of 'Jerusalem' are generally interpreted as some sort of evocative spiritual allegory, but Blake meant them literally; he really did believe that those feet in ancient times walked upon England's mountains green.

More conventional artists than Blake established the Royal Academy in 1768; among its members were Sir Joshua Reynolds and Thomas Gainsborough, plus a host of other painters featured on your grandparents' table mats. Developments in art were not separate from science in the way that they are today, it was all part of the wider journey to unlock the secrets of nature and the universe. The two came together with the methodical cataloguing and formal categorizing of biological species. Before this point *The Observer's Book of Insects* just had page after page saying, *Insect. Insect. Another insect. Horrible creepy-crawly thing. Pubic louse; at last one we recognize!*

From a little house in Bath, William Herschel discovered the first new planet since ancient times. He sycophantically named it *Georgium Sidus* (George's Star) but following intense lobbying from the Guild of Comedy Writers it was renamed 'Uranus'. While the country was in a logical sort of mood, it had decided that it was high time that Britain's calendar was brought into line with Europe's, with the result that 2 September 1752 was followed by 14 September 1752.* It's sometimes claimed people rioted about the loss of this week and a half, although there is no evidence of this. In fact the cry 'Give us back our eleven days' was meant as a joke. But the great thing about it was that if your child's birthday fell at the beginning of September, it saved you shelling out on any presents. 'Sorry,

---

* Although some other countries in mainland Europe had yet to make the switch too. The date in Greece was eleven days behind everyone else until 1923, while Russia's famous October revolution actually happened in November.

darling, there's nothing we can do. The government's abolished your birthday this year.'

All the great advances in science, maths, culture and philosophy combined to inform political theories and movements which ultimately found their expression in the American Declaration of Independence and the French Revolution. Only now with the benefit of hindsight is it possible to see the true value of the Enlightenment, of the ultimate triumph of reason over superstition. The intellectual and scientific rigour of the age set the benchmark for modern progressive societies; never again would self-indulgent mugs pore over their horoscopes or put their faith in quack medical treatments like crystology, scientology or the gimmicky pseudo-spirituality of herbalism, feng shui, ley lines and other hippy nonsense that apparently cures everything except gullibility. Well, not for a while anyway.

The Seven Years War: 'It'll be over by Christmas'

As war was declared once again, sweethearts kissed their brave soldiers goodbye before they sailed off to some faraway battle.

'Farewell, my darling. Who knows how long this mad war will go on . . .'

'Well, for seven years, clearly. It's the Seven Years War.'

'Till we meet again, whenever that may be . . .'

'Seventeen sixty-three. Seven years from now. It's really not that complicated.'

In fact fighting between French and British colonists in North America had been going on for a couple of years already, and early setbacks along the banks of the Ohio were a warning of greater defeats to come. The war began very badly for Britain. On land, Hanover was overrun by the French, who defeated 'Butcher' Cumberland, while in the Mediterranean Admiral Byng managed to lose the British colony of Minorca. To teach him not to do it again, he was court-martialled and shot. Voltaire jested that the purpose of this execution was *pour encourager les autres.** There was despair in London that Britain looked likely to lose the war, and the public clamoured for the one man they believed could turn around the country's fortunes. It was perhaps the first time that a minister was chosen by overwhelming public demand rather than the fickle patronage of the monarch.

William Pitt was the dominant politician of his age, but his career had previously been damaged by his outspoken criticisms of the King and the fact that Britain's foreign policy was being dictated by the needs of a minor German state that happened to be home to the monarch. But now Pitt became Secretary for War despite the royal family's dislike of this populist commoner. The public believed that Pitt (later called 'Pitt the Elder') was the one man with the strategic vision, energy and determination to turn around the course of the war and, sure enough, under his direction, Britain's fortunes seemed to change dramatically. The comparisons with Winston Churchill have been made by more than one historian.

It was Churchill who observed that the Seven Years War was the first truly global conflict, with colonial rivalries being fought out on four continents. In Europe, North America, Africa and India, European trading rivals fought for the largest market share of the latest business idea – overseas empires. In many cases, the acquisition of colonies was the by-product of a series of entrepreneurial business projects, not the outcome of one strategic national or military policy. It wasn't the British cabinet who decided upon military action in India, but the board of directors of the British East India Company.

'Right, chaps, item seven on the agenda: Mergers and Acquisitions. Clive?'

'Well, shareholders will be pleased to learn that we have completed the leverage buyout of our rivals, the "English Company Trading to the East Indies". Oh, and I should mention one other acquisition. The company is merging with India.'

---

* *To encourage the others* (from *Candide*). Voltaire also summed up Britain's ally Prussia as 'an army with a country attached rather than the other way round'.

'Merging with India?'

'Well, more of a hostile takeover bid actually, but for starters I'll be seeking the board's approval for funding of a small army and the conquest of Bengal in the next financial year.'

'Splendid. So item eight, the Christmas dinner. I thought maybe a curry . . .'

Britain's involvement in India had begun with the establishment of just a handful of small trading posts. But what started out as a few footholds on Indian territory ended up with the Brits completely over-ordering as usual.

'We'll have one Madras please, one Bengal . . . er, and a Bombay . . . And what's a Chota Nagpur?'

'That's a central Indian region, sir, very nice, lots of minerals and timber.'

'Yeah, we'll have one of those. And a Madhya Pradesh, and a Ceylon . . . Oh look, we'll just have the whole lot.'

Robert Clive was an unlikely military hero. He had been a minor clerk with the East India Company, who was so useless with a pistol that an attempt at suicide had failed, leaving him even more depressed than he was before. However, when it came to shooting at other people he was much more successful. In a determined bid for the coveted title of Employee of the Month, Clive secured the massive and lucrative territory of Bengal for the East India Company by an astonishing victory at the Battle of Plassey, in which just a couple of hundred company soldiers defeated the massive army of the local ruler who was supported by the French. Part of the justification for the military adventure was the infamous Black Hole of Calcutta, when captured British and native soldiers were imprisoned in a dungeon so cramped and unventilated that they could barely stand or breathe. The atmosphere wasn't lightened by one joker droning, 'This is Northern Line Information, we apologize for the delay which is due to an incident at Kennington.' Contemporary claims that over a hundred people died in the Black Hole have since been widely discredited, but the propaganda value at the time was enormous and the scandal was seized on by those seeking some moral justification for the actions of the paramilitary wing of the London

Stock Exchange. Now a rich and famous war hero, Robert Clive was promoted to become Governor of Bengal, became a Member of Parliament and then a peer and finally proved his all-round competence when he eventually succeeded in committing suicide, this time using his penknife. He was survived by his pet giant tortoise, which died in March 2006.

France had actually held the advantage in India, but that was now reduced to a few tiny outposts. In North America, however, the French situation seemed more advantageous. With territory in Louisiana and Canada, France was now attempting to hem in the British colonies with a string of forts between the Gulf of Mexico and the Great Lakes. Meanwhile Britain's American colonies were expanding rapidly westwards – it was clearly all going to end in tears. A 23-year-old commander called George Washington was employed to attack the French positions (it's always worth training up the locals – it can only ever help you later on). The key French stronghold was called Fort Duquesne, but once captured it would be renamed after Britain's dazzling war leader to become known as Pittsburgh. But it was in Canada that British forces achieved their most spectacular victory. With Captain Cook doing the map-reading, the English sailed up the St Lawrence River towards the French stronghold of Quebec. This hilltop fort was believed to be completely impregnable, but the heroic Brigadier-General James Wolfe hatched an ambitious plan to sneak his entire army up the sheer cliff face of the Heights of Abraham by night. At dawn the French were astonished to see an army of British redcoats facing them, and Wolfe led his men to a famous victory, though he was killed at the battle's climax. He had read 'Elegy in a Country Churchyard' the night before he died and wished he could have swapped places with Thomas Gray.* But frankly the poet would have been useless scrambling up a cliff face with a heavy gun in the middle of the night, he'd be all 'Don't tread on the flowers! Ouch, I've grazed my knee.' Britain's triumph in

* The verses were probably written in St Lawrence's Church in Upton, which today is not quite as pretty as it sounds in the poem, perhaps because the village has since been swallowed up by Slough.

Quebec and the follow-up victory in Montreal in 1760 ended French hopes of being a colonial force in North America. And if you ever find yourself in Quebec, it's worth asking the locals when exactly the French language ceased to be spoken in Canada.

So if you had to put a precise date to the point in history when Great Britain became top dog in Europe, 1759 would be as good as any. It was at this point, midway through the Seven Years War, when Britain's armies and navy won a string of military victories in different continents around the world, that saw Britain emerge with the coveted title of 'Most Powerful Country'. Pitt was dutifully modest as he accepted the trophy at the Annual Nation and Empire Awards. 'Ladies and Gentlemen, this award doesn't belong to me, but to all the people behind the scenes who worked so hard to make it all possible: Robert Clive, General Wolfe – wish you could've been here, Jim – General Braddock . . . Oh God, I'm bound to forget someone. But thank you everyone, it was a really strong field this year, so we're really proud to have won our first "Impy".' At the same ceremony, Britain also won 'Strongest Colonial Power', 'Best Technical Achievement' and 'Best Monarch Speaking a Foreign Language', while the 'Best Newcomer Award' was collected by Frederick the Great of Prussia.

George III: fluent in English, German and Gibberish

George II died in 1760 at the zenith of Britain's fortunes in the war. The throne passed to George III, who though young and stupid at least had the advantage of having been born in Britain and being able to speak English without sounding like a bad actor from *Colditz*. As George III got older, however, his English became a little harder to understand as the monarch's instructions to his ministers turned into a load of gabbled nonsense. At one point the mad King stopped his coach in Windsor Great Park and rushed off to shake the branch of a tree, whom he insisted was the King of Prussia.

George III (1760–1820) was actually the grandson of George II, the generation in-between as represented by the unfortunate Prince

Frederick having already died after being struck on the head by a cricket ball.* This had left something of a vacuum in young George's life, which was filled by the Scottish peer Lord Bute, who became young George's tutor after 'befriending' his mother Princess Augusta. When George III came to the throne at the age of twenty-three he made his former tutor his First Minister and the English press were aghast at this apparent Scottish takeover of the British government. Pitt meanwhile had resigned, frustrated at his inability to pursue the war as vigorously as he believed was required, and he was later furious that the Treaty of Paris allowed France the return of so many of her possessions. British forces had captured the lucrative sugar-producing colony of Guadeloupe,† the African colony of Senegal and Havana and Manila from Spain. But most of the territories gained in battle were surrendered at the conference table, allowing saloon bar bores to endlessly pontificate: 'See, what happened was, we won the war, but *we lost the peace* . . .'

However, France had been humiliated and her supremacy overturned. The French monarchy had lost its air of infallibility and within a couple of decades they would have lost their heads as well. Pitt is rarely credited as one of the causes of the French Revolution, but his part in the eclipse of France helped seriously undermine the ancient regime and ensure Dr Guillotin a sharp increase in sales of his new invention after 1789. In the peace treaty of 1763, France effectively surrendered her colonial claims in North America, while Britain gained Florida from the Spanish. From the tip of Florida to the uncharted wastes of Northern Canada, the whole Atlantic coastline was British. What could possibly go wrong?

---

* Although the lethal cricket accident has always been widely believed to be the cause of Prince Frederick's death, more rigorous historians claim that this is apocryphal and that he died from complications following an abscess on the lung. However, the abscess on the lung version should be discounted on the grounds that it is nowhere near as interesting.

† Such was the income from the sugar plantations on the island that in the ensuing peace treaty Britain dithered about whether they should let the French have Canada back or the tiny island of Guadeloupe.

The American Revolution: Britain loses War on Terror

The first War on Terror lasted from 1775 to1781. In the American colonies, local insurgents, hell bent on causing anarchy and destruction, began their cowardly attacks on the British peace-keeping forces. As the assassinations and bombings escalated, there were calls for the British government to withdraw its security forces, but despite being thousands of miles from home, the British army bravely refused to cut and run, trying instead to maintain the fragile peace so desperately desired by the vast majority of the peace-loving colonial settlers. In the warped mind of the extremists, they might have imagined themselves to be fighting some sort of 'heroic war of independence', but by any of the standards applied in the West today, the actions of those extremist militias was terrorism, pure and simple.

Of course such a biased and one-sided version of an independence struggle would never be tolerated these days, but these were the terms in which the British government saw the treasonous actions of the American rebels. And to begin with so did many of the American colonists. Most people making their way in the vastly different plantations had no burning desire to break away from Britain. They didn't like paying taxes but this was hardly unprecedented. There was no sense of 'American patriotism'; their strongest sense of identity was defined by the fact that they were European rather than 'Indian', and some had fought with Britain against the French a dozen years earlier. But in the decade after the Seven Years War, when Britain was riding high as the supreme colonial power, the arrogance and high-handed incompetence with which Britain treated her most significant colony pushed the moderate majority into seriously contemplating the previously whacky idea that the colonies could actually break away and simply declare themselves an independent country with no king, even if they were just a collection of loosely connected states with a system of government that no one had quite worked out yet.

In fact, given the small number of radicals at the beginning of the decade, and the apparently unassailable position of Great Britain at the end of the Seven Years War, it really was quite a monumental achievement to succeed in losing the greatest part of the British Empire so soon after having secured it. The British Prime Minister during this period was Lord North, a loud, enormous old Etonian, with bulging eyes and fat lips. He was the first Tory to get the job for a generation, and owed his position to his friendship with the King. Despite being somewhat intellectually challenged, George III had ideas about being his own First Minister and so Lord North was in the difficult position of explaining complex diplomatic or economic issues to brainless George, only to find himself thinking that the King's proposed course of action would surely make things worse. Even so it never even occurred to Lord North that this crackpot idea of an independent United States of America would ever come to anything. His family home is today occupied by American students studying abroad.

The road to war (avoiding toll)

The American Revolution was far from inevitable. Like everything in history except the death of Diana, the causes are complex and varied. But more than liberty, freedom and the pursuit of happiness, it was about tax returns. The snappy slogan coming out of the American colonies was 'No taxation without representation'. The simple argument was that if the colonies were being taxed by London, then they should have a voice in the British Parliament. American school history books might portray the war as a heroic stand for democratic principles, but we should remember that, just as in England, the moneyed classes were only interested in representation for themselves; none of them was advocating universal suffrage or votes for women.* The man who wrote 'All men are created equal' had the time to do this because all his slaves were earning him money back on his estate.

---

* Pennsylvania did draw up a state constitution that allowed universal white suffrage, but this was soon reverted to requiring a property qualification.

But the British government reacted to such demands with high-handed contempt, always opting for punitive measures when dialogue would have been more fruitful. Clearly there was some sort of culture clash going on here. If the Americans had said, 'Excuse me, I'm awfully sorry to trouble you, old chap, but would it be at all possible to have a tax rebate; I know it's a bore, but I'd be most frightfully grateful . . .' then everything could have been sorted out between gentlemen. The trouble was the Yanks shouted, 'Hey, buster, gimme a tax rebate!'; the English bristled at their rudeness and all-out war became inevitable.

The British government had thought long and hard about what might be the stupidest tax they could levy, and had come up with a tax on paper and documents. 'Yes, that'll work well. The editors are a bit critical of us at the moment, so I'm sure they'd appreciate a tax on their newspapers.' In fact, the so-called Stamp Tax, the levy that was to precipitate the total breakdown of relations between Britain and her colonies, was barely debated in the House of Commons; it was absent-mindedly voted through a thinly attended Parliamentary session without a second thought by a few drowsy MPs. But in the debating chambers of the colonies it was fiercely resisted. The very Whig ideas that the Americans had inherited from the mother country were now being thrown back at the English, whose ideas of liberty and Parliamentary representation clearly were not on the approved list of English exports.

Massachusetts was the most troublesome colony and so in 1769 the British sent a fleet to Massachusetts in a show of strength to anyone who was thinking of spelling Boston Harbour without the 'u'. The British redcoats (nicknamed 'bloodybacks') pitched their tents in the town and tensions grew between local lads and the squaddies. And then it snowed and one or two threw a few snowballs at British sentries, and – isn't it always the way? people get over-excited and go too far – the growing crowd started chucking lumps of ice as well, then bits of wood and rocks and, rather predictably, the soldiers responded to a baying and dangerous-looking mob by firing their muskets at them. Five locals were killed, sending shockwaves throughout the colonies. Every year on the anniversary of the '1770

Boston Massacre' the event is re-enacted by the Boston Society. Not with live bullets obviously, though the National Rifle Association is working on it.

The moderate Americans were struggling to defend British rule. Even though the Stamp Act was repealed, a tax on tea remained to signal the right of London to tax the colonies. A boycott of tea had some impact, but frankly, hardened pioneers of the wild frontier weren't really the type for camomile and fennel infusion. And so the Americans discussed how else this might be most effectively opposed. The moderates tried their best to explain their seventeen-point plan for renegotiation of customs duties but the other idea was easier to grasp. 'I say we storm the British ships in the docks and chuck all the English tea into the harbour!'

'Sorry, I hadn't finished explaining the fifteenth point yet—'

'Yeah, chuck the tea in the harbour!' shouted everyone in the meeting.

'Dressed as Red Indians!'

'Chuck tea in the harbour dressed as Red Indians? What sort of nutty policy is this?'

But sometimes an insane and pointless act is exactly what a political movement needs to stir things up a bit. So with a couple of moderates still shaking their heads in disbelief, the mob disguised themselves as Mohawk Indians (in the hope that they would not be identified), stormed on to three British ships and poured ten thousand pounds' worth of tea over the side. The 'Boston Tea Party' was a triumph for the Radicals, an act of enormous defiance with no loss of life.* The British were losing the PR war. What they really needed was a reporter down on the shoreline, giving moving accounts of the ecological disaster that this massive tea spill represented for local marine wildlife: 'This poor gannet is coated in Lapsong Souchong; that stranded otter's fur is thick with Earl Grey. The smell of bergamot is overpowering.'

Instead the British Government responded with more punitive

---

* Although many moderates were still shocked by such destructive behaviour. Benjamin Franklin offered to repay the cost of the tea out of his own pocket.

measures; a little clue to their attitude to American behaviour can be found in the name of the 'Intolerable Acts'. The punitive bills angered the colonists yet further, who began organizing military units. In April 1775 a stable boy in Boston overheard British soldiers intimating that tomorrow was going to be the day that they captured the rebels' arsenal, and he slipped away and told Paul Revere, a leading figure in the local Patriots. Paul Revere rode through the night, knocking on doors in every town that he passed through, warning everyone of the impending British action. The news spread like wildfire, church bells rang as a warning and the next morning American forces were ready for miles around. Another bloke called William Dawes rode out the same night in the other direction but, lacking the charisma and popularity of Paul Revere, everyone just said, 'Go away, it's the middle of the night', and so poor William Dawes is completely forgotten to history.

The British force came face to face with fewer than a hundred men from the Massachusetts militia. The British commander shouted, 'Disperse, you rebels, damn you, throw down your arms and disperse!' The American commander looked at the rows of heavily armed professional soldiers and then duly told his men to disperse. But some refused and most held on to their arms. The Americans had been instructed not to fire the first shot and the British commander was not keen to repeat the disaster of the Boston Massacre. But then came *the shot heard round the world*.* No one knows who fired it; most witnesses agree that it wasn't from the two sides facing one another, it was believed to have come from someone watching nearby. Maybe it was just an early car backfiring, but whatever the loud bang was, it was enough to start the American War of Independence. The Battles of Lexington and Concord were tiny skirmishes in military terms, but enough damage was inflicted on the British to give heart to the rebels, and the war had begun.

---

* The line comes from the 'Hymn of Concord' by Ralph Waldo Emerson, though the phrase was used again for the shot that killed Archduke Franz Ferdinand, precipitating the outbreak of World War One.

'War! Huh! What is it Good For?' (*Answer: Achieving freedom, justice and the creation of a new nation that would come to shape the whole future of mankind. Next question?*)

Unfortunately for the British, this was one war that the Americans didn't turn up late for. A 'Continental Congress' was held at Philadelphia, which appointed George Washington as overall commander of the American forces, a canny choice since the General had fought with the British and knew their strengths and weaknesses, plus he was supposed to have wooden false teeth which is always useful if you need a bit of kindling.* The General never had more than twenty thousand soldiers under his command at any one time; a fraction of the male population of fighting age, while the professional English army was reinforced with German mercenaries and negro slaves promised freedom if they left the American plantations to join with the British (a promise that was generally broken).

Britain's General Howe twice had the chance to capture Washington's army and win the war but failed to press home his advantage.

Washington had been stuck in New York City, and felt incredibly vulnerable, as anyone who has got lost in the Bronx after dark will understand. Food supplies were running low; sometimes the Americans' breakfast was only five waffles with cream and syrup on top. In a bold move recreated in the famous painting by Emanuel Leutze, Washington escaped across the Delaware River. In the picture the packed rowing boat features the future President standing up at the bows, which may look majestic but is actually really annoying if you are trying to row. The painting should be called 'George, sit down, you're making it really wobbly'.

By this point the Americans were fighting for more than just their rights under the British Crown, they were fighting for total independence for the thirteen colonies,† for the creation of a whole

---

* In fact Washington's false teeth were not made from wood, but from the teeth of elk and hippos.
† The Americans had invited the French Canadians to join them as a fourteenth colony, but were rebuffed. A different outcome at that meeting might have eventually resulted in the whole of North America being subsumed into the United States.

new country. The Declaration of Independence, signed on 4 July 1776, was a bold move so early on in the war, and alarmed many in the colonies. But it was a military necessity as well as a political aspiration. Why should France come and support some far-off rebels fighting for fairer taxation? But to see Britain lose the best part of her Empire was a cause worth supporting. The Declaration of Independence was a huge political gamble by colonial leaders fearing annihilation by British military superiority; a call to European powers to come to their aid. But it was a step too far for thousands of colonials. Many switched to the British side, many more left America for Nova Scotia or British possessions in the West Indies. But when the Americans scored a significant military victory at Saratoga, France was indeed persuaded to join the war, followed by Spain and Holland, leaving Britain hopelessly isolated.

With this war being fought three thousand miles from home the state of the British navy was crucial. Unfortunately the man in charge of the navy seemed more interested in gambling and playing cards than ensuring that British ships were in a fit state to fight a protracted war. I shall be remembered as the man who held on to the American Colonies, he thought. Forever more, my name shall be synonymous with British naval triumph and imperial glory. 'Now bring me a slice of ham between two slices of bread,' demanded Earl Sandwich. The savoury snack solution was a huge success. British naval strategy was a disaster. The Battle of Chesapeake Bay in 1781 was the last British naval defeat during the entire imperial age. Suddenly Earl Sandwich sat up and took notice. 'Chesapeake Bay? Now that would be a splendid name for a type of retriever.'

It was the temporary loss of control of the seas that proved decisive; until that point America had been helpless to prevent British warships blocking supplies while British forces could be moved up and down the Atlantic seaboard with ease. The French navy had improved greatly since the debacle of the Seven Years War, when it had consisted of two tatty fishing boats, some pedalos and a lilo. Now that the French navy could prevent the redeployment of British troops while supplying soldiers herself, the balance of the war shifted away from Britain. At Yorktown, Virginia, in 1781 came the decisive action of the war. Trapped in a narrow peninsula, the British army was outnumbered two to one by French and American troops, while the English escape route was cut off by French warships. The English held out hoping to be evacuated, but eventually they were forced to capitulate. The British commander attempted to surrender to the French general, who politely directed him towards the American George Washington. The story goes that the English soldiers marched to their surrender while their band played 'The World Turned Upside Down'.

When Lord North heard the news he shouted, 'It's all over, it's all over . . .' Two years later, under the terms of the Treaty of Paris, Britain and the 'United States of America'* formally acknowledged that 'by the grace of God and in the year of Our Lord 1783, we the undersigned hereby acknowledge that you say "pyjamas" and we say "pajamas", that you say "tomartoes" and we say "tamatas" and that furthermore, we should call the whole thing off.' George Washington became America's first president six years later and set the standard for virtuous and devoted public service that survives to this day.

The loss of the American colonies was a terrible blow to the British government. They could have little idea that the United States of America would one day become a key ally in two world wars and go on to produce seven series of *The West Wing* and *The Simpsons*, making it all worth it in the long run. Lord North lost a vote of no confidence in the House of Commons, while George III drafted a letter of abdication, though he never actually went through with it.

In France, King Louis XVI was delighted that his backing had been the decisive factor in bringing about this republican revolution. 'Ha! That'll teach the English King! And make sure everyone here in France gets to hear about how clever I was; helping those republicans overthrow their monarch!' Six years later, partly inspired by the success of the Americans and their ideals, French revolutionaries overthrew the *ancien régime*. The spread of republicanism to Europe would precipitate a twenty-year war and the final climax of seven

* This name had first been proposed by Thomas Paine.

hundred years of Anglo–French rivalry as Britain finally emerged as unquestionably the world's dominant imperial, naval and economic power. The only war that Britain lost during its period as top dog led to the creation of the country that would eventually replace it.

Pitt the Younger: Cub Scout, School Prefect, Prime Minister

The most likely candidate for Prime Minister to replace the disgraced Lord North was now the maverick Whig Charles James Fox, an extravagant larger-than-life radical who was openly critical of the monarchy and thus was hated by George III. Fox was a Parliamentary giant who deserves a greater place in the British national consciousness; a politician ahead of his time who argued against slavery, in favour of American independence and against the war with revolutionary France. In order to block this dangerous leftie, the King asked twenty-four-year-old William Pitt to become his Prime Minister since he had done such an excellent job as Milk Monitor. William's unemployed college friends found this appointment by the King particularly galling: 'As I said, it's who you know.' The son of the heroic war leader was mocked in the House of Commons and laughingly called a schoolboy but taunts about his immaturity soon disappeared as his administration demonstrated his fierce intelligence (plus his mum had gone in during half-term and had a word with the Speaker about bullying). Pitt remains the youngest Prime Minister Britain has ever had. He actually had an older brother who must have dreaded seeing the relatives at Christmas. 'I see your younger brother is already Prime Minister? And what are you doing with yourself, John?'

George III's mother had told him, 'Be a *king*, George,' which may seem an obvious suggestion since he was never likely to go into data-processing, but what she meant was that he should reassert the royal privileges that had lapsed under his two predecessors.

Pitt's appointment by the King did not have the support of the House of Commons but there was not much that they could do about it. Pitt lost a motion of no confidence but he chose to ignore it; he still had the support of the King. However, this position was less sustainable once George III started barking at the moon. It became vital to Pitt's survival that people didn't realize that the monarch was now as mad as a bucket of frogs.

'So how is our King this morning, Mr Pitt?'

'Never better, Mr Fox. Tip-top health. Most kind of you to ask.'

'He's not been chatting to any trees recently?'

'Trees? Oh, that! Yes, well, to be fair, you've not met the King of Prussia. He does look quite "tree-like". Easy mistake to make . . .'

'And I understand that his urine is green* and he is now tied up in a straitjacket?'

''Tis the height of fashion, Mr Fox. Green wee, white straitjacket, mouth clamp, large electrodes attached to the frontal lobes . . . Our cousins in Paris wear little else this season . . .'

In the early years of his ministry Pitt appeared to be quite progressive. In response to demands for fairer Parliamentary representation, he introduced a bill that would have curtailed the corrupt practice whereby Members of Parliament bought their seats in Parliament, leaving them to represent an empty field with just one constituent who the pedants pointed out was actually a scarecrow. The measure failed to get enough support from all the MPs from these so-called rotten boroughs, but marked Pitt out as a promising enlightened reformer. But amazingly, and some people today might find this hard to imagine, this particular politician started out seeming quite liberal but then shifted alarmingly to the right once he was in office. Within a decade, campaigners for political reform were being imprisoned without trial, while Irish nationalists were joining petty thieves on the twelve-thousand-mile journey to the new penal colonies of Australia.

Australia was founded as a rather larger than necessary open prison in 1788. The idea of an enormous land mass on the under-

---

* The fact that George III's urine was green has led modern opinion to hypothesize that he may have been suffering from porphyria. However, this is still only a theory, even though it is now often treated as fact.

neath of the globe added to the feeling that the world was being turned upside down. The uncharted land mass had been claimed for Great Britain eight years earlier by Captain Cook, who declared, 'I shall name this land "New South Wales" as the unspoiled virgin landscape reminds me of the coke-smelting works at Port Talbot.' Convicts had previously been exported to the American colonies, so Australia was established as a replacement for one of the more bizarre solutions to prison overcrowding to have been undertaken by the British government. The latest psychological theories held that criminals behaved the way they did because of deficiencies in their brain that were passed down through the generations. Members of the government genuinely believed that if the 'criminal class' was removed from Britain altogether then crime could be eradicated. Desperately cruel prison camps were created, where half-starved, overworked and abused convicts planned their revenge on the mother country by teaching their kids cricket, in order that they might regularly thrash England two hundred years later.*

Other colonial possessions were secured during this period. 'OK, so we've lost America. But look on the bright side, we've gained the Falkland Islands!' The American War could have been an even bigger disaster for Britain, but having given up on the colonies by 1781, British forces managed to hold off Spanish attempts to recapture Jamaica and Gibraltar, while English possessions in India and Canada resisted renewed French assaults.

But it was industry as much as empire that gave Britain the edge as it approached the end of the century. The world was about to be transformed, both socially and politically, and so in the late 1700s a few dignitaries gathered for the formal unveiling of the official plaque. There were a couple of speeches and then the King said, '. . . And so it gives me great pleasure to announce that we have now entered "The Modern Era".' He pulled open the little curtain, there was a light smattering of applause, and then millions of country folk

---

* In fact the rules for cricket were first written down in 1744: the Marylebone Cricket Club was founded a few months ahead of the colony of Australia to give us a bit of a head start.

picked up a few belongings and abandoned the countryside where they had been farming ever since Neolithic times.

The Industrial Revolution: the end of the world starts here

There is a presumption that, as history progresses, each generation experiences more change than the last; that not only is the rate of change ever faster, but that the actual degree of change is greater and greater with each passing century. Just look at the difference between children growing up now and their parents, we think. Today's kids have mobile phones and play computer games. Their parents had to use the house phone and play board games.* Incredible! In fact, recent generations have seen very little fundamental change during a prolonged period of peace and relative prosperity. Compare the stability of our own lifetime to the experience of someone born in 1760; they witnessed the entire transformation of their world from an agricultural society to an industrial one; after a thousand years in the same rural district their family moved from the countryside to some strange, rapidly growing city; they were answerable to a factory-owner instead of the local aristocracy; suddenly they had soot all over their faces instead of cow dung.

The origins of the Industrial Revolution are complex and disputed, but there are a few factors that historians come back to again and again. The great Eric Hobsbawm cites the growth in markets both in terms of Britain's domestic population explosion and the increasing access to overseas markets. The environmental determinists assert that it was the geographical proximity of northern England's coal reserves and iron ore to the established crafts such as gunsmithing and clockmaking that was the key to the Industrial

---

* Today's children are corrupted by all those horrible shooting and killing games in downtown Los Angeles, whereas in our day, entertainment was far more gentle and refined as Professor Plum went into the billiard room and was smashed over the skull with a candlestick.

Revolution taking off in Britain. Whereas my mum told me that the Industrial Revolution occurred because it was always raining: 'In hot countries you just go to the beach or play tennis, but in England you're stuck inside the garden shed, fiddling around trying to invent things.'

Britons might certainly allow themselves a little pride that the Industrial Revolution began here. The most fundamental change of human life in recorded history and it originated in Great Britain. Was it the creativity of British citizens? Was it the culture of social mobility and hard work that came from England's unique political freedom? Was it a religious belief system that promoted hard work, innovation and liberty? Whatever the many causes, we can pat ourselves on the back and think it's all thanks to us. And eventually the rest of the world followed Britain's lead; the global population exploded too, as did the burning of fossil fuels, and the destruction of the forests, and the polluting of the rivers and the fields, which will imminently be followed by the dramatic rising of sea levels, which will flood millions of square miles, creating death, famine, war and global meltdown. Well, obviously England just happened to be where it occurred first, I mean it could have been anywhere.

Of course James Hargreaves had no idea what he and others were starting when he invented his new multi-spool spinning wheel in 1764: 'Jenny darling, look what I've invented. I've named it the "Spinning Jenny", after you, my love!'

'You've named an automated spinning wheel after me?'

'Isn't that lovely?'

'What? So thanks to your invention, hundreds of textile-workers will become unemployed; huge factories will blight the landscape; children will be forced to slave in the mills for a pittance or pull coal carts underground until they are too ill from pneumoconiosis and millions will become dehumanized and die young and YOU WERE GOING TO NAME THE CAUSE OF IT ALL AFTER ME? Well, thank God you haven't sent off the patent yet.'

'Um, yeah, well, about that . . .'

Other key developments of the time had been the 'flying shuttle' (1733), invented by John Kay, and the Spinning Frame (1769) credited to Richard Arkwright, which he explained *employs a series of high-speed rollers to draw out the roving, before applying the twist via a bobbin-and-flyer mechanism*. At which everyone stared blankly, passed their teenage sons the instruction manual and asked them to work it out. The inventions were of course all prompted by the same simple motive: increasing profit. Maximizing production meant greater income in relation to wages paid out, and Richard Arkwright's Spinning Frame made him one of the richest men in England, even though he nicked the idea off someone else. These were all developments in the textile industry, which led the way in the growth of mechanization in other areas. But perhaps the most significant breakthrough was James Watt's steam engine, which was patented in 1769. The story goes that James Watt looked at the steam coming from the spout of a kettle and had a flash of inspiration.

'Eureka! That boiling kettle has given me an idea for an incredible new invention!'

'I know what you're thinking . . . a kettle with built-in water filter?'

'No, no; see the way the pressure builds up in the cylinder but is released through the spout—'

'Yes, yes, I see what you are saying. A kettle with a see-through section telling you how many cups of tea you can make . . .'

Sadly the story of James Watt being inspired by the kettle is a fairy tale, he merely improved earlier steam engines that had kept breaking down just after the extended warranty had run out. Like the Egyptians who had invented a primitive steam engine but only used it as a novelty executive toy, the Georgians didn't quite realize what they had stumbled upon. The mechanism that would power the whole Industrial Revolution was initially only used for pumping water from flooded mineshafts, but soon the steam engine would be powering everything: factory machinery, trains, boats and a little Mecchano traction engine that trained small boys to play with matches and bottles of meths.

To feed these machines, coal production multiplied four-fold in the second half of the century. Like every other measurable statistic, there is an almost horizontal line for hundreds of years, then a gentle increase at the beginning of the 1700s until the middle of the century when on every graph the y axis suddenly goes sky high. Population growth, miles of road, iron production, tonnes of shipping, miles of canals, number of sites for future industrial heritage museums: it all goes mad at the end of the eighteenth century.

Sir Richard Arkwright was just one of the new capitalist entrepreneurs growing extremely rich by the building of factories and mills. The factory-owners were very easy to spot as they were fat, and had big top hats and a cruel laugh that could be heard whenever they counted the enormous profits they made from using small children as fuel for their monstrous furnaces. Sometimes a poor country girl would come to one of them begging for work, and he would kiss her roughly and then throw her out on to the street with a menacing laugh as the girl pulled her shawl over her face in shame and told the orphans in her care not to give up hope. The cliché of the heartless factory-owner endures because it was a time when exploitation was incredibly easy. Large-scale industrialization had simply never existed before and so there were no rules by which it was governed. Even during the centuries of exploitation in the countryside, the aristocrats might occasionally have felt some sort of paternalistic responsibility towards the well-being of the peasants in their parish, but now the labourers were simply anonymous units who had arrived from different parts of the country, not known to their employers or their fellow workers. The Industrial Revolution happened without rules or regulation and it was half a century before anyone began to listen to the busybody liberal do-gooders asking if children's emotional and intellectual development was best served by working in steam-powered textile mills for sixteen hours a day.*

Yet still people came in their hundreds of thousands. Increasing mechanization in the fields drove down wages in the countryside, and if a few pennies more could be earned in the factories then it's

---

* The first Factory Act of 1802 said that young children could not work before six a.m. and after nine p.m., but since there was no record of births many factory-owners (or desperate parents) lied about children's ages. In any case there was no system of factory inspection set up, so the law went largely ignored.

not surprising that those living in rural poverty felt that they had no choice. And so wives flicked through glossy property magazines, going on about how the countryside was no place to bring up the children: 'Look at this darling, "Compact tenement building for rent, recently built next to sulphur-processing plant; two bedrooms, would suit three families with eight children each. All rooms have cold running water (down the walls), excellent ventilation via holes in roof and commanding views over the cesspit." And look, there's an article on life in the city. What's "rickets?" I wonder? Maybe it's the name of the local health club.'

Living conditions were incredibly harsh following the Industrial Revolution, but in pure financial terms, people were slightly better off. Life in the country hadn't been all scattering seeds in the sunshine, collecting warm eggs from fresh hay and then sitting around a glowing fire of an evening making corn dollies. People had been desperately poor, hungry and susceptible to disease. Now they were slightly less desperately poor, a bit less hungry and susceptible to a whole range of fascinating new diseases. In fact, improvements in medical science helped the population grow by about three million people in the second half of the century, and now the ordinary worker could expect to live to the ripe old age of thirty-nine. In the larger towns where previously only ten thousand chamber pots had been emptied out on to the street, suddenly the streets were running with the raw sewage of a hundred thousand people. Buying a Glade air freshener just didn't seem to make any difference.

As the chaotic sprawl of industrialization threw up new cities – Manchester, Glasgow, Birmingham and Liverpool – gradually the urban citizens would come to realize their collective power and press for better wages, humane working conditions and eventually residents' parking. Towards the end of the eighteenth century, as the Industrial Revolution began to really gather pace, the possibility of a major political uprising was a constant fear. Especially after the unforeseen rebellion that had already stripped the British of their American colonies, while over in France the whole political order was about to be turned upside down by a bloody revolution which would send shockwaves around the world and ultimately lead to terror, war and Michael Ball starring in *Les Misérables*.

The French Revolution: 'liberty, equality, military dictatorship'

In a sense the French Revolution is an interesting model for what might have occurred in Britain had the Stuarts won their battles with Parliament and an absolute monarchy survived. In the year of the storming of the Bastille, the Whigs celebrated the centenary of England's Bill of Rights, in which Parliament had established its supremacy over the monarchy. Throughout the following century the unusual political liberty enjoyed in Britain was a source of great pride to the English upper and middle classes, whose social and economic freedoms were a major factor in creating the roads, the machines and the factories that made Britain even richer. France had a political revolution partly because it lacked the very freedoms that had allowed Britain to have its own revolutions in industry, agriculture and transport. Obviously this wasn't the conscious reason why the French rose up; their cry wasn't for '*Liberté, égalité et une Spinning Jenny comme les anglais.*' But a century after England's 'Bloodless Revolution', the bankrupt French monarchy finally called a meeting of the French Parliament (which had last met in 1614) and was alarmed to discover that helping the King raise more money was not the only thing on the agenda. Four years later when his head was on the guillotine Louis XVI said, 'Do you know, I'm beginning to wish I'd never called that meeting of the États généraux'.

Of course there had been peasant uprisings before, but this was different. The soldiers guarding the King's palace looked through their telescopes and realized that this was no ordinary rabble: 'Look out, lads, it's worse than we thought! They've got . . . philosophy books!'

'Oh no, now we're sunk. Once they start quoting Diderot, Rousseau and Voltaire at us, the whole platoon will be trapped in an impossible philosophical paradox.'

This revolt wasn't just about the price of bread, it quickly escalated into a challenge about the whole nature of the government, the relationship of the individual to the state, the meaning of religion, even how illogical it was to have twelve months a year – it became a revolution about *everything*.

The English government were quick to respond to the tumultuous events across the Channel. The cabinet heard about it, tutted, and then carried on playing whist. But many in England were thrilled by what was happening. Wordsworth* later wrote:

> *Bliss was it in that dawn to be alive,*
> *But to be young was very heaven!*

Fox described the storming of the Bastille as by far *the greatest event . . . that ever happened in the world*, even if Edmund Burke predicted in 1790 that *some popular general will establish a military dictatorship in place of anarchy*. It took a couple of years for Pitt to realize that this high-spirited disturbance in Paris was actually quite a big deal. By the summer of 1791, the politics of the Revolution had swung sharply to the left† and hopes that the French were aspiring to a British-style constitutional monarchy were evaporating. In 1792 the monarchy was abolished and France declared a republic. Finally in January 1793, Louis XVI was publicly executed and his severed head held up before a cheering crowd. The royalists grudgingly conceded this was 'a setback' and set about updating the souvenir Louis and Marie Antoinette dolls at the Versailles Palace gift shop.

The stylish and extravagant French monarchy had been trend-setters for centuries, but this was one fashion that the crowned heads of Europe were less keen to follow. The British establishment was deeply shocked by the execution of a monarch, despite the fact that the English had chopped the head off their own King a century

---

* The undergraduate Wordsworth had actually been on a walking holiday in France in 1790 and saw events at first hand. On his second visit the following year he did his bit for Anglo-French relations by getting a French girl pregnant.
† Our concepts of 'left-wing' and 'right-wing' come from the French Revolution. Opponents of the Revolution sat on the right of the Assembly, radicals on the left.

and a half earlier. But their moral outrage was of course the cover for another emotion: they were terrified that they might be next.

The French Revolutionary Wars: not as pretty as they look in the paintings

The two nations came to this war from very different perspectives. The idealistic French wanted to export liberty, equality and fraternity; the English wanted to export tea towels. British textile manufacturers needed Holland, but before long the revolutionary forces had invaded and occupied the Low Countries and with their radical democratic ideas were greeted as liberators by the common people. This would be a new type of conflict; France was a whole nation at war and the numbers on the battlefields would be like nothing that had ever been seen before. The French soldiers also possessed a new secret weapon: conviction. Here was an army no longer populated by cynical mercenaries fighting for a week's pay and whatever they could steal along the way; all across Europe the French soldiers marched with enthusiastic idealism. The paintings of the time show the revolutionary soldiers sporting the tricolour of the Revolution, as the attractive female figure of Liberty led the way, inspiring the soldiers to the noble ideals of freedom and justice by having her bosoms falling out of her top. The French revolutionaries conquered most of Europe but it seems they still couldn't find a lady's blouse with securely sewn-on buttons.

In response to the French declaration of war, Britain brought together a 'First Coalition', an invincible line-up of all the major Western European powers whose experienced armies and pro-fessional soldiers would surely soon overwhelm these amateur revolutionaries. About five minutes later the alliance fell apart as each member went off and pursued its own agenda. Prussia used the crisis to expand its territories further; the Germans' surprise pact with Russia and their subsequent partition of Poland was a trick they would repeat again in 1939. Austria followed suit, hoping for a slice of Poland themselves,* while Holland and Spain would become puppet states of the French leaving Britain standing alone.

However, four years after the fall of the Bastille many royalists still held out against the Revolution. In 1793, a royalist uprising in Toulon was assisted by a British naval presence until a young Corsican artillery lieutenant named Napoleon Bonaparte succeeded in capturing the key Mediterranean port. In Paris his name was noted, and he was marked out for possible promotion. However, the post of 'Emperor of France, King of Italy, Mediator of the Swiss and Protector of the Confederation of the Rhine' was not one of the jobs on the list.

In 1794, the political situation in Paris took an ugly turn for the worse, establishing the traditional template for the next stage of most revolutions, whereby anybody who is vaguely interesting or out-spoken gets taken out and killed. It's a disturbing thought that in the unlikely event of a British revolution, those apparently harmless students selling Socialist Worker outside Woolworths would start off by executing the Prime Minister but would end up shooting Stephen Fry, Alan Bennett and Dame Judi Dench simply for being too popular. The mass executions of the so-called 'Terror' turned liberal British opinion against the Revolution, allowing everyone to go back to the far more comfortable position of simply being prejudiced against the French.

Some of the more curious mementoes from the French Revolution were assembled by Madame Tussaud, who used her skill as a wax modeller to create death masks of the countless victims of the guil-lotine which she brought to England in 1802. The mass executions were her inspiration for the famous 'Chamber of Horrors', and thanks to her we can still imagine being in the middle of the Terror, which clearly involved queuing for ages and paying well over the odds to look at a load of disappointing wax dummies.

The shocking accounts of the Terror made it even easier for the British government to become increasingly repressive and, following

---

* 'Austria' here of course means the massive Austro-Hungarian Empire, a major central European power, not to be confused with today's economy skiing destination.

decades of progress and liberalization, the atmosphere in Britain became markedly more reactionary. Opposition to the government or its pursuit of the war was interpreted as support for the extremists in France and often resulted in imprisonment without trial after habeas corpus was suspended in 1794. This had always been one of the key tenets of English liberty, that a person could not be arrested and held without charge, but now the authorities had the legal freedom to imprison peaceful advocates of democratic change.

A couple of years earlier Tom Paine's *Rights of Man* had sold a staggering two hundred thousand copies, but in the hysterical anti-Republic clampdown he was forced to flee to France to escape jail (where he was elected to the National Convention, opposed the execution of Louis XVI and ended up in a French jail instead).* Public meetings were banned, while the Combination Act made it illegal to form political societies or associations, which made the nascent trade unions illegal and led to the enforced break-up of countless Corresponding Societies (a sort of eighteenth-century chat-room that exchanged musings about the exciting developments in France). British freedoms were apparently too precious to be threatened by anyone exercising them.

Ireland: rebellion, union, and maybe a song about it later

One of the societies forced underground was the Society of United Irishmen, which frankly was an ambitious title for an independence movement founded in Belfast. However, the Irish rising of 1798 was one occasion when sectarianism was not at the forefront of the Irish independence movement. The organization had around a hundred thousand members all sharing one ambition: to break the link with England.

Its leader was Wolfe Tone who, despite his unusual Christian name, was neither a WWF wrestler nor star of ITV's *Gladiators*.

* William Blake urged Paine to flee the country after foreseeing his arrest in a prophetic dream.

Tone was a Protestant liberal inspired by the American and French Revolutions who came close to leading the Irish to independence (even if he turned up too late to join the fighting, got captured and ending up committing suicide). Unfortunately his organization was packed with informers who somehow managed to hide their real loyalty to the English Crown. 'I say, old chap, begorrah and top of the morning and all that. How about a pint of Guinness and some of that twiddly-dee fiddle music and then let's hear all about the plans for this rebellion so I can put on my tartan and play the bagpipes . . . No, hang on, that's not right . . .'

In 1796 a French force of around fifteen thousand attempted to land in Bantry Bay as Irish rebels rose up around the country. However, endless storms and poor coordination meant that the French army never got into port to support the rebels. Eventually the Irish decided they could wait no longer and rose up on their own and throughout 1798 small battles were fought across the country between British soldiers and rebels. There were significant anti-British uprisings from the Protestant inhabitants of Ulster, and part of Britain's strategy after 1798 was to drive a wedge between the Catholics and Protestants in the North.* But the decisive encounter finally came in Wexford at the Battle of Vinegar Hill when around fifteen thousand British soldiers and Hessian† mercenaries defeated the Irish rebels and went on a rampage of gang rape and murder, burning eighty rebels alive and destroying homes and livestock. The rebellion was probably the bloodiest period in Irish history, with up to thirty thousand killed in a few months.

If the weather had been a bit better in Bantry Bay, the presence of a sizeable French army might well have helped the Irish succeed just as the Americans had done fifteen years earlier and Irish history would have taken a completely different course. To commemorate

---

* Brigadier-General C. E. Knox wrote: *I hope to increase the animosity between Orangemen and United Irishmen. Upon that animosity depends the safety of the centre counties of the North.*

† 'Hessian' meaning that they were from the German area of Hesse, not that they were made out of the breathable coarse fabric that was briefly fashionable for table mats in the 1970s.

one of the great 'what-ifs' of Irish history, the abortive French invasion is commemorated in Bantry town centre, where today visitors can observe a large anchor from one of the original French ships with some bored local teenagers sitting on it smoking.

With outbreaks of violence rumbling on and fears of the French returning to Ireland, Pitt decided to solve the Irish problem with a union of the two Parliaments. The Act of Union with Scotland a hundred years earlier was deemed to have been a great success; Scotland had gone from strength to strength playing a disproportionately large part in the Enlightenment and the Industrial Revolution. However, Ireland had the added complication of religion; or rather of England's anti-Catholicism. Catholics were social pariahs almost on a par with paedophiles today, and in the case of Ireland's Christian Brothers, you got two for the price of one.

But 90 per cent of Ireland's population was Catholic; Pitt knew that unless Catholics were permitted to vote then Irish representation at Westminster would be meaningless and the situation would only worsen. However, there was one Protestant who was not prepared to concede this point. The increasingly nutty George III insisted that allowing Catholic emancipation would be a betrayal of his coronation oath, and his advisers (a pair of apple trees in the back garden) both agreed with him. In 1800 the first Parliament with representatives from all over the British Isles met in London, but one of its first tasks was to accept Pitt's resignation; for the new MPs were all Protestants elected by Protestants. Sectarian apartheid had been entrenched in law; using his allies at Westminster, a half-mad King had defeated the First Minister. 'Still, I think that's Ireland sorted. We won't be having any more trouble from that quarter . . .'

The diagonal red cross of St Patrick was added to the Union Flag, where it remains today representing the six counties of Northern Ireland that continue to be part of the United Kingdom, partly as a result of the divisions exacerbated after 1798.

'Erm, since we're redesigning the flag,' interjected the Welsh, 'maybe there could be something to acknowledge Wales?'

'What? Oh yeah, fair point. Leave it with us and we'll definitely get back to you . . .'

Napoleon's land army v Nelson's navy: home advantage crucial

It had been a great shock that the French had managed to get so close to landing a force in Ireland, since control of the seas was supposed to be the only advantage the British had in the prolonged war. But a couple of mutinies in the Royal Navy had left England exposed; the entire security of the country was suddenly in jeopardy because of some lefty union troublemakers who didn't like eating mouldy ships' biscuits and being flogged when they complained. Well, they should have thought about that before they chose to be bashed over the head and dragged on board unconscious.*

The British government had hoped that France's disorganized regime could not sustain a prolonged war effort, especially while the Austrian Empire possessed the largest army in the world. However, in 1797 the Austrians were driven out of their Italian territories following a stunning campaign by Napoleon, whose skills were now affecting the whole course of the war. France occupied the Rhineland, Belgium and much of Italy and all the European powers except Britain made peace with Revolutionary France. Britain was now on her own.

Napoleon Bonaparte was still only a military force at this point, although the politicians in Paris feared his ambition. This was a time when short men with a sense of inadequacy had to become rulers of all Europe to give themselves a little bit of power over other people; there were no jobs as driving examiners or aerobics instructors. However, in Horatio Nelson England had a naval genius to match the brilliance of Napoleon on the battlefield. Nelson had lost an arm in an engagement a few years earlier so Napoleon tucked one arm inside his shirt to make it fair. The two men would never meet in a direct

---

* Under this recruiting method – known as 'press ganging' – it was legal to kidnap men by force, by beating them up and dragging them on to the ship where they would awake to find themselves miles out at sea. More often, impressment involved able seamen being persuaded to join the navy where they would get better rates of pay than in the merchant fleet as well as a volunteer bonus.

engagement, but Nelson's achievements at sea prevented Napoleon from fulfilling his ambitions on land.

Apart from the fact that he spent the first two days of any voyage puking over the side, Horatio Nelson was born to be in the navy. He was the prototype maverick hero from a second-rate Sunday night TV drama; a brave and rebellious officer who sometimes felt compelled to ignore demands from his cowardly and bureaucratic superiors not to continue and then be proved right as he triumphed against all the odds. 'You may not play it by the book, Nelson, but you're the best goddamn fighter pilot/homicide detective/carpet-layer this unit's got.' At the Battle of Copenhagen in 1801 his superior officer hoisted a signal telling him not to attack. When this was pointed out to him, he put the telescope to his blind eye and claimed to see no such signal.* Then of course he proved his rather irritated boss wrong by winning a stunning victory.

But it was at the Battle of the Nile in 1798 that Nelson became a national hero. Successfully predicting Napoleon's intentions to invade Egypt, Nelson stumbled upon the French fleet in Abukir Bay and attacked at once, even though night was falling and he was sailing in shallow, uncharted waters. The French had anchored close to the land and, presuming that no captain would think it safe to sail even closer to the shore, their guns were not ready on that landward side. Nelson destroyed almost their entire fleet, leaving Napoleon stranded in Egypt with no means of getting his army home. No doubt the short ugly foreigner would have shouted in anger at his fawning courtiers, blaming everyone but himself and completely losing control in a very undignified manner instead of keeping a stiff upper lip and having a cup of tea as any British leader would have done.

Nelson's status was further enhanced when it was learnt that he had received a head wound in the battle and had waited in turn behind the ordinary sailors to receive treatment. Napoleon, on the

---

* Contrary to the popular image, Nelson did not wear an eye-patch; he just put the telescope to the eye that his colleagues knew was blind. On second thoughts, it's nowhere near as good an image; let's just say he put the telescope to his eye-patch.

other hand, abandoned his stranded army to rush back to Paris and lead a *coup d'état* and become a military dictator. So just to be clear, Nelson = Goody, Napoleon = Baddie. So now we know which side is going to win in the end.

Intermission: please note that war will resume in 15 minutes

The war between Britain and France had settled into something of a stalemate. Napoleon's cavalry units were rubbish out at sea and the British warships were not much better on land. A truce was agreed in 1802, which was more like a half-time break for both sides to get some oranges and listen to the team talk from their respective managers: 'Wellington: I'm going to move you out of India and put you in central Europe. Their star man is Napoleon; your job is to stop him. Nelson: you keep marking Villeneuve in the Mediterranean, stick close to him, don't let him past. Pitt: I know you thought you'd retired, but I'm putting you back on; come on, you're captain again, we need you out there.'

The Treaty of Amiens had recognized the French conquests on continental Europe, so if things had ended there the war would have been an indisputable French victory with the boundaries of France stretching from Rome to the Danish border. Britain also recognized France as a republic and the English monarchy at long last gave up its claim to the French throne. But peace lasted only a year, with Great Britain suddenly facing a different kind of enemy. The French Revolution was over. France had exchanged the dictatorship of a king for that of a man who would with characteristic humility crown himself Emperor and declare himself King of Rome for good measure. The Pope was sitting right near him; I'm sure he would have been more than happy to help.

Now at least the British could argue that this was a war against tyranny rather than the noble ideals of the Revolution. But with

Napoleon reorganized and his army re-equipped* the great general was finally focusing on Britain as his primary objective and a real sense of crisis built up across the country. An enormous army of ninety thousand French soldiers was massing in Boulogne, complete with flat-bottomed boats and leaflets advising them not to try British wine. Napoleon even had a special coin minted: 'Struck in London 1804' it lied. But he was confident that it could soon be distributed.

It would not be the last time that Britain would stand alone against a mighty continental power and, as always, the English Channel was all that stood between a conquering army and the subjugation of all Europe. ''Tis but a ditch,' said Napoleon when he saw the twenty-mile stretch of water. On the other side, a ragbag of local volunteers were drilling and marching with whatever weapons they could muster. The retired Pitt the Younger had found himself a new role as a sort of nineteenth-century Captain Mainwaring, organizing the 'Dad's Army' of the day. Until in May 1804 a messenger arrived with an urgent summons: the call had come for William Pitt to lead his country once more.

The prospect of a full-scale French invasion was enough to persuade King George III that, irrespective of past differences, he needed the best available man at the helm. The niceties of whether the Catholics had the vote or not seemed to pall into insignificance against the prospect of the English King being replaced by a French Catholic Emperor. Pitt set about improving England's defences, ordering the building of Martello Towers along the coast. These are the huge round military gun emplacements that today occasionally feature in property supplements about interesting architectural conversions under the headline 'Can a fortress become a family home?' followed by a very short article saying, 'Well, no.'

There was a brief moment of hope when Pitt formed an alliance

---

* During the brief interlude Napoleon had managed to raise some extra revenue by selling Louisiana to the Americans. The American President was forced to buy it after his wife had seen the advert in *Country Life*, though Napoleon managed to get the price up by pretending there was another couple interested.

with Austria, Sweden and Russia, but soon Napoleon's army was defeating the Austrians again and the invincibility of Napoleon was more terrifying than ever. When Pitt saw his niece looking at a map showing all the countries of Europe he told her to roll it up, it wouldn't be needed for another ten years. All over the continent, once proud and independent nations were cruelly being forced to have a clearly defined legal code and adopt the metric system. Only Britain held out for the right to drive on the left and overcook their vegetables.

All that Napoleon believed he needed was control of the English Channel for twenty-four hours, time enough to get his army across the strait, and then he would be unopposed in Europe and the world, taking not just Great Britain but all her possessions around the globe. For this purpose he needed the fleet of his ally Spain to join up with the French navy. British blockades had so far prevented this but then in the summer of 1805, the news came through that the French Mediterranean fleet had managed to slip past Gibraltar, and the Spanish and French fleets were in Cadiz. Nelson, only just back from a two-year tour of duty, set sail in mid-September as soon as his ship was ready. As the fleet sailed out of Portsmouth, onlookers knelt at the quayside and prayed. But there can have been fewer more inspiring sights than the vision of the great Horatio Nelson, standing on the quarterdeck of HMS *Victory* as she rose and fell with the swell of the sea, the Admiral turning green and then vomiting over the rail . . .

Many of France's best admirals had been executed during the Revolution on the grounds that they sort of owned a yacht, but the combined Spanish and French fleets still outnumbered the British. A significant number of British ships had had to stay behind to guard the Channel, while others remained on convoy duty or were in dry dock. But at dawn on 21 October, the two fleets came within sight of one another. With battle about to commence, Nelson sent his famous text message: *Englnd xpcts evry mn do dty:-*). The wind was gentle and there was a period of calm as the ships moved slowly towards one another. Captain Hardy* asked Nelson if his bright tunic and insignia didn't make him too easily identifiable. But all of

* One of Captain Hardy's descendants was Oliver Hardy, as in 'Laurel and Hardy'.

a sudden the firing began. Nelson's flagship soon cut through the middle of the French line at considerable risk to himself. The Admiral's genius for spotting weaknesses in the enemy's formation combined with the superior seamanship of the British crews created confusion in Villeneuve's fleet, and the British fleet was gaining the upper hand. Then only two hours into the battle, a French sniper perched up high on the rigging of the *Redoubtable* fired a musket ball into Nelson's shoulder. The shot went into his spine and Britain's greatest-ever naval commander collapsed on the deck. 'They have done for me at last, Hardy. My backbone is shot through.' Nelson covered his face as he was carried below, lest his men be demoralized by the sight of their leader dying. For four hours the battle continued while Nelson lay bleeding to death in the surgeon's quarters, his officers powerless to save him. 'Kiss me, Hardy,' said Nelson. There was a certain amount of embarrassed shuffling and then Captain Hardy thought, Well, it doesn't mean anything . . . and he leant forward and gave him a kiss. As one man who loves another, like a brother, as it were. 'Tell me Hardy,' continued Nelson, 'do you still have those leather trousers?'

The log of HMS *Victory* records: *partial firing continued until four-thirty, when a victory having been reported to the Right Hon. Lord Viscount Nelson, KB and Commander in Chief, he then died of his wound.* So Nelson lived long enough to learn that he had made Britain safe from invasion. The log continues: *ship then sailed home to become tourist attraction at Portsmouth Historic Dockyard; great day out for all the family, includes Harbour Boat Tour and 'Task Force South' Falklands Experience.*

On 4 November, a little schooner sailed into Falmouth Harbour with some monumental news. The British fleet of only twenty-seven ships had sunk or captured twenty enemy ships, but England's great hero had died at the hour of victory. 'Fine, but can you *not* tie your boat up here, this is a *private* mooring.' When the news reached London the death of Nelson tempered the joy of victory. But three days later when Pitt travelled to Guildhall to be toasted as the 'Saviour of Europe', such was the enthusiasm of the joyous crowd that mobbed his route that they unhitched the horses and pulled his carriage themselves.

'Actually this coach is much heavier than it looks, isn't it?'

'Yeah, is it too late to get those horses back?'

Eventually Nelson's body was brought home in a barrel of brandy and he was buried at St Paul's Cathedral, one of only five non-royals to receive such an honour, although that number may go up when the Beckhams finally pass away. He was placed in a wooden sarcophagus originally carved for Cardinal Wolsey, but which had remained unused after Henry VIII's chancellor had fallen out of favour. After all this time, it seemed a waste not to use it.

Just as the Battle of Britain would later prevent the Luftwaffe from gaining control of the skies before Hitler's impending invasion, Trafalgar ensured Britain's supremacy at sea, keeping Napoleon confined to mainland Europe and Britain unconquered as the rest of the continent's only hope of liberation. For soon there were no other allies. Just before Trafalgar, Napoleon had scored another stunning military victory at Ulm and a couple of months later he completely routed the Russians and Austrians at Austerlitz, a battle com-memorated by means of a Parisian railway station with a particularly unhelpful lost-property attendant.

The collapse of the coalition was too much for Pitt. He had laboured tirelessly on this alliance, and now his health deteriorated and he became delirious, shouting 'Hear! Hear!' from his bed to imaginary Parliamentary debates. His final words are disputed. The official account is that he cried out, 'Oh my country! how I leave my country!' although the less grand account has him musing, 'I think I could eat one of Bellamy's veal pies.' He was only forty-six, but then Pitt the Younger did everything early.

For two decades Pitt had dominated the British political scene, tirelessly organizing the British war effort and carelessly neglecting to get married or have a family. He'd been the one politician that the public believed could lead the fight against France; now he was gone and Napoleon was master of all Europe. The mood in Britain was increasingly despondent. British ships might still be free to sail the seas, but now there were no ports where they could unload their cargoes. Napoleon could not defeat Britain militarily, but he controlled enough of Europe to cripple the British economy through an organized trade blockade. Under the so-called 'Continental System' even former allies of Britain like Russia and Prussia agreed not to accept British goods. Politically aware shoppers across Europe would carefully read the labels to make sure they didn't break the boycott. 'Mum, I can't believe you've bought British apples; that is so fascist!' When Napoleon called England 'a nation of shopkeepers', he meant that trade was everything to Britain, not that he imagined every single Englishman ran a little corner shop selling fags, mags and Slush Puppies. Which makes it all the more surprising that the British Parliament took the far-reaching step of ending the one over-seas business that had brought England so much wealth during the previous couple of centuries.

Abolition of the slave trade: political correctness gone mad

Since the reign of Elizabeth but increasingly during the past 150 years, British ships had set off from Bristol or Liverpool and sailed to West Africa where the local residents had been helpfully rounded up by African businessmen to be exchanged for much coveted British goods such as guns, alcohol or Beatles memorabilia. Some of the slaves were prisoners of war from competing African states, others were outcasts within their own societies, convicts, or political oppo-nents of the local ruling élite. But many more were just unfortunate victims of kidnapping who could fetch a good price once they had been transported across the Atlantic in appallingly inhumane conditions. It is estimated that around twenty million Africans died before they even reached the slave market. Those that survived might often have to endure the brutal process of 'seasoning', whereby prisoners were tortured and deprived of food and sleep to make them compliant. The ships would then return to Britain loaded with the cheap produce of slave labour: sugar, coffee, cotton and tobacco, and the lucrative cycle would begin all over again.

And wouldn't you just know it, there were a few people who seemed to think that this example of British private enterprise was somehow not 'politically correct'. That it was somehow 'racist' to say that negroes could be slaves and white people couldn't. A few members of this liberal élite, who simply did not understand the ways of the countryside in the colonies, began a campaign to have the slave trade abolished. They focused on all the negative aspects of slavery, completely ignoring the fact that these Africans were being brought into contact with Christianity, given a job for life and were probably much happier than they would have been in war-torn Africa (being as it was ravaged by slave-traders). A campaign began in the 1780s with the monumental ambition of outlawing a trade that was completely accepted right across Europe and lined the pockets of many of the businessmen who populated the House of Commons. A group known as the Clapham Sect, led in Parliament by William Wilberforce, campaigned tirelessly with pamphlets, endless lobbying and public meetings at which former slaves would describe the conditions under which they had laboured.

'Well, I think we had a very interesting talk there from James about his life as a slave. So, James, if you could just stack all the chairs away, we'll be down the Rose and Crown.'

By 1807 they had succeeded in shifting public opinion sufficiently that when the Tories were briefly out of power, they were able to get a bill outlawing the slave trade through the House of Commons. The trade continued illegally for a while; if slave ships saw a Royal Navy ship approaching, they would simply throw all the slaves into the sea to avoid being fined. But the world's greatest slave-traders had set themselves against the practice, and would force the rest of Europe to abandon the trade at the peace talks at the end of the war. The institution of slavery continued across the British Empire, finally being abolished in 1833. The disappointing postscript is that there are reckoned to be more people living in slavery today than at any time in human history.

Wellington sticks his nose in . . .

There were two great war heroes to emerge from the Napoleonic

Wars. One is remembered with an eighteen-foot statue on a giant column in a London square named after his final battle. The name of the other lives on in a type of cheap rubber boot. The Duke of Wellington began life as plain Arthur Wellesley, younger son of a minor Protestant Irish family. The man who became a great English national hero was later dismissive of his Irish roots: 'Being born in a stable does not make one a horse,' he quipped. With few prospects he had entered the military and quickly rose through the ranks, serving with distinction in India, until he was given the job of leading a British force in Spain in 1808. The expedition was not a major offensive by the British government, it was barely acknowledged at the time, but bit by bit it wore away at Napoleon's military strength and gradually helped bring down the seemingly invincible dictator.*

Napoleon Bonaparte was not vain enough to believe he could rule most of Europe on his own, and was happy to delegate the day-to-day running of his various territories to the best possible candidates for the job. The fact that these people all had the surname 'Bonaparte' was pure coincidence. In Spain he had installed his useless brother Joseph; a move which greatly offended the proud Spanish. Spain refused to accept French rule but, unable to defeat the French in battle, they invented a word for a type of warfare that avoided pitched battles, conjuring up an unlikely image when Napoleon was informed that his army had been attacked by 'guerrillas'.

Britain did not possess a land army that could compete with the French and so her troops had been withdrawn from continental Europe in order to concentrate on domestic military duties, such as trying to keep a straight face at Horse Guards Parade while giggling schoolchildren whispered toilet-based swear words at them. But the popular uprising in Spain was an example that the English were keen to see followed across Europe, and so British troops were sent to lend their support. Lieutenant-General Wellesley landed in Portugal

---

* Napoleon later wrote of the Peninsular War: *This was what destroyed me*, perhaps overlooking the fact that he had foolishly invaded Russia without taking sandwiches.

(which had bravely defied Napoleon's demands that they cease trading with Britain) and, despite being heavily outnumbered by the French, he comprehensively defeated the French General Junot.

At this point Wellesley's superiors turned up and said, 'Righto, Wellesley, we'll take over now, thank you. So you've defeated the French? Splendid, well, we'd better give them a lift home then.' Instead of finishing the French off, the British generals negotiated an armistice so ludicrously gentlemanly that it involved the Royal Navy taking the French prisoners-of-war back to France with all their 'personal property' (namely everything they had looted from Portugal) at considerable inconvenience and expense to the British, so that those soldiers could be used against Britain again at a later date.

The scandal left the government reeling. Secretary of State for Foreign Affairs George Canning argued publicly with the Secretary for War Lord Castlereagh about whether more troops should be sent to Portugal and their rivalry became so heated that the two cabinet ministers ended up fighting a duel. Canning had never so much as held a pistol before, and unsurprisingly missed his opponent, while the Secretary for War managed to do his bit for the war effort by shooting his fellow minister in the thigh. Both men were forced to resign from the government, the Prime Minister resigned and was replaced by Spencer Perceval who continued the theme by being shot dead in the House of Commons by a crazed businessman who had been bankrupted by the war. It was all going very well.

However, Wellesley, elevated to Viscount Wellington in 1809, managed to keep his sizeable nose clean throughout; indeed his reputation continued to grow as he determinedly kept the Portuguese people onside by executing any British soldier who so much as stole a chicken or laid a finger on a local girl. This firm but fair approach won him the respect of his hosts and gained him the use of the Portuguese army to add to his meagre force of twenty thousand men.* Over the course of three years, the French poured

---

* However, he had less success cooperating with the Spanish; on one occasion the best chance for a decisive strike at the French was lost when the Spanish refused to fight on a Sunday.

350,000 soldiers into the Iberian peninsula, but failed to hold it in the face of determined Spanish guerrilla tactics and Wellington's skilful manoeuvres. The heroics and horrors of the war inspired great artists across Europe; Francisco Goya painted *The Third of May 1808: The Execution of the Defenders of Madrid*, Bizet reworked a story from the war to create his great opera *Carmen* while ITV1 produced *Sharpe* starring Sean Bean. By the beginning of 1812, Wellington held the most strategically significant fortresses to the south of the Pyrenees, and threatened the territory of France itself. With things going so badly in Spain, Napoleon decided that this would be a good time to pull out all his best troops and use them to invade Russia.

It is not easy to explain to the ordinary layman why the strategic obstacles to an invasion of Russia make it almost unconquerable, but Russia is what advanced military strategists term as 'very, very big'. Napoleon's unprecedentedly huge army of 650,000 soldiers counted for nothing in such endless territories, and with the Russians torching everything as they fled the advancing French were left without food and supplies. The Russians even let their own capital burn rather than let it fall into the hands of the enemy, which later led to a lot of arguments with the insurance companies. In October a humiliated Napoleon was forced to retreat and anyone heard humming the 1812 overture was in big trouble. On the retreat through the snow 170,000 French soldiers perished; but to a man of Napoleon's ego, these were mere statistics.

Meanwhile American patience had been stretched to breaking point by the British seizing American sailors and pressing them into service in the Royal Navy. In 1812 the United States declared war on Britain. However, it's probably fair to say that in 1812 having the United States declare war on Great Britain was perhaps not quite as big a deal as it would be today. This sideshow petered out with the end of the Napoleonic wars but not before the British had secured the future independence of Canada from the United States, burning down the White House along the way.*

---

* It is widely believed that the President's residence was painted white to cover up the blackened exterior, but this is a myth: the building was always white and was sometimes given that name before the fire in 1814.

Napoleon finally got back to France and seemed very touchy when his wife said, 'How was Russia?' His catastrophic retreat had inspired the formerly cowed allies to rise up once more. In October 1813 the French were defeated at Leipzig by the combined forces of Austria, Sweden, Prussia and Russia, and the French were pushed back across the Rhine. Wellington crossed the Pyrenees, winning a series of battles in south-western France, and by March 1814 Tsar Alexander I was in Paris and Napoleon abdicated and retired to Elba. The Corsican installed himself as the ruler of this tiny island close to his birthplace while Europe considered where it should go from here. Five or six million people had perished, whole nations were bankrupted, the ancient map of Europe was torn up – and all because of the inferiority complex of the little corporal. Frankly a pair of lifts under his insoles would have been a lot less trouble.

They think it's all over . . .

The company organizing the peace conference was desperate it shouldn't be cancelled. All the bottles of mineral water had been opened, lovely new writing pads and sharpened pencils had been carefully placed around the conference table and there were flip charts and maps all ready at the far end of the room. Then the news arrived that Napoleon had escaped from Elba and was marching to Paris with an army growing stronger by the day.

'We must leave immediately and raise our armies once more!'

'Well, I'm sure you'll want to discuss that *around the conference table* . . .'

'Saddle my horse, we march tonight!'

'But you can't cancel the whole conference! We're just serving the finger buffet . . .'

The allies had placed the younger brother of the beheaded Louis XVI on the French throne, as if everything could go back to the way it was before the French Revolution. Louis XVIII (they had carelessly missed out one along the way) was a particularly fat and cowardly monarch, and did nothing to inspire a stand against the dictator who had bankrupted their country. But he had lived through the Revolution and, having an experienced head on his shoulders, judged that the best way to keep it there was to run away very quickly. The French Marshal Ney was sent to capture Napoleon, saying he should be brought back to Paris in an iron cage, but switched sides when he found him. Twenty years of loyalty to the charismatic general were not easily forgotten, and thousands of seasoned soldiers and returning prisoners of war flocked to join Napoleon. Many of Wellington's best troops had been sent to fight the Americans, while the other European powers had been in the process of sending all their soldiers limping home with a roll of sticking plaster and directions to the job centre.

Napoleon moved with his characteristic speed and excellent military intelligence. He believed if he could attack the Prussian army before it joined up with the British and Dutch, he could defeat them all. The Prussian General Blücher was promptly defeated at Ligny on 16 June 1815 and Wellington fell back to a small Belgian village called Waterloo.

'What, like the Abba song, sir?'

'Shh, you're spoiling it.'

There was heavy rain the night before the battle and with most of his horses preferring the going good to firm, Napoleon waited to let the ground dry out before he attacked the British. Yet every hour he delayed brought the badly injured Blücher closer to joining Wellington. By late morning the French cavalry finally attacked, but the British squares held their positions; each man firing his musket then kneeling to reload while the line behind fired theirs. It was important not to get out of step. All day Wellington was seen glancing at his watch, wondering what had happened to the Prussians. At six o'clock in the evening, the French took control of the farmhouse at the centre of the British positions, and Napoleon sent in his undefeated Imperial Guard. Had they broken through as expected, the day may well have been Napoleon's, but the British infantry held its ground and the élite French forces came under intense fire. 'The guard dies, it does not surrender,' a French general is supposed to have shouted. However, this instruction made no mention of an extremely attractive third option which was to run away, and with the most feared soldiers in Europe retreating in chaos for the first time in the twenty-two-year war, Wellington stood up in his stirrups and gave the signal for the British to attack.

The Prussians had started to arrive amid the chaos of the battle-field, asking where they might be of most use, but everyone was very busy and it was hard to find the right person to talk to. There was not much daylight left but the substantial reinforcements meant the French situation was hopeless, and by nine p.m. Blücher met up with Wellington near Napoleon's former headquarters for a gloating con-ference. But Wellington later conceded that the battle had been 'the nearest-run thing you ever saw in your life'.

Napoleon fled and was eventually apprehended off the coast of Rochefort, where it was believed he was heading for the United States. He was exiled to the remote Atlantic island of St Helena, to an early, very basic version of Club Med. There he dictated his memoirs, which were obviously very much along the lines of: 'No, it was a team effort; honestly, I could never have done it all without you guys.' He died of stomach cancer six years later.*

Britain 'better than France': official

Britain had been at war with its larger neighbour on and off for around 750 years and had finally and conclusively won. For ever after, all French history books would graciously give Britain its full title of 'the United Kingdom of Great Britain (Better Than France)'. The next time the two countries met on the battlefields of Belgium a hundred years later, their soldiers would be fighting on the same side against a new European power whose unification had been precipitated by Napoleon's rule. But for now Britain emerged from

* Very famous people are of course not allowed to die mundane deaths, and so there have been endless conspiracy theories that he was poisoned by the British. But the arsenic detected in his hair follicles was also present in hair samples from twenty years earlier; the chemical was used in hair tonic, which is another reason why you should always try to buy organic.

the century of its most intense rivalry with the French as the unquestioned dominant military, colonial and industrial power of Europe and the world. Napoleon had failed, Britain had prevailed – and that is why today all of Europe drives on the left and uses miles instead of kilometres.

Britain had been able to endure twenty years of war against a larger, revolutionary army because of the social revolutions that had occurred at home. The enormous leaps in agriculture had improved food production sufficiently for Britain to avoid starvation during Napoleon's trade blockade. Industrialization allowed Britain to mass-produce the guns and ammunition required for a war fought on a larger scale than ever before and made Britain wealthy enough to subsidize the European land armies that England didn't have. The Industrial Revolution would now spread across a peaceful Europe. But despite the best efforts of the victorious allies, the French Revolution could not be put back in the bottle. The revolutionary concepts of equality and political liberty for all had spread around the world and would grow more powerful over the coming century. Nowhere were these ideas more potent than in Britain where the brutally exploited working classes were now gathered in large numbers in urban conurbations.

After the defeat of France, the British government no longer feared its enemies overseas. It was the enemy within that terrified the establishment. A bloody revolution seemed imminent as the unemployed soldiers drifted back from the Napoleonic Wars. The armies of the French Revolution may have been beaten, but its philosophy was unstoppable. And yet despite looking about to explode at several points during the nineteenth century, the long-feared 'British Revolution' never quite ignited. Though, like Waterloo, it was to be 'the nearest-run thing you ever saw in your life'.

8

Empire 1815–1914

How the Victorians established the world's modern template for imperialism, industrialized capitalism and association football

Every country has its golden age: Spain in the sixteenth century, France in the seventeenth century, Belgium in the . . . Well, anyway, several countries have had an era when their dominant position in the world brought immense wealth, influence and status. For Britain it was the 1800s. In the century between Waterloo and the First World War, Great Britain didn't have to clutch at straws by going on and on about the fact that they'd won Olympic gold in some poxy equestrian event. Britain was top. Head Prefect. Cock of the walk. The only world super-power. Like the United States today, except the rich were all fat instead of the poor.

The Napoleonic Wars were not yet over when a posh-looking envelope dropped through the door. *You are cordially invited to 'The Congress of Vienna'. Music by Beethoven and Ultravox. Dress: Military Casual.* Ooh, that sounds nice, they all thought, but of course when they got there they found that the conference was not actually in historic Vienna itself, but in one of those modern hotels beside the airport, and while they yawned through Metternich's PowerPoint presentation on 'Whither the German Confederation', the delegates wondered if they got to keep the nice sharp pencils and whether that Austrian lady taking the minutes would be at the dinner that evening.

In its way the Congress of Vienna is as important as the Battle of Waterloo; it decided the fate of thousands of square miles of territory, and guaranteed peace in Europe for much of the century. But somehow it hasn't inspired the same enthusiasm among military collectors; you can't buy little replica figures of hand-painted diplomats to put on the shelf above the telly. *Collect the entire set of conference delegates. Recreate the exact seating arrangements.*

By continually filling up the other delegates' wine glasses, Great Britain was able to secure a whole swathe of new colonies. The Cape of Good Hope and Ceylon were added to the Empire, Britain gained Tobago, Mauritius, Malta and the Seychelles, and was also granted Heligoland because no one knew where it was.* France was pushed back to her pre-war borders, received a large claim for compensation from the allies and told to get rid of those disgusting shower-tray toilets. But Castlereagh, heading the British delegation, insisted that the conference must be about peace rather than punishment. Despite pressure from the allies, French humiliation was avoided, Louis XVIII managed to pay the Invasion Charge within three years, permitting the Duke of Wellington to withdraw his occupying army and thousands of departing English soldiers bade farewell to their French sweethearts.

'*Au revoir, mon chéri*. Will you write to me?'

'Well, I would, luv, but a uniform postal system is another twenty years away.'

Britain was now in the Regency Period, named after the Prince Regent who'd assumed royal responsibilities in 1811 after George III was diagnosed by the royal physicians as having become irrecoverably 'bonkers in the nut'. The Prince gave his name to London's Regent Street, built by the great John Nash to cater for the growing need for Disney Stores and teddy bear shops. Nash's other projects included Trafalgar Square, the Brighton Pavilion, Marble Arch and an extension to 'Buckingham House', which was obviously quite a big one.

* Heligoland is a small archipelago off the coast of Germany. Not to be confused with Legoland, Windsor, which remains a British territory leased by the Danish.

There can have been no starker contrast to the fine Regency architecture than the chaotic, unregulated workers' dwellings being thrown up across Britain's industrial areas. The greatest conurbations had grown up in the Midlands, the North, South Wales and in Scotland's central industrial belt. In Manchester, rather unwittily dubbed 'Cottonopolis' for its endless textile mills, the sky was so dark from the blanket of sulphurous fumes pouring out of its brick chimneys day and night that people said the difference between the two was barely discernible. Under blackened skies, tonnes of raw sewage ran into open streams, so that the water as well as the air was poisoned. The shortlist was shrinking for Britain's 'Best Kept Village' competition.

Although science was making great advances, with Jenner developing the smallpox vaccine at the beginning of the century, medical knowledge could barely keep up with the new risks and epidemics brought about by industrialization and the unregulated urban sprawl. It's just as well Jane Austen was writing her novels in Hampshire, because they would have been a lot shorter had they been set in Manchester.

'Alas, Mr Goodly, I cannot grant you the hand of my fair daughter Leticia in marriage, for she has just dropped dead from sulphur poisoning.'

' 'Tis a great pity, sir, but you have other daughters, do you not?'

'There was Georgina, but she was crushed falling into the industrial rollers.'

'Rebecca?'

'Tuberculosis.'

'Fair Charlotte?'

'Cholera.'

'Ah yes, they say 'tis all the shite in the drinking water.'

It was the enormous gap between the rich and poor and the ignorance of what life was like in the industrial centres that did much to exacerbate social tensions after the war. The great liberal philosopher Jeremy Bentham argued for *the greatest happiness of the greatest number.* Everyone in Parliament agreed that this was a splendid idea for society in general and then went off to make personal fortunes by exploiting as many people as possible.

The British Revolution 1819: postponed due to inclement weather

Throughout the previous decades the Industrial Revolution had intensified to such a degree that people barely had time to think of a topical allegory for the political situation.

'I say, Mr Watt, since you invented your steam engine, the *pressure* building up in society has been reaching *boiling point*, and could now blow at any time.'

'Yes, you could almost say that the high-pressure boiler of urban society looks about to burst, sending rivets of social disorder across the nation, and leaving the shell of the post-war settlement a tangled, steaming wreck.'

However, political unrest was nothing new; in 1813 seventeen Luddites had been hanged for smashing modern machinery that they maintained put men out of work and reduced wages. The Luddites have been portrayed as simplistic wreckers and vandals, who imagined that by smashing new inventions they could halt technological progress. In fact their campaign was never so simple.

'So, Ned Ludd, you claim that your movement is not against modern machinery *per se*, but the way it has been used to break set wage agreements and lower the quality of textile production. Well, shall we get your claim about misrepresentation down on this new typographer machine?'

'Ooh no, I can't be doing with all that fancy technology. I'm actually a bit of a Luddite at heart.'

Having a quarter of a million ex-servicemen return home from the war did nothing to help the economic slump that came with the end of wartime production. But a government that had been set on papering over the cracks of the French Revolution in Europe saw every plea for fair wages, cheaper bread or greater representation as the work of dangerous revolutionaries.

An extensive network of informers made a good living from reporting revolutionary activity; these spies had a vested interest in over-dramatizing any dissent or minor disorder.

'I've found a radical, sir! Do I get my bonus?'

'What was he doing?'

'Writing to the council, sir. About a wobbly step. Filthy commie, they make me sick . . .'

The government made little distinction between peaceful protesters and advocates of violent revolution. At St Peter's Field in Manchester in 1819 over 60,000 demonstrators gathered with placards calling for Parliamentary reform, universal suffrage, cheaper bread and just the one saying 'John 3:16'. When the radical orator Henry Hunt got up to speak, soldiers were sent on to the platform to arrest him. This hardly calmed the atmosphere and, having been provoked by a bit of angry heckling, the cavalry felt compelled to charge into the crowd lashing out with their swords, indiscriminately killing eleven people and injuring at least four hundred more. The event was sarcastically dubbed 'Peterloo' after a slightly more distinguished episode in those same soldiers' careers four years earlier.

The Peterloo Massacre was a national scandal. Percy Shelley was inspired to write 'The Mask of Anarchy':

> Rise like Lions after slumber
> In unvanquishable number,
> Shake your chains to earth like dew
> Which in sleep had fallen on you –
> Ye are many – they are few.

The *Manchester Guardian* was launched to promote liberal interests in the massacre's aftermath. Now the government was really worried; poets and *Guardian* readers could prove an unstoppable physical combination. A series of extreme repressive measures known as the Six Acts were introduced to suppress all dissent. Habeas corpus was suspended once more, and the right to arrest without charge was widely used. Meetings of more than fifty persons required permission, and justices and magistrates were indemnified from any deaths they caused if people did not disperse when told to do so. Popular opinion was just wondering if the government had gone too far when a plot was uncovered to assassinate the entire cabinet and set up a revolutionary government.

The Cato Street Conspiracy of 1820 was betrayed by government informers amid accusations that the government had allowed it to develop knowing its exposure would help smear all calls for reform.

The Prime Minister, who had avoided the fate of his predecessor, was Lord Liverpool. Despite his name he was not a lovable moptop with a unique Scouse wit. Liverpool was a right-wing toff whose father had been a close adviser to George III ('Your majesty, I wouldn't chew that carpet if I were you'). Although his mother was Anglo-Indian, Liverpool was not a great friend of the outsider or the underdog, having opposed the abolition of the slave trade and votes for Catholics.

In 1815 his government had introduced the Corn Law, which banned the import of foreign wheat unless the price rose to eighty shillings a bushel. The law was designed to protect the incomes of English farmers but of course meant that the price of British wheat was kept artificially high. Bread was the staple diet of the British working class (alphabetti spaghetti came much much later) and so, with one protectionist measure, the government had brought real hunger to the very poor. It was one of those impossible moral conundrums: hungry masses or bigger profits for landowners? For another thirty years the Corn Law was to remain a political hot potato, which incidentally would have made a very nutritious alternative and they only take five minutes in the microwave.

George IV, Queen Caroline and Mrs Fitzherbert: a very crowded marriage

In 1820 King George III finally went to the great padded cell in the sky after fifty-nine years on the throne, making him the longest-serving monarch the country had ever had. There was much sadness at the final passing of the elderly, infirm King and as a mark of respect 'George the Third' became cockney rhyming slang for something you tread on down the park. At last the bloated boozer and opium addict the 'Prince of Whales' (as he was dubbed) became King George IV in his own right. He saw this as a chance to be finally rid of the wife he had only married back in 1795 because his dad and his ministers had agreed to pay off his massive debts and increase his allowance. George had had a number of mistresses, most notably Mrs Fitzherbert, whom he had secretly married ten years earlier even though she was a Catholic.

Despite her own extravagance and likely adultery, the persecution unleashed against the Queen by the bigamist King and his ministers made her something of a heroic martyr; to women in particular she was a very public symbol of the repression felt by all. She was accused of adultery but when the case against her disintegrated, the cabinet was forced to abandon the plans for divorce and the mobs in London celebrated by lighting fires and smashing the windows of cabinet ministers. But George IV was determined to keep his estranged wife (and first cousin) out of his coronation, while she was intent on being crowned Queen. In front of the entire British establishment and representatives of the crowned heads of Europe, the doors of Westminster Abbey were slammed in Caroline's face. Undeterred she dashed across the road to Westminster Hall where the royal party were gathered. There she banged on the doors with her fists, until she was eventually dragged away by force. It was all very undignified. Utterly humiliated and cast out of the royal family, the uncrowned Queen Caroline died just one week later. It was almost as if she had lived her life like a candle in the wind, and didn't really know whom to turn to when the rain set in.

George IV's popularity never really recovered but he made little effort to improve his public image – unless you count his desperate efforts to strap himself inside an enormous fifty-inch corset. He was described by the Duke of Wellington as 'the worst man I ever fell in with my whole life, the most selfish, the most false, the most ill-natured, the most entirely without one redeeming quality'. And then of course when he died, Wellington eulogized about his many wonderful qualities and everyone nodded in sombre agreement.

Before rock stars and matinée idols there was . . . the poet

With fat dullards like Lord Liverpool and George IV running the country, it's little surprise that the people looked elsewhere for their heroes. At which point, Lord Byron released his first collection of poems and mobs of screaming girls rushed through the crash barriers to get closer to the rebel poet, launching into a medley of his greatest elegies. Byron was a fantastically charismatic Regency idol, famously described by his jilted lover Lady Caroline Lamb as *mad, bad and dangerous to know*. At Cambridge University he had responded to a regulation forbidding dogs by keeping a pet bear. Emerging with a double first in Brooding and Being Handsome, he took his seat in the House of Lords and became one of the few Parliamentary defenders of Catholics and Luddites, even writing poetry on their behalf. Other works attacked the pompous establishment figures of the day like Wellington and Castlereagh, but it was Byron's sexual appetite that eventually made him a social pariah. He openly slept with men and women of all ages, falling in love with his half-sister and fathering a child by her. Visiting him in Italy Shelley wrote that he indulged in sexual practices which *are not only not named, but I believe seldom ever conceived in England*. To which the swift reply came *more details please*. In Venice Byron claimed to have bedded over 250 women in one year, in between swimming the length of the Grand Canal and writing poems and plays that developed his idea of the Byronic hero. Basically, if you were talking to a girl at a party and Byron walked in, you might as well have gone home there and then.

Lord Byron was the first modern celebrity, his face adorned china tea sets and ladies' lockets; had he come along a bit later they could have downloaded his poems as ringtones on their mobile phones. He was James Dean and Che Guevara rolled into one, but, as for all great pin-ups, dying young was unfortunately part of the deal. In his own version of *I'm a Celebrity, Get Me Out of Here*, Byron joined the War of Independence in Greece, and in the desolate marshlands of Missolonghi contracted a fever. The doctors administered leeches (egged on by Ant and Dec) but this only weakened him further and he died before he reached the battlefield. But his idealistic support for the Greeks only added to his heroic status and did much to win support for the Greek cause back in Britain.

Robert Peel told: 'We need more Bobbies on the beat'

Despite the best efforts of Lord Liverpool's government to massacre innocent demonstrators or kill the People's Princess by breaking her heart, there were a lot of capital crimes that were simply going unpunished because juries were refusing to convict. Although the twelve men good and true were only supposed to decide between 'innocent' and 'guilty', it must slightly affect your deliberations when you know that the young shoplifter will be taken from the courtroom to a place of execution and thence hanged by the neck until he is dead. I mean it was only a Mars Bar. Pilfering was just one of two hundred crimes that were punishable by death; impersonating a Chelsea Pensioner, scribbling on Westminster Bridge; chopping down a young tree; the hang 'em and flog* 'em wing of successive governments had held sway for decades, being tough on crime but very soft on the causes of crime along the way.

The new Home Secretary was no woolly liberal but could see that the situation was chaotic and unworkable. Robert Peel sprang from the new manufacturing class – his grandfather had got rich in the Lancashire textile industry, and growing up observing his father's factories Peel had at least met one or two working-class people, which is more than can be said for most of the cabinet. Peel reduced the

---

* Public flogging still occurred when petty thieves were placed in stocks or pillories, if the local Neighbourhood Watch were so minded. In 1817 it had been agreed that the spectacle of flogging women in the street be commuted to hard labour in the workhouse.

number of capital offences to four: murder, treason, arson in a royal dockyard and piracy with violence. I would have added 'pressing the button on the pelican crossing when you have no intention of crossing the road'.

In the Port of London, the bodies of executed prisoners were still left rotting on the gallows as a warning to others, but the government came to accept that this did nothing for house prices in the area. And it's hard enough getting your nervous seven-year-old daughter to sleep without having moonlit skeletons swinging in the wind outside her bedroom window casting their shadows on the wall. 'Darling, it's nothing to be frightened about, it's just the rotting corpse of a mass murderer. Now sweet dreams, dear . . .' So-called 'gibbeting' was abolished and more dignity was also afforded to living convicts as well, with the removal of iron fetters and improved conditions in the prisons.*

For those who were not locked up in Newgate prison or transported to Australia, Britain was still considered a free country, and an Englishman's liberties were fiercely guarded by those who gazed across the Channel and saw the military dictatorships of absolute monarchs on the continent. Like a standing army in peacetime, the idea of any sort of 'police force' had always been treated with instinctive suspicion. So it was in the face of fierce opposition that Peel introduced the Metropolitan Police in 1829.

Previously this work had been done by local volunteers and dodgy law-and-order enthusiasts, but that system only really worked in village communities where everyone knew one another. One thousand constables were introduced on to the London streets to direct tourists to Tower Bridge, tell people the time and pull over any liberated slaves driving an expensive car. Crucially the police were not to be armed, but were to have a whistle that they could blow in the foggy London back streets as bloodhounds barked in the near

---

* Peel's various legal reforms began when he first became Home Secretary in 1822 and continued through his two terms as Prime Minister ending in 1846. For convenience's sake the most notable reforms are all gathered here in one section, as 'Taking literary shortcuts' ceased to be a capital offence in 1824.

distance. It is of course from Robert Peel that we get the slang word 'Bobby' for policeman and well into the twentieth century the police were still nicknamed 'Peelers'. Sir Robert Peel's middle names were 'Bill', 'Fuzz', 'Pig', 'Filth' and 'Rozzer'. Although he is generally considered to be the father of modern policing, the city of Glasgow had had its own police force since 1800, and there was also a London precedent with the 'Bow Street Runners' that had been set up in 1749 by the novelist and magistrate Henry Fielding to arrest anyone trespassing on his genre. But it was the advent of the Metropolitan Police that led to police forces forming all across the country and established the structure, civic code and bizarre headgear that were to be copied across the British Empire.

Catholic Emancipation: Mother Teresa and Father Ted cease to be Public Enemies # 1

Peel may have been a progressive in matters of law and order, but the idea of letting Catholics have the vote was clearly going too far and he stepped down from the government and resigned his seat over the proposed step. With so few 'Papists' on the main island of Britain, this burning issue was fundamentally about Irish freedoms. The fear was that unless basic rights were granted to the Irish, the country might break from the Union altogether, become an independent state and completely out-perform Britain in the Eurovision Song Contest.

The King was also against equal rights for Catholics, which was a bit rich considering he had secretly married one, so he eventually asked the conservative Duke of Wellington to form a government. The hero of Waterloo was finally Prime Minister, but while he had been a brilliant military leader, he now found himself politically out-manoeuvred by the leader of the Irish cause. Daniel O'Connell was a Catholic lawyer and advocate of non-violent agitation against the Union with Britain. He stood in a by-election for Clare and was elected but then denied the right to take up his seat. Another by-election was held, and O'Connell won again. O'Connell threatened to have sixty Catholics elected to Westminster; the situation in

Ireland was growing critical, with civil war looming, and Wellington was faced with the choice of granting Catholic freedoms or preparing for a military conquest of Ireland. Wellington knew Ireland well (he'd even sat in the Dublin Parliament before the Union) and his years in the Iberian Peninsula had taught him the difficulties of imposing military might on a fiercely nationalist population. Eventually the Iron Duke persuaded the King that Catholic Emancipation was the only way forward. The fact that it was the fiercely patriotic Wellington advocating this step, the war hero who had previously resigned over the issue, was enough to persuade the King that there was no other choice, and amid scenes of jubilation in Ireland, Catholic Emancipation became a reality in 1829. Only the Tories could have got away with such a progressive step; to have had the move forced through by the liberals would have created too much division and suspicion. It's like the Conservatives having the first woman Prime Minister or New Labour introducing student loans – the other side could never have done it because it would have been too typical of them.

O'Connell continued his peaceful campaign for the repeal of the Union and at one point was jailed for sedition. He went on to become the first Catholic Mayor of Dublin since the reign of James II and the city's main drag was later named in his honour. Today, such is the amity and mutual respect between the two countries that on Saturday night, O'Connell Street is visited by countless English pilgrims in the form of stag parties who travel from Stansted Airport in order to puke up on the Millennium Spire.

It wasn't just in Ireland that the rise of nationalism was making itself felt. In 1830 a wave of popular uprisings spread across the continent after the French deposed their autocratic ruler and replaced him with his more democratically minded cousin. England too had a new King, as the unmemorable William IV (1830–7) filled in the gap between the Regency Period and the Victorian Era.

'So I suppose the style of architecture from my reign will be called "Williamesque", will it?'

'Er, maybe, your majesty . . .'

William, the younger brother of George IV, had ten children by his mistress, but being illegitimate they were not eligible for the throne. Had William's marriage to his actress friend been permitted by his big brother, there would have been no Queen Victoria, no Queen Elizabeth II and an entirely separate branch of the royal family would have taken precedence, eventually including the couple's descendant: Conservative leader David Cameron.

The Great Reform Act of 1832: democracy starts here

The general election that had to follow the accession of a new monarch saw a significant increase in the number of members committed to Parliamentary reform. Many voters had been inspired by revolutionary events on the continent, where the middle classes demanded a say in the running of their countries, got massacred and then shut up about it. Although England had had a Parliament since the thirteenth century, it represented wealth, not people. Indignant farm labourers would say to their MPs, 'It's almost as if you think your land is more important than the people who work it . . .'

'Yes. And your point is?'

During the centuries when the ruling class was made up entirely of landowners, allocating seats according to property had seemed like a sensible way for them to organize things, but since the Industrial Revolution, wealth and influence was no longer confined to the aristocracy while the Enlightenment and the French Revolution had introduced ideas of equality and democracy and other subversive notions that kept the King and the Duke of Wellington awake at night. Set against these modern criteria the House of Commons was laughably unrepresentative. There were MPs for bits of land that had long ago fallen into the sea. The only residents of Old Sarum in Wiltshire were twenty-seven rabbits and a badger. It was simply a hill with a ruined castle on it, which certainly saved a few bob on election leaflets. As well as these 'pocket boroughs' where the MP was simply chosen by a rich local patron, there were 'rotten boroughs' where the electors were so few that it was normal to pay them to choose you as their representative in the Commons. With no secret ballot and voting taking place over a period of weeks, bribery was not only endemic but accepted as perfectly normal.

There had been calls for Parliamentary reform for decades, and with huge new towns like Manchester, Birmingham and Leeds completely without representation, the situation had become intolerable. Voting was still seen as a privilege not a right, but there was also a practical dimension to the issue; you needed an Act of Parliament to build a bridge or a road, to establish a park or build a pier. Without an MP to introduce a bill on your behalf, proposing major projects was subject to long planning delays that we can only imagine today. The Duke of Wellington claimed the Parliamentary arrangement was already pure perfection. 'I cannot imagine how a better system might be devised,' said the member for Tellytubbyland.

Members promptly demonstrated what a great system it was by deserting him for the opposition to put the Whigs back in power. Both wings of the British ruling class were terrified of the masses and the constant spectre of revolution. It's just that the Whigs saw that by appeasing the middle classes, the revolution would be much less likely to happen as there would be no one to organize the firing squad duty-rota.

The new government was headed by Earl Grey, remembered today more for his taste in tea than his great achievements in government.

'Right, I propose to introduce a Reform Act that will add a quarter of a million adult males to the four hundred and thirty-five thousand existing voters—'

'Eurgh! This tea's disgusting. Did you rinse out the washing-up liquid?'

'Ah yes, 'tis the latest fashion, tea flavoured with bergamot. You'll get used to it. Now, most controversially of all, not all of these new voters will own their own property—'

'Eurgh, bloody hell; I can't drink this . . . Haven't you got any PG Tips?'

Tampering with the English cuppa and introducing notions of democracy was clearly going too far and the House of Lords repeatedly blocked Earl Grey's measure, while the King refused to create more peers to force the bill through. The Parliament of the landed gentry was leading the country to the brink. Throughout 1831 the mood darkened and the British middle classes began to turn the screws: 'Either you give us a say in things or we won't volunteer to be local magistrates any more.'

'They're bluffing! They'd never do it!'

'We mean it. No JPs, no sheriffs, no one to judge the "Britain in Bloom" competition . . .'

'Please, we beg you; think of the flower arrangers!'

The volunteers who made Britain's local government function were on strike. Many more withdrew their savings from the bank to create a financial crisis for the government. In some areas, political unions began drilling in the expectation of civil war.

Eventually even the Iron Duke* had to accept that the Lords' obstruction of reform was tearing the country apart and, having already resigned in favour of Earl Grey, he now urged many of his fellow Lords to cease voting against reform. As with Catholic Emancipation, it needed the ultra-conservative Wellington to effect radical reform.

The first reformed Parliament met in 1833 and the old guard said the place would never be the same again, which it wasn't when the building promptly burnt to the ground. All the newly elected MPs were still not familiar with Parliamentary convention and whispered, 'Is it normal for flames to be sweeping through the corridors like that?'

'Not sure; best not say anything, we don't want to show our ignorance . . .'

A great debate ensued about the type of building that should replace it. Classical styles as employed in Washington were rejected as having acquired revolutionary and republican connotations. Everyone was agreed that whatever the design, the whole thing

---

* Wellington wasn't called the Iron Duke because of any sort of resolution of character, it was a nickname he earned when he had iron shutters fitted to his windows to stop the mob smashing them during the Parliamentary reform crisis.

should encounter endless delays and go wildly over budget. Eventually they opted for Charles Barry's bold, gothic medieval-castle look featuring eye-catching towers, ornate stone carvings, intricate gold paintwork all surrounded by big grey, anti-terrorist concrete slabs.

The fresh intake of MPs gave the new House of Commons a more progressive reforming edge and one of the first acts of the new Parliament was the abolition of slavery throughout the British Empire. Only the trade itself had been abolished in 1807, slavery still underpinned the economy of colonies like Jamaica (where the local administration actually refused to free the slaves and had its constitution suspended). A massive twenty million pounds' compensation was promised by Parliament, which the freed slaves thought might be a start. 'No, the compensation's not for *you*. It's for the slave-*owners*.' The Christian middle classes were deeply offended by the very idea of slavery; Parliament wanted the workers of the colonies to enjoy all the liberties enjoyed by free-born Englishmen, of whom millions were now employed alongside women and children in factories and coal mines. New legislation prevented children under the age of nine from working in the factories, while those under the age of thirteen were limited to an eight-hour day. In the countryside, rural workers had seen their wages drop in an agricultural slump that had continued since the end of the Napoleonic war. Poverty and exploitation in the countryside led to riots with farm machinery smashed and hayricks burnt. When townies started turning up, straying off the footpath and leaving gates open, they got even more annoyed.

Although trade unions were no longer illegal, the government remained terrified of the idea of working-class organizations. When six men from the tiny Dorset village of Tolpuddle combined to protect their pitiful wages, they were prosecuted on the grounds that they had sworn an illegal oath, and duly transported to Australia. The ensuing outcry earned them 'Official Lefty Martyr Status' and ensured that for evermore they would be the subject of tiresome shouty plays by theatre-in-education companies doing bad West Country accents.

Wages were so low in the countryside that some agricultural workers were now being paid relief under the old Poor Laws. Since Elizabethan times the Poor Laws had allowed local parishes to pay out meagre sums to the aged and infirm, but now this ancient social-security system was supporting more people than the local rates could afford. The Whigs set about reforming the system, taking the administration away from thousands of individual parishes and bringing relief of the poor under governmental control. 'Right, if you could just fill out form DSS/13(b)/sp/1 "Application for Relief under the Reformed Poor Law 1834" we will have your claim assessed and processed within twenty-eight working days.'

The safety net in early-nineteenth-century England took the form of a cold brick workhouse. But, convinced that the work-shy poor would flock to the workhouses to live a life of luxury feasting on gruel and old root vegetables, the Poor Law commissioners ensured that the workhouses were sufficiently harsh to deter all but the most desperate. Families were deliberately split up, and the barest necessities for survival were grudgingly doled out by the workhouse guardians, who were generally cruel, fat men with enormous whiskers and names like Mr Grindpoor or Master Harshwhip. Dickens's *Oliver Twist* was written in this decade, and did much to bring the inadequacies of the Poor Law reforms to a wider audience. But then Dodger and Nancy sang 'Oom pah-pah!' and somehow everything seemed all right again. To stop cheeky cockney kids stealing silk handkerchiefs and then getting the entire marketplace caught up in an extended song-and-dance number, the reforming Whig government set about establishing some sort of schooling for the nation's poor. The Anglican Church and non-conformist organizations set up education boards that raised funds for the building of parish schoolhouses. It was that decision, to give the job of establishing the schools to the churches, that today has thousands of young parents attending church every Sunday, praying, 'Oh Lord, please let the vicar notice that I've turned up, so that I can get the kids into the local C. of E. primary school.'

It was to be many decades before education became compulsory: there was a deep-seated fear that educating the poor would make them dissatisfied with their lot in life; some even argued that the poor would be happier if they were kept in ignorance. Only in Scotland, whose education system was way in advance of the rest of the United Kingdom, was the majority of the population literate, which may go some way to explain the disproportionately high number of Scots making significant contributions to the worlds of science, literature and football punditry.

But the greatest changes in society were caused by factors outside of the government's control. The first census in 1801 had recorded a population of under sixteen and a half million. Just twenty years later it had risen to twenty-four million, despite the large numbers emigrating to America, Australia, South Africa and anywhere else you could have a barbecue without it raining. But the country was also shrinking, with improvements in communications bringing the regions within reach of one another. At the beginning of the Industrial Revolution thousands of miles of canals were cut across the English countryside, joining up the navigable rivers and creating a transport network for coal, freight and bearded men with pipes. But they'd only just finished painting the flowers on the side of the narrow boat when the entire canal system was superseded by the railways.

'Well, no question about what we're going to do with four thousand miles of disused inland waterways.'

'Quite. At last we have a national depository for supermarket trolleys.'

The opening of the first inter-city railway line was a major national occasion with the Prime Minister and members of his cabinet in attendance. It all went off very well apart from political riots and one cabinet member being run down and killed by the train.

'We apologize for the delay in the 1830 train from Manchester to Liverpool,' droned the tannoy. 'This is due to a cabinet minister on the track.' And all the passengers waiting on the platform tutted at hearing the usual excuses. Former President of the Board of Trade William Huskisson had been standing on the middle of the track chatting to the Duke of Wellington when Stephenson's Rocket*

---

* George Stephenson is often credited as the inventor of the train, but its evolution was a complex and protracted one. The ancient Greeks had rickety carts on wooden rails, which is not dissimilar to the London to Southend line today.

came hurtling along and turned him from the world's first train-spotter to the world's first railway casualty.

Despite this slight PR setback, railway mania soon gripped the country and by 1843 there were two thousand miles of track linking the industrial centres and creating whole new towns. One of these is today home to the Swindon Steam Railway Museum, where you can see exhibits of old rolling stock and life-size models of people waiting on a platform. If you want.

Victoria becomes Queen: 'It'll never last,' say critics

In 1837 William IV passed away with no surviving legitimate children to succeed him. They say the mourning continued for minutes. The throne then passed to his young niece who had never expected to be Queen. However, one eagle-eyed legal pedant noticed that Queen Victoria (1837–1901) was in fact a female, which barred her from the throne of Hanover, and so the 120-year-old constitutional link with the German kingdom was broken.* It seemed like a terrible wrench at the time, but I think we're probably over the worst of it now. Bye-bye Hanover; thanks for all the rubbish kings. After mad George III and his dreadful sons, there was some concern about the unpopularity of the monarchy, so it was with some trepidation that the Prime Minister Lord Melbourne waited to inform an eighteen-year-old girl that she was now Queen. The coronation of the country's longest-ever reigning monarch was a memorable affair but for all the wrong reasons. Nobody had thought to have a dress rehearsal and the various players stood in the wrong places and messed up their parts. The tiny Queen was handed the royal sceptre and couldn't believe that she was expected to carry something so heavy, and when the ruby ring was placed upon her finger it wouldn't fit.

Victoria became quite dependent on Melbourne, emotionally as well as politically. And Melbourne was more than happy to spend so

* Queen Victoria's first language was German, she learnt English later.

much time with the beautiful young Queen, especially having had his own wife run off with Lord Byron. Some even gossiped that the Queen was having secret sexual relations with the Prime Minister, which is one rumour you never hear in modern times, not even when Maggie was PM. However, Victoria's dependence on the Whig leader made it hard to adjust to a more formal relationship with his successor and when the Tory Robert Peel became Prime Minister a major political stand-off flared up over the Queen's choice of advisers. The so-called 'Bedchamber Crisis' sounds much racier than it was but for a while it gripped London society, and no doubt the women and children working in the coal mines talked of nothing else: 'The mineshaft is narrower up here, we have to push the coal truck on our hands and knees. Anyway, what was I saying? Oh yeah, the Queen cannot have ladies-in-waiting who are the wives and daughters of opposition MPs . . .'

'But Sir Robert cannot presume to dictate Her Majesty's choice of friends – hang on, the pit-prop's giving way, we're going to be crushed . . .'

Peel refused to form a Tory government while the Queen surrounded herself with Whigs and so Melbourne returned; basically the government of the day was decided by the whim of a twenty-year-old Sloane who didn't want someone different brushing her hair.

When the Queen Vic married her cousin Prince Albert of Square in 1840 her dependency shifted to her new husband and Peel was able to become Prime Minister the following year. The Queen wore a white dress for the wedding – a tradition that has continued ever since. But the first child was born nine months after the wedding, rather than the six months which is customary today. The royal couple went on to have a further eight kids, and nearly all of them were married into the royal houses of Europe. It became part of British foreign policy to place the Queen's children into the palaces of Moscow or Berlin, and as a special wedding present all their offspring were to inherit haemophilia from their mother. Nearly every royal family in Europe had to take great care not to cut or injure themselves, which is particularly difficult in a century when revolutionaries kept firing pistols at them.

The Chartists: 'I have a dream – but it takes too long to explain'

Radicals across Europe must have gazed with envy across the English Channel at the immensity and organization of the world's first working-class mass movement. 'At last, the workers have united! Are they storming the royal palaces?'

'No . . .'

'Have they seized members of the government and taken control of the army?'

'Not exactly . . .'

'So what exactly are the masses doing to overthrow the old order?'

'Er, well, they've organized a very big petition . . .'

Chartism was a very British radical movement. Agitators broke into armaments stores, dashed past the guns and helped themselves to all the clipboards. At secret training camps, volunteers were taught how to ensure that people didn't sign in the box where you were supposed to print your address. Their specially trained élite petitioners could strip down and reassemble a fountain pen in under fourteen seconds.

The movement sprang up from working-class disillusionment at the Great Reform Act of 1832. Fired up by their anger at working conditions in cities and the countryside and the way Poor Law reforms had driven the unemployed into the workhouse, the movement unified around the six points of the Charter that were drawn up by the movement's founders. These demands were:

1) Universal male suffrage (a suggestion to include votes for women in the campaign had been dropped very early on)
2) Constituencies of equal numbers (the Reform Act had still left huge discrepancies in Parliamentary representation)
3) Payment for MPs (so anyone could stand for Parliament, not just men with private fortunes)
4) An end to the property-owning qualification for MPs
5) A secret ballot (to stop intimidation and bribery)
6) Annual Parliaments (the only demand that was not finally met)

So when someone at a rally shouted, 'WHAT DO WE WANT?' they all had to shout the extended response while counting out all the demands on their fingers, until they got to five and the crowd went, 'Er . . . and what's the sixth one? Oh yeah . . . AND AN END TO THE PROPERTY-OWNING QUALIFICATION FOR MEMBERS OF PARLIAMENT!'

In 1839 a massive petition was presented to the House of Commons, but members voted not to even receive it. The upper-class majority were still appalled by having entrepreneurs and industrialists in Parliament, they certainly weren't going to listen to a representation from people who took sugar in their tea and had 'Mum' tattooed on their arms. The rejection pushed more radical elements in the movement towards violence. It didn't help that the Chartists often held their meetings in the pub; after a few pints their campaign slogan of 'Peace and order is our watchword' soon turned to 'Let's go and put traffic cones on all the statues' heads'. There was sporadic rioting and one disastrous insurrection did enormous harm to what had been perceived as a peaceful campaign. Armed Chartists stormed Westgate Hotel in Newport, South Wales, because, as every revolutionary movement throughout history has understood, once you have the Westgate Hotel, Newport, nothing can stop you. Newport Community Centre and the Baptist Chapel are bound to follow. It was claimed they intended this to be the signal for a national uprising, but in fact it was just a disorganized attempt to rescue some Chartist prisoners who were being held there. The authorities had packed the hotel with soldiers who fired into the crowd killing over twenty and injuring many more. The leaders of the uprising were sentenced to death (later commuted to transportation) and the Chartist movement became tainted and divided.

Two more Chartist petitions were presented, one in 1842 and a third at the climax of the movement in 1848, a year of revolutions all across Europe. Fifty thousand protesters gathered on Kennington Common, while the eighty-year-old Duke of Wellington organized the soldiers and cannons on every bridge across the Thames in case they defied orders to remain south of the river. Feargus O'Connor, their increasingly unreliable leader, claimed an unconvincing five million signatures had been collected for the final appeal, but with so many people involved it was no surprise that a few jokers had added one or two unlikely names to the list, including the Duke of Wellington, Mr Punch and Queen Victoria. (Or maybe her signature was genuine? You know what it's like: someone asks you to sign a petition; you agree just so as to avoid giving offence.) These irregularities were seized upon to discredit the enormous achievement of the petition and obvious strength of public feeling, making it easier for the government to once again dismiss the entire campaign out of hand.

The movement petered out; Feargus O'Connor died in a lunatic asylum and historians generally file the movement under the heading marked 'Disorganized failures'. But Chartism did succeed in the end; within twenty years there were major extensions of the franchise and all of the demands that they put on the agenda were eventually realized, with the exception of annual general elections, which frankly sounds like a bloody nightmare. The Chartists may have lacked a Martin Luther King, but they were the Civil Rights Movement of the UK; powerless protesters demanding democracy by peaceful means, even though their faith in Parliament was repeatedly shattered. What they lack is a modern minority championing their place in history. Women are drawn to the suffragettes, the Irish look back to the Home Rule movement, but white working-class men have not been allowed to see themselves as a historically oppressed minority. That's why there are fewer white vans with stickers saying *Remember the Chartists* than *Chelsea FC Pride of London*.

The Chartists' 'failure' is often contrasted with the success of the far more middle-class Anti-Corn Law League, a straightforward single-issue campaign that was so successful that these days you hardly ever hear politicians calling for the reintroduction of the Corn Laws. With the price of bread kept artificially high by this piece of protectionism, the league was able to claim that the law contravened the Lord's Prayer by denying the poor their daily bread. They made great use of the new penny post, probably inventing junk mail along the way, but even though the new Prime Minister Robert Peel may have been coming round to the idea of free trade, it was as much a national catastrophe as well as effective campaigning that finally saw the Corn Law abolished.

The Irish Potato Famine: where's Bob Geldof when you need him?

Ireland in the 1840s was further away from England than Ethiopia was in the 1980s. Today television pictures beamed by satellite can instantly convey the scale of suffering resulting from natural or man-made disasters around the world. Sadly, in 1846 there was no Ethiopian pop star to get all the top African singers to do a Christmas single for the starving millions in rural Ireland. Although the island was politically part of the United Kingdom, its faraway Celtic inhabitants were distrusted for their race, rebelliousness and religion. Irish peasants were among the poorest in Europe, and with so little land they had become dependent on potatoes as their staple food. The kids would rush home from working in the fields: 'What's for tea, Mum?'

'It's your favourite, lad! Potatoes!'

'Yummy, I love spuds. I wish we could have them every day.'

'Er, well, we do . . .'

Following a particularly wet summer, a fungus from America was discovered on the crop, and soon the blight had spread throughout the island (and to the Scottish Highlands too, whose suffering is often overlooked). The entire potato crop had failed and suddenly millions were facing starvation. A million died in a year, millions more eventually emigrated; indeed Ireland's population has yet to recover. The Irish language all but died out, but the survivors developed a burning sense of hatred for the English who in 1845 imported more Irish corn than would have been needed to feed Ireland's entire population.

But it seemed the rules of economics could not be suspended for the duration of this emergency. While reports came back to London about the dying bodies lying on the side of the road, it was explained that there was very little that could be done. 'The island lacks the infrastructure to distribute emergency food supplies'; 'It wouldn't reach the people who need it most'; 'There is too much corruption for relief efforts to be effective'. What is so striking about the 'explanations' given at the time is that they are exactly the same excuses that are used today as to why nothing can be done to alleviate the suffering in Africa. And yet only 150 years after the famine, Ireland became one of the most prosperous societies in the world; within a few generations its hungry peasants had gone from sleeping on mud floors in overcrowded hovels to living in plush white bungalows with central heating and satellite TV that they built themselves beside the ruins of the old famine cottages that still litter the countryside. Ireland's journey over the nineteenth and twentieth centuries proves that poverty and apparent hopelessness can be overcome and there is no reason that the same transformation could not be made to happen in Ethiopia or Sudan. Now if it rained for a whole summer in Ireland, the worst that would happen is that you'd be left with no choice but to visit the Skibbereen Famine Museum and Heritage Centre, and watch a video of Jeremy Irons in a chunky jumper describing just how bad it was.

But the Irish crisis finally gave Peel the opportunity to trigger the political earthquake that the shifting tectonic plates of the rural economy and manufacturing trade made inevitable. Throughout the 1840s the Anti-Corn Law League had gone from strength to strength; clearly wheat intolerance was the big issue for the middle classes. Effigies of Peel were burnt in public and in January 1843 an assassin burst into Peel's carriage and shot the Prime Minister dead. Except it wasn't the PM, it was his secretary riding in his boss's coach.* But Peel feared revolution, and now he opted to lower the price of corn. The much-feared Weetabix riots of '46 were averted.

The Repeal of the Corn Laws' significance wasn't just about the

---

* The assassin was actually a delusional madman who believed he personally was the subject of a massive international conspiracy involving the Pope and the Tory government. He should have just put it in a book; it would have become a number-one bestseller.

price of bread; it was a victory for trade over land, of the new merchant classes over the old aristocracy, of consumer over producer. As such it split the Tories right down the middle and an up-and-coming star of the Conservatives called Benjamin Disraeli launched such a fierce attack on Peel that the Prime Minister lost a vote in the House of Commons, resigned his office* and the Tories did not win another general election until 1874. It was the moment the political psychology of the century was defined. Free-traders, radicals, Peelites and Whigs would emerge as the dominant force under a new label 'the Liberals' to champion free trade, extend Parliamentary reform and then later believe in pretty well all the same things as the Labour Party while not wishing to mix with any working-class people.

Victorian capitalism: more fun owning a factory than working in one

The implosion of the Conservatives after 1846 does not mean that Britain suddenly grew into a liberal nanny state with free school milk and rubber matting under the swings. Victorian Britain continued its explosive development as an aggressively capitalist society – a unique and an entirely unplanned experiment in profit-driven industrialization. Nowhere else in the world had mankind ever had the opportunity to discover what would happen if you just left the rich to build lots of mills and factories, packed them with machines powered by coal and steam and then set the poor to work in them.

'Do you think we might need to regulate any of this?'

'Good God no, that's the worst thing you can do to business. Once you let the government start sticking its nose in, you end up with all sorts of petty rules and regulations, with bureaucrats suddenly turning up and droning on that according to Health and Safety

---

* Peel died in 1850 after being thrown from his horse. His country estate is now the Drayton Manor Theme Park featuring such rides as 'Shockwave' and 'Splash Canyon'.

regulations, rule 7b subsection 3, six-year-old girls are not permitted to pull coal carts underground for longer than sixteen hours a day or some other ridiculous bit of red tape.'

By the middle of the century, the government had taken the first steps to regulate the worst excesses of the new society they were still struggling to comprehend, but they were always many steps behind. Accounts of just how grim life was for the vast majority of the Queen's subjects filtered through in occasional government reports and often disbelieved anecdotal accounts, but the laissez-faire philosophy was so ingrained in the government that they would have considered it dangerously interventionist to put out a house fire. For example, millions of workers were paid in tokens that could only be exchanged for over-priced and shoddy goods on sale at the factory shop. A miner would have to rent his safety lamp, paying its actual value many times over during his working life. Trade unions may not have been illegal, but neither was dismissing anyone who joined one. At the beginning of the century the progressive mill-owner Robert Owen had attempted to create something more humane with New Lanark in Scotland, a community where the employees were well treated, properly housed and their children educated. Although he is often seen as one of the founding fathers of British socialism, Owen's attempt to unite Britain's workers as 'The Grand National Consolidated Trades Union' fell apart when they couldn't fit the name on the banner.

More radical solutions to the ills of the modern industrial society were being penned by Karl Marx and his colleague Friedrich Engels. It says something about the self-confidence of Victorian England that these radical revolutionaries, exiled from several European capitals, were free to write what they wanted in England.

'I am writing a book advocating the violent overthrow of the British capitalist state.'

'Fine, but could you please whisper because *this is* a library.'

Rather than wading through the Communist Manifesto, which failed to get selected as Richard and Judy's Book of the Week in 1848, overwhelmed bookshop browsers would have had the choice of Dickens, Thackeray, the Brontës, Elizabeth Barrett Browning,

Tennyson, Macaulay and John Stuart Mill. William Wordsworth was now the Poet Laureate although he died in 1850 from exhaustion trying to find a rhyme for 'daffodils'. All this time, Charles Darwin's manuscript of *On the Origin of Species* was sitting in a drawer in his office, which he finally got round to publishing in 1859.* Darwin's theory of evolution sent shockwaves through the worlds of science, philosophy and religion. Not only did it contradict everything that they held most dear about God creating man in his own image, it also told them they were all descended from monkeys, which created a certain amount of anxiety at Buckingham Palace as they wondered who was going to tell Her Majesty.

The visual arts were flourishing too, with the foundation of the Pre-Raphaelite movement, to provide dreamy soft-focus posters for the walls of female students in halls of residence. The great J. M. W. Turner died in 1851 and was later to have the Turner Prize named in his honour, so that his brilliantly atmospheric use of light and colour could be remembered with sharks in formaldehyde and Tracey Emin's messy duvet. Dickens's *Hard Times* or Turner's *Rain, Steam and Speed* may have provided snapshots of life in the middle of the nineteenth century, but society was changing so quickly that neither artists, philosophers nor governments could quite keep up.

The Great Exhibition: even more fun than the Millennium Dome

The rate of change and innovation, combined with the huge profits being made by the few, gave an air of hubristic self-confidence to the early Victorians that found its expression in the Great Exhibition of 1851. With a more gritty and realist director, the Great Exhibition could have been so much more interesting. 'Let's really show

---

* There is much speculation as to why Darwin took around twenty years to publish his great work. Some say he was anxious about society's reaction, others that he was finally prompted into publishing by similar ideas coming from Alfred Wallace. My own favourite is a recent theory that he never got round to it because 'he had a lot on'.

Victorian Britain for what it is. We can have displays of match-factory workers whose faces are rotting away from "phossy jaw". We could have real-life chimney sweeps, little boys with bleeding knees and elbows emerging from sooty fireplaces, coughing and spluttering before your very eyes. Or how about a parade of some of the hundreds of thousands of prostitutes plying their trade across Britain today, giving the lie to the myth of the upstanding morality of the model Victorian family.'

Sadly the gritty social realists never got a look-in at the Great Exhibition and so instead they simply had a massive public event celebrating and promoting Britain's advanced technological development, its huge manufacturing capacity, its colonial possessions and dominance of world trade. Frankly it was just showing off.

Prince Albert explained what was required in his now impeccable English: 'Big glass building needing we are,' and Sir Joseph Paxton designed the enormous glass structure that *Punch* magazine dubbed the 'Crystal Palace'. With days to go before the exhibition opened in Hyde Park the story goes that the whole enormous glass building became overrun with sparrows; thousands upon thousands of them were swarming around the Ancient History Zone and crapping on the life-size model dinosaurs. Every attempt to stop them getting into the structure had failed; the powers that be were at a loss at what to do. Finally Queen Victoria called for the elderly Duke of Wellington, who listened carefully to the distraught Queen and then calmly replied, 'Sparrowhawks, ma'am.' The problem was solved in an instant. This tale may be apocryphal, but passed into architectural folklore and 150 years later when they came to construct the Millennium Dome they were determined that the centre would not be overrun with sparrows or pigeons. Or visitors for that matter.

The Great Exhibition on the other hand was a huge success; attracting six million visitors, many of whom made their first journeys on trains to visit the attraction. In a way it marks the pinnacle of Victorian self-confidence, before the rise of Germany, Russia and the United States, before the Franco-Prussian War demonstrated that Britain was unable to control the balance of power on the continent, and before Prince Albert kicked the bucket and the

Queen went into an even longer period of mourning than the lady from the Scottish Widows adverts. The whole massive structure of the Crystal Palace was eventually reassembled in the South London suburbs in a determined attempt by one resident to have a bigger conservatory than his neighbour.*

British Empire: globe painters order extra pink

By the middle of the century, a quarter of all world trade went through British ports. Britain became the 'Workshop of the World' – that's 'workshop' in the manufacturing sense; it didn't mean that everyone was sitting on the floor in circles discussing what they had learnt from the non-violent direct-action role play. Britain was not just trading with its overseas possessions but also with an informal empire – a major factor in the rapid growth of the economies of the Balkans, the United States and Latin America was their trade with Britain.

With British manufacturing output expanding so rapidly, new markets were continually sought and new sources of raw materials always needed. The British Empire was conquered more by market forces than armed forces. Some possessions such as Gibraltar or Cyprus were seized by the navy or acquired at the post-war conference table for their strategic military value, but on the whole the pink bits on the globe were wherever British companies happened to have landed and managed to outdo other competitors.

Britain was increasingly moving towards free trade as the generator of wealth. One key political decision had been to allow merchant ships from any country to carry British goods. Overnight this removed the one major logistical constraint holding back growth; that there were only so many ships that could export British manufactured products. Suddenly ships from all over the world were sailing into British ports and seeking new markets for British goods.

* The Crystal Palace burnt down in 1936. Until the 1970s Crystal Palace football team were dubbed 'the Glaziers', which is hardly a nickname to get the heart racing.

Like Microsoft's early decision to allow anyone to design software compatible with Windows (while other software providers attempted to maintain total control and thus were left far behind) letting others do your work for you has always been the key to astronomical levels of growth.

The British Empire grew out of this expansion in private trade; just as today every Starbucks is a small individual franchise under one corporate logo, all the British trading stations began as unconnected adventures in private enterprise that used the Union Flag logo to protect themselves from a hostile takeover from the French Empire or Coffee Republic. Private companies shipping tea back from British plantations in India had the protection of the Royal Navy. Or if your trade was in something a little stronger, the British military would be employed to protect British traders selling opium. In 1840 British warships shelled a number of Chinese ports after their government had tried to stop the lucrative British opium exports from India to China. After repeated requests to halt the smuggling, the Chinese finally seized a large amount of the drug and set fire to it, which is sort of the point of opium, except that they weren't even attempting to inhale the smoke or pay for the privilege. China ended up paying huge amounts of money to stop British warships shelling Nanking, Britain gained Hong Kong and the opium trade continued. It was a bit like today's 'War on Drugs' with the minor difference that we were on the other side.

This style of 'gun-boat diplomacy', as it was ironically dubbed, was employed all over the world whenever British interests were at stake. Lord Palmerston became a very popular Foreign Secretary owing to his no-nonsense approach of sending in the battleships if foreign governments so much as spilt his pint. When a riot in Athens burnt down the house of a Portuguese man called Don Pacifico, Palmerston turned a local compensation claim into a major international incident. Pacifico had been born in Gibraltar and thus was able to claim British citizenship. British ships blockaded Greek ports and seized local shipping, prompting furious protests from neutral traders such as Russia and France, whose ambassador to London was withdrawn as a result. But in a marathon speech defending his rather over-the-top response to a delayed insurance claim, Palmerston cited the proud claim of a citizen of the Roman Empire, *'Civis Romanus sum'** ('I am a Roman citizen'), explaining that any inhabitant of the British Empire could now expect the protection of Britain's military might. After enduring one five-hour speech full of Latin quotes, MPs were never going to dare question his policies again.

Although we think of the century between 1815 and 1914 as a remarkably peaceful one, Britain was involved in countless military adventures, often more costly than the politicians at home had bargained for. Britain set the pattern for major powers mistakenly thinking that Afghanistan would be a pushover; just like Russia and America in more recent times, Britain learnt that invading Afghanistan was a bad idea. Or rather it didn't.

Afghanistan was important for its strategic position between Britain's rapidly growing Indian empire and expansionist Russia, which was alarmed by Britain's growing influence on its borders. When a pro-British Afghan leader was toppled in favour of an apparently pro-Russian one, British troops invaded, occupying Kabul in 1839 and putting their favoured puppet on the Afghan throne. But sending the army into the region was one thing, keeping control of the country was quite another. Now the Western commanders, who in any period drama on the subject would clearly have to be made to look a bit like George Bush and Tony Blair, were alarmed to find themselves out of their depth in Afghanistan. The British and Indian forces were compelled to surrender and were allowed to retreat through the icy mountain passes back to British-held territory, facing constant attacks, icy weather and food shortages. Out of sixteen thousand soldiers and camp followers, just one man made it back. He turned up half dead at the gates of Jalalabad with part of his skull smashed by an Afghan sword, although his life had been saved by his earlier decision to stuff a copy of *Blackwood's Magazine* into his hat. His heroic return is the subject

---

* President Kennedy made the same analogy during the Cold War, saying that the modern equivalent of *'Civis Romanus sum'* was *'Ich bin ein Berliner'*. Unfortunately that translates literally as 'I am a jelly-filled doughnut'.

of the bleak and evocative painting *Remnants of an Army* by Elizabeth Butler which today hangs in the Tate Gallery conveying the futility and tragedy of war with perhaps a little more power than *Carry On up the Khyber*.

Not content with one insane military adventure in the region, Britain's ongoing power struggle with Russia soon broke out into war in the Black Sea, a conflict that gave us Florence Nightingale, the Charge of the Light Brigade and a versatile item of knitted headgear.

The Crimean War: not worth it for the balaclava

Crimea is a small peninsula in the Black Sea, so clearly of major strategic interest to Britain. In fact the war against Russia originally looked set to take place in modern-day Romania, in response to Russian military advances along the Danube. But when Russia duly withdrew its forces, Britain and France had to find somewhere else to fight them. The wider picture was that the Ottoman Empire was in decline and that the Russians were gaining territory and strategic influence as a result, to the great concern of the British who liked things just the way they were.

For the first time since they fought Julius Caesar, the British and French were on the same side, but the rivalry continued as the two powers sought to outdo one another over who could be the most incompetent. It was a close-run thing, but Britain won the uselessness competition; the masterstroke being the delivery of five thousand left boots. By the time the war was over, there would be quite a few soldiers for whom one boot was all that was required.

Military operations were a disaster from the outset. The powers in London arrogantly presumed that their forces would quickly capture Sebastopol, and so the soldiers were not provided with winter clothing or provisions for a long siege. With the Russian winter descending, freezing soldiers preparing for the Battle of Balaclava were forced to cut eye-holes in woollen socks and pull them over their heads. Sebastopol still looked impregnable.

'What are we going to do, sir?'

'Well, I think we should wear them rolled down till it stops snowing; and when the sun comes out, we could roll them back up to make
a little woolly hat, see?'

'No, I meant in military terms, sir? The cavalry are here with their
commander, Lord Cardigan.'

'Ah yes, the battle. Now, Cardigan . . . ooh, I like the way your
woolly jumper has those little buttons down the middle . . .'

'Yes, because you can have it done up for when it's cold, and open
for when it's warmer . . .'

In the end the Earl of Cardigan led his men to one of the most
infamous disasters in British military history. In the famous 'Charge
of the Light Brigade', as recalled in Tennyson's poem, six hundred
men galloped the wrong way up 'the valley of death', where Russian
artillery could easily fire on them from both sides.* The Russians
presumed that the British soldiers must be drunk. Over a hundred
men were killed and even more injured; history has tended to put the
blame for this spectacular bit of aristocratic bungling at the door of
Lord Cardigan, although the ultimate command came from Lord
Lucan, which is not a name to fill you with confidence in the area of
health and safety.

The supreme commander in the Crimea was the elderly Lord
Raglan, a veteran of Waterloo who kept referring to the French as
'the enemy', at which his officers had to explain, 'Actually, sir, the
French are on our side.'

'What?'

'The French, sir. Not enemies, sir; allies.'

'Nonsense. We must attack the French at once.'

But at last the disasters of war were not going unreported back
home. Not only was the war photographed, but the advent of the
telegraph meant that a correspondent for *The Times* could send
regular reports back to Britain where his damning indictments
almost knocked the adverts for snuff and domestic servants off the
front page. The cumulative accounts of administrative bungling,

---

* As George Orwell noted later, it says something about the British self-image that
our most famous war poem commemorates a horrendous defeat.

the mistreatment of lower ranks and the stubborn adherence to stupid orders from London eventually forced the hopeless Lord Aberdeen to resign as Prime Minister and the more military-minded Lord Palmerston stepped into the breach. The only problem with the uncensored dispatches was that they were read by the Russians who learnt from the newspaper everything they needed to know about British troop movements.

Among those reading the distressing reports in *The Times* was a feisty woman who had appalled her upper-class family by helping the sick and dying instead of spending all her time fluttering her fan or writing long letters to her friends in swirly handwriting. Florence Nightingale* had been running a nursing home in Harley Street when a family friend who happened to be Minister for War asked her if she'd mind awfully going out to Russia and taking charge of the hospital in Scutari, near Constantinople. Nightingale transformed the image of nurses; previously they had been little more than menial helpers and nursing was often the occupation of repentant prostitutes. Here at last was an upper-class Englishwoman prepared to bring order and cleanliness to hospitals. Before Florence Nightingale you were more likely to die if you went to hospital than if they left you where you were – be it London or the Crimea.† This was just one of the many alarming statistics that Florence Nightingale demonstrated with her brilliant command of statistics and maths. She popularized the pie-chart and became the first woman admitted to the Royal Statistical Society, which must have made her the envy of dozens.

Nightingale only had to overcome prejudice against her gender; another heroine of the Crimea is less well known perhaps because she was less appealing as a national icon. Mary Seacole was a mixed-race Jamaican nurse whose offer to help in the Crimea was rejected by the

---

* Florence Nightingale was named after the city of her birth, a tradition that was continued with her unfortunate sister 'Parthenope Nightingale'.
† The Guild of Satirists have asked me to point out that today it is almost un-imaginable that anyone would leave hospital with an infection they did not have when they went in.

War Office. Undeterred, she raised her own funds to set up a treatment centre for the British wounded. She is cited in Salman Rushdie's *Satanic Verses* as an example of forgotten black history: *See, here is Mary Seacole, who did as much in the Crimea as another magic-lamping lady, but, being dark, could scarce be seen for the flame of Florence's candle.* Yeah, but Florence Nightingale hasn't got an ugly office block in Lambeth named after her.

Britain and France finally prevailed on the far-off peninsula and in the peace treaty that followed the Black Sea had to remain a neutral waterway, which must have been a great comfort to the British and French families who had lost around a hundred thousand soldiers between them.* The Crimean War had been totally avoidable and fifteen years later Russia was able to completely disregard the limitations imposed upon it. The treaty propped up the Ottoman Empire for a while, but in the Balkans in particular the Turks were rapidly losing control to the nationalists, and this would be the spark that ignited the Great War sixty years later. Somehow the image of the Charge of the Light Brigade, heroically galloping in the wrong direction, being massacred for no better reason than the fact that their arrogant commanders were barely on speaking terms, symbolizes the whole futility of this and so many other wars.

'The jewel in the crown' (has been nicked and taken to England)

British soldiers packing their bags to head home from the Crimea were still looking for their right boot when the message came through that they were being sent to India instead. The bit on the army recruiting poster that said 'Travel to interesting places' had neglected to add 'or wherever there are people who want to shoot at you'. In 1857 it was the one-hundredth anniversary of the Battle of Plassey

---

* The young Leo Tolstoy served with the Russian forces and the experience turned one of the greatest minds of the nineteenth century towards pacifism and non-violent resistance. In other words, his side lost.

and British supremacy in India. How can we best celebrate this? thought the locals. I know, let's kill all the English!

During the previous decades British possessions in India had expanded to include most of the sub-continent, making it the 'jewel in the crown' of the Empire. New provinces were acquired by maintaining the fiction of self-government through various local puppet rulers, but on top of the forty thousand British military personnel in charge of the Indian recruits, there was an army of British administrators and clerks. The image of the British colonial adventurer has never quite moved on from the plucky Biggles-type portrayed in the *Boy's Own Paper*, disarming the hysterical savage with a stiff uppercut to the jaw. In fact the British who went out to run the Empire were often the people who couldn't make it back home. What do you do with an untalented, rather dim young man whose expensive education has given him a completely unjustified sense of his own superiority? Send him out to the colonies where the racist infrastructure of empire means that he is boss no matter how inferior his intellect or ability. A quick reading of *Burmese Days* by George Orwell (based on his own first-hand experience) brings this obvious truth crashing into focus. The British Empire wasn't run by heroes and adventurers, it was administrated by small-minded, low-ability bureaucrats, who cherished the exclusiveness of the 'whites only' social club as the only thing in this world that was ever going to make them feel important.

It is no wonder then that resentment built up, particularly from the higher castes of Indian society, as they witnessed the enormous wealth of their country being shipped back to England. India's immense natural resources – diamonds, gold, silks and raffia-work table mats – helped make Britain the richest country in the world. The greatest diamond in history remains in the British Crown Jewels in the Tower of London. Mention the 'Koh-i-noor' to an Indian or Pakistani politician and they will tell you it is a symbol of centuries of imperial plunder. Mention the Koh-i-noor to an Englishman and he will tell you it's a curry house just off the High Street.

There was also growing disquiet about British missionaries seeking to convert the indigenous population to Christianity, the effects

of the railways on the rigid caste system and the increasing interference in charming traditional customs such as widows being burnt
alive at their late husband's cremation. For this reason the East India
Company needed to employ a quarter of a million Indian soldiers, or
'sepoys', who were paid to keep the peace in the territories that they
were currently stripping of all their material wealth or invade neighbouring provinces when the diamonds ran out. Among these soldiers
were both Hindus and Muslims and it would take something special
to unite them against their paymasters – but the Brits managed to
find it. In the end it was the tiniest of details that triggered a major
rebellion that cost many thousands of lives. The new Enfield rifles
had a greased gunpowder cartridge that had to be bitten open by the
soldier. A rumour went around that the grease was made from pig
and cow fat – deeply offensive to both Muslims and Hindus. When
sepoys were publicly stripped of their uniforms for refusing to let
this tallow touch their lips, it sparked a rebellion that quickly spread
to become the greatest crisis in the British Empire since the
American Revolution.

The rather insultingly named 'Indian Mutiny' (known in India as
the 'First War of Independence') did not consume the entire sub-
continent as the rebels hoped; indeed with so many cultures,
languages and races within India, Asian soldiers were pitted against
Asian soldiers in a very bloody war that saw appalling brutality on
both sides. But in 1858 when the colonial power had reasserted its
military hold over rebel areas, British reprisals for the rising were
savage and indiscriminate. Indians were tied over the mouths of
cannons that were then fired; whole villages were massacred if they
were suspected of having collaborated with the 'mutineers'; the
British revenge became known as 'the Devil's Wind'.

Our received idea of the British in India is of impeccably
mannered gentlemen in starched white shirts keeping a stiff upper
lip in the face of searing heat and flustered locals. But far away from
the reassuring image of Merchant–Ivory films and the comical
loyalty of Rangi Ram in *It Ain't Half Hot Mum* was a sustained
protection racket that went on for two centuries and needed military
brutality to enforce it.

Victorian imperialism also required and therefore cultivated a level of racism from which we have still not recovered. You can only be comfortable ruling a sub-continent if you imagine yourself to be inherently more civilized or cultured – it was the 'White Man's Burden' to educate and civilize these 'backward races'. So the next time you hear some racist abuse from a group of drunken football fans it is worth explaining the shameful legacy of imperialism to them because they will almost certainly thank you for putting them straight and sign up for a racism-awareness workshop on the spot.

After the Indian rebellion of 1857, the administration of India was taken out of the hands of the East India Company, and the period of the British Raj began under a government-appointed Viceroy with Queen Victoria eventually being proclaimed the 'Empress of India', which is pretty good going for someone who never went there. An extensive railway system was built and English imposed as the lingua franca so that 150 years later Indian call centres could ring us up to offer cheaper car insurance.

'Laissez-faire': French for 'No idea what to do'

Many of the useless upper-class idiots running the Crimean War or savagely suppressing the Indian Mutiny had become officers in the army because their parents had originally purchased their positions. As a direct result of the Crimean War, the sale of commissions in the British army was ended and the officers' training academy at Sandhurst has been packed with salt-of-the-earth working-class types ever since. The same aristocratic privileges had of course also applied at Westminster. Without the payment of MPs demanded by the Chartists (and finally achieved in 1911) only the very rich could afford to play at politics as a diverting sideline to running their estates, hunting foxes and catching venereal disease off Victorian prostitutes.

Lord Derby, who was Prime Minister for three short periods totalling four years, could chat to anyone for hours about card games, horses and billiards, but when anyone tried to engage him on matters of politics or government he became bored and distracted. Lord Palmerston was a dominant figure during decades of tumultuous change in Britain, but when it came to domestic policy was completely uninterested. Irritated by the constant demands for new legislation, he famously protested, 'We cannot keep adding to the statute books ad infinitum.'

Personalities like Palmerston, Lord Russell and Derby were as significant a factor in the formation of governments as general elections. If you had a stern look, wing collars and bushy whiskers you were in.* Cabinets were formed across the narrow political spectrum, wherever sufficient support could be found for a particular approach to the issues confronting the country at any given time. But one thing about Victorian politics that was better than the way we do things today is that politicians felt a greater loyalty to individual principles than to their political party. The only downside was that their principles were generally wrong; ministers had resigned in high dudgeon over giving Catholics the vote, abolishing rotten boroughs or lowering the price of bread. Now when the Chancellor William Gladstone attempted to reduce the tax on paper, his initiative was defeated in the House of Lords as it was feared that this would make cheap newspapers available to the masses. 'They might show young ladies on page three not wearing a hat.' Gladstone's creative response was to put all his fiscal measures into one Finance Bill, and so MPs had to vote for the whole package or none of it. He had invented 'the Budget' and for one day a year, kids' TV would be on BBC2 and journalists would indulge in their annual ritual of estimating how the changes in duty would affect the average Victorian family of Mum, Dad and the twelve kids.

The peace-loving Gladstone had been an unlikely chancellor for Lord Palmerston, who was all for increasing military spending. However, British land forces remained small for a power of Britain's

* The mid-Victorian period saw a great fashion for beards and characters like Marx and Darwin and W. G. Grace would be hard to picture without enormous amounts of facial hair. Eight members of Gladstone's first cabinet sported beards, which is a very useful fact if you are ever trying to get people to go home at the end of a long dinner party.

size and Gladstone continued to reduce income tax, hoping to abolish it altogether.* But Palmerston had good reason to fear the instability of the international situation. In Europe, German and Italian unification were steaming ahead, creating major new powers that would demand their say at the conference table. Civil war had broken out in the United States, and although Britain remained neutral, about one-fifth of the British population were involved with the cotton industry that was dependent for its raw materials on the exports of the southern states. Britain had pursued a policy of 'splendid isolation' which may have had the advantage of avoiding involvement in major European wars, but also left Britain completely powerless to affect events on the continent. Britain could only stand and watch when in 1870 Prussia completely overran France, shattering the balance of power on the continent, besieging the capital and condemning the animals in Paris Zoo to be served up as *girafe aux oignons*.

Palmerston did not live long enough to see the new European order. He had died in 1865, to be succeeded briefly by Russell, the last of the old-fashioned Whigs, who made way for Derby, the elderly Tory whose statue remains in Parliament Square so that parents can reply to their children, 'Who was Earl Derby? Well, he was a politician, erm, statesman, who – who was, er, very much *in the olden days*.'†

Gladstone and Disraeli invent 'Punch and Judy politics'

Gladstone and his great Conservative rival Disraeli represented the next generation of politicians, who would inherit the reins of

---

* Income tax had first been introduced during the Napoleonic Wars, after which it was abolished and replaced with greater indirect taxation which hit the poor hardest. Robert Peel had reintroduced income tax in 1842 as a 'temporary measure'.

† With a tenure of twenty-two years, Edward Smith-Stanley, the fourteenth Earl of Derby, remains the longest-serving leader of the Conservative Party. When his first cabinet was announced, the Duke of Wellington boomed, 'Who? Who?' in response to each name, and the government never shook off the 'Who? Who?' label.

government from the elderly gentlemen running the country from the House of Lords. Between them they would come to dominate late-Victorian politics as the two not-particularly-distinct camps evolved into the Conservative and Liberal Parties.

Gladstone was that rarest of politicians, one who moved to the left the longer he spent in the corridors of power. He started out as a Tory, opposed most of the great reforms of the first half of the century, including the Reform Act of 1832, but eventually came to believe in universal male suffrage. In 1840 he had taken up the slightly unusual calling of going out into the back streets late at night and trying to persuade prostitutes to give up their means of employment; a practice he continued even after he became Prime Minister, much to the anxiety of the PR managers at Downing Street. Speculation has continued as to whether his interest in prostitutes was entirely altruistic; in his diary he regularly sketched a picture of a whip, which some have suggested symbolized an interest in flagellation. Gladstone's other great hobby was chopping down trees, which remained his preferred means of exercise until he was eighty. So he'd quiz provocatively dressed prostitutes about their work and then go out and sweat and puff until the great thrusting oak flopped to the ground; but obviously the Victorians were completely at ease with their sexuality, it was all very healthy.

Even before they began their duopoly of the top job, Gladstone and Disraeli were dominating British politics. Disraeli had led the campaign against Gladstone's proposed electoral reforms and then when he replaced Gladstone in the cabinet introduced a far more radical measure himself. The 1867 Reform Act almost doubled the electorate, adding significant numbers of working-class voters to the electoral roll as the property qualification for voting was extended to ratepayers, lodgers and other people who wore cloth caps. Universal male suffrage may still have been some way off, but there were many Conservatives appalled by such a move, and one future Prime Minister resigned in protest.

With two and a half million voters now on the electoral roll, the days of bribery and coercion were over (particularly when secret ballots were introduced soon after). Disraeli established

Conservative Central Office and local associations were organized all around the country. They continued the political campaigning between elections, by pushing leaflets through letterboxes showing pictures of creepy social misfits calling themselves your 'Conservative Local Action Team'. This new, broader type of politics also required politicians who knew how to address a crowd beyond the House of Commons, and Gladstone led the way with his so-called 'Midlothian campaign', in which it was discovered that publicly denigrating your opposite number was far easier than explaining the complex intricacies of policy and finance.

During the passage of the 1867 Reform Act, an amendment to include women on the electoral roll was defeated, because it was realized that ladies were not interested in politics, only embroidery and kittens.* The National Society for Women's Suffrage was formed the following year just as women were about to gain the right to vote in local elections. Although it would be over sixty years before women got the vote on equal terms with men, they were making ground in other areas of society, becoming accepted at Cambridge and Oxford in the 1870s, and in 1873 mothers gained the legal right to have access to their children after separation or divorce, which had previously been cruelly denied by MPs (who never saw their own children after they had packed them off to boarding school at the age of six months and so couldn't really understand what the fuss was about).

Non-Anglicans were also being permitted to play a fuller role in society, with Nonconformists and Jews allowed into the House of Commons. Disraeli himself was of course of Jewish parentage, even though his father had had him baptized into the Church of England after a row with his synagogue, which you feel must have been quite a big one. 'What do you mean we don't believe the New Testament?' It is quite possible that his father had him baptized in order that he

---

* The move was proposed by the great philosopher John Stuart Mill, who was an independent MP for Westminster. His godfather had been the father of British liberal political philosophy, Jeremy Bentham, and Mill in turn was godfather to Bertrand Russell (grandson of the last Whig Prime Minister). See, even if you want to become a philosopher, it's down to who you know.

could advance in British society. But Disraeli was both a patriotic Englishman and proud of his racial origins. As a Sephardic Jew, Disraeli claimed a nobility that he argued made him an equal to the aristocrats with whom he rubbed shoulders in the House of Commons, although it's hard to imagine the English upper classes buying that one. Disraeli climbed to the 'top of the greasy pole' of politics, as he put it, despite the inherent anti-Semitism of Victorian society. Disraeli never forgot that when he stood for election in Shrewsbury in 1841 the crowd waved bits of pork on the end of sticks. But then Jewish people are always paranoid about anti-Semitism, I'm sure all that happened was that the voters were having a nice barbecue and as he passed they raised their sausages on skewers to give him a friendly wave.

In contrast to his great rival Gladstone, Disraeli had started out as a radical and ended up a Conservative, albeit a progressive and forward-thinking one. He believed in the potential of a political alliance between the aristocracy and the lower classes; the sort of cross-section you see at race meetings: upper class and lower class but no one in between. He was also a prolific writer and used his first period as leader of the opposition to dash off another novel. His books were not particularly well received, but he is probably the best novelist ever to become a prominent Conservative politician, which is quite an achievement in such exalted company as Edwina Currie, Ann Widdecombe and Jeffrey Archer.

The earnest and deeply Christian William Gladstone was the good angel on the shoulder of the British electorate. Disraeli was the devilish and far more entertaining voice of temptation, good times and patriotic pride. When Gladstone limited drinking hours the public got fed up with his worthy moralizing and Gladstone lost the following election declaring his party had been *borne down in a torrent of gin and beer.*

But his first term had been a very busy one, making up for years of indifference and downright laziness on the part of all the old guard who continued to achieve just as much now that they were all dead. The beginnings of a modern meritocratic society were gradually established. Exams were introduced for entrance into the

Civil Service, because the best way to find out who can run a government department is to get them to write an essay in Latin about Caesar's campaign in Gaul.

The justice system was overhauled and housed in the Royal Courts of Justice, which were built off the Strand. The Education Act of 1870 provided for the schooling of children between the ages of five and thirteen, the only minor disincentives being that attendance wasn't compulsory and that you had to pay. This was put right in the following decades, so all the property-developers suggesting they might turn those big empty Victorian school buildings into yuppy flats were told to come back a bit later. Because the first schools had been provided by the churches, the local authorities were now encouraged to fill the gaps. There were those who lambasted the government for failing to seize this moment to do away with faith schools altogether, but the anomaly survived. Victorian Britain was a deeply Christian society, even if the century gradually saw the end of Anglican domination. Up to half the population was now made up of 'nonconformists' such as Methodists, Baptists, Scottish Presbyterians, Unitarians and Quakers and an increasing number of Catholics with the large number of Irish workers now coming to England to work on the railways.

Bank holidays were introduced and now there was a range of sports that the Victorians could enjoy in their spare time. In June 1863 the Football Association had been founded above a pub in London, and by closing time they were moaning that the game had got too commercial. Although various ball games had been played for centuries, strict rules and regulations about stripy caps and waxed moustaches were at last laid down; now players risked a booking if they failed to smoke a pipe on the pitch. Football spread quickly from the upper classes to the masses, and when Blackburn Olympic beat Old Etonians in the Cup Final of 1883, it was heralded in the Blackburn local paper as *a victory for the manual working class* over *the sons of the best families of the upper class in the Kingdom.**

* The professional game emerging in the North of England quickly replaced the gentleman's amateur game in the south. Before that all the kids in Manchester had to support Surrey United.

The first FA Cup tournament had begun in 1871, in the same year that the Rugby Association was founded. Legend tells that earlier in the century, a boy called William Webb Ellis had been playing football at Rugby School when he suddenly caught the ball and then just ran with it. 'Hand ball!' shouted his opponents. However, being a public-school boy, William refused to accept that he was just a big cheat and claimed to have invented an entirely new sport. He later missed an open goal, sending the ball sailing over the net. 'I meant to do that! Er, it's a new sport. I shall call it "volleyball".' W. G. Grace was popularizing the more established sport of cricket, becoming Britain's first sporting hero in the process and in 1877 tennis began at Wimbledon, promising to provide many more English sporting heroes (expected any day now).*

Not content with living through a period when Britain was world champion in all the major sports by dint of being the only nation that played them, the electorate was growing uneasy about the country's inability to affect events in Europe and the contrasting constant meddling they saw at home. In 1874, Disraeli led the Conservatives to their first outright victory since he had helped split them in 1846.

'This is the first time we have won a workable majority since the repeal of the Corn Laws.'

'Amazing! Erm, just explain the repeal of the Corn Laws to me again?'

'Oh, for God's sake, I'm not going over all that again.'

Gladstone resigned the leadership of the Liberal Party although he would in fact go on to lead three more governments. The new Prime Minister was now a sickly sixty-nine year old. In 1876 he was elevated to the House of Lords as Lord Beaconsfield, so that he could at least have a nap from time to time. But although Disraeli declared that real power had come too late in life he still proved to be a busy reformer on the domestic front. The Public Health Act tried to do something about the terrible unsanitary conditions under which most people lived in urban areas, requiring house-builders to

* The name 'lawn tennis' for the sport was actually suggested by the future Prime Minister Arthur Balfour.

incorporate running water and a toilet, which always adds something to a home, I think.

The toilets were of course built outside, sometimes shared between several houses, which is a great way to get to know your neighbours. 'Would you mind if I went first, because I haven't got dysentery?' Incidences of cholera and typhus were sharply reduced as housing and sewerage systems were improved. Some slum clearance had begun around the country, most notably in Birmingham under its radical mayor Joseph Chamberlain, which led the way with municipal water and gas provision. Outbreaks of cholera had begun to be associated with contaminated water after studies by the physician John Snow.* Dismissing the theory that the disease was caused by 'foul air', Snow had noticed that an outbreak of cholera in Soho centred on one particular water pump. Thanks to his breakthrough, the supply of fresh clean drinking water was identified as essential to public health, and never again would anybody have to buy expensive bottled water and lug it all home like some Third World subsistence farmer.

Other reforms included the Factory and Workshop Act which outlawed the employment of children under ten years old while the Climbing Boys Act banned the use of children as chimney sweeps. Instead this work was to be done by adults, specifically cheerful tap-dancing cockneys singing 'Chim-Chiminey' who spoke with a bizarre East London/Californian/Serbian accent.

In 1867 a court had ruled that combinations 'in restraint of trade' were illegal, overnight destroying the whole point of the trade unions. Gladstone had remedied this with his Trade Union Act of 1871, but then made picketing illegal. This was reversed by Disraeli, who was keen to demonstrate that the Conservatives were the friend of the working man.

The London General Trades Council had been formed in 1860, followed the next year by similar bodies in Glasgow, Liverpool, Sheffield and Edinburgh. The early leaders of the trade unions were

---

* John Snow was an ardent teetotaller and so today is commemorated with a pub nearby named in his honour.

not revolutionaries; indeed, like their predecessors the Chartists, they believed that their efforts would all be wasted if they were tarnished with the stain of revolutionary violence. An active desire for respectability and propriety distinguished English working-class movements – unlike on the continent. In France a strike still hardly seems worth it unless they have set fire to a load of lorries in the middle of the *Route Nationale*.

There was also a growing republican movement, a reaction in part to the disappearance of Queen Victoria from the public arena ever since her beloved Albert died suddenly of typhoid in 1861. She remained in mourning for the rest of her reign, removing herself from London and the political scene and earning herself the nickname 'the Widow of Windsor'. She insisted that Albert's clothes continued to be laid out for him every morning, and none of her servants quite had the courage to say, 'He's dead, you mentalist; deal with it.' It was suggested that there might be some way of remembering him in Kensington Gardens; perhaps having his name on the back of a park bench or something. But the plans got a bit carried away and instead the bizarre 175-foot Gothic memorial was built opposite the Albert Hall. They also informed Her Majesty that her late husband's name would live on with Albert Bridge, Albert Embankment and the so-called 'Prince Albert', the piercing on the end of a penis between the fraenulum and the urethra. 'Oh, that's a lovely thought,' said the Queen, 'thank you so much.'

Disraeli did much to help nudge the mourning Queen back into the public's consciousness; she listened to his advice and allowed a level of informality that had been denied his predecessor. Queen Victoria found Gladstone deeply irritating and claimed he addressed her as if she were a public meeting. Disraeli on the other hand flirted with and flattered the Queen, giving her little presents like the Indian sub-continent. India got an empress partly because it was hoped that one overall figurehead might help bring some sense of unity to the disparate and diverse provinces, but also because it was simply a good way for 'Dizzy' to ingratiate himself with Victoria. The Queen was thrilled and probably relieved that she no longer faced the ignominy of being outranked by her daughter who was married to the heir of the new German Empire. Disraeli had presented the Suez Canal to her in much the same manner: 'It's yours, ma'am,' as if he'd just bought her a new pair of earrings.

In fact he had only purchased a minority stake in this particular timeshare, but he'd gone along to the talk on the promise of a free iPod, and the salesman quickly talked him into parting with four million pounds. As the route to India the canal was vital to British trade (four-fifths of its traffic was British) and the following decade Britain used the opportunity of an Egyptian civil war to seize military control of the French-built waterway. The following century the word 'Suez' would become synonymous with the crisis that overnight marked the end of Britain's status as a major world power.

But Disraeli made the late Victorian British people feel good about owning an empire. Like most politicians of the age he had not always been convinced of the merits of the British government spending so much money defending the trading interests of its private companies, but he could see the political value of imperialism as a way to stir the hearts of patriotic voters. He publicly regretted the autonomy that had been given to dominions like Canada and Australia, and advocated expanding the British Empire yet further, which had never particularly been government policy before. The myths that Disraeli expounded about Britain's place in the world, its right to rule the greatest Empire the world had ever seen, shaped Conservative thought for generations. His foreign policy positions initially won him great popularity; he warned that he was prepared to use force against the Russians threatening Constantinople, and to poor Gladstone it sometimes seemed that he was the only person appalled by the Prime Minister's vulgar jingoism.*

But it was just as well that all-out war in the Balkans was avoided

---

* The word 'jingoism' comes from a popular patriotic music hall song about this crisis:

> We don't want to fight, but by jingo if we do,
> We've got the ships, we've got the men, we've got the money too!

Back then, people's idea of a good night out was going along to have a good old sing-song about complex foreign policy issues.

because when British soldiers were forced to fight, it tended to end in disaster. A Second Afghan War was supposed to suppress troublesome Afghanistan, but the murder of the British Consul and all his embassy staff suggested that there was still some work to do on this. In South Africa, a Zulu uprising saw British forces completely overwhelmed and massacred. The government immediately dispatched Michael Caine and Jack Hawkins who despite being heavily outnumbered at the Battle of Rorke's Drift apparently stopped the African warriors in their tracks by singing at them: '*Men of Harlech, raise your voices, tum te tum, the words escape us . . .*' Rifles eventually triumphed over spears, but the idea of Britain's invincibility was badly damaged.

With an economic depression, and the realization that America and Germany were drawing level with Britain in terms of industrial output, Disraeli lost the 1880 General Election. He died the following year in order to embarrass Gladstone into organizing a memorial for him.

Although he was mistrusted by many (Joseph Chamberlain called him 'a man who never told the truth except by accident') Disraeli was a major figure in the history of British politics, defining modern Conservatism, the original 'One-Nation Tory' whose rivalry with Gladstone across the dispatch box set the tone for the oppositionist 'Yah-boo' politics which so earns the respect of the voters today.

Gladstone's second term, like that of Tony Blair 120 years later, was one of piecemeal social reforms frustratingly overshadowed by questionable military adventures overseas. The opportunity for far-reaching transformation of the country of the sort that had been piloted in Birmingham by Joseph Chamberlain was missed when the former mayor became one of only two radicals included in his government. (The other, John Bright, resigned from the cabinet in protest when Gladstone sent British troops into Egypt.)* Gladstone had previously been fiercely critical of Disraeli's colonialism, but found himself being dragged into various theatres of war around the

* The Quaker John Bright had come to prominence earlier in the century as one of the founders of the Anti-Corn Law League.

world that were beginning to demonstrate that the British Empire was overstretched and unmanageable. The stressed Colonial Secretary would just be trying to decide what to do about Afghanistan when someone would knock on his office door and say, 'The Boers are declaring independence in the Transvaal,' and then the receptionist would say, 'And did you get back to General Gordon about the Sudan?' and he'd sigh as he realized he was going to miss his evening classes *again*.

The British Empire™, now with added 'Africa'

Britain had planted the flag all over the world without necessarily having the military clout to defend its various claims. As we all know from experience, you can't just declare that you're the only drug-pusher on the estate unless you have enough muscle to kick out all the other crack-dealers. The British government had never set out to acquire an empire, and so were now rather alarmed to read the estimates from the Ministry of War for defending it all. It should also be stressed that the Empire was by no means central to the Victorian national consciousness in the way that we imagine it was. There were no maps of the Empire until the end of the century, propaganda still focused on English ideas of 'freedom'; the Glorious Revolution of 1688 was what made Britain special, not the amount of the world notionally ruled by the Queen. The only empire the schoolchildren were taught about in the classroom was that of Caesar and Constantine. In fact you can almost date the British Empire going into crisis from the point at which the English start going on about how great it is.

But from the 1870s onwards, despite the increasing difficulties of holding it all together, the idea of Empire for Empire's sake began to take hold in Britain. The estate agents suggested that the continent of Africa was a unique development opportunity, with large communal gardens, great transport links through the new Suez Canal, constant sunshine and endless sandy beaches known as 'the Sahara'. The new European nations saw this as their last chance to acquire any sort of colonies, even though these lands would cost more to administer than they would reap; what the Germans call *Torschlusspanik* set in: fear that the door was about to close and that unless they grabbed a piece of this action for themselves they might be left behind and the good people of modern Tanzania would never have the benefit of words like *Torschlusspanik*. British diplomats were alarmed to hear talk of the 'Belgian Empire', the 'Italian Empire' and the 'Hackney Empire'.

Despite Gladstone's apparent reluctance, Britain still emerged from 'the scramble for Africa' with by far the largest share of the continent's wealth; between 1885 and 1914 Britain took around thirty per cent of Africa's population under its control. Clearly as modern educated liberals we take no pride in having robbed and oppressed so many Third World countries. It's just that we can't stand by and say nothing while the French make out they did it more effectively than we did. The best that can be said for the British Empire is that at least the English were not as brutal as most of the other Europeans. The Germans occupying modern-day Namibia committed genocide against the indigenous Namaka people so successfully that today their name is not even recognized on Microsoft's spell-check.

Britain's industrial pre-eminence was now being seriously challenged by other major powers, with German steel production overtaking Britain owing to the demand for all the little spikes on their helmets. Britain was also experiencing a sustained economic depression and it was hoped that expanding the Empire would increase the balance of payments while maintaining the idea of Great Britain's dominance. It brought with it ideas of benevolent Christian civilization; taking the raw materials that the Africans couldn't use in exchange for a number of unexpected pregnancies. During this period Britain gained or consolidated its hold over South Africa, Zambia and Zimbabwe,* Botswana, Nigeria, Ghana, Gambia,

---

* Then called Northern and Southern Rhodesia, after Cecil Rhodes the business-man and colonialist who founded the De Beers diamond company and was a pivotal figure in the 'scramble for Africa'. Rhodes explained that the Anglo-Saxon race was the first nation on Earth and that the more of the world that was ruled by the English the better it would be for the world. Inviting him to the same dinner party as Mahatma Gandhi was a big mistake.

Uganda, Kenya, Sudan and Egypt as it pursued a policy of 'Cape to Cairo', which may have looked neat on a map, but caused all sorts of problems when you, the chaps on the ground, actually had to make it happen. Gladstone's popularity was irrevocably damaged by events in the Sudan where the Victorian hero General Gordon was killed, owing to the Prime Minister's reluctance to get dragged further into colonial wars. Gladstone's nickname 'G.O.M.', standing for Grand Old Man, got inverted to 'M.O.G.' for 'Murderer of Gordon', which is the sort of joke that gets a round of applause rather than a laugh.

Ireland: Parnell almost wins Home Rule, gets girlfriend instead

Eventually they decided that it was ridiculous to go all the way to East Africa to pursue disastrous colonial policies when Ireland was so much more convenient. Gladstone's first words when he had come to power back in 1868 had been that he would pacify Ireland. The fact that he talked in terms of 'pacification' rather than 'liberation' was symptomatic of the problem. 'The Irish Question' consumed his time as Prime Minister, and although Irish Home Rule came tantalizingly close, the chance of a united self-governing Ireland was lost, perhaps for ever. Had Charles Stewart Parnell not fallen in love with Kitty O'Shea, it is quite likely that Irish history would have taken a very different course.

Ireland was a rich country with a poor people. Landowners charged exorbitant rents for cold, leaky properties with a patch of scrub out the back; it was worse than being a student. In the late 1870s, a series of bad harvests threatened starvation for the few remaining Irish who hadn't emigrated to Boston. Evictions rose sharply; every day thousands of families were thrown out of their homes and left with a few belongings to sleep by the side of the road. This is why the Irish have never taken to camping holidays with the same enthusiasm as the English; it's not so long since they didn't have any other choice.

Militant nationalists began to organize around the issue of land.

The members of the Land League were very moderate in their approach: for example, they opposed the shooting of landowners because they might miss and hit the wrong person. Instead of openly using violence, the Land League organized a policy of ostracizing the worst landlords and their agents, ignoring them, refusing to work their land or serve them in shops. The first landlord to suffer this treatment was Captain Boycott.

'Hey, this could be a whole new word in the English language!'

'Yes, if landlords evict anyone we shall say that we are going to *captain* them.'

Boycott's 'persecution' by the Irish peasantry became a cause célèbre in Britain, and the government spent £10,000 deploying troops and policemen to allow imported workers to harvest his crop (worth around £350).*

The Honorary President of the Land League was Charles Stewart Parnell, leader of the Irish Home Rule group of MPs in the House of Commons and, according to Gladstone, 'the most remarkable' man he had ever met. Under Parnell's dynamic leadership, the Irish Parliamentary Party became Britain's first modern political party with party whips and oaths of loyalty ensuring that its members voted en bloc. They delayed and filibustered the ordinary business of the House of Commons, while back in Ireland a land war grew in which intimidation and violence escalated and the country became increasingly ungovernable. Gladstone's niece waved goodbye to her husband, Lord Cavendish, as he went to work for Uncle William as Chief Secretary for Ireland. On his very first day he and his assistant were found in Phoenix Park with their throats slashed. A group called the Invincibles claimed responsibility, which was also the nickname of Preston North End football club, which probably delayed police inquiries for a month or two.

The murders set back the Irish cause for years, particularly after *The Times* printed forged letters apparently from Parnell suggesting he supported the murders. The Liberals were turning away from

---

* *Captain Boycott* (1947) was the least successful film Clark Gable ever made. It was so rubbish that audiences boycotted it.

Parnell and the Home Rulers brought down Gladstone's government by voting with the Conservatives.

Gladstone had further widened the franchise so that now there were five and a half million voters on the electoral roll, but the divided Liberals fared disastrously in the general election. The radical Joseph Chamberlain was also a zealous believer in the Empire and the Union and stood as a Liberal Unionist, taking many of the party with him. Suddenly the large numbers of working-class voters had no candidates they could support, and the trade unions and the socialist societies began to consider forming a political party of their own.

Between the summers of 1885 and 1886 Britain had four leadership changes including a brief minority government under Gladstone. Although his Home Rule Bill was rejected by the Conservatives and defecting Liberals, the fact that it had been introduced at all was a source of great hope for the Irish cause. There was the issue of the Protestant Unionists in the North who were angered by the idea of Irish Home Rule, but Gladstone made it very clear that a minority could not dictate policy for the whole island. All Parnell had to do was bide his time until Gladstone had a sufficient majority and his goal was in sight.

But then disaster struck. Parnell was cited in a divorce case by Captain William O'Shea MP and the passionate love affair between his wife Katherine and Parnell was exposed in one of the most scandalous sex scandals ever to hit Westminster. Tabloid readers pored over every salacious detail of the sordid affair: they had taken tea together before eleven-thirty in the morning; there was no lace doily under the biscuits; she had taken her gloves off before shaking hands – it was pretty shocking stuff. For Parnell's devout Catholic supporters the adultery was a sin for which he could not be forgiven. In an attempt to reassert his authority, Parnell called a meeting of his party and demanded, 'Who is the master of this party?' to which the heckle came, 'Who is the mistress of this party?' Parnell was ruined. He died soon afterwards aged only forty-five, and hopes of Irish Home Rule were buried with him.*

* Like O'Connell before him, Parnell had been christened 'the uncrowned King of Ireland', even though his mother was American and he had a near-phobia about the colour green.

George V was later to comment, 'What fools we were not to pass Mr Gladstone's Bill when we had the chance!' For what is so significant about this moment of opportunity is that it preceded the whipping-up of Ulster Unionism by the British Conservatives. Within ten years, Protestant Ulster was demanding exclusion from any settlement. If Home Rule had been achieved under the Protestant Parnell and Gladstone, it would have been for the whole island, without the artificial border that was later to cause so much bloodshed. So the love affair between Charles and Kitty may have led to the creation of Northern Ireland. Let's hope the sex was worth it.

The Late Victorians: the last years of strange facial hair

When his dream of Irish Home Rule finally evaporated, the eighty-four-year-old Gladstone retired from government to take life a little easier, chopping down trees and translating Homer from Ancient Greek. He is still the only Prime Minister to have led four separate administrations; during which time he was Prime Minister for a total of twelve years. However, he did of course dominate British politics for far longer than this and it's something of a mystery that he does not figure more prominently in our national consciousness: a couple of statues, a few street names and that's it; he didn't even make the top one hundred *Great Britons*. Even an appearance in Channel 4's *100 Worst Britons* might have made him feel that he'd been noticed. At least a short recording of his voice is now available on the Internet as an MP3 file, but hopes are fading that it might knock the Arctic Monkeys off the top of the download charts. Perhaps as a pragmatist and rather stuffy Christian do-gooder, Gladstone's legacy was never going to be one to excite modern activists to rally under his modest banner of on-going cautious reform, even if he had far more effect on the Victorian era than the dumpy, sour-faced old bat after whom it is named.

Having been unable to bear his company for decades, the Queen did not even bother to consult him about a successor, and so in 1894, on the whim of a bigoted old widow* totally removed from London politics, Westminster was surprised to learn that the new Prime Minister was Lord Rosebery, a dashing and charismatic young millionaire and owner of a string of racehorses bought with his rich wife's money. Even though it was nearly the twentieth century, aristocratic Prime Ministers still emerged from a mysterious royal consultation process on the basis of who might work well with the other chaps at the gentleman's club that was the Houses of Parliament, rather than anything as subversive or vulgar as being elected leader by their party and then winning a general election. Indeed it was not until the 1960s that the monarch was removed from the process of choosing the leader of the Conservative Party. When the Liberal Lord Rosebery resigned (his main achievement having been to win the Derby twice as Prime Minister) the Queen asked the Conservative Lord Salisbury to form a government, just as her ancestor Queen Elizabeth had taken advice from Salisbury's ancestor William Cecil.

For despite the rise of the Victorian entrepreneurial businessman, the aristocrats still dominated politics and pretty well everything else in British life. When it came to 'ownership of large country estates', the lords, dukes and earls were way out in front of miners, mill-workers and little orphans who swept the railway crossings. Although many of the nouveau riche millionaires were subsequently given titles and admitted into the House of Lords, increasingly they no longer felt the need to acquire themselves a country estate, as land ceased to symbolize wealth in the way it had done for centuries. But by the end of the most tumultuous century in Britain's recorded history, the richest one per cent of the country still had around thirty per cent of national income, and according to income tax figures of the time, the upper and middle classes (approximately one-eighth of the population) had about half the national income. That left the vast

---

* Although she remained a widow in public, there has been much speculation that Queen Victoria secretly married her manservant John Brown, including anecdotal claims that Queen Mary the Queen Mother admitted burning the evidence in the royal archives.

majority of the working classes, around thirty-five million of them, barely able to afford lodgings, food, fuel and a pint or two to help them forget that they lived in Middlesbrough.

Although millions now had the right to vote, neither the Conservatives nor the Liberals made a very good job of representing the vast majority of the population by dint of the fact that they generally regarded the working classes as drunken, thieving, violent brutes, which in fairness only some of them were. Since the collapse of the Chartists, the political aspirations of the ordinary workers had been channelled into the trade-union movement, and by 1890 there were 350,000 union members all paying their subs and putting soot on their faces whenever the photographer from the *Daily Mail* came along.*

In 1889 a successful strike by London dockers raised the profile of unions representing low-skilled workers, rather than the craft unions that had been the first to be established. Many dockers were so malnourished that they would often just work for the first hour, and then opt to take their 5d to go and buy food. When they marched through London, dockers held fish-heads aloft to show what they could afford to eat. Which, to be blunt, was never going to encourage any middle-class sympathizers to march alongside them.

The unions were the only organizations with the financial clout to challenge the duopoly of the Tories and the Whigs. Previously all attempts to organize political representation for the working classes had failed to raise the money needed to subsidize a large contingent of unpaid MPs and so only a couple of 'labour' representatives hovered in the House of Commons bar looking for the dartboard: Battersea MP John Burns and Keir Hardie, a coal miner from the age of eleven, who founded the Independent Labour Party in 1893. To the left of Hardie's Christian Socialists was the Social Democratic Foundation founded in 1881, whose members included Karl Marx's daughter Eleanor, who could generally trump any debate by saying,

* The *Daily Mail* was launched in 1896 and quickly achieved a circulation of half a million. Part of founder Lord Northcliffe's winning formula was to give his readers a 'daily hate', giving rise to the nickname the 'Hate Mail'.

'That's not what my Dad used to say.'* And then running the book-stall at the Christmas Fayre was the Fabian Society, a group of left-leaning middle-class intellectuals including George Bernard Shaw and, later, H. G. Wells, who advocated socialism through the existing political system rather than by violent revolution. These groups were finally brought together at Finsbury Town Hall on 27 February 1900 with the expressed intention of forming a Labour Representation Committee to see a working-class socialist group in Parliament. Those delegates found themselves at the first ever Labour Party meeting.

'So, Mr Chairman, the momentous task before us—'

'ChairPERSON, I think you mean.'

'Er, yes, right, Mr, I mean Ms, er . . . anyway, the momentous task before us—'

'Point of order, Chair, is it not the case that our capitalist government is at this very moment supporting the plunder of the so-called "British Empire", and by sitting on these chairs made out of *Empire wood*, we are in fact supporting the very imperialism that we are setting out to overthrow?'

'Ahem . . . the task before us . . .'

'Er, would it be possible to meet on Tuesdays so there's no clash with my pottery classes?'

The Labour Party then suffered its first major setback five minutes after its formation when several members resigned in protest that the party had moved too far to the right.

But while Britain approached the twentieth century, its current leaders were still very much of the previous era. Lord Salisbury was a spectacularly complacent Prime Minister, who was so laissez-faire that he famously didn't recognize some of his cabinet ministers. During the winter, he disappeared to the South of France to be Prime Minister from afar, and the few reforms that did take place generally happened because he didn't take any interest in them. His

---

* Eleanor Marx died when she discovered that her husband was having an affair, and proposed a suicide pact. He agreed, supplied the cyanide, let her go first and then was free to enjoy the rest of his life with his new girlfriend. Honestly, men!

view of foreign affairs was similarly self-satisfied; he declared that *English policy is to float lazily downstream, occasionally putting out a diplomatic boathook to avoid collisions.* Just a few miles downstream was an enormous waterfall that went crashing into the River Somme. However, before the cataclysm of the First World War, Britain was to discover just how unprepared for modern warfare it really was; when an away fixture against the Johannesburg Young Farmers' Club nearly resulted in shock defeat for the British Empire.

The Boer War: the search for the good guys continues

Bart Simpson said that there were only three 'good' wars: the American Revolution, World War Two and the *Star Wars* trilogy. It is not surprising that the Boer War didn't quite make it on to this list; it was not a conflict that provides moral certainties to those searching for a simple struggle between good and evil. One side was led by Britain's General Kitchener, who used the opportunity to invent the concentration camp; on the other side were the Boers who later came up with apartheid. You feel that Nelson Mandela would have found it hard to take sides.

Joseph Chamberlain delicately explained the background to the Boers' mythical trek north after Britain abolished slavery throughout the Empire: 'the Great Trek took place mainly and chiefly because, in their own words, they wanted to wallop their own niggers.' Their presence in the Transvaal might have remained an irrelevance but for the discovery of gold at Johannesburg in 1886. Outsiders poured in from Britain and the United States, but were they interested in the beautiful countryside and the majestic wildlife? No, it was just money, money, money, and the Boers treated these 'Uitlanders' with almost as much contempt as they mistreated the native Africans. The British expats appealed to their government for protection, but hopes that the whole matter might be settled by negotiation fell apart when the British insisted that the Boers recognize their suzerainty, and since no one knew what that meant (a small canal? a skin disease? something off a French menu?) a quick colonial war seemed unavoidable.

The British were in for a shock. The Boers knew their terrain well, moved around quickly on horseback and were well armed with German-bought rifles. Soon the Boers had the upper hand, driving the British back with their superior weaponry and repellent accents. At Mafeking the besieged British forces were led by Robert Baden-Powell, who later went on to create the Boy Scout movement. He kept up morale by showing the men how to tie a woggle and singing, 'Ging-gang-gooly-gooly-gooly-watcha!' Clearly the heat and the hunger were getting to him. Further British disasters followed, including the Battle of Spion Kop* where some of the thousand British injured were carried by a young stretcher-bearer called Mohandas K. Gandhi. It was not until May 1900 that Mafeking was finally relieved, news of which prompted riotous celebrations back home. Britain's military superiority finally seemed to be prevailing as the major towns were taken. The Conservative government used this opportunity to go to the polls and in the so-called 'Khaki† election' of 1900 they were returned with a huge majority, much to the disgust of the Liberals and the new Labour Representation Committee, who hadn't even had time to come up with a proper name. The Conservatives' unofficial slogan was 'A vote for the Liberals is a vote for the Boers'.

But, unimpressed by the British government's support at the polls, the Boers refused to surrender, resorting instead to guerrilla tactics. General Kitchener, better known today as a First World War recruiting poster, came up with the ingenious solution of rounding up all the Boer civilians, their families and children into huge concentration camps where conditions were so abysmal that thousands of them died. Although the Union of South Africa was eventually absorbed into the Empire, somehow Britain seemed to

---

* 'The Kop' at Liverpool's Anfield ground was named after this battle, and the embankments at the grounds of many other football clubs also ended up with the nickname 'Spion Kop'.
† It had only just dawned on the British army that bright red tunics might make a soldier slightly easier to spot. This was the first war in which the army wore camouflage, although the muddy-coloured uniform had been used by some soldiers during the Indian Mutiny ('khaki' is the Urdu word for 'dusty').

have lost the moral high ground. Using the full force of the British Empire against a small community of farmers and then herding their wives and children into camps to die did not earn Britain the international respect that some might have hoped for. It reinforced a siege mentality in the Afrikaner community that later expressed itself in stubborn adherence to apartheid long after it had made the South Africans international pariahs for the second half of the twentieth century.*

For the cocksure British Empire, humiliation by a motley band of Dutch militias had been something of a shock and the grubby experience of the Boer War rather dampened the imperial fervour that had gripped Great Britain towards the end of the nineteenth century. But although it may not have been much consolation to the twenty thousand British (and Empire) soldiers who died in southern Africa, the war had been a crucial lesson for the British army. If the Boer War had been easily won, the First World War might well have been quickly lost. Only now did the army realize how totally under-prepared it was; it had had no general staff, outdated medical services and inferior weaponry, while German support for the Boers had made it clear where the next military threat might come from.

Victoria sees twentieth century: doesn't like it; dies

Three weeks into the twentieth century, Queen Victoria passed away aged 81. Millions were consumed with grief (except the few pedants still arguing whether the new century had started in 1900 or 1901). Few could remember a time when she had not been Queen, and the nation was said to be in deep shock, never expecting that this very, very old person would actually die. Following the huge national celebrations that had accompanied her Golden and Diamond Jubilees, another showpiece state occasion was organized: a full-scale

---

* Britain had played its own part in the establishment of apartheid. In the post Boer War settlement, it agreed to Boer demands for a colour bar in the constitution that would deny black natives the vote.

military funeral with all the crowned heads of Europe coming to mourn their grandmother/great-aunt/first cousin twice removed. Much of the pomp and ceremony that we imagine has its origins in the dawn of English history was actually invented during the Victorian era by royal stage managers: 'OK, darlings, I'm seeing soldiers in bearskins, and a pretty state coach with little men in white tights and red shortcoats. Oh, those cavalry jodhpurs are to die for!'

After Victoria was placed in her coffin, an alabaster cast of the hand of Prince Albert was placed in her hand, and a photo of John Brown was laid on her body just to provide a bit of gossip at the wake. Her fifty-nine-year-old son, now finally King Edward VII, later smashed all the statues and pictures of John Brown that adorned the various royal palaces.

The new King had grown increasingly frustrated at his endless wait for the throne and his mother's refusal to allow him any responsibility. Having no proper role he was condemned to a life of leisure and travel, while he caused embarrassment with outspoken comments on national issues and scandals surrounding his adultery. But apart from that there are absolutely no similarities between Prince Charles and Edward VII. Oh, apart from the fact that his mistress Alice Keppel was Camilla Parker-Bowles's great-grandmother. In Scotland he became just plain King Edward, as the previous six Edwards had not ruled north of the border, although many of them had visited from time to time to see the sights and kill everyone.

Edward's mistresses were all the more scandalous in an age when you were considered a bit racy if you didn't cover up the legs of the dining-room table. Today there are a number of beaches in Britain that permit nude bathing. It's incredible to think that only a hundred years before this became acceptable the Victorians dragged great big beach huts on wheels down to the water's edge so that bathers might climb straight from their changing room into the water without anyone seeing the bulges in their swimming costumes. Frankly, a Victorian version of *Baywatch* would have been rubbish.

Of course underneath the veneer of Christian respectability was a booming sexual sub-culture in which prostitution, rape and child abuse were rife. In 1885, the age of consent was raised to sixteen after

Parliament heard an account of a mother selling her thirteen-year-old daughter's virginity to an eager customer. An amendment to the same bill outlawed homosexuality, and it was this law that was used to prosecute Oscar Wilde a decade later. The moral panic had many more less celebrated victims. At the beginning of the Victorian era it is estimated that around half of all pregnancies were conceived outside marriage. Single mothers who had once been acceptable became social pariahs, which led to a huge increase in infanticide during the century. In 1895, 231 babies were found dead on the streets in London.

But despite the repression and the poverty, the relative income of the masses had marginally increased and the new age was one of optimism, technological advancement and ever-accelerating growth. Britain's population had grown from thirty-one million to forty-one million in the last three decades of the nineteenth century. London was now a city of over six million people, a bustling metropolis of crowds and horse-drawn cabs where everyone was in black and white and walked slightly too quickly. It had become a county in its own right in 1888 with the establishment of the London County Council; at the same time democratic local government was established at a grass roots level across the country, although Conservative ministers became alarmed at these outposts of 'municipal socialism'. Previously, upper-class Justices of the Peace had overseen matters at county level, but now elected councillors would do the job, including the provision of secondary education, which at last became properly funded during the first decade of the century. There were underground railways in London and electric trams in many other cities. Motor cars were appearing on the streets, while from America came news that the Wright brothers had flown the first aircraft, though it was not airborne quite long enough to serve a tiny portion of chicken and diced potatoes or watch a *Mr Bean* video.

In the first decade of the twentieth century hundreds of thousands of telephones were fitted in British homes,* and in 1901

---

* The invention of the telephone is generally attributed to Alexander Graham Bell. His first message was supposed to be, 'Mr Watson, come here, I want to see you.' Which met with the reply: 'Hi, it's Mr Watson here, I can't take your call at the moment, so leave a message after the beep and I'll get back to you.'

Marconi sent the first electromagnetic signal across the Atlantic, linking Britain to America by radio wave. Moving pictures had become a reality and the world's first purpose-built cinema was opened at Colne in Lancashire in 1907. Great advances were being made in medicine and hygiene; at Sandringham Prince Edward had had thirty of the novelty new flushing toilets installed (developed by 'Thomas Crapper', who clearly must have changed his name as a gag), while miles of underground sewers now meant that cesspits no longer leaked into the wells and springs, which did wonders for the sale of Buxton Spring mineral water. Although scientists were only just beginning to understand that microbes carried diseases, Joseph Lister dramatically reduced deaths from infection following surgery by using primitive antiseptics and the sterilization of surgical tools, while in 1896 X-rays revealed the tumours inside the human body that came from spending so much time playing with the new X-ray machine. To cap it all, in 1905 Albert Einstein explained that energy equalled mass times the speed of light squared and everyone just nodded and pretended that they had the faintest idea what he was talking about.

Although thousands were no longer dying of cholera or smallpox as they had earlier in the century, the average Brit was not exactly a health-conscious step-aerobics addict religiously eating their five portions of fruit or vegetables a day. Millions of people were still undernourished, sickly, nit-infested, toothless wrecks and frankly unlikely to win a modelling contract for Calvin Klein pants. The general population was also under-educated and poorly housed, average life expectancy was around forty-five for men and forty-nine for women, while the likes of Queen Victoria, Gladstone and Lord Salisbury all lived into ripe old age. But the poverty of the British people was not just an issue of injustice, it made Britain weaker in the face of increasing competition from other more recently industrialized world powers. A scandalous forty per cent of the recruits for the Boer War had been too unfit to serve in the army, and levels of literacy and numeracy left England lagging behind some of Britain's European rivals. There was only one agency with the power (and, many felt, the duty) to do something about all of this, and it wasn't the new Boy Scout movement. And in 1906 a government swept to power that would fundamentally and permanently change the relationship between the individual and the state.

Man tinkering in shed invents 'Welfare State'

It would be hard to say that Lord Salisbury's government had run out of steam, because it had never had very much steam in the first place. More an honorary board of directors than a busy legislative executive, the government of Robert Cecil, Third Marquis of Salisbury, had been nicknamed 'Hotel Cecil' since he had filled the cabinet with so many relations. It was his nephew Arthur Balfour who became his successor in 1902 when Salisbury retired to spend less time with his family. (The expression 'Bob's your uncle' probably comes from the fact that Balfour got all his political jobs from his Uncle Robert.) By far the most dynamic member of the government had been the Liberal Unionist Joseph Chamberlain, who had led the split from the Liberals on Irish Home Rule. It is one of the tragedies of this period that Chamberlain's intense patriotism found its expression in his enthusiasm for the British Empire, rather than in him turning his attention to improving the lot of the ordinary Englishman as he had done for the people of Birmingham. If 'Radical Joe' had stayed in the Liberal Party instead of leading the Liberal Unionists into the arms of the Conservatives, he would have surely become a great reforming Prime Minister, perhaps even stalling the pressing need for a Labour Party. But having split the Liberals, he now split the Conservatives and Unionists on the rather unglamorous issue of 'tariff reform'.

'God, that sounds boring,' said one of the backbenchers.

'Well, let me try and explain it to you,' enthused Joseph Chamberlain. 'Tariff reform is a bit like the Corn Laws, though not quite as thrilling—'

'Right. The thing is I've just remembered that I have to go and stand over there . . .'

The hot topic of increased custom duties on non-Empire foodstuffs was sufficiently controversial to make a number of Conservative Free Traders, including a young Winston Churchill, cross the floor of the house and join the Liberals. When people understood that what was at stake was an affordable loaf of bread, the government's popularity plummeted. Joseph Chamberlain retired from politics following a stroke, but both his sons would go on to lead the Conservative Party. Austen Chamberlain won the Nobel Peace Prize, while not to be outdone Neville was able to guarantee the nation 'peace for our time' after his meeting with that nice Mr Hitler.

Even under the marginally more progressive leadership of Arthur Balfour the complacent but divided Conservative aristocrats had felt as if they belonged to another age. So it was that in 1906 a political earthquake took place that utterly destroyed old-style Conservativism and brought modern, interventionist government to Britain. The Conservatives lost nearly 250 seats, including that of Balfour himself. For the first time there was a significant contingent of around fifty Labour MPs, who now organized themselves as a party in the House of Commons.* The new Prime Minister had a great array of political heavyweights in his cabinet: Herbert Asquith, David Lloyd George, Winston Churchill – 'And leading all these political superstars there is I, the Prime Minister, the most famous of them all: Sir Henry Campbell-Bannerman.'

'Exactly, Sir Herbert.'

'Henry.'

'Sorry. Henry. Sir Henry . . . Cummerbund?'

The new Labour contingent made its presence felt in the new House of Commons, perhaps because all the others were scared of being thumped by all these former miners and trade unionists. There was new legislation preventing employers from suing

---

* This figure includes trade-union MPs and others who allied themselves with Labour although there were plenty of divisions within the Labour grouping. 'How can you be "New Labour"? The whole party's only six years old.'

unions if they lost money during a strike (which is sort of the point) and the payment of MPs meant that the Labour Party would no longer have to fund their representatives by organizing frenzied jumble sales and ill-tempered quiz nights. Labour pressure brought the School Meals Act, allowing local authorities to provide free school dinners, on condition that the cabbage was unrecognizably overcooked and the dinner ladies all had a big mole on their cheeks with hair coming out of it. Medical inspection of children was also brought in; although it took them a while to learn not to shout out, 'Over here! This kid here! This is the one giving everybody nits!'

But the first Prime Minister to be constitutionally recognized as such was not to be very long in the job. After two years Campbell-Bannerman fell ill and resigned the Premiership, dying before he'd had time to move out of Downing Street. His last words were 'This is not the end of me', which everyone heartily agreed with, hoping he didn't notice them all raising their eyebrows.

Now that Britain was no longer ruled by a chap with a double-barrelled name, the business of social transformation could begin in earnest. The new Prime Minister was Herbert Asquith, a middle-class Nonconformist from Yorkshire, whose government ushered in the beginnings of Britain's welfare state. But the two key architects of these new reforms were two men from very contrasting backgrounds who would each in turn lead their country in a time of war. Lloyd George was a radical from the Welsh valleys in a time when having a Welsh accent was no impediment to getting on in British politics. Similarly, male-pattern baldness was no bar to the very top in the way it is in the current age of TV politics, or else we might have had to fight the Second World War without Winston Churchill.* Unlike Lloyd George, Churchill came from an aristocratic family.

---

* Since the age of television no bald man has been elected Prime Minister, although John Smith would probably have broken this rule had he lived. Defeated contenders include Sir Alec Douglas-Home, Neil Kinnock, William Hague and Michael Howard – Iain Duncan Smith was dumped before he even had the chance to lose.

Born in Blenheim Palace, he was a descendant of John Churchill, the first Duke of Marlborough. His father was Sir Randolph Churchill MP, and then there was Churchill the dog who did the car-insurance adverts. But the leader of whom the Conservative Party is most proud did much of his best work on the domestic front while he was a Liberal minister. Many of the more 'socialist' aspects of our modern welfare state – national insurance, health insurance and the minimum wage – have their origins during Churchill's period at the Board of Trade.

The real driving force behind these Liberal reforms, however, was Lloyd George. Inspired by schemes he had seen on a visit to Germany, the 'Welsh Wizard' introduced the old age pension, perhaps the most compassionate and desperately needed of the measures. Cynics had always claimed that previous steps to help the low-paid and unemployed had only been introduced by frightened governments desperate to head off a revolution. But an armed uprising led by elderly widows looked unlikely. Any angry mob attempting to storm Westminster could be easily reduced to tears by deploying five-year-olds singing 'Little Donkey'. Lloyd George was part of a government committed to social justice, even if the financial burden of bringing in his radical pension scheme for the over-seventies was somewhat eased by the fact that none of the poor actually lived that long. The trouble was that with all the other progressive measures they were bringing in – improving housing conditions, health provision and safety at work – life expectancy would soon start shooting up and then it would cost the Treasury a fortune. Quite honestly, it's not what you call joined-up government.

To pay for these radical measures (while simultaneously trying to keep up with Germany's rapid armaments programme), the Chancellor Lloyd George needed to find a very large amount of money from somewhere. 'Any thoughts, Winston? There must be one group of people with lots and lots of money out there somewhere.'

'Hmm . . . can't think of anyone. Anyway, must dash, I'm going back to my family's enormous country estate, where we're having a shooting party and all the servants will be serving us luxury five-course meals all weekend.'

'Oh well, it will come to me eventually . . .'*

Class War, Edwardian-style

Just as it had done during Gladstone's time in office, the House of Lords with its in-built Conservative majority was once again regularly blocking government measures. For centuries the aristocrats had considered themselves the natural governors of the nation. But as democracy had become more meaningful (with millions of British voters having just endorsed the Liberal programme), the will of the people had to prevail.

To tackle the problem of the Lords, Lloyd George came up with an idea that no one had ever tried before. He devised an interesting budget. The so-called 'War Budget' of 1909 (for a war on poverty) was a deliberately provocative though fiscally necessary measure designed to provoke the Lords into a battle in the one area where custom dictated that they had no remit: government finance. Lloyd George proposed a supertax for the very rich. On top of this there would be a land tax on the unearned increase in land values when they were sold for development or mining. He stopped just short of putting a tax on ermine robes, plus fours and monocles, but his intention was clear. The titled landowners of the House of Lords were going to have to go to the brink defending the thing closest to their hearts – their wallets. In fact the duties would have made a tiny dent in their wealth, but the Lords claimed that the measures were motivated by spite and class hatred. And they said this as if it were a bad thing.

The Upper House was clearly walking into a trap and Lloyd George relished the prospect of the fight. He toured the country

* In fact, Churchill was not personally rich by House of Commons standards, and had had to undertake a speaking tour of the United States to raise money to finance his political career.

giving speeches, describing the Lords as 'five hundred men, ordinary men, chosen accidentally from among the unemployed'. At a time when there was great concern that Britain needed to build more warships, Lloyd George claimed that a duke cost as much to maintain as two Dreadnoughts. When the Lords duly rejected the budget, Asquith called a general election, and the Liberals were returned to power, albeit without the huge majority they had gained in 1906. The Lords now feared for their survival and duly passed the budget, but the Liberal government had come too far to give up the chance to win this titanic power struggle. Asquith asked the King to create 250 new peers. Unsure what to do, the King died. For a brief moment the bitter divisions at Westminster were set aside for a period of mourning, although whether they were as courteous to one another at the funeral as should be expected is not recorded. Perhaps they solemnly followed the King's coffin whispering obscene insults and trying to trip each other up. The businesslike new King George V wanted to get everyone round the table and sort it all out, but the threat of hundreds of new members of the House of Lords remained. A list of prospective new peers was drawn up, and various well-meaning Liberals claimed that they hoped the drastic measure would not be necessary while they secretly wondered what title they should adopt and practised looking stately in the mirror.

In the end they were not needed. The Parliament Act restricted the power of the Lords, and ever since 1911, almost uniquely among Western democracies, Britain has effectively been ruled by just one chamber, with the House of Lords scrutinizing legislation, occasionally revising and amending but no longer constitutionally permitted to repeatedly reject an entire bill if the government is determined to get it through.* The in-built Conservative majority remained, but the aristocrats believed their detached overview of British society gave them a uniquely impartial position, which meant they'd only ever make a stand on really crucial issues like fox-hunting

---

* One other concession was that a government's maximum term of office was reduced from seven to five years, which is still the law today. However, governments rarely risk leaving it that long; the last Prime Minister to do so was John Major in 1997, and he suffered an even bigger wipe-out than the Conservatives in 1906.

rather than everyday trivial matters like the miners' strike or mass unemployment.

But the constitutional crisis had felt all the more worrying because it came at a time of increasing lawlessness and civil disobedience across the country. Clearly the more militant union activists heard about Conservative MPs angrily heckling the Prime Minister and felt that the revolution had finally begun. There were strikes around the country, including an infamous incident when rioting in South Wales resulted in the Home Secretary Winston Churchill sending in troops against striking miners; something for which he was never forgiven by many in the Labour movement.

'Hurrah, it is Victory in Europe, we have beaten the Nazis!'

'Hmph. I'm not waving at Churchill; he used troops against strikers back in 1910.'

Suffragettes' bold claim: 'Mental strain may not make ladies barren!'

Much of the civil strife came from the rather unexpected constituency of middle-class women. Lloyd George had campaigned against the Lords on behalf of the millions who had voted for the government; there were of course millions more who were still denied the right to vote by virtue of their sex. Today anyone suggesting that women should not be allowed to vote would be greeted with derision and outrage and would probably not be invited back to the book club. But throughout the late Victorian and Edwardian eras many believed, including plenty of women, that it would be most unbecoming of a lady to concern herself with politics.* Women were clearly biologically different to men, they

---

* Queen Victoria had written of *this mad, wicked folly of 'Women's Rights' with all its attendant horrors* and around 2,000 prominent women signed a women's 'Appeal against Women's Suffrage' published in 1889. It was genuinely advocated that by focusing her mind on traditionally male pursuits, a woman's biological ability to bear children might be adversely affected. Which is a polite way of saying 'These feminists are all barren lesbians, y'know.'

said, which made them physically unsuited to voting. It leaves you wondering which part of their body the men used to vote with.

But progress had slowly been made. Women were allowed to vote in council elections, for the elections to school boards, to become councillors, aldermen or mayors. Women's suffrage was coming at some point. Whether the action of the more militant suffragettes hurried it along or actually set it back is open to debate. History seems to have forgotten the mainstream, larger National Union of Women's Suffrage Societies led by Millicent Fawcett. The peaceful campaigns of the 'suffragists' were outshone by the dramatic tactics of the Pankhursts whose rival Women's Political and Social Union became known as the 'suffragettes' (a name that was originally coined as a term of abuse).

Emmeline Pankhurst had been infuriated when her daughter Christabel had obtained a degree in law, but had been denied a career as a lawyer because she was female. The Pankhursts* led a programme of civil disobedience that split the suffrage movement and alienated many women, especially after schools and other public buildings were set on fire. Windows were smashed, burning rags pushed through the slits of letter boxes, paintings were slashed (including, symbolically, *The Rokeby Venus* by Velázquez) and suffragettes chained themselves to the railings outside Downing Street and Buckingham Palace. Yet other women were inspired by the Pankhursts' courage and flocked to join the cause.

Women were arrested and imprisoned, but they responded by going on hunger strike. 'Oooh, I've lost five pounds in a week, soon I'll be a size double zero.' Rather wonderfully, Emily Davison sneaked into Westminster Hall and hid in a cupboard for the night of the 1911 census in order that she could give her official address as the Houses of Parliament. There is now a plaque inside that broom cupboard, although not many male MPs even know the memorial is there – you'd have to be looking for a broom to come across it.

* Emmeline and Christabel were joined by their young sister Sylvia who went on to become an active Communist and anti-colonialist, eventually moving to Ethiopia at the invitation of Haile Selassie. A third daughter Adela moved to Australia and became the co-founder of first the Australian Communist Party and later the fascist Australia First movement. But then that's a woman's prerogative.

A Women's Suffrage Bill was introduced in 1912, but fell when other voting reforms became caught up in the debate. (The suffragettes had lost much Parliamentary support following physical attacks on Asquith and other MPs.) The following year, Emily Davison lost her life as she threw herself under the King's horse at the Derby to the shock of the entire nation.* Public opinion swung back in the suffragettes' favour when the prison authorities began force-feeding the hunger-strikers. The government responded by passing what became known as the 'Cat and Mouse Act', whereby the hunger strikers were released and then rearrested to continue their sentence when their health had improved. The legality of this was dubious, but there was something of a shortage of sympathetic female lawyers to argue their case. 'Christabel, have you never thought of becoming a lawyer? All right, all right, I was only asking . . .'

Women would get the vote later that decade, but not before the protracted national trauma of the Great War had shown them every bit as capable of taking up key positions as the men. Britain was relatively early among Western democracies in granting votes to women: ahead of the United States (1920), France (1944) and Italy (1945). Swiss women didn't get the vote until the 1970s and as for Saudi Arabia, well, don't even ask.

1910–14: war clouds gathering over . . . well, Ireland actually

Two almost identical elections in 1910 failed to give the Liberals an outright majority and the balance of power was held once again by the Irish Nationalists who demanded Home Rule as the price for their support for Lloyd George's budget. (A couple of history books mention the Irish MPs' dislike of the increased duty on whiskey. I'm

---

* It may be that Emily Davison was not planning to kill herself but that she died attempting to pin a rosette on the galloping horse. She actually bought a return ticket to Epsom that day.

not sure what they might be inferring.) But though Home Rule could no longer be blocked by the House of Lords, Unionism had developed as a potent political force since the days of Parnell and Gladstone. Powerless at Westminster, the Conservatives did their utmost to whip up loyalist opposition, legal and illegal, as the Tory leader took the salute at a huge military rally put on by the Ulster Volunteer Force. The north-eastern corner of Ireland had become a completely different society to the rest of the island: industrialized, fiercely Protestant, with a preference for flutes and big drums over fiddles and bodhrans.

In April 1912 Asquith introduced a Home Rule Bill into the House of Commons. A great new ship had just been built by the Protestant shipbuilders of Belfast. 'Let this new unsinkable *Titanic* be a symbol of the Loyalists' ability to devise a solution for Ireland.' At the risk of spoiling the ending for anyone who hasn't yet rented the DVD, the *Titanic* sank on its maiden voyage. The captain was under pressure to break the record for crossing the Atlantic and so steamed on at full speed through the night despite warnings about icebergs. But after a massive gash was ripped along its hull, the liner began to sink, which is about the moment when they thought perhaps they should have put on a few more lifeboats after all. A desperate scramble for places in the boats ensued, with lower-class passengers discovering that the 'no-frills' super-saver-plus ticket had its downside. A string quartet continued to play on deck until the ship upended and broke in two and then Kate Winslet is on this raft and Leonardo is clinging on, and it's so sad . . .

The catastrophe stunned Britain, severely shaking the confidence of a nation already anxious about civil strife, German sabre-rattling and the growing crisis in Ireland. It was the most infamous shipping disaster in Britain's history and maritime regulations were changed as a result – but only after 1,500 people had lost their lives, including millionaire socialite John Jacob Astor, Benjamin Guggenheim and Mrs Bellamy from *Upstairs Downstairs*. That'll teach that actress to ask for a rise.

The ship's last port of call had been Queenstown in County Cork, a port that has since been stripped of any royal connotations and returned to its Gaelic name Cobh; an indication of the increasingly divisive and republican course that Irish politics was to follow. Thousands of loyalist Protestants were now drilling, well armed with imported German rifles. In the rest of Ireland, Nationalists formed into units and began gun-running operations of their own. Although the Home Rule Bill was stalled in Westminster, in March 1914 the leader of the Ulster Unionists Sir Edward Carson staged a melo-dramatic walk-out of the House of Commons to a standing ovation from fellow Unionists, declaring that he was leaving to head a provisional government in Belfast.

The British army officers in Ireland had been contacted by Conservatives at Westminster, who suggested that they might request not to take part in any suppression of a loyalist rising in Ulster, and when they were foolishly asked, fifty-seven of the seventy officers politely indicated that they would rather not take part. The Curragh Mutiny was watched with interest by the German government, who drew their own conclusions about the state of the British army.

Civil war seemed inevitable and in July three people were killed in an incident that seemed like the cue for civil war. But another shot, fired a thousand miles away in Sarajevo, was now echoing around Europe. While Britain had been gazing across the Irish Sea, continental Europe was suddenly plunged into crisis.

The slide into the First World War: 'Well, let's just see what happens . . .'

The Bosnian capital of Sarajevo will always be famous for one thing. But apart from the setting of Torvill and Dean's Olympic skating triumph of 1984, it was also the scene of the assassination that triggered the most terrible conflict that mankind had ever known. Riding in an open-top carriage, the Austrian Emperor Archduke Franz Ferdinand and his wife were shot dead by a Serbian student, presumably as part of rag week. The Austrian Empire had long been keen to crush the rebellious Serbs, and were now determined to use this crisis to go to war. Germany was allied to Austria (they still always give each other maximum points in the Eurovision Song Contest) and Russia was sworn to defend the Slavic nations of the Balkans. Russia was also formally allied to France, but a major rival of Turkey – it was clearly a highly volatile accident waiting to happen; you'd have thought the Health and Safety people would have taken one look at the whole precarious set-up and closed down the entire continent until it'd been made safe again.

Many years earlier the German generals had formulated a plan that in the event of war against the Franco-Russian alliance, they would have to strike first; quickly dealing a knock-out blow to France as they had in 1870 and then turning to deal with Russia, which would be slower to mobilize. The generals, not bothering with diplomatic or political niceties, decided that the quickest way into France was through Belgium, plus they'd gain access to all those delicious chocolates, and so massive army-sized railway stations had been built along the Belgian border. But ever since the little country of Belgium had been accidentally discovered by an English explorer in 1839, Britain had pledged to defend Belgian neutrality, indeed Gladstone had reminded Bismarck of this during the Franco-Prussian war, and the Germans had duly gone to Paris via the scenic route avoiding all the tolls on the motorway. But in 1914 Germany was too wedded to its military plans to listen to the nervous Kaiser suggesting that Britain might come to the aid of Belgium and France. Britain was a naval power, her little land army was of no military significance. Indeed Bismarck had joked that if the English army ever landed on the continent he would have it arrested by the police.

There were of course underlying economic and imperial rivalries between Britain and Germany, but these didn't make war inevitable. Britain was also rivals with France throughout much of the nineteenth century, but no war occurred. And the idea of an 'armed peace' has also been derided as making war unavoidable, but heavily armed opposing blocs did not go to war in the second half of the twentieth century. Looking back from our modern viewpoint, there is an arrogant assumption that the politicians of 1914 were incredibly foolish and that it was obvious they were sleepwalking to catastrophe. But a tangle of complex alliances, old treaties, local strategic and military considerations and rigid adherence to military plans meant that once one stray firework had landed in the box, the whole lot suddenly went off.

But having said that – *What were they thinking! They must have been insane*. A quick short war to sort it all out? Yeah, right, that always works. It has also been fashionable to blame Britain equally for the outbreak of hostilities; historians reacting against the anti-German propaganda that followed two world wars have sought to dig deeper and blame Britain's imperialism and urgent warship-building programme as an equally important factor. But, bluntly, the parental 'You're both as bad as each other' explanation does not wash. If you are looking for the causes of the First World War, I'd say Germany sending an army into Belgium and France was quite a big one. Austria–Hungary attacking Serbia must surely be a factor. The Great War *was* avoidable. But not once countries started invading one another.

What might have made them all search a little harder for a diplomatic settlement would have been some foreknowledge of the utter carnage that was to result from the world's first major post-industrial conflict. The last time all Europe had been at war, Britain had lost an average of 5,000 soldiers a year. But just a century later, 250,000 British and Empire soldiers would die on average every year on the battlefields of Europe. A foretaste of what was to come occurred at Mons in August 1914, just a few miles away from Waterloo. In Britain's first encounter of the Great War, over 1,600 soldiers of the British Expeditionary Force, the most élite troops in the army, were simply wiped out by German gunners. The over-whelmed British were forced to retreat and confident claims that 'it would all be over by Christmas' looked like naïve wishful thinking. Britain's golden century was over.

> *There's a whisper down the field where the year has shot her yield,*
> *And the ricks stand grey to the sun,*
> *Singing: — 'Over then, come over, for the bee has quit the clover,*
> *And your English summer's done.'*
>
> Rudyard Kipling, 'The Long Trail'

All change please

The First World War would irreversibly transform Britain. Before 1914, the state played very little part in the lives of the ordinary person, there was no military service as on the continent, there were no restrictions on travel, no passports or identity cards, any amount of money could be brought into the country or taken overseas. Immigration was unrestricted; foreigners could come and live in Britain without requiring visas or work permits. After 1914 the fate of the individual became tied to the fate of the nation as a whole. For Louis XIV 'the state' had been the individual of the Sun King. In Britain after 1914, the state was Mrs Edith Jenkins, 12 Station Road, Bognor. And the gentleman next door, and that family over the road and the kids kicking a football in the street. *L'état? C'est vous.*

Nearly every family would lose someone; three-quarters of a million British men were about to perish. But it was also the death of a certain kind of hope. The Great War shattered the centuries-old belief that all history was a gradual process of progress and improvement. Despite the exploitation of the Industrial Revolution, optimistic philosophers and politicians had seen its technological innovations as evidence of the theory of continual human progress – that, barring occasional blips such as the Black Death or William McGonagall's poems, humankind could not help but make their world a better place.

For in the course of little more than a century, man had seemingly conquered nature. Machines now planted the seeds and harvested the crops, wove the fabric and processed the food. Scientists had developed vaccines against diseases and theories to explain the universe. Man could travel faster than the quickest animal; he could fly through the air or travel underwater. The North and South Poles were being explored, the darkest interiors of Africa were mapped and messages could be sent almost instantly around the globe.

But the tragedy of the nineteenth century was that man's enormous technological and scientific advancement did not come with any equivalent moral and spiritual progress. Everything had advanced – except mankind's capacity for inhumanity. Oh, and

Dudley town centre, that hadn't improved, in fact it was worse. Britain had given the world the Industrial Revolution, and a new type of entrepreneurial capitalism, based on free trade and devolved imperialism; it had spread the ideas of individual liberties and democracy and the laws of Darwin, Adam Smith and the Marylebone Cricket Club. But for all the astounding growth in man's power, there had been no parallel increase in responsibility. The caveman with the club was now a caveman with a machine gun.

9

World Wars 1914–45

How Britain lost its power just as ordinary Britons finally won theirs

It is a common trick by historians to get attention for their work by controversially asserting the opposite of what everyone has always presumed about a given period. 'New research has revealed that the Vikings were in fact all lovely, cuddly charity workers and lollipop ladies who loved kittens and macramé' or 'Technically speaking Henry VIII was only married once, and to that wife he proved to be a doting and loving husband until the unfortunate incident with the axe.'

On this basis, this book is going to assert that 'Nothing happened in the first half of the twentieth century'. The decades following 1914 were a complete non-event as far as British history is concerned; things just pootled along as they had done for years, a leadership change here, a minor tax adjustment there, but apart from that it was all very quiet. Nothing much happened between 1914 and 1945 apart from the two most catastrophic wars the world had ever known, a disastrous economic slump, a fundamental change in relationship between the individual and the state, the advent of genuine democracy, the election of a radical Labour government, the arrival of the atomic bomb, Britain's decline as a world power and the invention of sliced bread, which was the best thing since – well, ever.

And the end of the Second World War is where this particular version of the story will end. Even though the history of Britain continues to be made every day (except last Thursday which was a particularly slow news day), the ultimate titanic struggle between good and evil seems like an appropriate climax to Britain's remarkable history. After that, moving on to John Major's Traffic Cone Hotline might feel like a bit of a let down. And rather neatly, Britain's ultimate victory over the Nazi Empire came exactly two thousand years after Julius Caesar arrived near Dover with his own ideas about a European superstate. Fifty-five BC to AD 1945 is precisely two millennia, and anybody who tries to claim that there is an extra year in there between BC and AD should be aware that the Romans used to throw pedants to the lions. ('What sort of lions?' they'd ask. 'Because there is more than one species.')

Throughout those twenty centuries, war was a constant feature of British life, whether between natives of the British Isles or against perceived enemies further afield. But never had it consumed the entire country as it came to in the twentieth century. By 1914 the magic of gunpowder had been combined with the mechanization of the Industrial Revolution. By the end of 'the war to end all wars' nearly a million Britons would have been killed.

The Great War: 'Great' prefix goes down badly in the trenches

The outbreak of the First World War was greeted by cheering crowds in the streets of the capital; outside Downing Street and Buckingham Palace thousands gathered to celebrate the end of a century of European peace. And isn't it always the way; there's invariably one Mr Negative who wants to put a big downer on the whole party atmosphere: 'Why are you all so happy? It's going to be awful . . .' Honestly, why can't people just go with the flow and enjoy the party?

Britain's popular military supremo General Kitchener was able to draw on his extensive experience of warfare in Africa to explain to everyone how they should now proceed against the Germans. 'When the enemy charges towards you, the trick is to fire your gun before the natives get close enough to throw their spears. Don't be intimidated by all the Germans whooping and banging their zebra-skin shields, just keep firing your rifle and they'll accept the King of England as their tribal chief within a week or so.'

There is only one thing worse than being unprepared for war and that is imagining you are ready when you are not. It was true that for a decade or so Britain and Germany had been engaged in a feverish arms race, which had resulted in Britain building eight of the most enormous warships the world had ever seen. The trouble was that these weren't much use in the fields of Northern France. The mud was bad, but it wasn't that bad.

Yet when it came to land war the British Expeditionary Force was reckoned to be the best trained, best equipped, most skilled army ever to march forth to war. The only problem was that there were only twelve of them. Not only had Britain never had a large army, it had no detailed plans for the recruitment and training of millions of men. Suddenly in the face of four million German soldiers, the 150,000 troops who made up the BEF did not look quite so invincible.

A dilemma presented itself as hundreds of thousands of raw recruits eagerly queued up at the army recruiting stations. Should Britain's crack troops remain at home to train them all? Or should this élite force, years in the making, be sent over to France to see what happened when they ran towards German machine guns? The professional soldiers were deemed too valuable to be kept out of action and they were immediately dispatched to France. Within three months more than half of the BEF were dead or wounded.

The first British soldier to fire a gun in the First World War is supposed to be Corporal Edward Thomas. Amazingly he survived the entire war, even though many of his comrades did not live to see the end of the first day. The Battle of Mons was a shock to both sides, but eventually the sheer weight of the German army proved too much. British forces were also under intense pressure in Belgium, a situation not helped by Winston Churchill turning up at the front and suggesting that he took personal command of the battle (which caused much amusement amongst his cabinet colleagues). Within a month the huge German army was just forty miles from Paris as the French cabinet departed for Bordeaux and the rest of the city prepared itself for occupation.

Then the Germans hesitated. Russia had done Britain and France the favour of launching a premature attack and German troops had to be rushed east. French troops had been ferried to the battlefields of the Marne, thousands of them in taxis, although it was not always easy to find a cabbie who would go south of the Somme at that time of night. Having looked so unstoppable the Germans were suddenly in full retreat and by mid-September English officers were confidently predicting that they would be on the banks of the Rhine within weeks.

'Message from reconnaissance, sir. The Germans are digging a trench.'

'A what?'

'A trench. You know, like a long hole in the ground, big enough for them all to take cover. Oh, and they've put a machine gun on top.'

'OK. Well, why don't we dig one of those, and then we'll just take it from there.'

The Germans had made the discovery that became the key to the First World War: that the combination of trench and machine gun created a barrier that was even harder to get past than a GP's receptionist. The solution was simple; just go round the side. But then they built another trench. When the Germans attempted a counter-attack, the British and French built trenches too and then tried to bypass the Germans and thus occurred the so-called 'race to the sea', during which each side repeatedly attempted to outflank the other until there was a line of trenches all the way from Switzerland to the English Channel.

'So now what do we do?'

'Er, hang on, let me read the orders from HQ. Ah, here we are, we are all to "sit here for three and a half years firing shells at each other until millions of people have died".'

'Well thank God our commanders know what they're doing.'

Trench warfare: even less fun than camping

The soldiers of the First World War didn't live in the trenches for four years; they would only spend a fraction of their time at the front, perhaps a week at a time, before being rotated with soldiers in the support lines or in the reserves. But the intense experience of being huddled together in a muddy hole while people fired shells at you did much to break down the class barriers that had existed before the war. Junior officers and privates co-existed in an animal-like proximity that taught them to respect and learn from one another. For example, the British upper classes did not generally use the Anglo–Saxon swear words prior to being herded into trenches with the common people. But when a huge explosion goes off right next to your ear, expletives such as 'Golly!' and 'Cripes!' don't quite express the shock and anger provided by the F word. Cigarettes became popular with all classes after the First World War; prior to 1914 most people consumed their tobacco in pipes. It is still con-sidered bad luck to take three matches to light a cigarette. For it only took the tiny flare of one match for a German sniper to spot you, on the second match he'd take aim and at the third match you'd be dead. And still there were no health warnings on the packets.

The danger didn't only come from the enemy. With sanitary con-ditions even worse than those at Glastonbury Festival, there were outbreaks of dysentery, typhus and cholera. 'Trench foot' was a com-mon complaint caused by prolonged immersion in the flooded trenches. Soldiers' feet would swell up, turn blue and sometimes develop gangrene and require amputation. But so hellish was life on the Western Front that any soldier carried away on a stretcher was looked upon with envy. Today the expression 'to shoot yourself in the foot' is taken to suggest a foolish accident. In fact there was nothing accidental about it; deliberately destroying your own foot was a sacrifice worth making if it got you into a hospital bed and away from the front line and probably death. Other soldiers might be driven insane by the noise, fear, sleeplessness and gore. But the treatment for post-traumatic stress disorder was still in its infancy back then and over three hundred soldiers were shot at dawn for 'cowardice' or 'desertion'.*

By Christmas 1914 the stalemate in France was total. Both sides were dug in and facing each other along an endless line of muddy trenches that would barely move more than a few miles one way or the other. It was all quiet on the Western Front but for the sound of German conscripts singing bloody Christmas carols. 'Oh no, not "Little Donkey", I preferred the sound of artillery.' But then, from the other side of no man's land, some English soldiers joined in. Eventually some Germans proposed a Christmas truce in order to bury the dead lying in no man's land. *You no fight, we no fight* said the signs held up above the trenches. *Merry Christmas* came the reply. Cautiously the enemies emerged, until before long they were exchanging cigarettes and drink and then someone produced a football and a mad kick-about ensued. Back in the studio, the pundits moaned about the state of the pitch and England's search for a left-footed midfielder. The famous football game itself ended in a draw. And then the Germans won on penalties.†

How wonderful it would have been if at that moment, with all those soldiers having seen that their enemies were no different to them, they had simply refused to return to their positions. If they had all agreed simply to throw away their guns and let there be peace on Earth for all mankind. And then maybe all the squirrels and bunnies would have hopped around and baby deer and songbirds

* Gertrude Harris was three years old when her father Private Harry Farr was shot for cowardice at the Somme. Medical evidence pointing to obvious 'shell-shock' was ignored during his twenty-minute trial. Ninety years later his daughter finally saw him receive a posthumous pardon. All 306 British and Empire troops executed were pardoned in 2006 despite strong opposition from inside the Ministry of Defence.
† In fact there are various conflicting versions of different games. One account has the final score as '3–2 to Fritz', while others say there were up to fifty a side and no one kept score.

could have sung along to the Christmas carols and Disney songs and there would have been no more war ever again. The trouble was that the German midfielders were putting in dirty fouls and reckless two-footed tackles and diving to try and get a penalty, and after a bit of pushing and shoving, a punch was thrown and before long full-scale war had resumed along the four-hundred-mile front.

'Business as usual' (except people are trying to kill you)

In the early days of the First World War, the names 'Passchendaele' 'Gallipoli' and the 'Somme' had yet to earn their iconic status. The place names that were greeted with a sombre reverence for their wartime suffering were 'Bridlington', 'Scarborough' and 'Hartlepool'. German ships bombed the seaside resorts, finally caus-ing all the pennies in the Copper Cascade to tumble down into the coin tray as the supervisor shouted, 'Oi, you're not allowed to nudge the machines.' Windows of boarding houses were shattered and there were a few casualties as the reality of the war was brought home to the ordinary population. In 1915 the first Zeppelins appeared over Britain, huge grey airships that weren't even advertising Fuji Film; but had come to drop bombs on British towns and cities. Though the damage was slight compared to the bombing in the Second World War, it was hard to offer this up as consolation at the time.

The shock that civilians were now being targeted helped paint the beastly Hun as a barbaric monster. From occupied Belgium came stories of nuns being raped and babies having their hands cut off, all eagerly believed though later shown to be completely fictitious. (And so in the Second World War when stories of horrific atrocities emerged, many who heard them were deeply sceptical even though this time they were all true.) With increased secrecy and censorship, all sorts of ludicrous rumours were believed. A million Russians had apparently landed in Scotland and were marching the length of the country to join the Western Front. People claimed to have seen these Russians themselves, passing through their village 'with snow on their boots'.

By 1915, stories of another miraculous salvation began to spread. It was five hundred years since the first gun had ever been fired at an English soldier at Agincourt, just a few miles from the first battle of the Great War. Under the fields of this corner of Europe lay British soldiers from the campaigns of Edward III, the Duke of Marlborough and Wellington. And now at this key moment in English history, the ghosts of Agincourt had been seen rising up from the ground and intervening on the English side. Visions of medieval English bowmen had been seen by the soldiers; St George had appeared in the sky to inspire the English as the so-called 'Angels of Mons' conclusively proved that God was on the side of the English.

These stories of apparitions and heavenly bodies were widely believed at the time, although in fact their origin lay in a fictional short story written as reportage in the London *Evening News*. But once this fairy tale had been taken literally, many soldiers became convinced that they too had seen the angels, and the patriotic value of this divine intervention was so good for morale that everyone was happy to go along with it. Sadly, St George later got shell-shock and was shot for deserting his post.

However, the public weren't completely stupid. During a campaign to reduce alcohol consumption, George V was persuaded to take the 'King's Pledge', promising that he would set an example by not drinking for the duration of the war. No one else followed suit, and the short war turned into a very protracted war, made even longer for His Majesty by everyone going, 'Cheers, George, lovely drop of wine by the way; you not drinking? Oh, that's right, you did that pledge thingy, didn't you? Bad luck. Do you mind if I have yours?'

Convinced that alcohol consumption was affecting the production of munitions, the government introduced stricter licensing hours. Pubs would only open for a couple of hours at lunchtime and then close earlier at night in the hope that all those factory-workers handling high explosives might sleep in their beds rather than the gutter. This drastic step was brought in as an emergency measure just for the duration of the First World War. So when peace returned and you came out of the cinema at 11.01 p.m. and fancied a drink and a chat about the film, you were permitted to do so after November 2005.

But at the beginning of the war the country was more intoxicated by the flush of patriotism sweeping the whole country. Queen Mary appealed to the women of the Empire to knit three hundred thousand pairs of socks for the troops, because she'd made a start and it looked like it was going to take her ages. 'Your country needs YOU!' declared the famous recruiting poster featuring Lord Kitchener directly pointing at whoever read it, whether an 18-year-old man or a slightly alarmed 87-year-old lady.* Having seen thousands of highly trained British soldiers wiped out by machine guns, a million young men thought, That's the life for me, and volunteered to replace them. But without sufficient accommodation or equipment, recruits slept in tents through the winter and trained with sticks; pointlessly drilling and receiving outdated instruction from the Victorian upper-class soldiers who were too old to go to the front. As it turned out, filling the enthusiastic volunteers with disillusionment and cynicism was about the best preparation they could have had for the life they would endure in the trenches.

The front line was about to get even more terrifying when in 1915 poison gas was introduced by the Germans. Some of the first gas used was chlorine, which the powers-that-be believed could be neutralized by ammonia, most readily available in human urine.

'So what you're saying is that we have to wee on to our hankies and hold them over our mouths and noses.'

'Don't be ridiculous, we would never ask you to do anything so disgusting. Private "Spotty" Spencer here has already wee-ed on to some of his old army socks for you.'

Gas masks became standard issue as more horrific, heavy gases were introduced that filled the trenches and lingered in shell holes. Like was returned with like; indeed, by the end of the war the British had launched more gas attacks than the Germans. The introduction

---

* Margot Asquith, the wife of the Prime Minister, intensely disliked Kitchener, declaring that he was not a great man, he was a great poster.

of gas warfare was not exactly a tactical masterstroke by the Germans: '*Ja*, you see, the prevailing wind in Europe is westerly, so if we introduce gas warfare, it will get our British and French enemies in the West.'

'Doesn't a westerly wind blow *from the West*?'

'Does it? Oh *Scheisse!*'

Gallipoli: Australian volunteers told 'too late to change your mind'

When Winston Churchill became Prime Minister in 1940, there were some who thought the appointment was the final nail in the coffin for Great Britain and the Empire. Given his record in the First World War, this was an entirely understandable position. Although he can't be held entirely responsible for the debacle that was Gallipoli, he was the man who pushed it through and was convinced of the brilliance of this bold and surprising strategy. But there was a very good reason why nobody was expecting the British to land a massive force on the Dardanelles peninsula in the Eastern Mediterranean. There was absolutely no point in doing so.

'But if we knocked Turkey out of the war we could send supplies to Russia!'

'We don't have any supplies to send.'

'OK, but we could send an army into the Balkans to march all the way to Germany.'

'We don't have a spare army. And they would never make it if we did.'

With stalemate in France, the idea of opening a second front had gathered momentum as ill-fitting historical analogies were made with the Duke of Wellington's Iberian campaign. In the spring of 1915 British, French and Empire* troops landed at Gallipoli, despite

---

* There were large numbers of Australian and New Zealand troops at Gallipoli. The day of the landing, 25 April, is today a national holiday in both countries.

having no landing craft, no maps of the peninsula and no training for invading a hostile coastline. The Turks were expecting the landing. One little clue had been the British ships ceaselessly bombing the coast beforehand.

It might have been hard to imagine a more hellish place than the Western Front, but at Gallipoli the British and French governments had succeeded in contriving one. The troops were even more exposed and vulnerable, with nowhere to fall back except into the sea. The narrow rocky peninsula gave them no option of fighting on a wider front, and up on the higher ground the Turks poured men and ammunition into their superior positions.

All through the scorching Mediterranean summer the Allies tried to get beyond the aptly named 'Cape Helles', as the rats and flies fed on the thousands of bodies piled up in no man's land. In the lulls between attacks and counter-attacks Allied soldiers were picked off by Turkish snipers or died of disease. Only after eight disastrous months was the peninsula finally evacuated, leaving behind the bodies of 44,072 Allied soldiers.

Churchill, despised by the Conservatives as a turncoat, was demoted and later forced out of the government. His stock was so low, few expected that it could ever recover. The minority Liberal government was no longer credible, and Asquith was forced to enter into a wartime coalition. Gallipoli didn't just kill thousands of ordinary soldiers, it helped kill the Liberal Party. A short meeting at Westminster ushered the last-ever Liberal government out of office. They started going on and on about proportional representation about five minutes later.

Coalition government: 'Let's pool our weaknesses'

It wasn't just the army leadership that was ill equipped to deal with total war. Herbert Asquith lacked the vigour and flexibility needed for the national crisis. He was also the first Prime Minister for over a century to appear on the government front benches the worse for drink. (And he thought the nickname 'Squiffy' was just a pun on his surname.) Like most of his cabinet he remained wedded to the idea of laissez-faire as the only form of government, even when his country was engaged in a world war. His Liberal-led coalition was not much more effective than his previous government, with the exception of the first British politician to have the official title of 'Minister'.* When the generals blamed their failure to advance on a shortage of shells, the newspapers took up their cause, whipping up the scandal as public opinion turned against the War Office. Lloyd George now took charge of munitions and, under his dynamic and inventive leadership, production was transformed. Lloyd George was the only man in the cabinet who knew how to talk to the unions, but he cultivated friendships at all levels, with newspaper proprietors and rich businessmen, and lots and lots of attractive young women who must have been crucial to the war effort somehow. Before long the country was producing more shells in three weeks than it had previously produced in a whole year. The generals were soon able to fire as many shells at the German lines as they wanted. And it made no difference whatsoever.

'Daddy, what did YOU do in the Great War?'

Having won their campaign over shell production, the newspapers searched for another major cause around which fevered public opinion might crystallize. Deciding that it was a bit early for 'Asylum-Seekers Are Eating our Swans' or 'Diana Inquest Denied Dodi Diaries' they landed on the issue of conscription. Since the outbreak of war, the army had had more recruits than it could possibly cope with, but the idea that the nation was being let down by slackers and cowards was appealing in its base simplicity. Factory-workers had been given special badges or armbands to show that they were not cowards but were deemed essential for war work on the home front; you could wear a Mining Badge, a Munitions Badge or

* Before Lloyd George became 'Minister for Munitions' everyone in the cabinet was 'Secretary of State for this' or 'President of the Board of that'.

just your Robertson's Golden Shred Golly Brooch and hope nobody looked too closely. But the clamour continued to send all able-bodied men to the place where this status would rapidly be altered. It was even suggested that the upper classes might do without chauffeurs and footmen. The butlers were needed on the front to announce the arrival of enemy offensives: 'There's a German army at the front door, sir. They say they wish to become the dominant European land power and extend their imperial and industrial influence to eclipse the historic world empires.'

Lloyd George knew a populist cause when he saw one and, turning his back on his Liberal and Labour allies, he threw his weight behind the conscription campaign. Early in 1916 amid cabinet resignations and party splits, compulsory military service was brought in for all men between eighteen and forty-one for the first time in British history. Three thousand conscientious objectors were put into 'labour camps' and a small number of Marxist objectors were put in the army, where they were court-martialled and sentenced to death for refusing to obey orders. They only evaded the firing squad by the last-minute intervention of the Prime Minister.

With so many men away at the front, women were now taking an increasing number of the jobs traditionally done by men. Two million women entered employment during 1915, working in factories or as 'clippies' on the buses, where they didn't just take the fares but really listened to people about where they wanted to go on this journey. There were women employed in the mines and docks, although in Liverpool women dockers withdrew when men refused to work with them. Unions in the traditional heavy industries were assured that this arrangement was only for the duration of the war. But the office-workers did not have quite the same industrial muscle, and the long-serving male clerk disappeared for ever. Once bosses had experienced having a young female secretary working late in the office, they suddenly became fierce supporters of the emancipation of women.

For many women the First World War was the most wonderful, fulfilling thing that ever happened to them. They felt a sense of liberation and purpose, and some guiltily admitted that this terrible war had been the happiest time of their lives. These positive memories had to be suppressed after the war, for they did not chime with the experience of the heroes from the front. A whole nation may have been at war, but only the remembrance of the men counted afterwards.

Conscription was not to apply to Ireland, a tacit admission that despite over a century of Union, the population did not consider themselves part of the United Kingdom. Hundreds of thousands of Irishmen did however volunteer (more from the South than the North), responding to the romantic notion that this was a war to defend the 'little countries of Europe', like Belgium, Serbia and, well, Russia. Home Rule was about to become a reality and the Irish would surely earn their independence through their loyalty and service. Well, apart from those fellahs with the German rifles planning to kill all the Brits.

The Easter Rising: egg hunt cancelled due to attempted revolution

Because of everything that followed the events of April 1916, the Easter Rising acquired a hallowed status in the history of the Republic, despite the fact that at the time it was seen by most of the Irish as an insane posture by a motley band of unrepresentative extremists. There was no questioning the rebels' courage; they were prepared to take on the entire British army at the point when a fully mobilized Britain was in possession of the greatest army and navy it had ever possessed. They knew they might well be slaughtered, but believed (correctly as it turned out) that some sort of heroic self-sacrifice committed symbolically at Easter might inspire the whole nation.

So on 24 April the rebels marched to the Dublin General Post Office to declare independence. But isn't it just typical, you get stuck in the queue behind the lady who's buying a postal order but only has loose pennies at the bottom of her purse and then the miserable clerk closes the counter. To the bemusement of passers-by Patrick Pearse declared Ireland a republic on the steps outside. About a thousand volunteers had occupied key positions around the city and the British forces were caught by surprise. The rising was a mixture of murderous intent and amateur farce. One of the rebels was the proud owner of a beautiful de Dion-Bouton car, which he proudly drove to the scene of the uprising, where its burnt-out remains could later be seen amid the smoke and rubble. Another rebel hijacked a tram to take him to the rebellion, then counted the passengers on board and insisted on paying all their fares. Wax effigies were stolen from a nearby shop to prop up in the upstairs windows of the rebels' HQ, so that when the British forces did finally arrive, they were confronted with the bizarre image of King George V, Queen Mary and General Kitchener pointing rifles back out at them.

Two flags were raised above the General Post Office, the traditional green flag with the Harp lager logo and another which most people had never seen before: a green, white and orange tricolour in the tradition of the revolutionary flag of France. For five days the rebels held out in their various strongholds, hoping in vain for German reinforcements until they were finally forced to surrender. Five hundred people had been killed in this apparently insane uprising and the citizens of Dublin booed them as they were marched out of the smoking buildings. The turning point of Irish history came not from the rising, but from the English response.

Throughout May the rebel leaders were executed by firing squad, including one who was shot strapped to a chair because he was too injured to stand. Irish public opinion had been all for a constitutional settlement, for Home Rule under the Crown. But the endless executions delivered Ireland into the hands of the Republican Sinn Fein. Of the revolutionary commanders only Éamon de Valéra was spared, being as he was a United States citizen. The British authorities, hoping the USA might come into the war, were eager not to alienate American opinion and so, almost by accident, Ireland's future President was sifted from the martyrs of the General Post Office.

British naval supremacy postponed until – well, for ever

Without the Easter Rising, the war and British politics in general might have taken a very different turn. For the Irish rebels inadvertently saved Lloyd George's life. The future Prime Minister was due to visit Russia with Lord Kitchener when the Irish crisis meant that the War Minister had to go alone. The ship struck a mine off the Orkneys and Kitchener's body was never recovered.

The British people were devastated. But as the British cabinet led a period of sombre national mourning, they privately couldn't believe their luck. The rude and arrogant Kitchener had been a complete pain in the neck; he wasn't up to the job but they couldn't possibly sack such a massively popular symbol of the war effort. Then they'd had this idea of sending him to Russia: 'Kitchener, we have a very important job for you. We want you to sail across that heavily mined bit of sea, very close to German waters.'

'You mean the sea where all the enemy submarines are?'

'Are there? So there are! Golly, well, try to avoid the submarines *and* the mines then.'

'And this is definitely a very important mission?'

'Definitely. Asquith borrowed one of the Tsar's gramophone records. And he wants it delivered back to him in person.'

In fact there was no shortage of conspiracy theories that it was the British establishment who contrived the 'accidental' sinking of Kitchener's ship; others blamed Irish Republicans or the Jews. But you can't help but think that what with it being the First World War and everything, the *Germans* might have perhaps had the means and the motive. For Kitchener's ship wasn't the only vessel to succumb to the German navy. The U-boats were targeting anything spotted in enemy waters, British or otherwise. The scandalous sinking of the giant cruise ship *Lusitania* off the Irish coast had led to the death of 1,400 civilians, many of them Americans. German bakers' shops were burnt down in London; anyone with a German surname was at risk of being lynched by the mob. 'You don't think my surname sounds a teensy bit German, do you?' asked the King nervously.

'Saxe-Coburg-Gotha? Hmm, now you mention it, it might

subconsciously suggest some sort of Germanic undertone. Perhaps you should change it to something more English-sounding, like, say, the location of your family's ancestral castle?'

'Perfect. I shall be "George Royal-Borough-of-Windsor-and-Maidenhead".'

Britain had spent the best part of its pre-war defence budget on eight mighty battleships, but they could do nothing to stop the German mines and submarines. In fact the Dreadnoughts were so valuable that they didn't want to risk taking them out of port for most of the war. The only major engagement between the two mighty navies was inconclusive, although the Royal Navy suffered more losses at 1916's Battle of Jutland than the Germans. The hulls of the British ships had been built with thick, impenetrable armour. But nobody had pointed out that, fired at long range, the enemy missiles would land from above, so perhaps they should have thought about making the decks out of something more protective than papier mâché. The Dreadnoughts were the Trident missiles of their day; expensive status symbols of no practical use in battle.

The war could not be won at sea; it could not be won on a second front in Turkey or the Balkans. And Field Marshal Haig believed that the only reason that a decisive breakthrough had not occurred on the Western Front was because all previous attacks had lacked sufficient 'weight'. Now his theory was to be put to the test. Thanks to him, the Great War would surely end in 1916 after his conclusive victory at the celebrated Battle of the Somme.

The battle would indeed be famous. But not for the reason that Haig anticipated.

The Somme 1916: *The unreturning army that was youth**

Today when people talk of 'living through hell', it usually means that their appeal against unfair dismissal has been delayed, or the builders next door have been very noisy for several weeks. For the millions of

* From 'Prelude: The Troops' by Siegfried Sassoon.

soldiers in the trenches of the First World War, their experiences of Hell on Earth were beyond anything those of us born into Britain's most blessed generation can possibly imagine.

Lives not lost were often lives ruined, for the physical and psychological scars of war stayed with the survivors for ever. Pretty well every family in the country lost a son or a brother or a father, whether they were rich or poor. In fact the mortality rate among junior officers was higher than average; even the Prime Minister's son was fighting in France, and was now about to lose his life as just another victim of the single greatest wipe-out ever experienced by the British army.

The plan for the Battle of the Somme was not the most tactically advanced or complex ever conceived by a British general. Two years into the war, Douglas Haig had finally come up with a strategy that he believed would end the stalemate of the Western Front.

'We blow up all the Germans and then advance into their lines.'

'That's it? That's the battle plan?'

'Absolutely. Sorry it took so long, but I'm sure you'll agree it was worth the wait.'

'Let me just get this straight. We subject their positions to such an intense week of artillery pounding that you're saying none of them could possibly survive. And then our troops take their positions by simply running towards them?'

'No, no, not running. Walking. We wouldn't want anyone tripping up and hurting themselves.'

It seems incredible that the army of the Somme were told to walk towards the German positions, but Haig was totally confident that there would be no opposition.

'I tell you what, Douglas. If it's so safe, why don't you go first?'

'What?'

'If you are so sure that there will be no Germans coming out of their shelters to fire machine guns at us, why don't you be the first to stroll over to their positions?'

'Oh well, I, erm, I don't often go up to the front itself. Not really my bag, old man.'*

* In fact Haig never visited the front line.

On 1 July 1916, after five days of heavy pounding, the British guns finally stopped. At 7.30 a.m. the whistles were blown and the first waves of soldiers climbed up the ladders out of their trenches and walked towards the German machine guns. By the end of the day there were over fifty thousand casualties, with nineteen thousand of Kitchener's eager volunteers lying dead within seconds of their first experience of any action. Haig had said that if the initial attack were not successful he would abandon the entire offensive but instead he stubbornly continued to send wave upon wave into the slaughter zone, convinced, as the weeks turned into months, that a breakthrough was imminent.

By the time the Somme offensive petered out in the November mud, the British army had suffered four hundred thousand casualties; the distance gained worked out at about two lives for every centimetre. Haig would have been appalled by this statistic. 'The British army work in feet and inches!' The Battle of the Somme wasn't unique among the battles of the First World War; it was simply the worst example of pointless slaughter in the endless war of attrition. For the French, the carnage at Verdun is equally totemic, but in battles at Ypres, Passchendaele, Loos and many others the pattern was much the same. The generals considered it a victory if the Germans lost more lives than the Allies, no matter that both sides were still pretty much in the same place at the end of it all. But for the British the Somme was a turning point in the psychology of the war. The tone of the war poets, for example, turns from innocence to despair at the pointlessness of it all. For the surviving volunteers who had faithfully answered Kitchener's call, there was no longer any escaping the fact that nobody at the top seemed to know what they were doing. Now that this was plain to see, surely this terrible war could not be allowed to go on much longer?

But they weren't even halfway through.

'Calm down, dear! It's only a world war'

Despite the desperate situation Asquith seemed unable to move up a gear or even get into gear at all. The Conservative leader Bonar Law had rushed out of London to see the Prime Minister one Monday morning to find him at a country house playing bridge with three ladies. Fortunately for Britain there was one politician who could see what needed to be done and knew that he was the only person who could achieve it.

David Lloyd George was a giant of a man; an electric dynamo in a world of grandfather clocks. Having laid the foundation of the welfare state in peacetime, he transformed the efforts of a country at war, first as Munitions Minister, then Secretary of State for War, until at the end of 1916 he finally became Prime Minister, the first ordinary unprivileged Briton ever to do so. The political machinations that got him the top job were complex and secretive; this upstart son of a teacher from North Wales did not have the support of many of the gentlemen in government. But with the support of Labour MPs and just enough key figures at Westminster, after three days of wrangling he emerged as the head of the new coalition government.

It was a very British coup. In the same month that Rasputin was removed from his position of influence in Moscow by being poisoned, shot, bludgeoned and then drowned in a freezing river, Asquith was simply approached by some chaps in wing-collars who said, 'Listen, Squiffy old chap, not sure you're still top-notch and tickety-boo. Would you mind awfully . . . ?'

Lloyd George was not a party leader and owed his position to his support in the country rather than at Westminster. More of a president than a prime minister, he was criticized for employing so many unelected officials – the precursors to today's 'special advisers' – whom he housed in the back garden at Downing Street and in huts in St James's Park, the so-called 'garden suburb'. In many other ways Lloyd George was a very modern politician. But if Britain's national saviour had had to survive under today's media spotlight he would have lasted about five minutes. The 'Welsh Wizard' was as dynamic in his love life as he was in government. His wife had stayed in North Wales when he became an MP, which he failed to take as his cue for a lifetime of celibacy. There were also financial scandals, most notably his brazen sale of peerages which resulted in the practice finally being made illegal. It was this law that almost led to the prosecution of Tony Blair until he was suddenly acquitted of mis-using the honours system by the Duke of Scotland Yard, OBE, KB, VC.

Soviet Russia quits 'capitalist war' to hold poorly attended meeting above pub

World war had spread around the globe as the two team captains took turns to pick sides from the minor countries lined up on the touch-line.

'Turkey, we'll have you,' said the Kaiser.

'Pick Italy, they're good,' whispered France into England's ear.

'OK, Italy, you're on our side.'

'Bulgaria.'

'Portugal.'

'Oh, I was going to pick them. OK, er . . . Switzerland?'

'Nah, they never play.'

It was three years into the war when the United States finally turned up, and it was England's pick. 'That's not fair, if you're having America, you can't have Russia as well!' and so it was agreed that the new Bolshevik government in Russia would make peace with Germany, and then Britain would send troops to fight the Russians instead of supporting them. A few other American countries came in on the Allies' side after the United States, but few historians seem to think that it was Guatemala's entry into the war that swung it.

It had been the submarine war that had brought America in on the Allies' side in April 1917, but Germany had gambled that if they ignored US threats and sank neutral ships they could starve Britain into submission before America's entry could make any difference. They came very close to succeeding. At this point one ship out of four leaving British ports failed to ever return. Neutral ships were refusing to come to British ports despite the best efforts of the politicians: 'Are you going to let yourself be put off by a pack of German U-boats and thousands of hidden mines?'

'Well, yes, we thought we might.'

Food stocks were falling dangerously low, with only six weeks' supply of wheat remaining. Unless the situation was somehow drastically changed, Britain would be starved into surrendering at some point in the summer of 1917. Lloyd George was desperate for the men at the Admiralty to come up with some innovative suggestions, but these varied from 'Nothing we can do, I'm afraid' to 'More than my job's worth, quite frankly'. The Prime Minister became persuaded of the merits of trying out a convoy system so that merchant ships travelled together protected by the navy. The shoulder-shrugging Admiralty said convoys were completely unworkable, producing misleading statistics that included even the Isle of Wight ferry in the merchant ships that would need navy protection. But Lloyd George overruled his minister and his department and the system worked brilliantly. Only one per cent of convoy-escorted ships were sunk. Starvation or surrender was just averted and it was only the political will of the Prime Minister that had forced this policy through.

'Yeah, all right, we have to admit that we were *partly* in the wrong.'

Britain occupies Iraq: 'We're not coming back here'

There was only one old-fashioned war hero to emerge from the First World War. 'Lawrence of Arabia' was a man of many talents, inspiring the Arabs to rise up against the Ottoman Empire, co-ordinating their various revolts to assist the British war effort and getting David Lean to make a very, very long film about it. It took a couple of years before his espionage work bore fruit, and even longer in the Director's Cut.

'Lawrence is just going to ride towards us from the horizon.'

'OK, I'll put the kettle on.'

The Ottoman Empire was now collapsing on all fronts and Britain was able to acquire the valuable oil fields of Mesopotamia.

'You're only invading because of the oil!'

'Yes. Obviously. Oil is crucial to our economy. What's your point?'

Britain drew a few random borders on the atlas and decided to call this territory 'Irak'; apart from having to change the spelling, everything went swimmingly ever after.* While Britain was sorting out the Middle East, the army entered Jerusalem in 1917 and the famous 'Balfour Declaration' proposed the idea of a Jewish homeland in Palestine; *it being clearly understood that nothing shall be done which may prejudice the civil and religious rights of existing non-Jewish communities in Palestine.* They were really on a roll. 'We'll just secure long-term peace in Cyprus and Beirut and then I think our work here is done.'

March 1918: Germans go ahead with minutes left on clock

The year in which Berlin finally chucked in the towel had begun with the Germans looking about to win. In the spring of 1918, with Russia now out of the war and America not yet effectively in it, Germany launched an all-out assault on the Western Front. The idea of the Germans attacking during a war seemed to catch Haig completely by surprise. The line was pushed back forty miles and the Germans were once again within striking distance of Paris. In Westminster, a panicky government raised the age of conscription to fifty and against all advice tried to enforce it in Ireland. The Irish MPs withdrew from Westminster, never to return.

The government decided it was time to take the gloves off and began sending over little balloons with notes tied to the string. While British troops were in full retreat, untrained for war on the move or military tactics out of the trenches, German civilians were finding balloons in their back gardens with notes promising that the English would be really nice to them if they surrendered. But the Germans had novel propaganda methods of their own. It was around this time

---

* In 1920 Britain attempted to put down a rebellion in Iraq by using RAF bombers. Aerial bombardment is one British invention that hasn't yet been commemorated on a special set of stamps.

that the nervous British establishment became aware of the existence of the so-called 'Black Book': a list of 47,000 perverts in senior positions in the British establishment. Judges, generals, ministers; pretty well anyone who was anyone was listed alongside details of their preferred sexual deviation. When news of this book leaked out during a libel case, the ordinary British public were shocked. 'Only forty-seven thousand?!'

But the exhausted German nation could not sustain their attack. Plus it must have been demoralizing to have Costa Rica and Honduras declare war on you as well. 'And now Haiti and Liberia as well? Why is everyone against us?'

'Because you started a world war that resulted in the needless death of millions, killed thousands of neutral sailors and civilians with your submarines and mines and introduced poison gas to modern warfare.'

'Yes, *but apart from that?*'

In late summer 1918, under the overall command of the French Commander Foch, the Allies began pushing Germany back. The first significant numbers of US troops had arrived, albeit supplied almost entirely with British equipment. One American recruiting poster of the time said *U.S. Marines – First in France.* One or two French and British soldiers might have had something to say about that. A mass breakthrough of tanks occurred at Amiens, heralding the end of the very brief but bloody age of trench warfare. The tank had made an inauspicious debut on the battlefields of Europe two years earlier at the Battle of the Somme.* Its supporters had wanted to wait until these secret weapons could be deployed in significant numbers, but Haig had been desperate to throw everything at the front. On their first outing only twenty-one tanks had limped into action and the element of surprise had been blown. More than half the tanks available had not even made it as far as the front; these clumsy British-made vehicles were initially very unreliable and

---

* During the secret development of this weapon, British designers pretended they were building a new type of large water tank. This became shortened to 'tank', and the name stuck.

temperamental, constantly breaking down even if the garage had just done a full service.

'Typical British bloody car industry. Can't we put a BMW or a VW engine under the bonnet? They're much more dependable.'

'Not sure that would go down very well at the moment.'

In the autumn of 1918 more dramatic advances were being made in what Churchill had called the 'soft underbelly of Europe'. After a major British victory in September, the Ottoman Empire surrendered in October 1918; pipped to the post by Bulgaria, who everyone had forgotten was in the war anyway. Italian successes against the Austrian-Hungarians were knocking Germany's most significant ally out of the war and, with no army to send to this new front, the German military high command lost heart. Unable to defeat Britain and France on the battlefield, the Germans thought they could at least really annoy them, and so began armistice negotiations with just the United States. For three weeks, America unilaterally conducted peace talks without its Allies. France was publicly furious, while Lloyd George decided it was probably best not to criticize President Wilson. Which has pretty well been the relationship between America, Britain and France ever since.

It all fell apart very suddenly. The German navy mutinied; there were uprisings in Berlin and elsewhere, and with commanders refusing to guarantee that German troops would defend their own government, the Kaiser fled to neutral Holland. Two days later armistice terms were decided upon at 5 a.m. and it was agreed that war would end at 11 a.m. that morning.

'The war to end all wars' (Yeah, right)

At 10.58 a.m. on 11 November 1918, George Lawrence Price (Serial No. 256265) was shot dead by a German sniper. The Canadian private is widely believed to be the last soldier to have been killed in the First World War. Two minutes later the guns fell silent and Europe was at peace.

The world would never see such madness again, they pledged. But recovering from a mustard gas attack in a German military field hospital, an insignificant Austrian corporal was appalled that the war had ended while the German army remained undefeated in the field. His name was Karl-Heinz Pfammenschmidt and he would go on to become a maker of the finest jam doughnuts Salzburg had ever known. In the bed next to him, however, was another Austrian corporal whose name was Adolf Hitler. He would have very little direct impact on the Salzburg doughnut business.

Back in Britain the end of the war seemed to come suddenly and unexpectedly. People rushed out on to the streets; cheering crowds rode around on open-top buses and the scenes of national jubilation were like nothing the country had ever seen. Bonfires were lit in the street; indeed the foot of Nelson's Column is still scorched with the marks of one such fire. Complete strangers had sex in public; as the great historian A. J. P. Taylor said, *They were asserting the triumph of life over death.* Or they were just shagging. Suggestions that these scenes be re-enacted every year in memory of the war were not taken up by the British Legion. Instead, on the anniversary of the armistice, Britain's war dead would be remembered with two minutes' silence, interrupted only by one person's mobile phone going off and its flustered owner saying, 'Terribly sorry, sorry, everyone . . .' The British Legion, formed in 1921, took as its symbol the poppy; chosen because the first signs of life on the scorched muddy battlefields had apparently been the blood-red specks of this humble flower. Obviously you have to allow a certain amount of artistic licence; there must have been all sorts of grasses and weeds springing up, but you wouldn't want Remembrance Day ruined by everyone trying to pin stinging nettles to their lapels.

Of course in 1918, people didn't need paper flowers or cenotaphs to remember the war; three-quarters of a million young men had lost their lives, and everywhere could be seen the limbless or blinded survivors. The apocalyptic horseman of War had finally returned to his stable and then said, 'OK, Plague, your turn.' In the latter months of 1918 more people around the world died of an influenza epidemic than had been killed in the entire war. In Britain 150,000 people died from so-called 'Spanish Flu'. Lloyd George himself had nearly succumbed immediately after the armistice, spending ten days in bed in Manchester Town Hall, which is not the first place you would choose to fall seriously ill.

Perhaps if he had died then his heroic status would have been preserved for ever, for the Welsh Wizard's subsequent years in office were to diminish his standing. But Lloyd George is to the First World War what Winston Churchill is to the Second: the dynamic, visionary and determined leader without whom Britain might have capitulated. Both men were flawed geniuses, but their contrasting status as national heroes has as much to do with how we feel about the wars they won as to what they personally achieved. Churchill led us through an apparently black and white conflict that we feel proud to have fought and won. Lloyd George won an unnecessary war we would rather forget. And so the British people voted Winston Churchill as the Greatest Ever Briton while Lloyd George came in at a scandalous number 79, only just ahead of Johnny Rotten and Sir Richard Branson.*

But we should remember the First World War, perhaps more than any other, because it is possibly the starkest example of what can occur when politics goes wrong. Just like us, the Europeans of 1914 had thought they were the most advanced society ever to have lived on Earth. They had great literature and architecture, they had science and philosophy and a car with a roof you could pull down when it was sunny. But the same society that produced the novels of E. M. Forster and Marcel Proust and the music of Debussy and Mahler created the slaughter fields of Verdun and the Somme. Few people had seriously entertained the idea that such terrible things were possible, perhaps because the very scale of the horror was too awful to entertain. And today we bury our heads in the sand at the thought of all-out nuclear war or environmental meltdown, telling ourselves that such horrors could never actually be permitted to happen. But this is the triumph of hope over experience; the First

---

* However, one shouldn't take these polls too seriously. In the American equivalent, United States citizens collectively decided that the Greatest Ever American was Ronald Reagan, God help us. The Canadians voted for Tommy Douglas. Er, obviously.

World War proved that the idea of the sky falling on our heads isn't some ridiculous apocalyptic impossibility. Sometimes the sky really does fall on our heads; sometimes we bring it crashing down upon ourselves.

Election Special (because now you're allowed to vote)

The general election of 1918 was a truly historic occasion, even if the country wasn't in much of a mood to celebrate it as such. Democracy had finally come to Britain. Earlier in the year, more voters had been added to the electoral register than in all the nineteenth-century reforms put together. The Chartist dream of universal male suffrage had finally become a reality; the ordinary man at last had the right to vote, which was the government's way of saying, 'Sorry about the cock-up with those trenches and all that.'

'Oh, that's quite all right, don't worry about it.'

Women's suffrage had also been overwhelmingly accepted almost without a debate in a free vote in the House of Commons. After all the struggles of the Suffragettes, it was something of an anti-climax, although of course it would never have been on the agenda in the first place had so many women not campaigned with such determination. However, just to annoy them, the men decided that women would not get the vote till they were thirty. Otherwise the men would have had to endure the terrible prospect of there being more women voters than men, and all the laws would have been about remembering to take things up the stairs instead of just walking straight past them.

For a century, the establishment had maintained that the ordinary people could not be trusted with political power, and now that moment had come the party leaders appealed to the electorate's basest instincts by whipping up the anti-German sentiment across the land. Deep down the politicians knew that Europe and Britain's best interests would be best served by a peace that preserved German dignity and economic viability, but frankly that didn't play as well at the hustings as 'Let's hang the Kaiser!' The heroes sent to their deaths in the First World War were described as *lions led by donkeys*. Now that responsibility for the government was to be shared with those lions, they quickly demonstrated that there was a little bit of donkey in all of us.

The election was essentially a huge vote of thanks to Lloyd George, whose popularity was such that he could have stood as the leader of the Monster Raving Loony Party and still won most of the seats in the country.   Instead he opted to continue the wartime coalition with the Unionist Conservatives. This put him in opposition to the other Liberals, who were still led by Asquith, and Labour too decided that it would prefer to fight on its own terms. Fatally, the great radical Lloyd George had tied himself to the forces of reaction rather than reform. He won overwhelmingly, promising 'a fit country for heroes to live in' but within a couple of years there would be two million unemployed and the Conservative majority would realize that there was nothing to stop them making Lloyd George one of them.

... But you can displease all of the people, all of the time

Lloyd George's peacetime administration satisfied no one. The left were hoping for the sort of progressive reforms that he had pushed through before the war, but any attempts to move in this direction were opposed by his Conservative majority on whom he depended for his position. In the coal mines, the Welsh Wizard was now seen as a traitor; the mines had been placed under state control during the war, but Lloyd George defied an independent enquiry that suggested this situation be made permanent. The coal mines were Britain's biggest employer, and when the miners lost a bitter strike in 1921, wages fell in other industries too. More and more of the heroes of the trenches were finding themselves on the scrapheap and if Lloyd George hadn't extended unemployment benefit, it is quite possible that the violent uprisings happening all over Europe would have been duplicated in Britain.

There were some advances in housing and education. Local

authority housing was subsidized, and the school leaving age was set at fourteen. This is why primary education still ends at the age of 11, because anything shorter than three years of secondary education would not have been viable.

'Right, young man, you'll soon be fourteen. What are you going to do when you leave school?'

'Well, sir, I thought I would join the unemployed and hang around on street corners looking menacing . . .'

But Lloyd George wasn't just stymied by his political bedfellows, the exchequer didn't have the money to spend on an extension of the welfare state. The days when a Britain emerged victorious from war richer and stronger were over. Worse still, Britain had borrowed from the United States but lent money to the Tsar. 'Hey, Russia, can we have our war loan back now?'

'*Nyet*. We do not recognize capitalist debts.'

'No, seriously, joke over. Can we have the money?'

'All usury is theft from workers by capitalist banks.'

'He *is* joking, isn't he?'

Towards the end of the war, civil war in Russia had made it seem possible that the Bolsheviks might be toppled. In the hope of bringing the Russians back into the war against Germany, Britain had sent a small number of troops to assist the rebel White Russians. Not enough to make any difference, but just enough for Britain to be cast as the oppressor of the people's soviets for evermore. Labour MPs protested about this interference and now a war-weary government brought the soldiers home. Obviously Lenin was all, 'Hey, no hard feelings, we're communists, you're capitalists; let's agree to disagree.'

Some hoped that future wars might be averted by the creation of the League of Nations; a half-hearted attempt to create an international forum that was doomed to fail when the United States and the Soviet Union sent their apologies. Many in America had disliked the fact that their historical policy of isolation had been overturned by President Wilson. But it is barely possible to be a major world economic power without becoming a major political and therefore military player as well. America was twice forced to confront this reality in the first half of the twentieth century – just as

China will have to in the first half of the twenty-first. So there's something to look forward to.

The mistake of 1918 was thinking that Germany could be kept out of the equation. The two dominant themes of the period were 'Revenge' and 'Never Again'. Unfortunately these two ideas were contradictory. The retribution exacted at the peace conference at Versailles made everyone feel a bit better for a while. The only downside, admittedly quite a significant one, was that it would lead to another world war twenty years later.

Britain had insisted that the German navy be surrendered and it was now being held in Scapa Flow in the Orkneys. But there in 1919 the entire fleet scuttled itself; the German admiral ordered his captains to blow up and sink their own ships rather than let them fall into the hands of their former enemies. The rusting hulks of fifty-odd ships are still there, providing, incidentally, an invaluable source of uncontaminated metal for space satellites. Only steel forged before the first nuclear detonation in 1945 is completely free of radioactive isotopes (background radiation affects the highly sensitive sensors used in space communication) and so many of the tiny specks orbiting over our heads in the night sky contain recycled bits of the German Imperial Navy from the First World War.

The Kaiser learnt of the demise of his great navy at his new home in Holland where he eventually lived just long enough to see the Netherlands occupied by the Nazis. The Allies had wanted him extradited so that he could be tried and executed but the Dutch Queen thought this a rather vulgar idea.

The war and its aftermath brought new governments to pretty well every country from the Western Front to the Sea of Japan and created whole new countries such as Czechoslovakia and Yugoslavia. Perhaps in future, hot-headed declarations of war might be delayed if they made the new countries really difficult to spell. In Britain too, the borders were about to be redrawn. After more than seven hundred years, Irish independence was finally about to become a reality.

'Do you know what, in a funny sort of way, I'm going to miss all those political battles.'

'Well, I'll tell you what. Let's just hang on to six counties in the North. Just as a memento of all those happy years together.'

There was this Englishman, this Irishman and this American . . .

Ireland had pleaded for autonomy for so long that it had simply become impossible to ignore. Like Mrs Doyle in *Father Ted*, if a nation spends enough time saying 'Go on, go on, go on, go on, go on . . .' eventually it wears you down. Opinion in Ireland had hardened after British attempts to enforce conscription and the martyrdom of the 1916 rebels. Sinn Fein had eclipsed the moderate Home-Rulers, explaining in their historic native tongue why Eire must break completely free, and then saying it all again in English because nobody understood Irish any more. In the election of 1918, Sinn Fein won nearly three-quarters of the seats* but did not come to Westminster, gathering instead in Dublin at the Dáil.

'The what?'

'It's Irish for Parliament.'

'Of course it is. I knew that.'

'And de Valera is our Príohm Aire.'

'National Airline?'

'President.'

'Exactly.'

The new assembly levied taxes, passed laws and was immediately accepted by the majority of the Irish people. Post office workers unilaterally redirected the official post of the British Governor's office to the Irish Parliament and frankly the British rulers in Dublin were left feeling more than a little embarrassed and unwanted. De Valera's

---

* Amongst these was Countess Markievicz, the first woman elected to Westminster, though generally not counted as the first woman MP since she did not take her seat. The best thing to do if you are running a quiz night is to leave the wording of this bit of trivia really vague, in order that there are lots of over-aggressive arguments after everyone's had a few drinks.

young rival Michael Collins organized the Irish Republican Army for the coming military battle, receiving financial support from Americans who fully understood the complexities of the Irish situation because they had a grandfather from Irishland. Only the Soviet Union recognized the new country, and Washington declined Irish offers to mediate. A rather piqued British government declared the Irish Parliament illegal, and sent over the infamous Black and Tans, the notoriously brutal auxiliary police officers, so-called for their improvised and rather fascist black and khaki uniforms. These quasi-military policemen were generally recruited from all the meatheads who were judged to be too vicious and indiscriminately violent to become night-club bouncers. They were given carte blanche to do whatever it took to subjugate the population, even if French idioms might have been a little beyond them. If one of their number was killed by the IRA, they executed random civilians, burnt down town centres and tortured suspected sympathizers. The name still causes such revulsion in Ireland that in 2006 when Ben and Jerry launched an ice-cream with the name 'Black and Tan', they were forced to apologize for the offence given in the Republic of Ireland and stress that the ice-cream flavour had no intention of repeating the torching of Cork City.

With law and order having collapsed and murder and random reprisals taking place over much of the country, the British government sought a settlement, offering Ireland Dominion status under the Canadian model, with six of the nine counties of Ulster allowed to opt out of the Irish Free State if they chose to do so.

'Ireland without Ulster? That would be like the Nolans without Denise!'

De Valera had sent Michael Collins to the British negotiating table, to save himself being tarnished with the inevitable compromise that would follow. 'Michael, you know whoever signs an imperfect treaty with the British might be assassinated by the hard-liners?'

'It's a risk I suppose we'll have to take.'

'Actually, I'm busy next week. Oh and when you come back, could you use the R585 road out of Béal na mBláth, and slow right down as you pass the old stone cottage.'

Such is the power of the cinema that it has almost become accepted as fact that de Valera arranged the assassination of his great rival. In fact there is no proof of this, even though it is heavily implied in Neil Jordan's film of Collins's life and premature death. The movie also shows the British sending armoured vehicles into a Gaelic football game to shoot indiscriminately into the crowd, when in fact they were on foot. But hey, let's not fall out over things in the past; I mean, that's never been the Anglo-Irish way.

The Irish Free State officially came into existence in December 1922. The Irish problem was solved for evermore, and there really are leprechauns counting their gold underneath the blackthorn bush. It had been promised that the hastily improvised partition would be reviewed and revised, but it remains to this day. Most of the bizarre European borders sketched out after the Great War were abandoned in the 1990s. Only the arbitrary line between Britain and the Republic in Ireland still remains. But as I am sure Martin McGuinness would agree, there's only one thing more stupid than the border between Britain and Ireland and that's killing people over it.

The Unionist Conservatives who made up most of Lloyd George's government never really forgave him for allowing the secession of Ireland, and like Peel and Gladstone before him, Ireland destroyed Lloyd George. And as for granting Dominion status to those dusky-coloured chaps in India, well, the bloody lefties could just forget it. Indian independence would probably have come a quarter of a century earlier had Lloyd George managed to work with Asquith and his fellow Liberals. But by 1922 the Conservatives were tiring of the cuckoo in the nest, and it took a small crisis in the Eastern Mediterranean to finish him off. A crisis had blown up between Turkey and Greece, and Lloyd George wanted to use British troops to intervene. Everyone else in the country was sure that this reminded them of something that had happened a few years earlier. 'Hmmm . . . a small local dispute in the Balkans, Britain gets involved. It definitely rings a bell . . .' The unions threatened a general strike if war was pursued and the Conservatives met to consider their loyalties. Britain's first democratically elected Prime Minister didn't fall from power following another general election or great debate in the House of Commons – it was a private meeting in the Carlton Club that decided to dump him. No Liberal Prime Minister ever held office again.

So when exactly did they form the 1922 Committee?

When Lloyd George heard the result of the Conservative MPs' vote he resigned immediately. So did the leader of the Conservative Party, Austen Chamberlain, and many of the cabinet.* And so it was that a rather unexciting Scottish businessman was called to kiss the hand of the King, although by now they were wondering if this ancient tradition wasn't just a little bit, you know, gay.

'I still like girls though.'

'Oh, me too. Girls, football, cars, military history; all that stuff . . .'

Andrew Bonar Law had led the Conservatives once before, but now he was to have the shortest term of office of any Prime Minister in the twentieth century. His cabinet were formed from whoever was left after all that excitement down at the Carlton Club and though there are lots of famous names in there, unfortunately when the PM was looking down the list he didn't check whether that was *the* Viscount Peel or *the* Lord Salisbury. Churchill called his cabinet 'the second eleven'. Bonar Law died a year later, and was buried in Westminster Abbey, where Asquith quipped that the Unknown Soldier had just been joined by the Unknown Prime Minister.

The most interesting thing that they did was allow the silent movie

* However, the Conservatives' 1922 Committee, or 'the influential 1922 Committee' as it is always called on the news, did not originate here. It was actually constituted in 1923, taking its name from the election of the previous year. In fact it is just a rather grand name for all the Conservative MPs stuck on the backbenches, because none of them liked the name 'Political No-Hopers and Embittered Outcasts Committee'.

cameras into Downing Street for the first time, which (rather wonderfully) the British Film Institute recently stuck up on YouTube. As silent movies go, stilted footage of old men with moustaches having a meeting isn't quite up to the slapstick knockabout that the genre demands. The ministers walk into the room and sadly the Keystone Cops do not follow them in and bash them over the head with truncheons. Neither does the chair collapse and the cabinet table tip up. Instead the captions ratchet the hilarity up another notch: 'The Duke of Devonshire (Colonies) discusses a point with Viscount Peel (India)'.

But the very existence of this film shows that times were changing. These politicians were considered very modern and perhaps a little too casual when some of them actually called each other by their Christian names. Top hats and tails were out, three-piece suits and ties were in. Even the King swapped his crown for a bowler hat. George V came across as far more businesslike and practical than his haughty forebears. He attended the Cup Final every year, never once punching a rival fan, and it was he who began the tradition of giving a Christmas message on the wireless.

'To all of you I wish a happy Christmas and nerry mew year – Oh fuck, can we go again?'

'No, you're going out live, your majesty.'

The radio was a new feature in the British drawing room; the number of radio licences went up from 125,000 in 1924 to nearly 2 million two years later and by the end of the thirties virtually every home had one. The BBC morphed from the British Broadcasting Company into a public corporation in the mid-twenties, and the values it espoused were very much those of the church-going upper-middle classes. Radio announcers could not be unleashed upon a microphone unless they were wearing a dinner jacket, and there were to be no regional or working-class accents. Attendance at church dropped, pubs and social clubs suffered because clearly no working man would want to miss the live radio commentary of the Oxford v Cambridge Boat Race.

The first politicians to speak on radio shouted at the microphone as if they were addressing a large public rally, but it was Bonar Law's successor Stanley Baldwin* who was the first to master the chatty fireside style that this intimate new medium required. 'Hmmm . . . This is the midnight hour . . .' he'd whisper over his mug of cocoa. 'You're with me through the night here on Premier FM, talking about tariff reform after this classic from the Carpenters . . .'

Rather thrillingly, the big debate of the day was 'Tariff Reform' versus 'Empire Free Trade'. Remakes of *West Side Story* would have pitched the Import Protectionist Gang against the Empire Preference Posse as this fanatical tribal division split the Westminster Village. Would Britain do better if imports were taxed, or would the free flow of goods to the Dominions increase orders from the factories? Clearly passions were always going to be running high. Three times in as many years these issues were put to millions of new voters: 'You wanted a democracy? Well, you asked for it.'

The last of these three elections saw the Liberals effectively knocked out as a political party, even if their policies and values continued to predominate whichever side happened to be in power. Even Asquith and Churchill lost their seats,† while Lloyd George finally became the leader of what was left. The Liberals never completely disappeared, providing a valuable service for all those people who rejected Conservative values but were too appalled by the working classes ever to vote Labour.

The horrific spectre of the servants actually moving above stairs suddenly loomed into view when the minority Tory government fell in December 1923. The tradition of asking the second largest party to form a government suddenly seemed a rather alarming idea now that this was made up of oiks in replica football shirts with naked ladies tattooed on their forearms. All sorts of bizarre ideas were suggested to keep Labour out of power: 'We could have a

---

* Stanley Baldwin had not been in the cabinet for long but was chosen by the King over the more experienced Lord Curzon, as it was felt that it was no longer possible to have a Prime Minister who sat in the House of Lords. Lord Curzon was not exactly in touch with the common man. During the Great War when he had seen soldiers swimming, he had expressed astonishment that the lower classes had such pale skin.

† Churchill was replaced by Britain's only ever 'Prohibitionist' MP.

Liberal–Conservative coalition under Austen Chamberlain or Balfour', 'We could have a non-Parliamentary government of "National Trustees" ', 'We could make a rule that you can't be in the cabinet if you leave the telly on during mealtimes'. But in the midst of the secret lobbying, the King was firm that this was a job for Ramsay MacDonald.

'What, the clown from the hamburger ads?'

'No *Ramsay* MacDonald. The Labour leader.'

Labour take office: pass the smelling salts

On 21 January 1924 the King noted in his diary that it was twenty-three years since his grandmother Queen Victoria had died, and he wondered with some amusement what she would have thought of the socialists forming a government. In Britain the left did not finally come to power through revolution or a popular landslide, but at the invitation of the monarch. The majority of the cabinet were of working-class origin, few had any political experience and they even felt compelled to rent posh outfits from Moss Bros for court occasions. They were a minority government with no real power, and the civil servants were less than enthusiastic about enacting any radical policies. In fact as head of the security services Ramsay MacDonald actually asked if he could see the secret file that had been kept on him but he was refused and he didn't like to ask again.

The main task of the minority Labour government was to try and look sensible and moderate, so that they might be trusted with real power at the next election.

'What if we had a red rose instead of a flag?'

'No, they'd never fall for that.'

Perhaps because he was stymied at home, MacDonald concerned himself with foreign affairs, particularly in Germany where inflation was a teensy bit of a problem. As the German economy collapsed the price of bread reached the price of 200,000,000,000 marks, though with a bit of haggling you could usually get the baker down to

199,000,000,000 if you had the right change on you. MacDonald played a part in the renegotiation of Germany's war reparations, and under his government Britain finally recognized the government of the Soviet Union. But it was the perceived association with Russian communists that was to keep Labour from winning the election that the minority government was soon forced to call.

Four days before polling day, the *Daily Mail* published a letter apparently from leading Russian Communist Zinoviev which 'proved' that the Labour government would play a part in bringing about proletarian revolution in Britain. For a few eagle-eyed students of Russia, the clues were there that this letter was a forgery:

> Greetings Fellow Red–Under–the–Bed–type Socialist Persons. This damaging letter is just to confirm that we definitely have secret lefty-conspiracy with our Britisher Labour Party comrades to make everyone in capitalist England wear little furry hats and eat beetroot. All members of British Soviet will have big bushy eyebrows and give four-hour speeches about glorious tractor production in Leningrad. And it will always be snowing.

The letter caused a sensation, massively boosting the Conservative vote, and helping to put Stanley Baldwin back in Downing Street. Obviously the *Daily Mail* was careful never to print anything untruthful about the labour movement ever again. But eighteen months later British workers and the Conservative government really would be locked into a titanic struggle which many feared was the beginning of a revolution. Indeed, it was an attack upon the trade unions in the *Daily Mail* which precipitated a breakdown in talks between the TUC and the government. The edition would not even be printed. Suddenly the whole country was paralysed by the only general strike Britain has ever experienced as foreign observers waited for the bloodshed to begin.

The General Strike: workers down tools; everyone else down pub

The new Conservative administration under Stanley Baldwin was called 'the government of the old men', which seems a strange way of trying to distinguish it from all the others. This reassuring, pipe-smoking cousin of Rudyard Kipling was the only rich industrialist ever to become British Prime Minister. Back when concern had been riding high about the size of the war loan, he had set an example by personally donating one-fifth of his personal fortune to the treasury. Strangely all the rich businessmen who were *not* in the government chose not to copy him.

His surprise appointment on returning to power was making Winston Churchill the chancellor. Churchill had been elected as an independent, and apparently thought the PM was offering him the chancellorship of the Duchy of Lanchester. The country's finances had been in pretty desperate shape since the Great War with high unemployment and poor balance-of-trade figures. Churchill's solution was a return to the gold standard and nobody dared disagree in case they said something that showed they didn't have the faintest idea how this worked. The gold standard was the guarantee that all the paper currency in circulation was secured by its equivalent value in gold reserves. Above the Queen's head on our banknotes it still says 'I promise to pay the bearer the sum of ten pounds' but if you attempted to test this during a royal walkabout, it's unlikely that she would start handing over bits of jewellery.*

The effect was to make British exports too expensive, and Britain's greatest industry, coal mining, suffered a further slump. Down the years the mine-owners had become enormously wealthy but now with coal prices dropping they demanded the miners take a pay cut or work longer hours. The miners' leader responded with the defiant 'Not a penny off the pay, not a minute on the day'. When a government-backed enquiry came down on the side of

* This promise is actually signed by the Chief Cashier of the Bank of England, but he's too shy to have his face on the notes.

pay cuts, the Trades Union Congress called a general strike.

The response was overwhelming and universal. On 3 May 1926 millions of ordinary union members stopped work for no personal advantage or chance of private gain, despite virtually every newspaper telling them to defy the strike. They did so out of a sense of solidarity with mineworkers they would never meet, and a feeling that natural justice was not being observed. Instead of the situation exploding into revolutionary violence, a rather jolly holiday atmosphere prevailed in the May sunshine. Students and other middle-class volunteers were enjoying the short-term novelty of driving buses or sorting the mail, while strikers were reported playing football with the police. Key medical and agricultural workers were kept in place and there was little bloodshed, despite Winston Churchill's best efforts to stir things up by getting armoured vehicles to drive through the centre of London. Churchill thrived on such conflict and for ten heady days he edited the provocative government propaganda sheet the *British Gazette* which described the strikers as 'the enemy'. Churchill had wanted to take over the airwaves, but the BBC kept its independence by not being independent. It self-censored any news it feared the government might not like and that well-known radical agitator, the Archbishop of Canterbury, was kept off the air in case he tried to see both points of view.

There was no revolutionary intent on the part of the TUC leaders, who had never really wanted the strike in the first place. They'd felt compelled to show their support for the miners, but now that the doomsday weapon had finally been demonstrated they were keen to put it back in the box as soon as possible. 'The workers! United! Will never be defeated!' went the chant. 'Unless their leaders unexpectedly cave in for no apparent reason!' It was almost as if the TUC had been frightened by its own success. Without consulting the miners, the TUC suddenly ended the stoppage after nine days following an empty assurance from Baldwin that there would be no victimization of strikers. This promise was of course broken, and there followed a raft of anti-union legislation, not to mention a great deal more suffering on behalf of the miners who stayed out until November when hunger and poverty finally forced them back on reduced wages. Like the First World War, Britain's only ever general strike was a credit to its people, while its leaders were spineless and dithering on one side and duplicitous and vindictive on the other. Final score in the Police v Picketers football match: Policeman 7, Strikers 0 (10 players arrested and detained in back of police van for 90 minutes).

Things fall apart; the centre cannot hold

The 1920s have an image of bohemian ballerinas reclining on chaises longues, smoking cigars and deciding to become lesbians. Even if the lives of surrealists or the Bloomsbury group were a million miles from the impoverished existence of ordinary people, it was a time of great intellectual development in the Western world. In the British Isles, where literature had always been the predominant art form, writers got together to appreciate the paintings of Pablo Picasso or whistle along to the symphonies of Stravinsky – but eventually had to admit: 'Sorry, I just don't understand any of this at all.'

'Exactly. And that's what we should be doing with our writing.' Then they all went off and wrote stream-of-consciousness novels and experimental poetry and their editors were too embarrassed to tell them to completely start again.

The leading movement of the early twentieth century was the 'We'll Just Have to Take Their Word For It' movement. Whether it was the writing of James Joyce or Virginia Woolf or the incomprehensible theories of Einstein or Freud or the economic analyses of John Maynard Keynes, the British people appreciated the huge leaps being made in the arts and science without having the faintest idea what any of it meant.

'Oh yes, T. S. Eliot. Well, he's clearly a genius . . .'

'Have you read *The Waste Land* then?'

'Er, well, no, but *you just have to take their word for it*. I do read some poetry though. I love the one where Christopher Robin has wheezles and sneezles . . .'

The most popular art form of the era was of course the cinema. With 90 per cent of the films coming from the United States there were concerns about the Americanization of British culture, even if Hollywood's greatest movie star Charlie Chaplin was a British export. (Later in his life he was accused by the rabid McCarthy witch-hunt of 'un-American activities', which would seem reasonable for someone who was from South London.) With the first 'talkie' appearing in 1927, the music hall and theatre continued to suffer, although the plays of Noel Coward and J. B. Priestley continued to cater for the middle classes (or anyone else who was prepared to pay that much for a programme and an ice-cream). Early attempts to simply record West End plays for transmission on the radio were a failure, and soon plays were written especially for the wireless. The BBC also pumped orchestral music into the home, in the hope that excited teenagers would gather round their sets to listen to the latest smash hit from Sir Edward Elgar.

Like other modern luxuries the radio was bought using the new craze for hire purchase. This opportunity of spending beyond your immediate means was far from respectable, and the goods were often delivered in unmarked vans.

'What's that in the plain box? Are you buying things on hire pur-chase?'

'No, no, honestly; it's just sex aids and pornography; I'd never buy a phonogram on h.p.'

Car ownership increased on a similar basis. At the beginning of the 1920s there were about a hundred different producers of auto-mobiles in Britain and one of the revelations of the General Strike was that Britain's total dependence on the railways was over. One simple change of law allowing cars to be parked on the street instead of in private garages transformed the market for cars. By the end of the 1920s there were a million cars on the road. No driving test was required and there were more road deaths than there are today.

Private enterprise brought competition but also chaos. The provision of electricity was one example; voltage varied widely even within the same towns and there were twenty-three different types of plug for an electric fire. Imagine such a ridiculous variation today; it would be like having loads of different mobile phone chargers kicking around the house. Despite the consumer boom and the apparently upbeat atmosphere, the post-war economy was not in good shape. For most of the country, the 1920s was a time of poverty and bitter realization that the huge sacrifices of the Great War had all been for nothing. The spectre of unemployment or wage cuts hung over most workers, and the General Strike had demonstrated the limits of union power. Perhaps the next decade might be different, they hoped. Perhaps the 1930s would be a time of full employment, growing prosperity and world peace. You have to admire their optimism.

The Great Crash of 1929 (investments can go down as well as up)

It was at a rather excitable public meeting that the right-wing Conservative Home Secretary William Joynson-Hicks found himself struggling to defend unequal voting rights for men and women. Finally he ran out of arguments and just said 'Oh all right then'; thereby committing the government to granting the vote for women at twenty-one. Rather than be seen to break their word, the infuriated cabinet now felt compelled to honour this spontaneous promise, even though they were all against the idea. And so even though some people still had two votes, 1929 saw Britain's first truly democratic election. OK, so the party that got the most votes came second, but you can't expect miracles.

Baldwin had fought the 1929 election campaign using the current road safety slogan 'Safety First'. Considering how lethal the roads had become it is not very surprising that voters were not very reassured. For the first time ever, Labour won the most seats, even if they again did not have an outright majority. The second minority Labour government included the first-ever woman cabinet minister and member of the Privy Council, Margaret Bondfield, who was made Minister for Labour, with special responsibility for making the sandwiches. Oswald Mosley, the former Conservative and Independent MP, joined the Labour government, and one of the more bizarre and disastrous political careers began to go badly wrong.

Oswald Mosley is up there in the all-time Worst XI of British Villains, alongside James Hewitt, Dr Crippen and the supermarket planner who decided to put the fromage frais with the cheese instead of with the yoghurts. It could all have been so different. Mosley's radical proposals for tackling the massive unemployment faced by the incoming Labour government were creative and bold, a major programme of public works not dissimilar to the New Deal that followed in Roosevelt's United States. But does he get any credit for this? No, he does not. You resign in a sulk and go off to form just one fascist movement, allying yourself with Hitler and Mussolini, organizing anti-Semitic marches through the Jewish East End and employing thugs to beat up your opponents and suddenly you're Mr Bad Guy.*

MacDonald was too timid to push for anything so radical as Mosley's major programme of works so the government limited itself to building a public lido in Hyde Park, making a few concessions to the miners and authorizing an extension of pensions and unemployment benefit. Mosley's place in the government was taken by a rather more unassuming man called Clement Attlee.

MacDonald was keen to show that Labour could be an acceptable government and so continued with the unacceptably inadequate policies that had necessitated the formation of the Labour Party in the first place. He was enjoying being Prime Minister and went to America where he received a ticker-tape parade in New York. It's not clear what he said to them, but immediately afterwards Wall Street crashed, share values plummeted around the world, America called in its loans and the entire Western world went into economic meltdown.

The Great Crash of October 1929 was a mean trick by the capitalists to play on Britain's minority Labour Government, but at least some of them had the good grace to jump out of the New York

---

* Oswald Mosley was related to Elizabeth Bowes-Lyon, the future Queen Mother, though she probably thought he was a bit of a woolly liberal.

skyscrapers as their entire fortunes disappeared. Europe's economy had never really recovered from the Great War, and now a fatal over-dependence on American banks was exposed. 'Dear Europe, Please be advised that your account has now exceeded its overdraft limit. We now require full repayment of all the loans of the last decade. P.S. Your account has been debited a further $20 to pay for this letter.'

Labour had been elected in the belief that they might be better at tackling unemployment, but by August 1930 it had shot up to over two million. With tax revenues falling and benefit bills increasing, the country was plunged into a dire economic crisis and the government couldn't even flog off all the national utilities because they'd neglected to nationalize them last time Labour were in office. Even the King took a fifty-thousand-pound pay cut for the duration of the crisis, which was a blow to those plans to get the loft converted at Buckingham Palace.

There is only one person you can turn to in such an emergency. 'Get me the chairman of the Prudential Assurance Company!' said the Prime Minister, showing that he could be pretty dynamic when the moment arose. 'This calls for a national audit!' The man from the Pru predicted a massive (and it now transpires an exaggerated) budget deficit, and suggested huge cuts in unemployment benefit, which was very helpful of him. The publication of Sir George May's report came just as banks were collapsing across Europe and now, to make things even worse, the pound came under intense pressure. One of Germany's million-mark notes had been held up in the House of Commons as a reminder of where economic collapse could lead.

The cabinet was deeply split on how to tackle the complex economic crisis. As former trade unionists and campaigners many of them were not particularly used to making harsh financial choices: 'I say we kick out the Tories!'

'We *did* kick out the Tories.'

'Well, what about calling a general strike to overthrow the government?'

'We are the government.'

'Oh, well . . . we could go on a march? And demand that the economy gets better?'

Confidence in the Labour government was not strengthened by the fact that most of the cabinet's only experience of high finance was playing Monopoly.* But now the argument was a little more significant than who was going to be the little dog. Nine ministers resigned rather than implement the suggested 10 per cent cut in benefits that would hit the poorest. Clearly the government could not go on. Ramsay MacDonald went to the King to offer his resignation.

Had George V simply accepted, the political history of the 1930s might have been very different. Instead, the King is supposed to have suggested to MacDonald that he head a 'National Government' to lead the nation through this crisis. Everyone had been expecting a Conservative–Liberal coalition to form a government but after ten years as Labour's leader, Ramsay MacDonald suddenly turned his back on the party that made him, and went into partnership with their sworn enemies.

'Nya-ha-ha-ha!' cackled the evil royal family, rubbing their hands in conspiratorial glee. 'That will split the lefties down the middle; they will be kept from power for ever, we rich will get richer and the poor will get poorer and all those jewels and gold will be mine, all mine!'

'They're already yours, George.'

'Yeah, well, whatever.'

At the ensuing 1931 General Election, Labour was wiped out; 556 supporters of the National Government were elected (470 of them Conservatives) and the official Labour Party was reduced to a rump of just 52 seats. Two years earlier it had seemed that the party of the ordinary British worker was on an inexorable upwards curve that would end in its domination of British politics. Now it looked quite possible that Labour would never recover. MacDonald was now expelled from the Labour Party, cast as the greatest class traitor in

---

* In fact Monopoly didn't arrive in Britain until 1936, becoming a huge hit as it trained middle-class children for a lifetime of discussing property prices.

the history of the movement. But did those high-minded socialists dwell on this betrayal? Did the idealists and dreamers let themselves become consumed with bitterness and hatred towards their former leader? Well, yes, they did.

The Great Depression: 'Oh, just snap out of it'

It seems as if it rained more in the 1930s. The 1920s had been an endless string of glorious summer afternoons passed dreamily punting on the River Cam or having picnics listening to jazz on the wind-up gramophone. Suddenly in 1930, the weather changed. Now it's all cold and damp and everyone's shuffling around with their collars turned up, puffing on dog-ends and rubbing their hands together in the freezing smog.

'Eee, does tha remember t'nineteen twenties, lad? All that dancin' t'Charleston, and drinkin' cocktails at t'endless pool-side parties an' that?'

'Aye – grand times they were, mon; who'd 'a thought we'd go from Brideshead College, Oxbridge, t'bein' on t'scrapheap for rest o' oor lives, like?'

'Aye lad, tha degree in Classics and t'Aestheticism be no use once t'shipyard closed.'

The areas hit worst by the slump were in the old industries of shipbuilding and the cotton mills. But all over the country the poor were affected by the severe economic downturn. Not only did the unemployed see their benefit slashed, public-sector workers suffered pay cuts as wages were driven down across the board. At Invergordon in Scotland, the lower ratings of the Atlantic Fleet refused to obey orders in protest at the severe cuts. There were violent clashes between police and demonstrators in various cities across the country, including the capital, where rioting broke out among five thousand protesters outside Battersea Town Hall: 'We demand restoration of full unemployment benefit. And that this building be renamed "Battersea Arts Centre", and become a leading venue for ground-breaking off-West End theatre productions.'

In Jarrow unemployment hit 75 per cent and later in the decade the town was to organize the most famous of the hunger marches to London. The 'Jarrow Crusade' achieved little and was ignored by the government; the local MP, the diminutive Ellen Wilkinson, who had marched alongside her constituents, was allowed to talk to the House of Commons for three minutes before they moved on to other business. But the marchers had a modest heroism that won the admiration of thousands along its three-hundred-mile route. As they headed into the south of England, welcoming committees organized food and lodgings for the Geordies, donating boots and clothing and applauding them on their way. 'You know, they didn't touch that hummus and ciabatta; I thought they were supposed to be hungry?'

The economic crisis showed no signs of letting up. Investors preferred the security of gold to Britain's over-valued currency and when the banks reported they were about to run out of reserves, a bill was rushed through Parliament to take Britain off the gold standard. Like the sudden exit from the European Exchange Rate Mechanism in 1992, 'going off gold' was a humiliating moment for Britain. The pound fell from $4.86 to around $3.40, and Britain's status as the world's leading economic power looked unlikely to return. Trotsky had predicted that the next world war would be between Great Britain and the United States, but England found it far less trouble to politely hand over the running of the world to the Americans and try not to offend them too much after that. In fact, after the shameful deed had been done, everyone rather wondered what all the fuss was about, and many other countries (including the United States) soon abandoned the gold standard as well.

Another economic sacred cow would soon have to be slaughtered as the balance of payments continued to suffer. In September 1932 the government felt compelled to place tariffs on imported goods. This was the end of the great Victorian tenet of free trade, the policy that was believed to have brought Britain so much wealth during the previous century. From now on when you bought clothes in New York, you'd have to cut off all the price labels and wear them as you strolled through the 'Nothing to Declare' channel at customs. Special trading concessions were granted to the Empire; countries like Canada and New Zealand had continued to do most of their trade with the mother country, for sentimental reasons as much as anything. But like the over-valued pound, the Empire was actually becoming more trouble than it was worth.

Doesn't 'Empire' sound a bit, well, *imperialist*?

The collapse of the Labour government had also had great signifi-cance for millions of people on the other side of the globe. The chances of India gaining dominion status diminished with a Conservative-dominated cabinet. In terms of territory, after the Great War, the British Empire was the largest it had ever been, with gains in the Middle East and former German colonies in Africa. But the map is deceptive, with various degrees of self-government now in place in the former colonies, and Britain lacking the military power to defend what it still directly ruled. The granting of independence to the colonies was done using Whitehall's patented 'Racist-ometer'. You pointed this handy device at the map of the British Empire and it told you the local inhabitants' skin colour and religion so that you knew whether they were civilized enough to rule themselves or not. Early on, the white colonies like Canada and Australia were peacefully granted Dominion status within the 'Commonwealth', which evolved into full independence with promises to buy all their lamb or maple syrup. The despised Catholic Irish were only allowed to rule themselves after more than a century of strife, but the dark-skinned Hindus and Muslims of India were kept waiting even longer. Between the First and Second World Wars, India's Congress movement, led by the remarkable Mohandas Gandhi, sustained a peaceful campaign of non-violent resistance for which both sides owe an eternal debt of thanks.

Gandhi was repeatedly imprisoned by the British, perhaps most famously for breaking the British legal monopoly on salt production. Dressed only in a loin-cloth, the frail looking old man led a 240-mile march to the sea, where he and his supporters were openly planning to boil up sea-water to make their own salt, which is about as revolutionary and provocative as it gets. Gandhi made it clear that he was prepared to die for the right to make salt, because there are some things you just can't compromise on. The civil disobedience campaign spread across the country, leading to the imprisonment of fifty thousand Indians. Although some concessions were made in the Government of India Act in 1935, Britain failed to take the hint that they had very much outstayed their welcome.

Few people were as adamantly opposed to Indian independence as Winston Churchill, who resigned from the shadow cabinet in protest at the merest whiff of a concession to India. For the rest of the 1930s he remained an isolated figure, particularly as he began his unpopular demands for Britain to rearm in the face of the growing military threat from Germany. 'For God's sake, Winston. We had one big war with Germany. We're not going through that again.'

Bloody Fascists

However, in 1933 Hitler came to power in Berlin, Japan quit the League of Nations followed by the Germans. MacDonald went to Rome to meet with Mussolini and rather disappointed his embittered former Labour Party colleagues by failing to sign up with the Fascists. Back in Britain Oswald Mosley's party of 'vitality and manhood' held their largest rally to date in Olympia. The *Daily Mail* had run the headline 'Hurrah for the Blackshirts!' although they were a little less enthusiastic after Mosley's storm troopers were filmed beating up anyone who disagreed. At the so-called Battle of Cable Street in 1936, around seven thousand Mosley supporters were prevented from marching through a predominantly Jewish section of the East End by a massive turnout of over a hundred thousand anti-fascist demonstrators. Barricades were built in the street, and children rolled marbles under the hooves of police horses or burst bags of pepper in their faces to stop the police escort for the anti-Semites. The march was abandoned.* 'I was moved to tears to see bearded Jews and Irish Catholic dockers standing up to stop Mosley,' remembered one local eyewitness later. In the 2006 local elections, the British National Party doubled its number of councillors, many of them elected in the East End of London.

Mosley felt unready to compete in the 1935 general election, and urged his supporters to abstain under the slogan 'Fascism Next Time'. As it turned out, next time would be in 1945, after the Fascists had caused the deaths of over a hundred million people, laid waste most of Europe and Mosley had been locked up as a Nazi sympathizer, so next time would have been a bit of a long shot as well.

Ramsay MacDonald limped on as Prime Minister until 1935, but cabinet meetings had all got a bit awkward. Most of the Liberals had resigned from the government over free trade, leaving just this illegitimate son of a farm labourer in charge of a cabinet packed with Conservative toffs.

'So, Lord Snooty, how was your weekend?'

'Spiffing, thank you, Sir Percy; huge house party, bagged a few pheasants, probably got the kitchen maid pregnant. What about you, MacDonald?'

'Och, well, I stayed in at home, because, well, I wasnae invited anywhere, and I dinnae have the smert clothes in any case . . .'

Baldwin had been the effective power behind the throne and took over just before the general election, which was just as well since MacDonald lost his seat to the official Labour candidate. MacDonald had resigned the premiership on health grounds and was advised to take a sea trip to restore his strength.

'How was your husband's health cruise, Mrs MacDonald?'

'Er, well, he died.'

Labour had made respectable gains in the 1935 election, but the Liberals were not even able to contest more than one in four seats. A

---

* The government banned political marches in uniform and so the British Union of Fascists responded by marching holding up their black shirts on coat hangers, which is just being deliberately uncooperative.

massive Tory majority was returned, still under the notional title of the 'National Government'. 'It's such a shame the other side have to get all political,' said the politicians.

The mood of national unity had been augmented by the King's silver jubilee, but the seventy-year-old King was nearing the end of his reign. Always a heavy smoker, the King had suffered from bronchitis and emphysema and people tutting and blowing the smoke away. In January 1936 he became increasingly ill and the doctors advised a trip to Bognor Regis to take the sea air. To this suggestion the King is supposed to have muttered the memorable response 'Bugger Bognor'. However, secret papers opened fifty years later revealed that his final hours were far more scandalous than this. With the King comatose and fading fast there were concerns about the timing of his imminent death. If he held on for too long, the death of the sovereign would end up being reported in the evening papers, along with the gossip and racing results. The King's physician Lord Dawson unilaterally decided that it would be far more appropriate for the death to be announced in *The Times* and other more dignified morning papers, so he hastened the King's death by administering a lethal injection of morphine and cocaine. The only other person to know of Dawson's decision was the attendant nurse who refused to give the injection herself.

Of course it was all done out of respect for the monarchy. It could be argued that another way of respecting the King might have been not to kill him . . . George V's last words were 'God damn you' and technically speaking this episode makes George V the last British monarch to have been murdered, even if cocaine and morphine effect a slightly gentler death than that of, say, Edward II.

Edward VIII now became king. In his later years George V had despaired of his eldest son's inability to settle down and his succession of affairs with married women. He was reputed to have said of his eldest son, 'After I am dead, that boy will ruin himself in twelve months.' On this point the old King was wrong. It would be eleven.

The abdication crisis: they thought *their* royals were scandalous?

The royal family changed a great deal in a half century. In 1936 the new King was forced to abdicate the throne of Great Britain in order to marry a divorced woman. In 1992 the heir to the throne announced he would be separating from his wife following an adulterous affair, while his sister Anne announced her intention to divorce, as did their younger brother Andrew, whose wife was photographed topless having her toe sucked by her financial adviser. Thank goodness the British government made the stand it did fifty-six years earlier or standards might really have slipped.

Edward VIII was a popular Prince of Wales and in contrast to his gruff old dad, had been a debonair 41-year-old bachelor who enjoyed the company of society women. He had done his best not to offend anyone while he was Prince of Wales, commenting on a tour of Australia that the aborigines were *the most revolting form of living creatures I've ever seen!! They are the lowest known form of human beings & are the nearest thing to monkeys.* Like many in the upper classes he was impressed with the dynamic governments of Nazi Germany and Fascist Italy, and he gave Hitler the fascist salute when he met him in Germany in 1937. There has been speculation as to whether Hitler intended to place Edward back on the throne as a puppet ruler if he successfully conquered Britain.

But for most of his short reign the only controversy surrounding the King was his outspoken criticism of the poverty he saw in Wales when he visited a mining community. 'Something should be done' was his detailed policy suggestion, although the offence this caused to Baldwin and his cabinet could not have helped in the stand-off that was to follow. During the first ten months of his reign he continued his royal duties, appearing everywhere with his American companion Mrs Wallis Simpson. The stuffy English establishment decided that she was a hard-bitten opportunist divorcee, which made her totally unacceptable as a potential Queen of England – but she had won the heart of the King. When in October she finally divorced her second husband, Baldwin was firm with the King that His

Majesty couldn't possibly be her third. But Edward wasn't listening; he was dreamily doodling a great big heart with 'Eddie 4 Wallis 4 Ever' in the middle.

'Your majesty, you have to think of your position as Head of the Church of England . . .'

'But I lurrrrvvvve her. She's so luuuurvely . . .'

'Ahem. Your majesty, you're not just the Prince of Wales any more.'

'Hmmm, *Wales*. Sounds a bit like *Wallis*, doesn't it?'

Throughout these months not even a hint of the scandal appeared in the British media; there were no long-lens photos of them snogging, no tabloid journalists recording the lovebirds on the telephone saying, 'You hang up first.'

'No, you hang up . . .'

'No, you hang up . . .'

Nor were there any *Panorama* interviews featuring Wallis Simpson biting her lip as a tear ran down her face, but then the BBC had only begun broadcasting television programmes in August and only three people had tellies anyway. However, the newspapers were desperate to break the story. And in December when the Bishop of Bradford nonchalantly commented that the King was 'in need of God's grace', the editors tried to pretend that the story had burst into the public domain and the scandal suddenly exploded upon an unsuspecting British public.

Despite the fact that the entire Anglican church had only come into existence owing to the divorce of the eighth Henry, the eighth Edward was told he would have to abdicate before he married a divorced commoner. The Church of England still forbade marriage to its ordinary divorced members, how could its Supreme Head marry a divorcee? All the Dominions had been consulted and were strongly against the marriage, except the Irish Free State, whose response was: 'You seem to have got us confused with someone who gives a toss.' And so just eight days after the story had broken, the love-struck King went on the airwaves and confirmed to his stunned subjects that he had abdicated, while various TV producers fought each other over the serialization rights for a lavish costume drama. The throne passed to his younger brother George VI, while 'the Duke of Windsor' as he was now to be known married Wallis Simpson the following year, and during the war was dispatched to the Bahamas as its Governor to stop him saying embarrassing things about how very smart those Nazi uniforms looked. He lived until May 1972, so just long enough to see T. Rex get to number one with 'Metal Guru'.

Give appeasement a chance

Baldwin had been Prime Minister three times; the fact that all we remember of him is his role in the abdication crisis says something about how little impact he made. He saw the new King crowned in 1937 and then stood aside for Neville Chamberlain, his long-standing understudy in the role of 'dull man in a suit'. Baldwin saw his reputation diminish as he was cast as one of the 'guilty men' who had appeased Hitler. After the war he made one of his last public appearances when a statue was unveiled to him. The crowd cheered him as he arrived, but Baldwin, now very frail and deaf, asked, 'Are they booing me?'

But it was his successor who was to become permanently associated with appeasement – or feeding the crocodile in the hope that it will eat him last, as Churchill described the policy. Neville Chamberlain had actually been something of a modest social reformer, making minor improvements to housing and education policies, but foreign affairs kept getting in the way. For example, the government planned to raise the school leaving age to fifteen, and they even set a date for this: 1 September 1939.

'Right, put that in the diary; we must make sure we keep the day completely free.'

'Hang on, the German ambassador's scrawled something else in on that day. "Invade Boland." Who's Boland?'

'That must be "invite Boland" – he's obviously going to invite Mr Boland to our school-leaving-age thingy . . .'

Hitler had begun rearming immediately on coming to power in 1933. Under the settlement of 1919 Germany was forbidden to have an air force, but soon the fighter aircraft were rolling off the end of the production line and Britain didn't object because they were too embarrassed to say the word 'Fokker'. The German Führer was openly working towards air force parity with Britain, a standing army five times the size of that permitted by the treaty and a navy as large as Britain's. The only explanation is that Adolf Hitler must have neglected to read the Treaty of Versailles properly, otherwise he surely would have been mortified at this diplomatic faux pas: 'Oh no! I've just discovered that we shouldn't be doing any of this. Oh God, I am so embarrassed, they must think me so rude . . .'

Britain's objections did not look particularly resolute: 'Right, I'm warning you, you better not take one more step, or else!' In 1936 Hitler sent his troops into the demilitarized zone of the Rhineland. 'Right that's it! That's the last time we're letting you off . . .' Two years later Germany marched into Austria. 'I mean it; you make one more move and there'll be trouble . . .'

The Anschluss with Austria met very little resistance, unless you count Baron von Trapp defiantly singing 'Edelweiss', while Julie Andrews goes all watery-eyed watching from the wings. Germany was now a major European military power but there were many in the British establishment with their own anti-Semitic tendencies who rather admired the Nazis and saw them as a necessary bulwark against Communist Russia. It seems incredible that the politicians of the day were not completely clear that Hitler and the Nazis were the bad guys; I mean, if ever you watch a film and a character appears wearing a Nazi armband, that's always a sure sign he'll turn out to be one of the baddies later on.

The European situation was complicated by Fascist Italy. Clever British diplomats thought that if they were nice to Mussolini then he would avoid forming an alliance with Germany. So Britain cravenly recognized Italy's rights as conquerors of Abyssinia (modern-day Ethiopia) – and then Italy joined an alliance with Germany. The liberal democracies stood back and watched while Hitler and Mussolini helped the Spanish Fascists overthrow the legitimate socialist government of Spain. The Spanish Civil War provoked strong emotions in Britain, with thousands of courageous individuals volunteering to fight on the Republican side including the writers Laurie Lee, Stephen Spender and George Orwell. Although if they were anything like most of the writers I know, it's no wonder the Republicans lost: 'Right, pass me the battle plan, we must attack at once!'

'Er, yeah, I'm just rewriting it actually, I was never completely happy with it . . .'

But standing up to the Fascists wasn't a left-right issue. A strong pacifist element in the Labour Party was convinced that rearmament had been a cause of the Great War, while on the right, Winston Churchill, now in the Conservative Party, became increasingly credible as his dire warnings about the 'Naaarrrsies' looked to be coming true. The policy of appeasement reached a shameful climax in 1938 over German claims regarding large chunks of Czechoslovakia. Neville Chamberlain flew out to Munich to meet with 'Herr Hitler', Mussolini and the French Prime Minister: 'You know what? I've just realized that we never invited anyone from the Czech government.'

'Oh yes, how careless of us! Well, I'm sure they'll be more than happy to go along with whatever we decide.'

Chamberlain caved into German demands to take German-speaking Czech regions into his Third Reich when Hitler gave his word that he had no further territorial demands in Europe.

'OK. Erm, why have you got your fingers crossed?'

'Oh, zat? Ha, oh, it's just to remind me to do something later . . .'

Britain's rulers were so desperate to avoid war, they actually allowed themselves to be persuaded of the merits of the aggressor's case. 'Yes I know you're only five feet tall and he's an amateur bare-knuckle boxer. But to be fair, you *did* spill his pint and look at his bird. Now go outside and let him beat you up.'

But Chamberlain returned home a hero, waving his extended warranty agreement, declaring, 'I have in my hand a piece of paper signed by Herr Hitler himself that is a receipt for the gift of Central and Eastern Europe. Hang on, that doesn't sound right.' The Prime Minister promised his people 'Peace for our time' although they weren't told that 'our time' meant approximately eleven months. Huge crowds cheered the great Prime Minister who would surely be an English hero for evermore.

And who can blame them? It's easy for us to criticize the politicians for being too desperate to avoid war, but given the carnage their generation had witnessed in the trenches, the enormous sense of relief was understandable. We cannot criticize the leaders of 1914 for not preventing war and then criticize the leaders of 1938 for not rushing into it. Actually, on second thoughts, that's a far more comfortable position. Yeah, if it was us, we would have started the Second World War much, much earlier, but we would have definitely found a way to avoid the First World War altogether.

Six months later Hitler invaded the western half of Czechoslovakia claiming that he was 'just making it neat'. Chamberlain's piece of paper had meant nothing; Hitler was a big fat liar (although it turned out that wasn't the worst thing about him). Conscription was introduced in Britain without a murmur and re-armament was now at full pace. A quick look at the map made it clear that Poland was probably next, and finally Britain took a stand, guaranteeing to come to Poland's aid.

'So how will you do that then? Will you get the train through Germany or what?'

'Look, we're just saying we'll come to your aid. We haven't worked out all the details yet.'

Britain was hoping that Germany could never invade Poland without provoking the wrath of the Soviet Union, but when the Nazi–Soviet Non-Aggression Pact was signed in August 1939, Britain and France were stunned. Several Communist Party members imploded trying to justify the surprise alliance. War was clearly days away. Poland was invaded on 1 September and the British government politely suggested a withdrawal so they might perhaps all have another conference. There was no response. Chamberlain did not lead the country into war, he was reluctantly dragged into it by Parliament and popular opinion.

On the evening of 3 September the Prime Minister addressed the British people from the cabinet room in 10 Downing Street. The radio broadcast was a very flat, serious affair which really could have used a bit of livening up by the producers of Kenny Everett or Radio 1's Steve Wright in the Afternoon.

> This morning the British Ambassador in Berlin [SHORT BURST OF 'DEUTSCHLAND ÜBER ALLES' PLAYED ON A KAZOO] handed the German government a final note [COMEDY RUSTLE OF PAPER, GERMAN MAN SAYS 'OOOH, DANKE SCHON'] stating that unless we heard from them by eleven o'clock [CUCKOO CLOCK] that they were prepared at once to withdraw their troops from Poland [MARCHING FEET], a state of war would exist between us [CROWD GASPS]. I have to tell you now that no such undertaking has been received [BIG RASPERRY] and that consequently this country is at war with Germany [DISAPPOINTED CROWD: 'AAAAHHH!'].

In fact once Chamberlain had conveyed this grim state of affairs, he immediately turned the subject round to himself and began an extended self-justification of his disastrous policies; reminding the nation of all the hard work he had put in to make sure that a major European conflict was avoided. Except that it hadn't been. Britain was at war but this time nobody was cheering in the streets. The veterans of the First World War were not going to celebrate sending their sons off to the battlefields of France. Now the army was mobilized, gas masks were being issued, the air force and navy were on high alert. Oh, and rear lights happened to become compulsory for night-time cyclists on the same day. They wouldn't want anyone getting hurt.

The Second World War (see History Channel for further details)

When it comes to writing about the Second World War the historian suddenly encounters the problem of a lack of secondary sources. You go into the history section of the airport bookshop, but have they got a single book on the Second World War? I mean, you'd think there might perhaps be one slim volume on *The Fighter Aircraft of the*

Battle of Britain or *Warriors of the Third Reich;* just one copy of *Sex Spies of the Nazis* or *The eBay Guide to Nazi Insignia*. 'No, we've got lots of stuff on the First Reich,' shrugs the assistant, 'and a few books on the Second, but no, I've never heard of this "Third Reich" you're interested in.'*

Such has been the impact of the war upon our culture and our national consciousness that it has become hard to separate out the recycled myths from some of the occasionally grubby realities. The British people really did rise to the challenge of the Second World War, showing great unity and courage in a just and necessary war. But British airmen didn't really hide out in a French café run by the Resistance and waitresses in stockings and suspenders saying ''Allo 'Allo' in comedy French accents.

The narrative of the war with its twists and turns is now so well worn it is hard to remember that for those living through it, 1939 till 'whenever-it-might-end' was a time of endless uncertainty and surprises. 'Would the Germans drop gas on British cities?' 'Would Spain join the Axis Powers?' 'Would Hitler annex the German part of Switzerland?' None of these things came to pass but all seemed more likely than the invasion of Russia, Pearl Harbor or Hiroshima.

And yet to begin with nothing happened. The RAF dropped some politely worded leaflets over Germany. The Air Minister blocked a plan to deprive the Nazis of timber by setting fire to German forestry with the outraged response: 'Are you aware it is private property?!' Barrage balloons floated eerily over British cities but more people were killed by road accidents caused by the blackout than by enemy action and a surreal sense of anti-climax overtook the country in what the American papers dubbed 'the phoney war'.

The city streets were even more quiet for the sudden departure of so many children. One and a half million schoolchildren and carers had been evacuated from the expected targets of German bombers and billeted in the countryside. It is hard to imagine that many of the

---

* Just in case you've ever wondered, the First Reich was the Holy Roman Empire from around 800 to 1806; the Second Reich was the Kaiser's Empire declared after the Franco-Prussian war in 1871. They decided not to have another Reich after the Third one, the whole 'Reich' brand was a bit tainted by then.

old people alive today were once bewildered children clutching some sandwiches and a gas mask, waving goodbye to their parents on a chaotic railway platform. Their tickets were blank; no destination was given. After a long and tiring journey, they were lined up in church halls, resolutely clinging to a sibling's hand as they waited to see which stranger would pick them out and adopt them for the duration of the war. Some children were lucky enough to gain a caring 'Auntie and Uncle' who treated them with love and kindness, encouraging frequent letters home and visits from their mothers. Others, of course, suffered years of cruelty or child abuse. And today, while overbearing parents are in and out of the school office fretting about whether little Jemima should sit next to her best friend in Maths, the grandparents must look on and think, We were just bundled on to a train with a label tied to us, not even knowing what *county* we were going to live in for the next few years.

Chamberlain proved to be as inept in the running of the war as he had been at avoiding it. Labour refused to serve in any coalition with him as Prime Minister, so the only significant changes to his government were the return of two future Prime Ministers: Winston Churchill and Anthony Eden (who had resigned in 1938 over appeasement). Churchill had been hoping for the war office but had to be content with the Admiralty. In fact the Royal Navy was the only one of the services to see significant action during the first six months of the war and Churchill was lucky that the unpopular Chamberlain got the blame for a series of disasters at sea rather than the minister directly responsible. 'Mayday! Mayday! HMS *Belfast* has struck German mine! Request urgent assistance that we be towed up the Thames to be kept as visitor attraction for tourists and school trips!'

In April 1940 Chamberlain made a fantastically complacent speech asking what had happened to the promised German attack. Now they 'had very little margin of strength still to call upon', he confidently declared, Hitler had 'missed the bus'. Chamberlain had just approved Churchill's plan for the navy to move in on Norwegian ports to stop iron ore being exported to Germany. But Hitler was not going to miss this particular bus. On 9 April, the Germans got up early and caught the Oslo Hoppa, seizing the Norwegian capital and all the country's airfields and key installations within a few hours. British troops finally landed but it was too late. The Nazis installed a puppet government under the Norwegian fascist Vidkun Quisling, who unsurprisingly turned out to be a bit of a quisling. Every year the Norwegian government sends Britain a giant Christmas tree as a thank you for its help during the war. It's not clear whether this annual gesture is meant sarcastically or not. Britain and France had suffered their first military defeat of the war and powerlessly watched the Nazis overrun Denmark as well. What were the Allies to do now? They had to take some sort of initiative: 'All right, watch this then . . .' and Britain invaded Iceland. Oh no . . . Hitler must have thought. Now the Third Reich has nowhere to look at geysers and bathe in naturally heated pools.

The Norwegian humiliation provoked fury in the House of Commons. Chamberlain was taken aback by the level of anger on his own side; quoting Oliver Cromwell, one senior Tory declared, 'You have sat too long here for any good you have been doing. Depart, I say, and let us have done with you. In the name of God, go!' Labour decided to force a division and a hundred Conservatives voted against the government or abstained. Chamberlain was holed below the waterline, even though he limped on for a couple of days failing to patch together a new coalition.

Chamberlain wanted his fellow appeaser the one-armed Lord Halifax to be the new Prime Minister. So did the King. But this would only work if the other obvious candidate, Churchill, was prepared to serve under him. Churchill, Halifax, Chamberlain and the Tory chief whip then came together for a meeting that would determine the whole nature of the war. When Chamberlain asked Churchill if he would serve under Halifax, Churchill sensed that this was an attempted stitch-up. With sailors drowning at sea Winston could hardly say 'No' and refuse to do his bit. But if he said 'Yes', then completely the wrong sort of man would be handed the job of leading the country at a time of deep national crisis. So he simply said nothing and stared out of the window. Was he thinking about it? they wondered. Had he not heard the question? The loaded silence endured for two whole minutes. Finally Halifax could bear the embarrassment no longer and admitted that it might be difficult for a peer to become Prime Minister at such a time. And so the King was instructed to send for Winston Churchill. That day, the Nazis rolled into Holland, Belgium and Luxembourg. France was completely exposed. It was just as well the new Prime Minister always enjoyed a challenge.

Ask Churchill!

Churchill's arrival in the House of Commons was cheered only by the Labour benches. He talked of 'blood, toil, tears and sweat' and Members wondered if he was about to launch into an advert for washing powder. With the Germans already crossing the French border, the new Prime Minister's unambiguous policy was 'to wage war by land, sea and air'. His unwavering aim: 'victory at all costs'. This was more than just rhetoric; it was a message to the glum-looking appeasement faction who had still hoped that a separate negotiated peace could be made with Hitler, irrespective of the fate of France.

Churchill created a coalition government bringing in a number of senior Labour and Liberal figures. For the key role of Minister for Defence he appointed Winston Churchill. He would be in direct control of military affairs as no other Prime Minister had been before him. A new vigour was felt throughout Whitehall, people dashed down corridors, worked longer hours and would have had their lunch at their desks if Pret A Manger had had a branch in Westminster.

Despite the fact that the Germans had overcome Poland in a couple of weeks, an opinion poll showed that more than three-quarters of the British people believed Britain would win the war. Perhaps it seemed unpatriotic to predict defeat to a pollster, but this sense of confidence was about to be shattered. By the time the Dutch had looked up 'Blitz' and 'Krieg' in their Flemish/German diction-aries, the Germans had occupied most of Holland and were closing the net around Belgium.

The French had placed an enormous amount of confidence in the impenetrability of their 'Maginot Line'. This was an impressive string of gun emplacements, concrete forts and anti-tank defences that apparently made France 'uninvadable'. The only tiny criticism that might be raised against it, and maybe this is just being picky, is that it stopped two hundred miles short of the coast. But surely no German army would be so cunning as to go round it; for when did Germany ever invade France via Belgium? Apart from last time? They considered ways of making it clear that the border with Belgium was also out of bounds, putting up some little 'Keep off the Grass' signs or a little six-inch-high white picket fence like the one around the flowerbeds, but even this, it seemed, might not have been enough to halt the Nazi tank commanders.

Run rabbit run*

The bulk of the British army had advanced into Belgium, where they were dependent on the French holding the line to the south. But on 13 May, the heaviest air bombardment the world had yet seen was concentrated on a narrow strip of the front near Sedan. Stunned and demoralized, the French forces were overcome by the German attack and the retreat and disorder spread along the line. By 16 May, the German officers were advancing further than their orders permitted. The French Prime Minister telephoned Winston Churchill and told him that France was beaten. Churchill immediately flew to Paris to try and stiffen his resolve but witnessed the French government burning its archives and preparing to evacuate the capital.

'Where is the strategic reserve?' he asked them.

'There is none,' they replied.

Churchill later described this as the most shocking moment of his life. When he finally heard that France had surrendered he wept.

* The song 'Run Rabbit Run' was released in October 1939 and the lyrics were interpreted as a sarcastic comment on the effectiveness of the Luftwaffe. At that point the only death caused by German air raids was a rabbit on the Shetland Islands.

The German tanks just kept going and kept going, and to their own astonishment on 20 May they reached the point where the River Somme flows into the English Channel. Now the British army and the best of the French troops were cut off. Without supply lines or support they fell back to the port of Dunkirk. Perhaps this might be the place to show a bit of the old Dunkirk spirit.

There seemed to be nothing to stop the Germans capturing the entire British army. But then to his generals' astonishment Hitler ordered his army to halt. There has been much debate about Hitler's reasons for this strange order. Did he want the British to be allowed to escape? Did he suddenly feel a bit guilty about having been a tad over-aggressive? Some have speculated that Hitler hoped to keep the British army intact for the day that he dreamt of when the British Empire and Germany would unite against his real long-term foe, the Soviet Union. These theorists usually follow this assertion with another pint and a packet of pork scratchings, before moving on to insist that the moon landings were actually filmed in the Nevada Desert. The more credible explanation for the order to halt is that Hitler was concerned by the degree to which his commanders were acting beyond their orders in the field, and that he was petulantly trying to show that he was in charge of operations. Either way, it was a crucial delay that bought the British desperately needed time.

Over 330,000 Allied troops were trapped in this tiny corner of north-eastern France, trying to take what cover they could from the German fighters strafing the beaches and the town. The Royal Navy was under intense bombardment in the approach to the port and the British plan to evacuate its troops was based on the grim realization that there would only be time to rescue about 45,000 of them. It just had to be accepted that the vast bulk of the army would become prisoners of war. For the port of Dunkirk only had room for so many ships to evacuate the troops and the Royal Navy couldn't get any-where near the beaches where the army was waiting on the dunes.

Then the soldiers on the beach beheld the 'miracle of Dunkirk'. Through the fog emerged hundreds of ordinary little boats: a volunteer fleet of English boating enthusiasts in their pleasure craft; fishing boats; river ferries; RNLI lifeboats; private yachts and cabin cruisers. The boats' owners had heard the call on the wireless for small craft to cross the Channel to assist in the ferrying of soldiers from the beaches to the larger ships. The response was way beyond anything the government had expected: an amateur armada of hundreds of 'little ships' sailing directly into the war zone of the English Channel, manned by the boats' civilian owners who insisted on making the crossing themselves, guided by the beacon of the burning town. The surreal pictures of Operation Dynamo only begin to show the scale of the task facing them. Huge snaking lines of soldiers, wading out into the waves, hoping there would be room for them on the next boat, never knowing if that would be the last. Overhead the Royal Air Force did their best to fight off the scream-ing Stukas that were firing on the defenceless boats (although around seventy were sunk). The RAF lost 177 planes, the Royal Navy lost six destroyers, the French lost three, but with the French and British soldiers bravely fighting on the outskirts of the town and holding off the Germans, the entire British army was successfully evacuated.

Many of these little boats are still around today; tied up in quiet Thameside villages or pootling about in the estuaries of the south coast. There's one moored in Ramsgate harbour that was piloted by a father and his teenage son, who went back time and time again under heavy enemy fire. Just reading the modest little plaque makes you want to cry.

The defeated soldiers arriving at the English ports were treated like heroes and given whatever food people could cobble together from their rations. Churchill had insisted that the French and British be evacuated on equal terms, and over 120,000 French and Belgian troops arrived in England along with around 218,000 men of the British Expeditionary Force. The propaganda value of the civilian response was immense. So proud were the British of the successful evacuation and the instant myth of the plucky armada that Churchill actually had to remind people that evacuations didn't win wars. People forgot that most of the returning soldiers had crossed the Channel on large ships as the legend of the little boats became dis-torted and the 'spirit of Dunkirk' devalued by over-use. But in June

1940 the army was unexpectedly saved. As the last ships pulled out of the harbour, the Germans moved in. Now the Channel ports had all fallen and the Germans were laying plans for the invasion of Britain and Italy declared war on Great Britain. Churchill had only been in the job a month. 'Is it always like this?'

On 14 June the Germans entered Paris and Ingrid Bergman stood up Humphrey Bogart at the railway station. Before long Hitler was being filmed in the French capital for the German newsreels.

'OK, Mr Hitler, *Ein Führer in Paris* take one; and try not to look too smug.'

'Not too smug, OK, *ja*.'

'Hmm, that's nice where you're standing but I think it might be even better if you had the Eiffel Tower *behind you*, because I think the Eiffel Tower really says "Paris", don't you?'

'Oh, *ja*, OK, so standing here, looking at what I've conquered, exceeding the achievements of Frederick the Great, Bismarck and Hindenburg?'

'That's perfect, but you're looking a teensy bit smug again . . .'

The French were made to surrender in the very railway carriage in which Germany had signed the Armistice in 1918. The Germans had even gone to the trouble of putting little name cards on the table to show the French where they were to sit. 'Oh good, I'm next to General Huntzinger, I like him . . .'

France was out of the war, and would play no further significant part, despite what the French school history books might later say about the entire war being won single-handedly by the French Resistance: 'Battle of Stalingrad? Germans defeated by the French Resistance.' 'Iwo Jima? Japanese island conquered by the French Resistance.' It later became politically necessary to give France a role in the post-war settlement, but in 1945 when the defeated German generals were made to surrender to representatives of the victorious Allies, they were astonished to see the French included.

Britain 0, Germany 4

In June 1940, Britain was on its own. The army was safely back in Britain, if depleted and disorganized. The situation was made worse by a worrying realization by one of the generals: 'Buffy, you haven't seen all our tanks and armaments and troop carriers and everything, have you?'

'Oooh no, I haven't, you don't think you might have left them in France?'

'Well, that's what I'm beginning to wonder. Piers, old chap, you didn't pick up all the British army's equipment when we were leaving Dunkirk, did you?'

'I don't think so, it's hard to remember it was all such a rush . . . You didn't maybe just leave them on the boat?'

The entire British army had to be equipped again from scratch. An appeal went out for scrap metal to be handed in at public depots. Clearly the RAF had a plan to bombard German cities with garden railings, bed frames and tin potties. Most of the metal collected was actually useless for turning into munitions, but it helped morale to be doing *something*.

On the same principle, back gardens were converted to vegetable plots and civilians volunteered for service as Air Raid Wardens or members of the Local Defence Volunteers. The Home Guard (as it became known) had been formed in order to provide an élite force of well-intentioned pensioners to hold up the invading Nazi storm troopers by telling them meandering anecdotes. The government expected a maximum of 150,000 men to volunteer but ten times that number had come forward by the end of June, such was the sense of duty and eagerness to play a part. Among them was a fifteen-year-old boy called Jimmy Perry, who would later co-write the sitcom that would define the popular image of this 'Dad's Army'. To begin with they drilled with garden tools and broomsticks, and if Hitler had invaded they could at least have ensured that the beach looked tidy beforehand. But while the partisans in Yugoslavia later tied down twenty-five German divisions from their hiding places in the mountains, English seaside resorts don't really have the right terrain for prolonged guerrilla warfare. They could have hidden behind the ice-cream kiosk for a while, but eventually one fears the Third Reich might have overpowered them.

No part of society could remain unaffected by the war. Women too were expected to play their part, whether in the auxiliary services such as the 'WAAF' created in June 1939 or in the factories or the fields as 'Land Girls'. The popular image of the Land Girls is all sun-kissed English roses turning hay in the sunshine and looking radiant in gingham headscarves. In fact work in the fields was gruelling and unglamorous and morale was often low. But all of this revealed something quite different to the situation that had come to pass in France. Britain had an absolute determination to continue fighting the war at all costs, even from Canada or India or Africa should the British Isles be overrun. The French army had fought with determination and courage, and their soldiers continued to battle on after the fall of Paris. But the French leadership had been resigned to defeat from the moment the Germans broke through at Sedan. English suggestions of making a stand in Paris or moving the government to French North Africa were met with a spineless shrug. So what was the difference between the resolute mood in Britain and the defeatism that overtook France? The answer can be summed up in two words: Winston Churchill.

Churchill's entire life had been building towards this moment. He was a natural fighter, who in peacetime had often crassly opted for conflict when conciliation would have been smarter. But now it was a war between democracy and fascism, and his pugnacious certainty was an inspiration. In the 1930s he had sounded histrionic; now he was simply historic. On 4 June he rose in the House of Commons and set out at great length the series of disasters that had befallen the British army. The message was bleak; the mood was sombre. But his detailed explanation of Britain's hopeless position was not softening them up for the announcement of peace overtures or some compromise with the conquerors of Europe. The point was that no matter what happened the fight would continue: 'We shall defend our island, whatever the cost may be. We shall fight on the beaches, we shall fight on the landing grounds, we shall fight in the fields and

in the streets, we shall fight in the hills; we shall never surrender.'
Britain had no equipment, a shattered army – and yet somehow its
MPs were standing in the House of Commons cheering.

A Britain led by Chamberlain or Lord Halifax would probably
now be making a humiliating peace with Hitler. The long
embarrassing silence that secured Churchill the premiership a
month earlier was surely the most important two minutes in British
history.

The Battle of Britain: flying *not* safer than crossing the road

In 1909 Louis Blériot won a competition organized by the *Daily Mail*
and became the first man to pilot a plane over the English Channel.
There was anxiety at the time that Britain's historic moat could now
be so easily breached. Only thirty-one years later hundreds of
German planes were in the sky above Britain, bombing airfields,
cities and factories in preparation for the invasion of Britain.

Being the modest sort of chap he was, Hitler had been surprised
by the speed of his own success in France and so no detailed plans
existed for the invasion of Britain. On 12 July he instructed his
commanders to buy a copy of the Dover *A-Z* and start scribbling
warplanes and tanks on it as they made exploding noises. The only
prerequisite to 'Operation Sealion', as the invasion of England would
be called, was that the Luftwaffe must have control of the air.

The Battle of Britain was not a battle in the conventional sense; it
was given this epic title by Winston Churchill to provide some overall context to the hundreds of separate engagements that were taking
place in the skies during the summer of 1940. From well-kept
country gardens in Sussex and Kent, civilians tried to make sense of
the first-ever military conflict to take place entirely in the air. The
vapour trails silently snaked this way and that; it was barely possible
to see which plane was which. But the liberty of those squinting up
at the sunny skies was entirely dependent on the few pilots who were
charged with the task of beating the German Luftwaffe.

The Germans' first targets had been the airfields, and Britain learnt that parking all your aircraft in a nice straight line might look very neat, but it made it a lot easier for a single enemy plane to destroy the whole lot in one go. The targets were widened to factories, radar stations and eventually the civilian population. On 13 August 1940 a total of 1,485 German aircraft flew across the Channel: the Luftwaffe called it 'the Day of the Eagle'. The German military machine was littered with stupid names like this: 'Wolf's Lair', 'Lightning War', 'SS Death's-Head Unit'; the Nazi Party had the intellectual sophistication of a fifteen-year-old Heavy Metal fan.

Invasion barges were lined up along the French Channel ports, while German troops practised amphibious landings. Hitler had timetabled the invasion for September. At 8.07 p.m. on the evening of 7 September the British secret codeword 'Cromwell' was sent to military units across the country. This was the message that the German invasion had begun. Church bells rang out as a signal that it was under way; army units prepared; Home Guard volunteers gathered for action. No landing came. It was a false alarm. Instead hundreds of German aircraft flew overhead in the direction of London. They weren't carrying paratroopers, but bombs.

The modest British air force was deployed with the greatest possible efficiency thanks to two earlier breakthroughs. One had been the invention of radar, patented in England in 1935. In 1939 satellite dishes were erected across the country to defend civilization; fifty years later they were stuck on the sides of houses to mark its demise. The other unknown advance had been the cracking of the Germans' apparently 'unbreakable' Enigma code. Enigma was endlessly studied by a group of mathematicians, crossword enthusiasts, chess champions and early computing pioneers. 'You see; you called them nerds at school, but you're grateful to them now . . .' Much of the work on Enigma had been done by a young Polish mathematician before the war, and once Britain's brilliant cryptologists had entered Hitler's mother's maiden name and his year of birth for the PIN number, they were in.

Britain was also fortunate that not one single German spy was effective on the British mainland during the entire war. Four secret agents were landed by boat to report on British coastal preparations, but they were immediately identified as foreigners when they failed to hover anxiously at the shop counter making sure they weren't pushing in. Others were caught and immediately redeployed as double agents, one of them later receiving the Iron Cross from the Führer for his excellent intelligence-gathering that England was planning to invade Patagonia and abolish Wednesdays.

It was hard for either side to know for certain how many enemy aircraft their men had shot down. But the British and Allied pilots were consistently inflicting greater losses than they sustained themselves, despite the strange decision to paint a big red, white and blue target on the side of every British plane. The air force had been unfairly criticized during the Dunkirk evacuation but now the pilots became national heroes. 'Never' – said Churchill famously – 'in the field of human conflict was so much owed by so many to so few.' Aircraft production had reached such a pitch that Britain actually ended the Battle of Britain with more planes than it had when the battle began. On 17 September Hitler postponed the invasion of Britain 'until further notice'.

The Blitz: 'Britain can take it!' (You mean there's a choice?)

It did not particularly feel as if control of the skies belonged to Britain with German bombers now dropping their payload over the East End of London. On 7 September the Luftwaffe began fifty-eight nights of consecutive bombing of London. Judging from the popular culture that has grown up around the Blitz, the initial effect of the bombs was to make everyone talk in an exaggerated cockney accent: 'Gor blimey luv-a-duck, them Jerry bombs is raining like cats and dogs ternight. 'Allo, Queen Mum, you come ter entertain us down 'ere? Budge up, Reg, Her Maj's gonna give us a sing-song. Take it away Liz . . .'

'My old man's a Marquis, he wears a Marquis' hat . . .'*

The King and Queen had declined suggestions that they might want to join the significant numbers of toffs who had decamped to Canada for the duration of the war, and now they took the trouble to go down to some of the homes in the East End to see how the front and back rooms had been creatively knocked into one. Churchill too visited the scenes of devastation and shouted, 'We can take it!' to the irritation of one or two people who were already in a bad mood at losing their home and all their possessions. Giving them the V sign was the final insult.

London was woefully under-prepared for this type of in-discriminate bombing, and more anti-aircraft guns were quickly organized to fire pointlessly into the sky to cheer people up a bit. Barely any German bombers were brought down by the so-called ack-ack guns, but at least their existence panicked some German pilots into dropping their bombs before they reached their targets, which was bad luck for a man in a remote cottage in Sheerness.

At the depressing and predictable wail of the air-raid siren, families gathered under the stairs or dashed to the Anderson shelters at the bottom of the garden. These were cramped and rather damp government-issue shelters that were dug into the garden and covered with earth. Many of them still survive, although now they are more commonly described as 'Bijou one-room London apartment: £250,000'.

The shortage of shelters (or gardens to put them in), led to many Londoners spontaneously heading for the Underground stations at the sound of the sirens. The government initially tried to halt this unexpected flood, as no one could work out how much to deduct from their Oyster Cards, but eventually they came to see that the public had solved the shelter shortage for themselves. Tens of thousands of bunk beds were made available and Henry Moore's atmospheric pictures captured the gloomy dehumanizing effects of

---

* This is slightly incorrect on several points: (a) her father was an earl not a marquis, but it just doesn't scan as well; (b) she wouldn't have been known as the Queen Mother until after the death of her husband in 1952; and (c) she did not in fact go into the Underground to lead a singalong cockney knees-up.

so many faceless strangers driven below ground. The scenes of desperate and over-tired Londoners crammed together on tube platforms are recreated today every evening and morning rush hour.

A children's song about the Great Fire of London had always said it would come again another day, and in 1940 this folk prediction came true. On the night of 29 December a greater area was destroyed by fires and explosions than in 1666 as 1,500 separate blazes raged around the capital. St Paul's Cathedral, which itself had been built upon the ashes of the first Great Fire, was iconically photographed rising above the smoke as fire crews battled to save it. A dozen Wren churches were not so lucky.* Other London landmarks hit at other points during the Blitz included Buckingham Palace, Westminster Abbey, the Old Bailey and the Houses of Parliament. Both the historic Westminster Hall and the nineteenth-century House of Commons were ablaze on the same night and there were only enough fire-fighters to save one of them. As a gesture to anarchists every-where, the House of Commons was left to burn to the ground, although not with the politicians still in it.

The Blitz wasn't all heroic stiff upper lips and cheerful cockneys rescuing kittens from the rubble. Some charming souls took the opportunity of an air raid to go and burgle their neighbours; others fought over somewhere to shelter. But nothing brings a society together like a clear and indisputable evil and generally petty local differences faded in relation to the rather justifiable resentment that people felt towards the Germans. Enormous and heroic efforts were made by those who lived through the Blitz, risking their lives as they rescued trapped survivors, fighting the fires or tending the injured or simply hysterical. On the worst night in London, three thousand people lost their lives – more people than died in 9/11 – as London became the target of state terrorism on a nightly basis. For the first three years of the war, more civilians were killed than servicemen.

But the attempt to break British morale, if that's what it was, did

* One of the destroyed churches, St Mary Aldermanbury, was rebuilt brick by brick in the United States. Every seventeenth-century detail is perfectly recreated, right down to the neon flashing sign saying 'God hates Communism and Gays'.

not work, even after the bombing spread to other ports and towns. Coventry was so comprehensively bombed that the Germans coined the word *Coventriert* for the destruction of a city. Ports like Plymouth, Portsmouth, Swansea and Liverpool were devastated. The population of Plymouth decamped to Dartmoor to sleep in the open air every night as their city was repeatedly bombed. It would be hard to claim that the pre-war beauty of Plymouth was recaptured by 1950s architects. A whole series of targeted raids on historic towns saw the destruction of Exeter, York, Norwich, Bath and Canterbury. As well as dropping bombs all over Britain, one lone Messerschmitt dropped an unexpected extra over the countryside of Scotland. Rudolf Hess, the Deputy Führer of the Third Reich, suddenly turned up and was arrested by a Scottish farmer with a pitchfork. Hess had apparently come because his horoscope had predicted he would personally bring about peace between Germany and Britain, which seems a tall order for every single person who was Taurus. Hess was taken to England, where interrogators quickly decided he was a mental case, which was about the only thing Britain and Germany agreed on throughout the whole war. At the post-war Nuremberg war trials he was sentenced to life imprisonment and ordered to become the subject of 312 nutty conspiracy theories. This demented member of the British Royal Family/Russian double-agent/alien from the Planet Zog lived a miserable life in solitary confinement until he finally committed suicide in 1987.

As a shell-shocked Britain struggled through 1941, it was still alone in the war, without adequate equipment or defences, short of food and with no prospect of striking any meaningful blow against the enemy. German conquests stretched from the Arctic Circle to the Mediterranean; there was nothing that Britain could do but clear up the rubble and try to keep building tanks, guns and planes in the hope that perhaps Adolf Hitler might make some sort of silly mistake. By the end of the year, he had invaded Russia and declared war on the United States, which as mistakes go were both quite big ones.

The Battle of the Atlantic: Germans put das Boot in

The island status that kept Britain safe from invasion also made it dependent on shipping for its food and materials. Merchant seamen risked their lives keeping Britain supplied with their vital cargoes of tobacco. During the time of Napoleon or the Kaiser Britain had come close to starvation, but now the enemy's sea power was stronger and far more deadly.* The brains behind the *Unterseeboot* campaign was Admiral Dönitz, who would go on to become Hitler's successor as leader of the Third Reich, although the job description was not quite as attractive by May 1945. Dönitz employed U-boats in packs around a convoy, which was far more effective than dispersing lone submarines to wait outside ports. The Royal Navy escorts seemed powerless to prevent the terrible toll on merchant ships heading for Britain. Depth charges were dropped against the German submarines, but this only seemed to make the crew jolt slightly for a moment and grip on to a rail, while any sudden leaks could be stopped by turning a great big metal wheel as they did their best to shake off the giant squid that was also attacking the sub from the other side. Or maybe I'm just getting my films mixed up. There were occasional successes against the U-boats, most notably in May 1941 when a British crew captured a German submarine complete with Enigma machine and documents. This heroic story was re-created in the 2000 film *U-571*, with the only slight historical alteration that the vital breakthrough was achieved by the American navy rather than the British.

However, the right to distort history for evermore was one of the rights that Britain signed away to the Americans in return for what-

---

* A great opportunity to acquire the French navy had been lost in July 1940 when negotiations between British and French commanders were badly handled. Britain could not risk this fleet being added to the German navy and issued an ultimatum to the French ships to sail to Britain or the Caribbean. When all these orders were not obeyed, the Royal Navy attacked the French ships in Algeria with the loss of 1,300 French lives. It had been the ruthlessness of this act that had convinced Washington that Britain had the stomach to continue the war alone for as long as it took.

ever help neutral America was prepared to give us. President Roosevelt had been re-elected in November 1940 on a promise to keep the United States out of the war. 'We are definitely neutral . . .' he kept having to explain to his isolationist Congress. 'We are just giving Britain fifty destroyers to use as novelty paperweights and doorstops.' Such were the legal niceties of neutrality that it was not possible for America to fly military aircraft to Canada, but it was decided it would be legal to fly them to the border and then push them over the line! Britain was understandably a bit short of cash at the time and so a certain amount of bartering and pleading was involved.

'So what can you give me in return for fifty destroyers?'

'Er, I haven't actually got any money, but we could swap them for this attractive "Let's Save France!" badge.'

Churchill, half-American himself, exploited his friendship with Roosevelt to the full. He put him down as his best friend on MySpace and the two of them spent hours chatting away on MSN. America acquired use of British Caribbean bases in return for ships and, under an arrangement called 'Lend-Lease', equipment was sent to Britain in exchange for an I.O.U. note and a big coffee mug that said 'World's Number One Country'.

Shock as World War spreads round world

America also gave assistance to China who had turned up to the Second World War far too early in 1937. Relations between the United States and expansionist Japan were rapidly deteriorating as the latter took over former French Indo-China. 'Why can't places like Vietnam just be left alone?' argued the Americans. The war was also spreading to North Africa with Britain invading Italian-held Libya. The Germans might have occupied France with its fine food, wine and its beautiful cities packed with art treasures. But Britain had the Sahara.

Italy's rather unheroic entry into the war in June 1940 turned out to be more of an irritation to the Nazis than a support. The Germans were forced to step in to rescue the situation in North Africa, and Britain was pushed back out of Libya by Field Marshal Rommel.

'Mussolini, why don't you have a rest from invading places . . .' suggested Hitler.

'But we're only trying to help. Actually, you couldn't give us a hand in Abyssinia, could you?'

Italy had also invaded Greece but had been beaten back. Britain sent troops to support the Greeks but Hitler quickly overran the Balkans and fifty thousand Allied troops had to be hurriedly evacuated.

'So this time we managed to take all our equipment with us, did we?'

'Nope.'

Britain withdrew to Crete, but were again forced to evacuate following a German invasion. The humiliating disaster in the Balkans had reminded people that this was also the reckless Churchill of Gallipoli. But his sentimental decision to ride to the rescue of 'the cradle of democracy' did have one unforeseen consequence. Germany's secret invasion of Russia had to be delayed by six weeks, the conquest was not complete by the time the severe Russian winter set in, and thus eventually Germany lost the Second World War. So it wasn't all bad.

We always said we were great mates with the Bolsheviks

Britain could not reveal that it had broken Germany's secret codes, but still informed the Kremlin that Russia was about to be invaded. Stalin declined to fall for such a fiendish capitalist trick: 'Oh yeah, right, I really believe you . . .'

'No, honestly, trust us. Hitler is going to attack you this summer.'

'Of course he is – and did you know they've taken the word "gullible" out of the dictionary?'

Even after the invasion had begun, Stalin still refused to believe his front-line officers. 'Oh, don't tell me you're in on this gag too . . .'

But news of Hitler's invasion of Russia was met with jubilation in

Britain. The far left switched from demanding an end to this imperialist war to shouting 'Second front now!' Churchill didn't hesitate to commit Britain to an alliance with Russia although he tried to remember to limit references to 'our fight for freedom' in future speeches. In his book on the Second World War he later wrote: *If Hitler had invaded Hell I would make at least a favourable reference to the Devil in the House of Commons.*

Sheer geographical logistics made it hard for Britain to do much to help the Soviet troops being pushed back towards Moscow. Britain did, however, successfully send a convoy of supplies to the northern Russian port of Archangel, even taking an oil tanker with them to refuel all the ships, skirting German-held Norway as they did so. Getting insurance for that trip was a nightmare.

Churchill was now convinced that Britain would ultimately be victorious, especially with the United States' neutrality being stretched to breaking point. Yet throughout the summer and autumn of 1941 Germany seemed unstoppable as it raced across huge areas of the Soviet Union. Only on 5 December did the Russians finally win a victory against the Germans on the outskirts of Moscow, and the Nazis would never again get so close to the Soviet capital. Two days later Japan bombed Pearl Harbor.

America joins World War (slightly less late than last time)

'I stick my neck out for nobody,' says Humphrey Bogart in *Casablanca*. But you can't help thinking the American will join the struggle in the end. Whatever *Casablanca* might mean in Spanish, away from the real White House, most Americans were still keen to keep the United States out of any foreign war. All this changed on 7 December 1941. The Yanks might have guessed something was up when all the staff at the Japanese Embassy in Washington packed up their things on 4 December, destroyed their codebooks and headed for home. But the annihilation of America's Pacific Fleet in Hawaii, killing 2,400 Americans, still came as a total shock to the United States and the world.

From our modern perspective, Japan's decision to launch an unprovoked attack on the world's foremost industrial power seems like an incredibly stupid thing to do. And back in 1941 it looked like that too. Japan's increasingly hubristic military government had thought it could win a quick war if it struck a decisive early blow against America – and then the United States would somehow disappear and not bother them again. Churchill had promised America that if they were attacked Britain would declare war on Japan 'within the hour'. Because of the time difference between London and Washington, he actually managed to declare war on Japan at an earlier hour than the United States did. Two British warships were immediately sunk by the Japanese who were advancing on British colonies in the Far East.

Despite Roosevelt's personal support for Churchill, America's war with Japan did not automatically mean war with Germany. Indeed there was a strong sense in the United States that they had their own war now, conflict in Europe was so 1930s. Fortunately America wasn't given any choice; Hitler's hubris exceeded even that of the Japanese government and the Führer promptly declared war on the United States. Conquering half a continent does that to a man. And so the lines were drawn: Germany, Italy and Japan versus Britain, Russia and the United States. Fascist Totalitarianism v Liberal Democracy.

'What about Russia?'

'Shhh!'

'Pacific' meaning 'peaceful'

In a contest between the Empire 'where the sun never set' and the Land of the Rising Sun, something was going to have to give. Hong Kong fell within weeks of Pearl Harbor and Britain's key Pacific base at Singapore was now seriously exposed. At the southern tip of the Malay peninsula, Singapore had huge guns pointing out to sea to prevent a nautical assault. Unfortunately the defences of the city had not been designed to prevent anyone having the discourtesy to come in via the back door. Japan didn't invade from the sea, they just came down the peninsula. For this rapid invasion the Japanese possessed a fiendish secret weapon: the bicycle. Tanks and fighter aircraft are one thing, but anyone who has attempted to walk through a pedestrianized shopping centre will know that the bicycle can be a terrifying assault weapon. The crack Japanese cyclists rode on the pavements, went straight through red traffic lights; the British pedestrians never stood a chance.

The British and Empire troops were discovering that the Japanese adversaries had no respect for the usual rules of combat. Their soldiers had been taught to die rather than surrender and thus despised any European soldier who had allowed himself to fall into the hands of the enemy. At Hong Kong, British captives had been tied together in groups and then bayoneted to death. There were reports of hundreds of Australian POWs being ritually beheaded. Unfortunately the greatest capture of British forces in the history of the British army was about to be achieved by this brutal opponent. With the fall of Singapore 130,000 British and Empire troops were captured at a stroke. Only a fraction of them would return home alive.

The fall of Singapore was the greatest single capitulation in British history; a political and military disaster which would have toppled less secure leaders. The idea that Britain had the might to defend its scattered Empire had been exposed as a sham. But closer to home Britain was not faring any better. In North Africa, Rommel captured Tobruk along with 35,000 Allied prisoners and now there were serious questions about Churchill's handling of the war. He faced a vote of confidence in the House of Commons, and the government lost a series of by-elections to Independent candidates as voters showed their dissatisfaction with the progress of the war. Britain badly needed something, somewhere to go right. In August Churchill was persuaded to replace the arrogant and remote leadership of the British Eighth Army in Africa. The new commander was an unconventional general called Montgomery. A photograph from 1918 shows this unknown soldier standing behind Winston Churchill at a parade. Now this diminutive soldier from the ranks was about to transform Churchill's war and become a national hero along the way . . .

'Monty', as he became known, had previously raised a few eyebrows in Ministry circles for his innovative methods. He was reputed to have set up brothels, with regular medical inspections, for the 'horizontal refreshment' of his troops, rather than just letting them take their chances with unknown prostitutes. He made a point of appearing before the ordinary soldiers as often as possible, easily identified in his trademark beret as he worked hard to bring about a sense of cohesion between the various units. Morale in the 'Desert Rats' was transformed even before Britain inflicted its first land victory against the Germans at the Battle of El Alamein in October 1942. Montgomery had accurately predicted the length of the twelve-day battle and the number of casualties. It was later remarked that we never won a major battle before Alamein and we never lost one afterwards. This fact may have more to do with the concurrent reversal of German fortunes at Stalingrad, but finally it seemed the tide was turning.

Now Churchill felt able to give a speech announcing that 'This is not the end. It is not even the beginning of the end. But it is, perhaps, the end of the beginning . . .' at which everyone nodded earnestly, not quite having the courage to say, 'Sorry, you lost me there, can you go over that again . . . ?'

And it's 1, 2 , 3, What are we fighting for?

Into this euphoria came the Beveridge Report, the blueprint for a 'Welfare State' that would care for the entire population 'from the cradle to the grave'. Part of the risk of having Labour ministers in a coalition government was that they might go off and commission some lefty report to look into social security provision after the war. Beveridge was a Liberal economist and presented his radical vision with the language and demeanour of a moderate academic gentleman. He set out detailed plans for a compulsory national insurance scheme that would pay for a 'National Health Service'; there would be unemployment benefit, sickness pay, universal pensions and everyone would get a big bag of sweets and a ride in the Duke of Kent's new car.

The report became a bestseller overnight. The timing could not have been better; belief that the war could actually be won was coupled with a vision of a society worth fighting for. A subtle change was taking place in British society; popular opinion was moving markedly to the left. Any Conservative politician advocating a return to massive unemployment and poverty as had been experienced after the last war would have found the *Question Time* audience shaking their heads in firm disagreement. The alliance with Russia meant that for a short while the normally staid and conservative BBC ended each evening with a rousing chorus of 'The Internationale', and taxi drivers would bore you rigid with their oppressive liberal views: 'I'll tell you something about the Polish immigrants – they come over here and become Battle of Britain heroes, and, well, where's it going to end? Next they'll be helping us liberate all Europe.'

The war also gave people the opportunity and perhaps desire to improve themselves intellectually, reading Penguin paperbacks, joining the Left Book Club or pretending to like all the long boring bits of the classical symphonies on the radio. Despite the shortages of the war, standards of living had actually gone up for the vast majority as wages rose and mass unemployment vanished. The most significant deprivation was the change in living standards felt by the better off. The poor had always endured shortages – their ration book had been an empty wallet. People were also healthier now that limits were placed on the family allocation of meat, butter and profiteroles. Fish was the only meat not rationed; children were given cod liver oil, milk and concentrated orange juice; and for those evacuated to the countryside, there was fresh air and exercise. The only slight negative on the family health front was the German bombs landing on your house and the fact that Dad was being shot at by the Japanese army in the jungles of Burma.

Meals in restaurants were 'off-ration', although there were strict limits as to what could be served. During the war the government set up 'British Restaurants': local authority cafés that provided basic low-cost meals to the general public. For who better to run your favourite bistro than the council?

'Yes, I'd like egg, bacon and chips please, and a cup of tea.'

'No, I'm not from the Meal-Planning Department, I'm from Catering Control – first we have to do a statutory assessment to ensure that the meal application falls within local authority guidelines. If you put your lunch request in by the second Tuesday of the month it should be ratified by the time of the next meeting of the council's Comestibles Committee, which are organized on a bi-monthly cycle.'

These restaurants continued to be a feature of the English high street for many years after the war. In the 1940s, few words sat together as uncomfortably as 'British' and 'Restaurant' but the ordinary people must have felt a pang of socialist pride as they sawed away at the smidgeon of gristle on their plate. 'All right; these restaurants may be rubbish, but they belong to us – to the people! Actually, shall we go to Lyon's Corner House instead?'

'The beginning of the end . . .' (Part One)

Nineteen forty-three was the year when the torch of world leadership was passed over to the United States. In early 1942 American munitions production was still less than the British. By the end of 1943 it was four times greater. When Britain finally invaded France, overall command would be in the hands of an American.

In the meantime a significant part of the British war effort was directed at the bombing of Germany, almost because there was not much else they could think of doing. You have to wonder if Bomber Harris ever gave a moment's thought to his carbon footprint. Sir Arthur Harris had been made Air Chief Marshal in February 1942 and became a zealous advocate of the type of bombing that virtually wiped out whole German cities. Both sides continued to rain bombs on each other's civilian centres, in perhaps the most militarily pointless dimension of the whole war. The damage to German war production was less than 10 per cent, while the demands of the bombing campaign on Allied war production were around 25 per cent. On both sides it probably helped strengthen the resolve of the civilian populations, making Hitler stronger not weaker. It would have been better if Britain had never dropped a single bomb on German civilian targets, although it might have been hard to propose such a progressive argument to a London mother who'd just seen her entire family killed by a direct hit on her home.

Throughout 1943 the real deciding battle of the Second World War was being fought far away on the Eastern Front. The very same soldiers who had been filmed parading down the Champs-Elysées in Paris in 1940 were nearly all to die a cold and hungry death at Stalingrad. Stalin was pressing for a second front in Europe, and even the Americans were eager for an early landing in Northern France. Churchill, for once in his life, was cautious. There are those who believe that the Allies' reluctance to open up a second front was a cynical ploy to let Communist Russia be left to fight itself to exhaustion, until the British and Americans stepped in at the end with powerful military machines intact. However, this position is mainly held by people who sell newspapers outside Woolworths on Saturday mornings.

British and American forces were now too deeply tied up in the sideshow of North Africa to make an assault on France possible in 1943, and so the Allies had to make do with an invasion of Sicily.

'These Sicilian chaps, don't you have a few of them in America?'

'Er, yeah. We generally try not to upset them.'

The Americans had been bombed by the Japanese, decided to deal first with the Germans, and ended up fighting the Italians, who were no threat to the United States whatsoever.

To confuse the enemy, a novel deception was attempted using the dead body of a homeless Welsh alcoholic.* His corpse was dressed in the uniform of a British army major and on his person were placed the invented plans for a fictitious invasion of Sardinia. The body of 'The Man Who Never Was' was found 'washed up' on a Spanish beach. The plan worked perfectly, the documents quickly found their way to the military leadership of the Axis Powers who continued to believe that Sardinia was to be the main target long after Allied forces were securing their positions in Sicily.

* It can't be confirmed for certain that the body used was that of Glyndwyr Michael, and this claim only emerged long after the book and film of *The Man Who Never Was*.

With the Italians demonstrating that they couldn't win at home as well as away, Mussolini was overthrown in July 1943 and the new Italian government began suing for peace. For a moment it looked as if the whole of Italy might just drop into the Allied sphere, but once again, Hitler was forced to come to the rescue of his annoying Fascist comrade. He invaded Italy from the north, reinstalled Mussolini, who apologized and said it definitely wouldn't happen again. The Italians were deeply confused. 'I'm sorry, so whose side are we on now?'

After an invasion on the 'toe' of Italy in September 1943, the Allies took the heel and secured the ankle. Then they moved up to the bit where the laces are, before deciding they had probably worn out the 'Italy is shaped like a boot' analogy. Severe losses were endured at Anzio and Monte Cassino where the seven-hundred-year-old monastery was regraded from 'World Heritage Site' to 'wonderful investment opportunity, recently levelled for redevelopment'. The hilltop stronghold was finally taken in May 1944 and the Allies entered the Italian capital in the first week of June. The fall of Rome should have been a historic and symbolic moment in the narrative of the war, but the soldiers who had pulled off this heroic feat failed to get the acclaim they deserved. For the very next day, the largest-ever seaborne invasion force in the history of the world set sail for northern France.

'Ah!' said Churchill. 'That's why it says "D-Day" in my diary.'

6 June 1944: British get to the beach before the Germans

Throughout late 1943 and early 1944 a massive deployment of American servicemen and equipment built up in Britain. Eisenhower, the Supreme Allied Commander, joked that it was only the barrage balloons that stopped the island sinking altogether. Three years earlier Britain had dreaded invasion but now another sort of invasion had taken place; one and a half million American servicemen were billeted across the country in preparation for the attack on France. A recently republished guide was issued to all American servicemen explaining the subtleties of British society and advising them to avoid boasting to the British Tommies about how much they were paid. It explained that the British are reserved, not unfriendly, and that 'bloody' is one of the worst swear words there is. It extolled the difference between the two cultures, urging sensitivity, humility and caution before concluding, 'Look, just wait a few years and then you can come back and fill up every high street with Drive-Thru McDonald's and Tex-Mex bars.'

For the deeply segregated American army, the British attitude to black soldiers was a revelation. Many white Americans found it hard to cope with seeing a negro gentleman being invited for tea at the vicarage or dancing with white girls at the village dance. The young women of England, where eligible men had been in short supply during the war years, found the American soldiers had surprisingly forward ideas about how they might further Anglo-American relations. With money in their pockets and smart new uniforms, the American G.I.s had that certain something that the English women found irresistible. It's called chocolate. 'Over-paid, over-sexed and over here' was the abiding complaint against the Yanks from the majority who weren't having it off with them in the hay barn. Sixty thousand English women became G.I. brides, and many others were left broken-hearted as they waved their sweethearts goodbye. 'If only he had left me something to remember him by,' they wept as they wondered why they were feeling sick in the mornings.

If you wanted to get a sense of the awesome scale and chaos of the D-Day landings, you could do a lot worse than watching the first half an hour of Steven Spielberg's *Saving Private Ryan*. Will Tom Hanks make it on to the beach and survive the hail of bullets killing his comrades wading ashore? Well clearly, yes he will, he's the star of the film; they'd be stupid to kill him in the first five minutes. Two hundred thousand men were involved in one way or another in the D-Day landings (two-thirds of them British), as 156,000 men stormed the beaches of Normandy, some quickly gaining a foothold, others pinned down on the beaches by the strength of German resistance. Incredibly, Winston Churchill had been determined to be among those dodging the bullets on the very first day, and nobody could talk him out of this mad idea. Finally it fell to the King to forbid his First Minister to go; the very last time a monarch over-ruled a British prime minister.

The weather was so bad the Germans were convinced no invasion could be imminent, and so Rommel spent 6 June in Ulm celebrating his wife's birthday. 'Why are you being called away this time? It's just work, work, work isn't it? What's so important that it can't wait a few days?'

The Germans had been convinced that the landings were going to be two hundred miles to the east where the English Channel was narrowest. All the double agents working in England had confirmed these plans, and huge formations of tanks were photographed wait-ing in Kent. What the German spy planes could not deduce was that these were actually inflatable dummy tanks, which are rubbish in battle because they can't fire shells and they puncture really easily. It was some time after the Allies had gained a foothold that the Germans were persuaded to move the bulk of their forces from the Pas de Calais to Normandy.

One of the first towns to fall was Bayeux, but they had removed the ancient tapestry recording an earlier occasion when a conquering army successfully crossed the English Channel. This town was the first in France to be visited by Charles de Gaulle, leader of the Free French, who had infuriated Churchill throughout the war by being just like him.

But progress was not as quick as hoped and by the end of June only a narrow part of the Cherbourg peninsula had been occupied. The optimism in Britain was also tempered by a lethal new threat, the V-1 flying bomb or 'doodlebug' whose engine could be heard droning over the capital until the noise suddenly cut out leaving everyone below waiting for the imminent massive explosion. This was followed by an even more powerful and terrifying flying bomb: the V-2 rocket, which just landed out of the sky with no warning whatsoever. Both caused massive casualties for no military gain and the evacuation of London that ensued was even greater than during the Blitz in the early days of the war. Fortunately the launch pads were captured before the Germans had a chance to test out their experiments of launching rockets containing chemical weapons. The scientists who developed this lethal rocket technology were later captured and given the only possible punishment. They were whisked off to the United States to help develop the American space programme.

British and American boffins had been making huge advances of their own. In 1940 scientists from California and Cambridge discovered a new element which they called 'plutonium' after the recently discovered planet Pluto. It was given the abbreviation 'Pu' as a schoolboy joke, which passed unsuspectingly on to the periodic table. The first atomic bomb was tested in July 1945 and the following month the experiment moved on to a densely populated Japanese city.

Now the net was closing around the Axis Powers; Japan was being pushed back in Burma where at one point it had threatened India. Some of the British and Empire soldiers who fought for years against the Japanese in the jungles of South-East Asia were a little resentful about how little attention they subsequently received for their ordeal in the theatre they claimed was 'the forgotten war'. Russia was racing through Poland, while on the Western Front Paris was liberated in August 1944 with German officers defying Hitler's orders to raze the beautiful city to the ground. French girls gratefully threw their arms around the liberating soldiers who had to explain, 'No, mademoiselle, you are intoxicated with the ecstasy of liberation and it would be unfair of me to take advantage of such a situation.'

Perhaps now . . . thought the British population in occupied Jersey and Guernsey, we will finally be set free. The Nazis had moved into the Channel Islands in June 1940 to take advantage of their favourable tax regime and low crime rate. Britons under occupation provided no smaller proportion of collaborators than any other country, as the Nazi war machine seized control of their crucial new potato industry and oiled navy blue jumpers. But now the islanders hoped liberation would come. In fact, the German fortifications were so strong that even after three million Allied troops had crossed the Channel, it was simply not worth sacrificing the lives and resources required to send tanks into Sark, especially when no motor vehicles are allowed there anyway. So it was that these little bits of Great Britain remained under Nazi occupation even after the fall of Berlin.

In September an over-ambitious attempt to bring an early end to the war by seizing the bridges over the Rhine with a massive drop of paratroopers proved to be 'a bridge too far' in the eponymous words of one of the commanders. Judging from the 1970s film starring Sean Connery, Elliott Gould, Dirk Bogarde, James Caan and Michael Caine, the élite Allied special forces seemed to be getting on a bit and could have done with losing a bit of weight before they went parachuting into occupied Holland.

In December, Hitler launched a counter-offensive and pushed the Allies thirty miles back in the so-called Battle of the Bulge, thus providing a lazy strap line for slimming magazines half a century later. Although the initiative was soon regained it meant that the Russians now looked certain to reach Berlin first, with all the political ramifications that that would later bring. Frankly the long-term interests of Germany would have been far better served if Hitler had concentrated all his efforts on the Eastern Front but could you tell this fascist dictator anything?

There were many in Germany now keen to make a separate peace with Britain and America, but the Allies had agreed to demand unconditional surrender on all fronts. America and Russia weren't going to fall out now, they were saving that till about a week after the end of the war. In early 1945, 'the Big Three' – Churchill, Roosevelt and Stalin – met in Yalta in the recently liberated Crimea with a big map of Europe and a marker pen. Britain had originally gone to war in defence of Poland, but now the Western Allies could only extract vague and easily broken promises that free elections would be held in Poland. 'Why does Stalin laugh every time the translator explains our desire for a democratic Eastern Europe?' Churchill satisfied himself with keeping Greece out of the Communist sphere of influence, and when a popular uprising took place there, Britain sent sixty thousand troops to suppress the communists. In a sense those troops were the first to fight the Cold War, even though few people had any sense of the titanic power struggle that would follow the defeat of Germany.

In January 1945 the Russians liberated Auschwitz, and the massive scale of the Nazis' organized genocide against the Jews was revealed in all its horror. Throughout the latter part of the war there had been increasing rumours about the organized gassing of Jews, gypsies, homosexuals and others who didn't fit into the Nazis' idea of Aryan perfection. The claims of genocide were so extreme it had made them hard to believe, and now the idea that an advanced European culture was capable of systematically murdering six million Jews was so appalling that it didn't just confirm the total evil of the Nazis but left a deep and permanent scar on our view of humanity itself. The British, American and Russian governments had in fact known that some sort of extermination camps existed, but they are generally absolved from any blame for their failure to bomb the camps or their railway lines on the grounds that they had to concentrate on military targets. However, this defence does not stand up to a great deal of scrutiny when one considers what happened next: the pointless massacre of perhaps a hundred thousand German citizens in the historic and harmless city of Dresden.

The RAF had begun the war dropping leaflets and were now dropping incendiary bombs with the deliberate intention of creating an apocalyptic firestorm that would suck the oxygen from anyone who didn't burn. Such is the rapid dehumanizing effect of war on advanced civilized societies. This operation was the brainchild of Bomber Harris, and there was much disquiet at his methods as the war ended. Harris became the only war leader not to be given a peerage immediately after the war, and no specific medal was minted for the bomber crews. An attempt to salvage his reputation eventually took place under the Thatcher and Major governments, and a statue to him was unveiled in 1992. It required a police guard as it was regularly graffitied, usually with the word 'Shame' (unless the artist was just a fan of the 80s acid house band 'Shamen' who kept being disturbed just before he'd finished). There has been a debate ever since as to whether the British and American bombing of Dresden constitutes a war crime. The simple answer is no, because it was committed by the side that won.

The river Rhine was crossed in March 1945 while in the East the

Russians were closing around Berlin. The narrow failure of a plot to take Hitler's life the previous year was now costing hundreds of thousands of lives as the war stumbled to its chaotic and brutal end. On 28 April Mussolini and his mistress were killed by Italian partisans and strung upside down for all to see.* The following day in his bunker deep under the rubble of Berlin, Adolf Hitler married his girlfriend Eva Braun, but the atmosphere never really lightened: 'Come on, everyone, cheer up, this is supposed to be a wedding party!' In an attempt to share her new husband's interests, Eva Braun committed suicide alongside him the very next day. Hitler had also killed his pet Alsatian 'Blondi', which with the fifty million deaths that the war had already caused seems an unnecessary extra.

The Führer had instructed the U-boat hero Admiral Dönitz to continue the struggle, who now declared 'We fight on!' Privately Dönitz must have opened the books and discovered that Hitler hadn't left him with a great deal to work with. The 'Thousand Year Reich' surrendered a week later. Victory in Europe came on 8 May 1945.† Gathered around wireless sets in Britain, families listened to the chimes of Big Ben before a BBC announcer introduced the Prime Minister, 'the Right Honourable Winston Churchill', although you'd have to be pretty uninterested in politics not to know that by now. In a slow and steady voice, Churchill listed at length the various British, American, French and German signatories of the peace agreements and where they had been signed, while at home all the listeners were going, 'Yes, yes, skip all that . . . just tell us who's won!' He was humble and grateful to Britain's allies, singling out the Russians for their immense contribution. 'We may allow ourselves a brief period of rejoicing,' he suggested, though not actually offering to buy every-

* His granddaughter Alessandra Mussolini has continued the family interest in far-right politics. In 1992 the former *Playboy* cover girl was elected to the European Parliament on the irresistible combination of making the trains run on time *and* being topless.
†VE Day was supposed to be 9 May, so the Western Powers could announce it at the same time as the Russians. But an American reporter broke the story that the war was over, and the British and American governments could hardly tell the dancing crowds to go back into their homes until tomorrow. VE day is still commemorated a day later in Russia.

one the first drink himself. 'Long live the cause of freedom!' he proclaimed. 'God save the King!' And then everyone quickly switched
the radio off because next up it was *You and Yours*. In Britain the
crowds poured out on to the streets, a million thronged down the
Mall and around Buckingham Palace, where the King and Queen
were joined by their daughters and the Prime Minister. As in 1918
there were bonfires and spontaneous street parties as the public
rejoicing went on long into the night. And next morning they woke
up with a hangover, looked around at bombed-out, bankrupt Britain
and said, 'Oh God, this is going to take ages to clear up . . .'

Their finest hour?

The Second World War has acquired a unique and hallowed place in
British history, not purely because the war itself turned out to be so
just, but also because of the extraordinary heroism of the servicemen
and civilians caught up in it. It is not possible to record all the acts of
courage and self-sacrifice that ordinary people made for the common
good: women fire-fighters who stood their ground when buildings
were crumbling all around them; teenagers who toiled away for hours
helping move the rubble in the search for survivors of the Blitz;
pensioners ready to die firing a shotgun at the enemy 'as long as I
take one with me'. The ordinary British people showed themselves to
be resourceful, unselfish and modest, yet incredibly heroic, in a way
that is hard to imagine looking at that snarling driver who made
obscene gestures to you as he cut you up at the traffic lights. Never
again would there be such a sense of unity and purpose in Great
Britain. Back in 1940 Winston Churchill had said that future
generations would look back and say 'This was their finest hour.'
And he was quite right.

Today we are all products of the Second World War. Not just
culturally, having grown up in the Britain that came out of it, but
literally, in the sense that nearly everybody born in the past sixty
years probably owes their very existence to some chance meeting of
their parents or grandparents caused by the social disruption of the

war or its aftermath. For the ageing generation that lived through such an incredible six years, it is no wonder that it has continued to be the defining experience of their lives. But for the rest of us, the vast majority, it is perhaps time to let it go. It's important to remember history, but not to live in it. Britain standing alone in 1940 was the result of a humiliating military disaster; it is not the basis for a European foreign policy the following century. Germany is a modern, cultured democracy making a major contribution to arts, science and the reliability of motor cars, and we demean ourselves more than them by printing tabloid headlines about Hitler and the Blitz every time we have to play them at football. Having said that, it doesn't seem likely that the British are going to change, so it might be simpler if the Germans just threw in the towel and agreed to play along with all our tiresome wartime stereotypes for evermore. It would certainly make the European Parliament more entertaining if every time a German MEP spoke he had to put a little comb to his upper lip before shouting, '*Achtung! Achtung! Hände hoch, Schweinhund*, for you ze var is over I think.' The British MEPs would clap with delight and amusement, shouting, 'Do the walk! And the arm! Do the goosestep thingy with your arm in the air.'

The war in which liberal democracy took on fascist totalitarianism was refashioned as the definitive battle between good and evil. All the hypocrisy and moral ambiguities that total war entails were blown away by the Holocaust and the Nazi and Japanese conduct of the war. No wonder the British have wanted to pore over it again and again in films and comics and displays by the Bombing of Dresden Re-enactment Society. Great Britain led the world through its darkest hour, refusing to give up even when all seemed completely lost. Even after the British Tommy had been captured, the struggle went on. If the films are to be believed, every British prisoner of war in captivity successfully constructed a twin-blade helicopter out of yoghurt cartons, landed it at Piccadilly Circus, hopped out and asked to be sent straight back to the front. In 1944 a mass breakout occurred at Stalag Luft III at Zagan in Poland in which seventy-six prisoners got out before the seventy-seventh was spotted and a panicky German guard, probably with a scar and a barking Alsatian, raised the alarm.

As anyone who has been stuck in front of the telly all afternoon on Christmas Day will remember, *The Great Escape* ends with the cold-blooded massacre of fifty of those who tried to escape.

'Do you think it was worth the price?' says Flight Lieutenant Hendley at the end of the film.

Group Captain Ramsey replies: 'Depends on your point of view.'

This clipped, understated British response captures the entire moral debate between the contrasting responses to Nazism. What did those fifty prisoners achieve by escaping and ultimately being murdered? Did they not also have a responsibility to give themselves the best chance of returning safely to their wives and families by sitting out the war as prisoners? That was the pragmatic reasoning of collaborationist Vichy France. But surely the very level of evil of a culture that murdered captured prisoners in cold blood meant that every individual had a higher duty to oppose that regime by whatever means it could, however suicidal. That had been the position of Britain since 1940. Unfortunately not as many people dwell on this existential dimension of the film as the bit where Steve McQueen jumps the fence on the motorbike.

Britain's lone stand against the evil of Nazism gave it moral authority for a generation after the war. But although people might respect you for what you did in the past, they tend to respect you even more if you have a great big army standing right behind you in the immediate present. America and Russia were the great powers now; the big three who met up to discuss the future of Europe were really the big two and a bit. Britain may have been flush with Brownie points, but it was completely and utterly overdrawn at the bank. Two world wars in the first half of the twentieth century (neither of them conflicts that Britain had been forced to fight in) had totally exhausted and bankrupted Great Britain and stripped it of any real super-power status.

But what had been the value of all that Victorian greatness if the ordinary Englishman had generally lived a short and wretched life; powerless, exploited and hungry? The vast majority of Britons would have swapped the entire British Empire for a full stomach and a little security for his family against poverty and disease. Britain was about to lose India and gain the National Health Service; how could the latter not be a greater source of pride to the true patriot? The victory of the First World War had ultimately been a hollow one for those who had made the greatest sacrifices; now a more permanent, meaningful triumph was about to be secured. Britain had lost much of its power, but ordinary Britons were about to seize theirs.

Election results live (three weeks after voting)

Summer 1945. A railway station somewhere in the Midlands. Labour has just won a shock election victory. A young public-school boy clicks his fingers at a porter and shouts, 'My man?'

'That's all over now,' replies the porter. 'You can't talk to us like that any more.'

This exchange, true or not, entered popular mythology because it illustrated a major change that had just taken place in the psychology of the British nation. 'The people' had taken over. For what had happened in July 1945 was a very understated, polite and restrained British Revolution.

The Americans have 1776, the French have 1789, but despite (or rather because of) such milestones as Magna Carta, the summoning of Parliament, the execution of Charles I, the Glorious Revolution of 1688 and the Great Reform Act of 1832, Britain had never experienced one cataclysmic violent and permanent overthrow of the *ancien régime*. It would have been just too rude. Instead the English waited and waited, gaining extra little freedoms here, winning minor rights and responsibilities there; until finally, in July 1945, the British Revolution came along when everyone was least expecting it. The rebel forces queued politely at the polling stations and then simply voted for a completely different sort of society.

Churchill had suggested that the wartime coalition continue until the defeat of Japan in the Pacific, but with the expectation that this might take another eighteen months, Labour refused and withdrew from the government. A general election was called for July and the widespread presumption was that the national saviour who led the Conservatives would win it overwhelmingly. Election day was 5 July 1945 but the ballot boxes remained sealed and guarded for three weeks while the forces' votes from around the world were returned home. In those battered black boxes was a surprise that no one had foreseen. The Labour Party had won a landslide election victory and Winston Churchill was out. The great war leader was devastated. The King told him that he thought the people were most ungrateful while Mrs Churchill suggested that it might be a blessing in disguise. 'At the moment' – replied her husband – 'it seems quite effectively disguised.'

We lazily think of the right to vote as the key indicator of a free society, but that only provides the potential. The incremental widening of the franchise between 1832 and 1928 hadn't automatically made people free; it is what the voters did with that power when they finally gained the confidence that made the difference. A detailed paper on the Beveridge Report had been found in Hitler's bunker, with a note stating that the plans were superior to any system of social insurance dreamt up by the Germans. Labour were also committed to state ownership of major industries, a universal entitlement to pensions, child benefit, legal aid and the abolition of birching and flogging for young offenders, which was clearly namby-pamby liberalism gone to extremes.

'At last!' declared the miners. 'Now that the coal mines are owned by us, we will never have to go on strike again!'

'Rejoice!' celebrated the commuters. 'The railways belong to us, the people! Never again will that surly bloke at the ticket kiosk be rude and unhelpful!'

The Education Act of 1944 had established the principle of free secondary education, and now the school leaving age was raised to fifteen. Two hundred and fifty thousand homes had been destroyed in the Blitz but within weeks former armaments factories were turning out prefabricated dwellings. Whole new council estates began to be built, and the planners were determined that these would be decent homes with bathrooms and inside toilets, with the added option of using the lift if you'd had a few beers. If there was a row of beautiful Victorian houses with a big bomb crater in the middle, great care was taken to make sure that the new house was thrown up with modern bricks, metal windows and a flat roof, so that it looked completely wrong. They claimed they were building a New Jerusalem. Nobody liked to ask why on earth they would want to recreate a bombed-out Middle Eastern war zone, split with religious strife and factional infighting. Probably because it wouldn't have sounded as visionary to proclaim: 'We shall build a New Guildford.'

Most symbolic and enduring of all would be the National Health Service, which came into being on the third anniversary of Britain's most celebrated election. The idea was a simple one, but nothing like it existed anywhere in the world. A universal health-care system, free at the point of delivery, available to all, irrespective of income or status or even nationality. There would be a rush of people who went to see their doctors about complaints they had endured for years but could never afford to do anything about. And lots of lonely old widows decided that it was quite nice to go and chat about themselves to a friendly gentleman for half an hour, and so made a point of doing it on a weekly basis with some excuse or other for the next sixty years.

These were the meaningful freedoms that eventually evolved out of the British Revolution of 1945: security and dignity in old age; insurance against unemployment or sickness; the freedom of choice provided by a decent education system. Of course the quest for these rights is an ongoing one that continues into the twenty-first century and the millions of ordinary people who voted for Attlee's government certainly didn't see an overnight transformation in their wealth and prospects. Rationing didn't end; in fact it got worse, with even bread becoming rationed soon after the war. And of course 'freedom' itself is a highly subjective concept; the liberation that would come for some would mean increased restrictions for others. Who is to say which definition of liberty is the most valid? The post-war government might have struck significant blows for freedom from poverty, illness, ignorance and homelessness; but on the other hand they restricted the freedoms of the very rich to take large amounts of capital out of the country. How can anyone say which is the more fundamental human right? (Bearing in mind that these rich people are probably wearing top hats and a monocle and talking in stupid accents.) Alas, it is just one of those impossible philosophical and moral paradoxes for which there is no right or wrong. But at last the dreams of so many generations of idealists were being put into law; they were creating a society beyond the wildest dreams of the Chartists or the Levellers or the peasants marching behind Wat Tyler. The only slight blot on the horizon, it was pointed out, was the prospect of all-out nuclear war between the new superpowers that could end all life on earth, but then there're always people who'll manage to find something negative to say about any situation.

Relax! It's the Atomic Age

Churchill was not the only war leader who wouldn't be at the peace conference after the war. President Roosevelt had died suddenly in April 1945, at the beginning of a record fourth term. The new President Harry Truman did not want a long-drawn-out Pacific war with all the US casualties this would involve, especially with expansionist Russia having just declared war on Japan. It was in this context that Truman decided to use his brand-new atomic bomb that had only become ready a few weeks beforehand. Under an agreement made at Quebec in 1943, the atomic bomb could not be used without British consent. The new American President was either unaware of this condition or chose to ignore it. Just to give the impression that consultation had taken place, Clement Attlee rang up and left a message on the answerphone telling him to go ahead.

After two nuclear explosions killed around two hundred thousand Japanese civilians, the Second World War finally ended on 14 August 1945. There were more street parties and celebrations, tempered with the chilling realization that a terrifying new type of war had been born at the close of the old. Few people understood quite what had just happened at Hiroshima and Nagasaki, they were just grateful that this weapon had brought a speedy end to the years of war. Although it was probably not top of the list of concerns of the citizens of flattened and radioactive Japanese cities, American

Lend-Lease ended immediately after VJ Day, and Britain was suddenly plunged into a dire economic crisis. Truman had no intention of subsidizing Britain's gradual return to normality, especially now they'd elected a socialist government. This was a bit of a shock to the British, who thought that giving out gum, Hershey bars and billion-dollar loans was what the Yanks were for. The King's speech had just announced the nationalization of the Bank of England. It was a shame there wasn't any actual money in it.

When they elected a Labour government, the voters of Britain had turned away from foreign affairs towards domestic issues, but much had to be done on the international scene too. There would be independence for India, and the chaotic withdrawal from Palestine in the hope that if we just left them to it, everything should sort itself out there pretty quickly. Around this time a duplicated letter began to fall through the letterboxes of various newly independent governments:

A personal invitation to you, **Ceylon**, to join the 'British Commonwealth Club'. Membership of this exclusive organization is open to all alumni of the British Empire. You will receive a smart lapel badge, use of our attractive clubhouse in Holland Park conveniently situated just **5,000 miles** from your capital **Colombo** (*check*) plus a quarterly newsletter keeping you up to date with which other members of the Commonwealth are busy murdering one another.

Britain also played a key role in the establishment of the United Nations, which held its inaugural meeting at Central Hall in Westminster in January 1946.

'Now what shall we call ourselves? Britain? Great Britain? Is "Great Britain" over-stating it a bit now?'

'What about the United Kingdom? Then we'll be placed next to the United States and we can be filmed sitting next to them nodding in agreement at whatever they say.'

The deliberations at the UN would be predominantly in English; the language of a little island off the north-west coast of Europe would become the common tongue of the whole world. The values established in Britain would eventually triumph too, as the whole globe aspired to a combination of the Whiggish ideals of liberal democracy and the industrialized capitalism that was forged in Britain's Industrial Revolution. Even the sports played all around the world were popularized and defined by the British: football, rugby, tennis and golf. Credit where it's due though, the French did come up with boules.

When Julius Caesar had landed near Dover two thousand years earlier he was venturing beyond civilization to a backward, barbaric island on the edge of the world. Little could he have imagined that it would be this island that would one day spread its ideas, inventions and culture around the world; that the reach of the Roman Empire would be as nothing to the global domination of these Britons. Or maybe he did imagine it, but there just wasn't the Latin vocabulary for him to say, 'Believe me, chaps, one day this lot will invent the steam engine, cricket and the internet.' In the two millennia in between, the British people fought foreign invaders and battled for freedom from home-grown tyrants. They endured serfdom, the Black Death, endless wars and a lot of drizzle. How much all those events have shaped the British, or how much our national character has shaped our history, it is hard to say. Perhaps it was good luck that the terrible religious civil wars between Protestants and Catholics were fought out across much of Europe, but never significantly in England. But again, centuries later, when the titanic power struggle between communism and fascism was tearing other countries apart, nobody in Britain wanted to know. Perhaps there really is a profound gentleness in the British character that instinctively backs off from revolutionary violence and religious extremism.

Finally it seemed that the country was at peace abroad, and at peace with itself. With the troops still coming home from around the globe, the nation's leaders, its ministers, generals, the Commons and Lords, the King and his daughter the future Queen Elizabeth II gathered in Westminster Abbey for a service of thanksgiving and remembrance, while the ghosts of all their predecessors looked on.

Buried under the flagstones were the dusty bones of British kings and queens from Edward the Confessor right up until Queen Anne's square coffin took the space meant for all her successors. Keeping them company down there were great prime ministers like the Pitts and Gladstone, writers from Geoffrey Chaucer to Charles Dickens, plus countless other representatives of centuries of British genius from Sir Isaac Newton to Charles Darwin.

What would these great Britons of the past have thought of the enormous victories that had been secured by their descendants? Did the ghosts of Good Queen Bess and Henry V feel a swelling sense of patriotic pride as they listened to the hymns echoing down into the abbey vaults?

'Oh gawd, they're singing "Abide With Me" again . . .' moaned Edward I.

'It's so bloody dirgy. I wouldn't mind if they knew the words, but they do the first line, and then it's just mumble mumble mumble.'

' "Rest In Peace," they said. I haven't had a moment's peace since I got here,' whined Thomas Hardy.

'Too bloody right,' chimed in Mary Queen of Scots. 'If they're not singing and praying, they're walking back and forth over your grave . . .'

'Exactly,' said Henry II. 'Tourists, school trips, bloody royal weddings. You'd think they could at least put some carpet down . . .'

'Well why don't we actually do something, instead of just whinge-ing about it?' snapped William III. 'Why don't we storm up there and smash the windows and tip over the tables and set fire to the place?'

An embarrassed silence fell over the catacombs.

'Well, sir,' ventured the Unknown Warrior, 'because that's not the British way . . .'

Rudyard Kipling nodded in agreement.

'So what is the British way?' said Pitt the Younger.

'Eh?'

'What exactly *is* the British way? If we don't much go in for violent protest or massacres or revolutions, but then we encounter some-thing that makes us really angry; what are we supposed to do?'

The national heroes glanced at one another, looking for an answer.

'Well . . .' explained the Unknown Warrior, 'we moan about it to each other for a while . . .'

'And then what?'

'Well . . . Maybe a letter to the local paper?'

'Yes, and a petition . . .'

'Or, if one felt very strongly about something, there's always the poster in the front window.'

Contented murmurs of agreement echoed around the room as the opening bars of the National Anthem struck up in the abbey.

'Yes, and we usually get there in the end. You just have to be a little bit patient about these things . . .'

'Splendid,' said a voice at the back. 'Why don't I put the kettle on?'

BIBLIOGRAPHY

I haven't reproduced seven pages of obscure book titles here because a) I didn't read that many and b) I hoped that if I offered a 'selected' bibliography you might presume that I'd ploughed through many more volumes than I actually did. Despite my affected snobbishness about the internet, I found it an incredibly useful tool, even if you have to treat the 'facts' in the same way that you would if you'd just asked a bloke in the pub. But particularly helpful were www.learningcurve.gov.uk, www.historytoday.com, www.spartacus.schoolnet.co.uk, www.bbc.co.uk/history, www.british-history.ac.uk, and of course Wikipedia, which is generally pretty reliable except for its list of major female movie stars who have slept with a fifteen-year-old blogger called Kevin.

General

Briggs, Asa, *A Social History of England* (London: Weidenfeld and Nicolson, 1983)

Carr, E. H., *What is History?* (London: Macmillan, 1961)

Fraser, Rebecca, *A People's History of Britain* (London: Chatto & Windus, 2003)

Giddens, Anthony, *The Class Structure of the Advanced Societies* (London: Hutchinson, 1973)

Kearney, Hugh, *The British Isles: A History of Four Nations* (Cambridge: Cambridge University Press, 1989)

Kee, Robert, *Ireland: A History* (London: Weidenfeld and Nicolson, 1995)

Lee, Christopher, *This Sceptred Isle 55 BC–1901: From the Roman Invasion to the Death of Queen Victoria* (London: Penguin Books & BBC Books, 1997)

Marshall, H. E., *Our Island Story: A History of Britain for Boys and Girls, From the Romans to Queen Victoria* (London: Galore Park in association with Civitas, 1905, republished 2005)

Morgan, Kenneth O. (ed.), *The Oxford History of Britain: Revised Edition* (Oxford: Oxford University Press, 2001)

Paxman, Jeremy, *The English: A Portrait of a People* (London: Michael Joseph, 1998)

Roberts, Geoffrey, *The History and Narrative Reader* (London: Routledge, 2001)

Thompson, E. P., *The Making of the English Working Class* (Harmondsworth: Penguin Books, 1991)

Trevelyan, George Macaulay, *A Shortened History of England* (Harmondsworth: Penguin Books, 1972)

Introduction; Ancient and Roman Britain; Dark Ages/Saxons

de la Bédoyère, Guy, *Roman Britain: a new history* (London: Thames and Hudson, 2006)

Burgess, Colin, *The Age of Stonehenge* (London: Dent, 1980)

Campbell, James, *Essays in Anglo-Saxon History* (London: Hambledon Press, 1986)

Cavill, Paul, *Vikings: Fear and Faith in Anglo-Saxon England* (London: HarperCollins, 2001)

Dyer, James, *Ancient Britain* (London: Batsford, 1990)

Higham, N. J., *The Death of Anglo-Saxon England* (Gloucestershire: Sutton, 1997)

Mattingly, David, *An Imperial Possession: Britain in the Roman Empire 54 BC–AD 409* (London: Allen Lane, 2006)

Salway, Peter, *The Oxford Illustrated History of Roman Britain* (Oxford: Oxford University Press, 1993)

Thomas, Charles, *Celtic Britain* (London: Thames and Hudson, 1986)

Wilson, David M., *The Anglo-Saxons* (London: Thames and Hudson, 1960)

Wood, Michael, *In Search of the Dark Ages* (London: BBC Books, 1981)

Normans

Chibnall, Marjorie, *Anglo-Norman England 1066–1166* (Oxford: Blackwell, 1986)

Crouch, David, *The Normans: The History of a Dynasty* (London: Hambledon and London, 2002)

Harvey, Barbara (ed.), *The Twelfth and Thirteenth Centuries 1066–c.1280* (Oxford: Oxford University Press, 2001)

Lindsay, Jack, *The Normans and Their World* (London: Hart-Davis, MacGibbon, 1973)

McLynn, Frank, *1066: The Year of the Three Battles* (London: Cape, 1998)

Stafford, Pauline, *Unification and Conquest: A Political and Social History of England in the Tenth and Eleventh Centuries* (London: Edward Arnold, 1989)

Middle Ages

Barber, Richard, *Henry Plantagenet* (Woodbridge: Boydell Press, 2001)

Bevan, Bryan, *Henry IV* (London, Rubicon Press, 1996)

Bevan, Bryan, *King Richard II* (London: Rubicon Press, 1990)

Hilton, Rodney H., *Class Conflict and the Crisis of Feudalism: Essays in Medieval Social History* (London: Hambledon Press, 1985)

Jones, Terry & Ereira, Alan, *Medieval Lives* (London: BBC Books, 2005)

Prestwich, Michael, *Plantagenet England 1225–1360* (Oxford: Clarendon Press, 2005)

Turner, Ralph V., *King John: England's Evil King?* (Stroud: Tempus, 2005)

Tudors

Bindoff, Stanley T., *Tudor England* (Harmondsworth: Penguin Books, 1950)

Elton, Geoffrey R., *England under the Tudors* (London: Methuen, 1974)

Hoak, Dale (ed.), *Tudor Political Culture* (Cambridge: Cambridge University Press, 1995)

Innes, Arthur D., *England under the Tudors* (London: Methuen, 1950)

Tittler, Robert & Jones, Norman (eds), *A Companion to Tudor Britain* (Malden, Mass.: Blackwell in association with The Historical Association, 2004)

Stuarts

Ashley, Maurice, *The English Civil War: A Concise History* (London: Thames and Hudson, 1974)

Farmer, David L., *Britain and the Stuarts* (London: G. Bell, 1965)

Hibbert, Christopher, *Cavaliers and Roundheads: the English at War, 1642–1649* (London: HarperCollins, 1993)

Lockyer, Roger, *The Early Stuarts: A Political History of England, 1603–1642* (London: Longman, 1989)

Miller, John, *The Stuarts* (London: Hambledon and London, 2004)

Purkiss, Diane, *The English Civil War: A People's History* (London: Harper Press, 2006)

Vallance, Edward, *The Glorious Revolution, 1688: Britain's Fight for Liberty* (London: Little, Brown, 2006)

Revolutions

Dickinson, H. T. (ed.), *Britain and the French Revolution 1789–1815* (Basingstoke: Macmillan, 1989)

Rule, John & Wells, Roger, *Crime, Protest and Popular Politics in Southern England 1740–1850* (London: Hambledon Press, 1997)

Smith, Hannah, *Georgian Monarchy: Politics and Culture 1714–1760* (Cambridge: Cambridge University Press, 2006)

Speck, William A., *Stability and Strife: England 1714–1760* (London: Edward Arnold, 1977)

Empire

Black, Jeremy (ed.), *Britain in the Age of Walpole* (London: Macmillan, 1984)

Black, Jeremy, *Walpole in Power* (Stroud: Sutton, 2001)

Cowie, Leonard, W., *Hanoverian England 1714–1837* (London: G. Bell & Sons, 1967)

Edwards, J. R., *British History 1815–1939* (London: G. Bell & Sons, 1970)

Hobsbawm, Eric J., *The Age of Empire 1875–1914* (London: Weidenfeld and Nicolson, 1987)

Matthew, Colin (ed.), *The Nineteenth Century: The British Isles 1815–1901* (Oxford: Oxford University Press, 2000)

World Wars

Clarke, Peter, *Hope and Glory: Britain 1900–2000* (London: Penguin Books, 2004)

Gilbert, Martin, *The Second World War* (London: Weidenfeld and Nicolson, 1989)

Hobsbawm, Eric J., *Age of Extremes: The Short Twentieth Century 1914–1991* (London: Michael Joseph, 1994)

Silkin, Jon (ed.), *The Penguin Book of First World War Poetry* (London: Allen Lane, Penguin Books, 1979)

Sked, Alan & Cook, Chris, *Post War Britain: A Political History 1945–1992* (London: Penguin Books, 1979)

Taylor, A. J. P., *English History: 1914–1945* (Harmondsworth: Penguin Books, 1975)

Watson, Janet S. K., *Fighting Different Wars: Experience, Memory, and the First World War in Britain* (Cambridge: Cambridge University Press, 2004)

Acknowledgements

This book would not have been possible without the wonderful staff and resources of the London Library where much of it was written. I would also like to thank Bill Scott-Kerr, Georgia Garrett, Mark Burton, Pete Sinclair, Sarah Whitfield, Richenda Todd and most of all my wife, Jackie, for her support and encouragement and for pretending that she was remotely interested in the fact that the Nazis still occupied the Channel Islands after the fall of Berlin.

Index

Gallipoli, 376, 379–80, 448
Gama, Vasco da, 161
Gandhi, Mohandas, 341n, 350, 419–20
Garter, Order of the, 101, 105–6, 116
gas warfare, 378–9
Gaveston, Piers, 98, 99
General Strike, 409–111, 412, 413
Genghis Khan, 90
Geoffrey of Monmouth, 25n
George, St, 110, 180, 225, 377
George I, King, 138, 225–7, 228, 234
George II, King, 226n, 234–5, 238, 240, 249
George III, King: accession, 249–50;
   American War of Independence, 153, 252,
   258; Catholic policy, 273; death, 295–6;
   madness, 249, 260, 273, 291, 295, 308;
   Napoleonic Wars, 277
George IV, King (*earlier* Prince Regent), 291,
   296–7, 300, 301
George V, King: choice of PM, 406n, 407,
   416; Christmas messages, 405; death, 422;
   economic crisis, 415; Irish policy, 345, 384;
   Lords crisis, 360; name, 385–6; WWI, 377
George VI, King: accession, 425; choice of PM,
   432–3; King's speech, 470; response to 1945
   election, 467; WWII, 443, 457–8, 463, 471
Germans, 46–7, 341, 351, 365–7
Gibbon, Edward, xii
Gibraltar, 224, 261, 278, 319
Gibson, Mel, 95
Giles, Johnny, 181
gin, 236, 333
Gladiator, 20n
Gladstone, William: African policy, 341, 342;
   Belgian policy, 366; career, 330–1, 333, 335,
   339, 345, 354, 472; Chancellor of
   Exchequer, 329–30; Irish policy, 342–5, 364,
   403; Midlothian campaign, 332; reputation,
   342; social reforms, 339; Trade Union Act,
   336; Victoria's view of, 337
Glasgow, 266, 300, 336
Glastonbury, 26
Glencoe, massacre, 221
Glendower, Owen, 119–20
Glorious Revolution, 138, 210–11, 217, 222,
   340, 466
Gloucester, 62, 88, 107
Gloucester, Duke of, 220
'God Save the King', 238, 473
Godwin, Earl, 43, 44
gold standard, 409, 418

Gordon, General, 340, 342
Gordon Riots, 243, 244
Gould, Elliott, 460
Government of India Act, 420
Goya, Francisco, 285
Grace, W. G., 329n, 335
Gray, Thomas, 248
Great Britons, xii, 345
Great Crash, 414–16
Great Depression, 417–19
Great Escape, The, 464–5
Great Exhibition, 317–19
Great Fire of London, 201–2, 207, 444
Great Plague, 200–1
Great Trek, 349
Great War, *see* World War I
Greenland, 33
'Greensleeves', 145
Gregory I, Pope, 28–9, 30
Grey, Earl, 303–4
Guadeloupe, 250
Guardian, 294
Guevara, Che, 297
Guggenheim, Benjamin, 364
Guillotin, Dr, 250
gunpowder, 125, 128, 177, 371
Gunpowder Plot, 176–9, 207
Guthrum, Viking leader, 35, 36
Gwynne, Nell, 199

Hadrian, Emperor, 13
Hadrian's Wall, 12–13, 31
Hague, William, 357n
Haig, Field Marshal Douglas, 386, 387–8, 392
Halidon Hill, Battle of, 102
Halifax, Lord, 432–3, 440
Hampton Court, 146, 197
Hancock, Tony, 46
Hanks, Tom, 457
Hanover, 213, 226, 234, 245, 308
Harald Bluetooth, 41n
Harald Hardrada, King of Norway, 51
Hardie, Keir, 347
Hardy, Captain, 278–9
Hardy, Thomas, 472
Harfleur, siege, 123, 124
Hargreaves, James, 263
Harold II, King, 44–5, 51–5, 61
Harris, Sir Arthur ('Bomber'), 454, 461
Harris, Gertrude, 375n
Harris, Rolf, 116

INDEX

INDEX

Second World War, *see* World War II
Sedan, Battle of, 439
Senlac, 53–4
serfs, 60–1, 107, 114–15, 471
Seven Years War, 245–9, 251, 252, 257
Shakespeare, William: comedies, 199;
  Elizabethan age, 169; *Henry V*, 123, 124,
  143; *Henry VIII*, 143, 172n; *Macbeth*, 172;
  Richard II, 111n, 118; *Richard III*, 118, 132,
  135, 138
Shaw, Bernard, 127, 348
Shelley, Mary, 243n
Shelley, Percy, 294, 297
Sheriffmuir, Battle of, 227
Shrewsbury, Battle of, 120
Sicily, invasion of, 455
Sidney, Sir Philip, 237n
Simnel, Lambert, 142
Simpson, Bart, 349
Simpson, Wallis, 423–5
Singapore, 450–1
Sinn Fein, 401
Six Acts, 294
slave trade, 281–2, 295, 305
slaves, 14–15, 61, 170, 183n, 305, 349
Sluys, Battle of, 103
Smith, Adam, 242, 369
Smith, John, 357n
Snow, John, 336
Social Democratic Foundation, 347
Somme, Battle of the, 349, 376, 386–8, 393, 396
Sophia, Electress of Hanover, 220
South Africa, 307, 339, 340, 341, 349–51
South Sea Bubble, 231–3
Spanish Armada, 162–3, 166–8, 211
Spanish Civil War, 426–7
Spanish Inquisition, 158
Spanish Succession, War of, 219
Spender, Stephen, 427
Spenser, Edmund, 169
Spielberg, Steven, 457
Spinning Frame, 263–4
Spinning Jenny, 263, 267
Spion Kop, Battle of, 350
Stainmore, Battle of, 39
Stalin, Joseph, 448, 455, 460
Stalingrad, Battle of, 437, 452, 455
Stamford Bridge, Battle of, 51–2
Stamp Tax, 253, 254
Stanley, Lord, 137, 138
steam power, 264

Stephen, King, 68–71
Stephenson, George, 307
Stirling Bridge, Battle of, 95
Stirling Castle, 96
Stone Age, 3–4
Stonehenge, 5–6
Stonewall riots, 99
Strathclyde, 25, 38, 63n, 72n
Stravinsky, Igor, 411
Straw, Jack, 112, 114
Strongbow, 72
Stuart dynasty, 172n, 173, 219–20, 222–4
submarine war, 385, 386, 390, 446
Sudan, 340, 342
Suez Canal, 338, 340
suffragettes, 312, 332, 361–3, 397
Sussex, 26, 31, 52, 57, 195
Sutton Hoo, 27–8
Sweyn, King, 41

Tacitus, 20n
tanks, 393–4, 458
tariff reform, 355–6, 406
Tasman, Abel, 191n
taxation: American Revolution, 251, 252–4,
  257; Anglo–Saxon, 40, 44; Civil War, 189;
  income tax, 330, 346; Lloyd George's
  policies, 359; Magna Carta terms, 91;
  Norman, 59, 62, 64; of Jews, 94; on alcohol,
  236; on land, 359; on paper, 253, 329; on
  wool, 93; Parliament's role, 173, 214, 224;
  poll tax, 112, 113, 115; Roman, 8, 19;
  Saladin Tithe, 75; Scottish, 221; supertax,
  359; under Charles I, 183, 184; under
  Edward I, 93, 96; under Edward III, 106;
  under Henry III, 91; under Henry VII, 143;
  under Henry VIII, 151, 152; under Richard
  I, 79, 80
Taylor, A. J. P., 395
Tennyson, Alfred, Lord, 317, 323
Tewkesbury, Battle of, 133
Thackeray, William Makepeace, 316
Thatcher, Denis, 212
Thatcher, Margaret: government, 185, 461;
  poll tax, 115n; portrait, 234; privatizations,
  151–2; reputation, 39, 309; trade union
  relations, 111
Thomas, Corporal Edward, 372
Times, The, 323, 324, 343, 422
Tinchebray, Battle of, 67
Titanic, 364

Tobruk, 451

Tolpuddle Martyrs, 155, 305

Tolstoy, Leo, 19, 325n

Tone, Wolfe, 271–2

Tories, 205, 222, 228, 301, 309, 315, *see also* Conservatives

Tostig of Northumbria, 51

Tower of London: Anne Boleyn's execution, 150; built, 58; Crown Jewels, 326; Great Fire, 201; heads outside, 96; Henry VI in, 129, 132, 133; Peasants' Revolt, 112; Princes in, 135, 136; prisoners, 174, 208; Richard II in, 115

Townshend, Viscount 'Turnip', 235

Towton, Battle of, 132

Trade Union Act, 336

trade unions: *Daily Mail* attacks, 408; General Strike, 409–11; general strike threat, 403–4; leadership, 336–7; legislation, 305, 336; miners' strike, 361; political representation, 344, 347; Robert Owen's work, 316

Trades Union Congress (TUC), 408, 410

Trafalgar, Battle of, 278–9, 280

trench warfare, 373–5

Truman, Harry S., 469

Tudor family, 119, 138

Tull, Jethro, 230, 233

Turner, J. M. W., 317

Turnpike Act, 228

Tussaud, Madame, 270

Tyler, Wat, 112–14, 155, 469

Tyrrel, Walter, 66

Ulster, 181, 185, 272, 345, 365, 402

Ulster Volunteer Force, 364

unemployment, 398, 409, 414–15, 418, 453

Union Flag, 273

United Irishmen, Society of, 271

United Nations, 470–1

United States of America: Churchill in, 359n; cinema, 412; civil war, 330; creation, 242n, 252, 256, 258; gold standard, 418; League of Nations, 399; New Deal, 414; rise, 290, 318, 319, 454; United Nations, 470; war with Britain (1812), 285; women's suffrage, 368; WWI, 390, 394, 399; WWII, 445, 447, 449–50, 459

Unknown Warrior, 404, 472–3

V-1s and V-2s, 458–9

Vandals, 17

VE day, 462–3

Verdun, Battle of, 388, 396

Versailles, Treaty of, 400, 426

Victoria, Queen: accession, 308–9; children, 309; death, 351–2, 354, 407; Empress of India, 328; Era, 301; Great Exhibition, 308; husband's death, 318–19, 337; marriage, 309; name, 11; PMs, 308–9, 337–8, 345–6; view of women's suffrage, 361n

Victory, HMS, 278–9

Vienna, Congress of, 290–1

Vikings: Alfred's campaigns, 34–6, 37; arrival, 32–4, 46, 47, 107; Athelstan's campaigns, 37–8; Danegeld, 40, 42; Danelaw, 36–7; Eric Bloodaxe, 39; massacre of, 40–1; violence, 33–4, 370; voyages, 33–4

Villeneuve, Admiral, 279

Vinegar Hill, Battle of, 272

Visigoths, 17

VJ Day, 470

Voltaire, 241, 245–6, 267

WAAF, 439

Wade, George, 238

Wakefield, Battle of, 130

Wales: absorbed, 221, 273; Athelstan's wars, 38; Black Death, 108; Celts, 12, 25, 29; Civil War, 191; Edward I's conquest, 94–5, 96; Glendower rebellion, 119–20; Henry Tudor's landing, 137; kingdoms, 38, 72n, 94; Offa's dyke, 31–2; religion, 29; Viking raids, 34n

Wales, Prince of, 95, 104

Wallace, Alfred, 317n

Wallace, Sir William, 95–6

Walpole, Sir Robert, 226, 233–5, 237–8

Warbeck, Perkin, 142

Wars of the Roses, 111, 118, 128, 133, 137, 141

Warwick, Earl of (the Kingmaker), 133, 134

Warwick, Earl of (son of Clarence), 142

Warwick, John Dudley, Earl of, *see* Northumberland

Warwick Castle, 179

Washington, George, 248, 256, 258

Waterloo, Battle of, 287–8, 289, 290

Watling Street, 36, 228; Battle of, 11

Watt, James, 264, 293

Welch, Raquel, 3

Wellington, Duke of (Iron Duke): Byron on, 297; Chartists, 311–12; Crystal Palace